Volunteer Training
For Courts and Corrections

by

JAMES D. JORGENSEN

and

IVAN H. SCHEIER

The Scarecrow Press, Inc.
Metuchen, N.J.   1973

Library of Congress Cataloging in Publication Data

Jorgensen, James D
　　Volunteer training for courts and corrections.

　　1.　Volunteer workers in corrections--Study and
teaching--Addresses, essays, lectures.　I.　Scheier,
Ivan H., joint author.　II.　Title.
HV9275.J65　　　　364.6'07　　　72-11517
ISBN 0-8108-0570-7

Major contributions to the readings which
formed the backbone of this book were made by
Judith A. Berry, Assistant Director of the National
Information Center on Volunteers in Courts, and
Ursula Davies and Kathleen Wells.
　　We also benefited from contributions by
Louise Allen, Robert Hamm, and Gloria Kroeger.
　　For editorial and typing assistance we are
greatly indebted to Kathy Blackwelder.

Dedicated

TO THE VOLUNTEERS OF TODAY

In their legions, serving troubled fellow humans,

and, with hope,

TO THE VOLUNTEERS OF THE FUTURE

TABLE OF CONTENTS

LIST OF REPORTS

Supplementing and illustrating the text are the following "reports," originally part of the National Court Volunteer Training Project Preliminary Report series, sponsored by the Office of Juvenile Delinquency and Youth Development, U. S. Department of Health, Education and Welfare.

PREFACE

Within a period of a few short years our courts have begun to experience a revolution. In the tradition of revolutions, the outcome has been a redistribution of power. In this case the power of the ordinary citizen to influence the lives of troubled people has been channeled into our courts and correctional systems. The movement has been typified by quiet deeds of ordinary people who are determined to give of themselves in helping the people who come through our criminal justice system. As counselors, advocates, friends, and in many other roles, these men and women have come fourth in increasing numbers as volunteers. Their service has been a tribute to the spirit of free participation that exists in the American conscience.

Today, literally thousands of men and women stand ready to enter voluntary service to our judicial and correctional systems. A 1967 Harris Poll revealed that over one-third of a nationally representative sample of 1200 people said they would be willing to perform volunteer correctional services. If we truly have a third of our people willing to help offenders, we potentially have a most powerful weapon with which to combat recidivism. However, if good intentions paved the road to hell, they could just as well fail to open the road to solution of the problems of crime and delinquency, unless these well-intentioned people are prepared to understand the offender, the judicial system, and the society in which both exist.

This involves training, and that's what this book is about: training volunteers to enter the service of some of our most crucial institutions--correctional agencies, prevention service, and our courts. Survey statistics have consistently confirmed that this vast contingent of volunteers is comprised of intelligent, successful, well-adjusted, and happy self-actualizing people. They are attempting to fulfill needs beyond the levels of physiological satisfaction and safety. They are looking for new experiences, albeit at times out of occasional boredom or a feeling that their lives lack personal meaning.

We have in America one of the best educated popula-
tions in the world. Potentially they possess the ability to
be helpers, not only to offenders but to the very institutions
that must ultimately bear the burden of dispensing justice.
This potential, we feel, can be amplified many times over
through good programs of volunteer training.

As this is written, an estimated 200,000 volunteer
citizens contribute time and effort in some form to probation, parole, detention facilities, or to correctional institutions. By the time this is published, this number may increase by 50%; such is the growth of correctional volunteerism. These volunteers work in juvenile courts with children
of ages ranging from ten to eighteen, in youth service bureaus, juvenile detention centers and institutions, as well as
with adult offenders in probation, parole, and institutional
settings.

The authors, while envisioning the volunteer himself
as the ultimate target and the reason for this book, wish to
stress that the volunteer trainer should be the primary and
immediate consumer. It is the trainer rather than the
trainee who must interpret and adapt the principles and contents of this material to his individual and unique volunteer-
training situation. No two court volunteer programs will be
identical, and the presentation of absolutely standard materials is an exercise in futility. The trainer alone must
judge the relevancy of any training model for his own application. It is hoped that the materials in this book are in
such form as to provide the consumer with guides for action, not recipes. Indeed, this is true of any facet of
volunteer coordination. (The reader is referred to the book
Using Volunteers in Court Settings in which Dr. Scheier
emphasized this point also.)

This book is meant to be a resource book of readings,
a reference rather than a continuous text. While it can be
read consecutively from cover to cover, it will probably be
best utilized when consumed in parts.

Most of the readings in this book grew out of the
National Court Volunteer Training Project, 1969-1971, spon-
sored by the Youth Development and Delinquency Prevention
Administration, Social and Rehabilitation Service, U.S.
Department of Health, Education and Welfare. This grant
was awarded to the Boulder County Juvenile Court, Boulder,
Colorado, Judge Horace B. Holmes presiding, and the Na-
tional Information Center on Volunteers in Courts. The

purpose of the grant was (1) to train probation staff in procedures for the effective management of volunteer programs in probation work, with particular emphasis on the training of court volunteers, and (2) to train probation professionals as volunteer trainers--that is, to provide them with the information techniques and general consultive guidance necessary for effective and realistic training of local volunteers working with court probation departments.

Many readers have already had access to the preliminary report series emanating from this project in 1969-71. The present book is geared to update these reports where necessary, supplement them where feasible, and reorganize the reports in a more logical order for the convenience of the reader. It is the conclusion of the authors that this material should be made available now, even if not in perfect form. For it is now that the volunteer movement is entering its most crucial expansion period, and thus we wish to share what we know about training, realizing that the field is moving rapidly, and training techniques which are being developed in other areas than the courts and with which we are not familiar, may have great relevance to court volunteers.

A word about the experience and background of the authors is perhaps in order here. Several different people, out of their specialized experiences, have contributed to several of the readings in this book. As for the principal authors, Mr. James Jorgensen is an Associate Professor of Social Work at the Graduate School of Social Work, University of Denver, where he has been since 1964. He teaches in the area of social work practice and is responsible for the corrections program at the school. He was the Director of Social Services at the South Dakota State Training School from 1961 to 1964 and was a Child Welfare Worker in that state from 1958 to 1961. Mr. Jorgensen and his colleague, Professor Alex Zaphiris, developed the training model utilized in the large volunteer program begun by the Denver County Court in 1966. He also has directed the training program for the Jefferson County Court and has been involved as a volunteer trainer of volunteers for PARTNERS, a private organization providing volunteer services for the Denver Juvenile Court. In all he has personally trained over five thousand correctional volunteers. He was a Senior Consultant to the National Court Volunteer Training Project, and in that capacity has appeared at numerous regional and national meetings relating to the utilization of volunteers in correctional settings.

Dr. Ivan Scheier, a psychologist, has been a court volunteer for eight years at Boulder County Juvenile Court. He was Director of the National Court Volunteer Training Project and is currently Director of the National Information Center on Volunteers in Courts. Both authors have a number of previous publications in the court volunteer area.

What we have experienced in this movement has, we believe, equipped us to offer some contribution to court volunteer training. But, as trainers, we would be the last to foreclose on future opportunities for learning. As authors, we too have much to learn about learning, and we cordially invite the reader to learn along with us by his participation in the work of this book.

I: INTRODUCTION

Chapter 1

BASIC CONCEPTS AND PURPOSES

Why should court volunteers be trained? What should
the objectives of volunteer training programs be? What content should such programs entail? How should training be
delivered? These questions are now very much open to discussion as volunteers become the interest of more and more
courts.

In regard to the first question, "Should volunteers be
trained?" it would have to be admitted that the authors cannot point to any study which would prove that volunteers that
are trained perform better than those who have not been
trained. A point of view which is sometimes expressed is
that training may tend to destroy the humanity at the core
of the transaction between the volunteer and the offender.
This point of view deserves consideration. Indeed training
programs can have a reverse or undesirable effect, particularly if trainers and training programs do not address
the humanness of the helping process for which the volunteer
is being prepared. Those who have worried about training
the natural decency out of people have rendered an important
service to all of us involved in training volunteers in that
they have forced us to reexamine some of the basic premises
of our training programs.

The process of training, if it is to be advocated,
must have a rationale. The training must ultimately sub-
stantiate the rationale. Through evaluation, it must be
determined whether the training has accomplished the goals
set initially. Our major rationale for training is based on
a widely accepted precept that people who are prepared for
future experiences perform better.

Beyond this we could definitely justify the training of
volunteers to work with offenders. We have a duty as trainers to replace fantasy and ignorance with reality and

11

knowledge. Volunteers in fact want and demand training.
They feel a need to know about the court as an organization,
its goals, its clientele and its problems. They want to understand the behavior of the people the court is serving and
they want training that is geared to enhance their skill in
performing their particular tasks, whatever they may be.
We know that people who work in organizations for a living,
as most of us do, seek ways of finding the means within
that organization to grow and enhance themselves. We have
no reason to believe that the volunteer expects any less.
[See Chris Argyris, Integrating the Individual and the Organization, New York: Wiley, 1964; 330 pages.]

    A great deal has been written about training in in-
dustry. There is little question but that training makes far
more productive, efficient, and effective organizations. We
must conclude that the practical verdict of usage substantiates
the importance of volunteer orientation and training. Morrison's survey found that 149 of a sample of 153 courts had
a pre-service orientation program, while 120 of the same
sample provided in-service training. [See June Morrison,
"The Use of Volunteers in Juvenile Courts in the United
States: A Survey," Volunteer Administration, 1970.] Consensus, then, finally justifies for us the need for training
for volunteers in corrections.

    A spinoff of training which may or may not be a jus-
tification is the potential a training program provides for informing the community about correctional systems. The
criminal justice system has remained rather closed to citizen inquiry and scrutiny. It has not responded to questioning,
and has remained somewhat aloof from criticism. Citizen
training has potential for impact beyond the scope of volunteer services. What the ultimate payoff of the trained
volunteer might be in terms of system change is an interesting query. It is our premise that a core of trained
volunteers in any community is an asset and a fundamental
step towards public education regarding the social problems
of crime and delinquency. (And a number of courts deliberately admit observers to their volunteer training programs
for this reason.)

    Training has within it another important side benefit,
that of screening. For this reason, training should be
demanding. It should have within it the potential to discourage "joiner" types and retain those who are more intent
on becoming helpers. Trainees should be expected to involve

themselves, to complete the course of study, and to contribute to their own learning. The extent to which trainees immerse themselves in training may provide an index to their ability to stand up under the demands of service later. The testing component of training should not be ignored. If the trainer has reason to believe that training is triggering unusual behavior in a trainee, it is important that there be appropriate follow-through at that point. It is far better to screen at this point than later.

We recognize that the word "training" carries with it a semantic problem. It implies, for many, conditioning to work on an assembly line; to others, possibly it means taking unique individuals and transforming them into anonymous people who perform routine, dull tasks. Our own position is a more common sense one, we believe: Training is any relatively systematic and planned effort toward preparing people for a job. While we will tend to use the term "training," we would be satisfied with any term the reader prefers which clearly denotes the understanding of "orientation" and "job preparation."

The second question we have raised is the question of the objectives of volunteer training. Our operating premise is this: volunteer training must have as objectives (1) the provision of knowledge (2) the development of skills, and (3) change of attitudes on the part of the volunteer. Granted, these three areas are interrelated. If one has greater knowledge, he may or may not change his attitudes, which may or may not result in greater skill in performing a certain task. At any given point in training, however, it is helpful if we can state what the training is geared to accomplish.

Program objectives dictate differential training. A volunteer entering a program where counseling is the main objective will need intensive training in this area. A volunteer who is expected to be a recreation leader may need less preparation in counseling and considerable training in group dynamics. They may both need extensive orientation to understanding deviant behavior. The ability to individualize and particularize training from this perspective is obvious.

Thus the ability of trainers to design individual training assignments to mesh with general training becomes an important attribute of the trainer. He must understand the nature of the tasks of each trainee and become proficient in

relating this task to the knowledge-attitude-skill configuration
mentioned earlier.

Knowledge: What does every volunteer need to know?
This question must be asked by the trainer as he considers
the tasks being asked of the volunteer.   What does a volunteer need to know if he is going to be a counselor, a tutor,
or a case writer? Ultimately the trainer is faced with the
recognition that training must provide general knowledge or
core knowledge which must be given to everyone, plus specific knowledge which will be given depending on the tasks of
specific volunteers.

All volunteers must have a working knowledge of the
organization of which they are a part.   This means they
must know something of its structure, its goals, its personnel, and its relationship to the greater social institutional
environment.   Beyond this volunteers need knowledge of the
process by which the organization handles its clientele.   Additionally all volunteers need knowledge of the particular
problems being addressed by the court or correctional institution.   The volunteer must learn to see the problem of
crime and delinquency as being more than the sum total of
X number of people behaving in a delinquent way; he must
see these people as part of a larger whole, that whole being
the known forces in the community that produce crime and
delinquency.   Specific knowledge might deal with problems
such as alcoholism, drugs, runaways, etc.

Skills: The skill element of training is the most difficult, because skills are developed as a result of doing,
and doing is really the process of performing the specific
volunteer task.   To the extent that doing can be incorporated
in training, skills can be developed.   Often this part of
training is dealt with more in the in-service phase of volunteer training.   Later chapters will concern themselves with
doing as a part of training.

Attitudes: Training can change the attitudes of volunteers.   A study of training of Denver County Court Volunteers indicated that volunteers who initially felt that fines
and jail sentences were deterrents to committing more offenses were less inclined to feel this way after training.

Our experience would indicate that volunteers are for
the most part moderate, non-primitive people.   They may
take certain correctional practices for granted because they

feel too unfamiliar with corrections to take issue with what
is being done. Thus their attitudes are the result of lack of
information rather than deep-seated prejudice towards offender groups. Like the rest of the population they may seek
simple answers to complex problems, yet they are open to
information and thus they are good candidates for attitude
changes.

Our third question is that of the content of volunteer
training. Content is of course related to training objectives,
but beyond that many other factors ultimately dictate what
training content will emerge.

One of the variables is that of who is being trained.
The volunteer trainer will find it helpful to assess his trainees in terms of age, educational experience, culture, etc.
as he proceeds with training. It is not suggested that
classes be segregated for training based on the above factors,
although there may be instances where this would be advantageous. For example in one training program a group of
Chicano law students were being prepared to render specific
help to Chicano misdemeanant offenders. In this instance,
little benefit would have accrued from making the class het-
erogeneous. The level of understanding of the Chicano culture and the judicial system required no training in this
area; thus, training time was more efficiently consumed by
introducing the class to community resources for Chicano
people and methods of referral and follow-up.

Generally it is beneficial in training to have a hetero-
geneous class. Middle Americans can learn from Americans
of lower socio-economic classes and middle-aged people can
learn from the young, as can people from mixed racial and
ethnic backgrounds learn from one another. In instances
where there is a proper "mix, " the trainer must be sensitive
to the need of direct training at a level where there is something for everybody. In terms of breaking classes into work
groups he should be aware of the potential for utilizing this
mix in terms of specific training tasks.

A master's thesis written by a group of students at
the University of Denver Graduate School of Social Work
showed that volunteers tended to live at the edge of the city
and in suburban areas while the offenders they worked with
lived closer to the core of the city. This would suggest that
training should be geared to help the volunteer understand the
neighborhood in which his charge lives. But more importantly

the cultural pluralism that features this country requires the
attempt to recruit and train people indigenous to the neighborhood.   Judge William Burnett of the Denver County Court
suggests that preliminary studies in that court indicate that
reduction in re-arrest rates may be associated with pairing
volunteers and offenders closer to each other in social class.

While content of training will be addressed in later
chapters of this book, it is sufficient to say at this point
that each community, each court, and each class constitutes
a unique entity which will dictate the content of volunteer
training.   It is indeed the thesis of this book that training
must be individualized and this includes, of course, the content of training programs.

The last question we would like to address in this
chapter is that of how to deliver training that has the greatest impact.   We will examine this topic in some detail later,
yet we would like to re-state here that the differentials we
have mentioned as to content also apply as to method of
delivery.   Many means of training are open to the imaginative trainer.   We will be emphasizing throughout this book
the need to question many of our time-honored means of
teaching.   We know that faced with short training periods,
we must find highly efficient ways and means of helping the
volunteer internalize training.   This requires much more
than information-giving in lectures.   It does require training
that utilizes the small group as a definer of reality and a
trainer that is comfortable with small groups as training
entities.   It requires trainers that can utilize multi-media
in speeding up the training process.   In short, we must
come to grips with the fact that short time periods must not
be allowed to curtail the impact of training.   We can package training in such a way as to have impact even with time-
limited training.

As we proceed to cover the above points in more detail, we would like to orient the reader to our plan for the
remainder of the book.   We hope to provide the reader with
a time perspective within which the trainer can begin to see
training opportunities.   We will examine each of these in
more detail in the hope that each contact between the court
and the volunteer can be viewed as providing training opportunities.

While time in itself is important, we feel that the
media through which training is conducted is fully as

important.   Thus we will look at the ways in which training
can be conducted.   Films, tapes, lectures, role playing and
many others will be looked at in terms of their relevance to
volunteer training.

Lastly we feel an obligation to the trainer to help him
look at the resources in his community that might be of assistance to him in putting together the kind of training program that entices new volunteers.   Additionally we wish to
stress the importance of ongoing evaluation of training programs.   The following chapters are not intended to finalize
the state of the art, but rather to open up to the reader the
thoughts, opinions, and in some cases the findings of those
who have trained volunteers during this important beginning
period.

II: LEARNING OPPORTUNITY OR CONTACT POINTS, FORMAL AND INFORMAL

Chapter 2

FORMAL PRE-ASSIGNMENT TRAINING

Elsewhere in this book (Chapter 3) a reading (Report IV) entitled "Training Locales for Court Volunteers: Nine Opportunities Over Time" refers to a specific training locale, the formal pre-assignment training class. It is with the content and delivery of this type of class that we will concern ourselves in this chapter.

In this chapter, one reading summarizes trends in terms of typical material covered in training in 350 courts using volunteers. This will orient the reader to what has actually been done in the way of court volunteer training today, regardless of how it may or may not conform to what might be considered "ideal." Finally, the reading "Training the Court Volunteer: One Model" (Report II) and the training outline used in the Denver County Court volunteer training program (Report III) will provide the reader with some fundamentals of the design of training programs which are thought out beforehand and are not just <u>ad</u> <u>hoc</u> programs.

What should be the content of a volunteer training course? We believe that the learner should be oriented to the whole before being exposed to the parts. But what is this whole? We suggest that crime and delinquency are the main parts of it. Within that whole also is the criminal justice system, which manages the social problems of crime and delinquency. Related to the criminal justice system, of course, are the people being processed by it. These people are characterized by behaviors which must be understood and related to through change strategies. In essence, then, training should be related to all of the above and, we believe, in the order given.

The diagram below perhaps will give the reader a clearer picture of the whole and the parts, including the volunteer as well as the offender.

The Components of Training

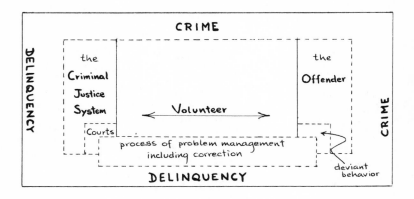

Crime and Delinquency

Many misconceptions exist regarding the nature of crime, the extent of the problem, its meaning, and its impact on society. The volunteer, like all of us, is more crime conscious today than ever before. The media daily relates accounts of crime; "law and order" are bywords; FBI uniform crime statistics are drummed into all of us regularly. Our trainee comes primed with much information and misinformation.

Training should help put crime and delinquency in perspective. The trainee need not be bored with statistics that would soon be forgotten, but he can be introduced to some of the basic material from good references such as The Challenge of Crime in a Free Society and the supporting Task Force Reports. Rather than presenting this material in an inflammatory way by depicting the fact that a serious crime is being committed every few seconds, for example, we believe that this material can be presented in an honest and challenging manner. It would seem to us that a basic teaching point would be to inform the trainee that crime as a social problem is not even being managed, to say nothing of being controlled. Volunteers need to know for example, that one of every five children faces the prospect of a Juvenile Court appearance before his 18th birthday, or that half of our arrests are for drinking-related offenses. Our goal in dealing with the topic of crime in training is to reflect the fact that human beings commit crimes, and these human beings are coming into court with increasing regularity, and are processed by a system which now includes the court volunteer.

Neophyte trainees, beyond this, should be given some frames of reference with which to view crime and delinquency. Details on all the numerous theories of crime are beyond the scope of volunteer training, but crime and delinquency can be discussed briefly from the viewpoints of sociology, psychiatry, anthropology, etc. without detailed theories. Many new volunteers' understanding of crime is based on a rather personal frame of reference, which often leaves the trainee closed to new information. Rather than providing the trainee with a "new" frame of reference, it is suggested at this point that training be geared to providing some new perspectives: we think the vision of the volunteer should be expanded to include alternative ideas rather than seeking to replace or supplant his present ideas. For as we know, ideas are evaluated (and often discarded) on the basis of agreement or disagreement. Thus we feel that training should introduce ideas, but not indoctrinate.

The Criminal Justice System

The preceding diagram depicts the criminal justice system as a part related to the greater whole of crime and delinquency. In using the term "system" we are aware that one of the attributes of a system is that there is an integration of the parts. The criminal justice system perhaps then should not be considered as a true system in that it is notorious for the lack of interrelatedness or linkage of the parts to each other. For example we find often that institutional personnel mistrust judges and probation officers, while parole departments play down the role of the institution.

While there is not always interrelatedness, there does appear to be a relationship among the subsystems in that what happens in one subsystem does affect other subsystems and ultimately the entire system. As an example, a

successful probation program will probably reduce the intake
of the institution and ultimately affect the parole caseloads,
which could have repercussions on the money allocations
within the entire system.

Our objective in training the volunteer is to provide
him with a perspective of the criminal justice system that
takes him from the act of arrest through the entire process
to ultimate reintegration of the offender into society.

The Offender

It is to be noted that the diagram places the offender
opposite the criminal justice system. This "part" is of extreme importance to the volunteer in training because he is
the target of the volunteer's efforts. "Offender" or "criminal" or "delinquent" are, of course, emotionally charged
words. There may be serious objection to their use, in
that with repetition they conjure up possibly distorted images
which may have the effect of alienating the trainee from the
person he is supposed to help. Yet we know of no way
around this except to stress in training that we are talking
about people who, like us, have flesh, blood, hopes, de-
sires, and problems.

Whatever way is chosen to orient the volunteer to the
offender, it is important that it has the effect of humanizing
the offender to the class. Later in this book we will discuss some means of accomplishing this. Suffice it to say
at this point that we need to present the offender in such a
way as to make his behavior comprehensible rather than
bizarre. Obviously we are less inclined to fear something
we comprehend. Behavior that is comprehended is often behavior that can be identified with, even though it is not approved.

While we do not suggest that volunteers are necessarily antagonistic to offenders, we do believe that in many
cases they are ignorant about law violators and that they are
like most of us in being ambivalent about their reactions to
them. Our goal in training is at least to create a greater
receptiveness to the offender, and we believe that moving
from general to specific material provides us with a greater
chance of accomplishing this. If the offender can be viewed
in the perspective of a greater society that produces crimi-
nality, then the offender can be better understood.

The Court

In our diagram we have placed the volunteer between the court, as a part of the criminal justice system, and the offender. The volunteer is of course most concerned with the particular court for whom he will be working, and he obviously needs to understand this specific organization in terms of its tasks, personnel, operating technology, and structure. But it is also a necessity that training be directed toward helping the volunteer understand the court in relation to the other components of the criminal justice system. The court receives people as a result of their being charged with violations of the law, and it processes these people in ways that direct other agencies and institutions to enter the picture. Thus, a complete view of the court in relation to the local criminal justice system is vital. Connected to this also is the need to understand the local system as part of a state and national system. The volunteer of course must ultimately see his role in relation to all of this.

A training program may, for example, be addressed in part to depicting the process whereby a juvenile court receives referrals from a juvenile bureau of a police department. How these cases may be disposed of, the differential utilization of welfare departments, mental health centers, and correctional facilities might also constitute part of the curriculum, as would the process of using the facilities of the court.

Problem Management

Problem management is presented in the diagram as a process carried out by the criminal justice system. The offender becomes a part of this process as does the volunteer.

In this part of training the volunteer needs to develop an understanding of the alternatives the court has, in terms of legal sanction as well as from the standpoint of what is feasible for the offender himself and the available community resources. Community resources, since they are often inadequate and yet are at some point important in the process of problem management, should be introduced and explained to the volunteer. Our suggestion to make this most meaningful is to present these resources in relation to individual

problems. In other words, if a particular offender's problem is health, then the health resources in a particular community should be explained in terms of their problem-solving
capacity in relation to this problem. Problems with legal,
financial, educational, employment, and psychiatric dimensions can be explained in the same way. The point that should
be stressed in training is the present stance of the community in relation to these problems. What should emerge,
hopefully, is a clear picture of the adequacy or inadequacy
of the community response. Volunteers can be an important
force in the development of additional resources, if they are
made aware of the need for these resources during training.

Since so many of the volunteers in corrections are
being asked to assist around processes of probation, parole,
and institutional care, training should be geared to provide
an understanding of these processes. By this we mean an
understanding of the rationale of the above as management
processes as well as corrective tools. We will discuss this
in more detail later in the book.

Correction

Our diagram depicts correction as a part of problem
management. For the volunteer it is the most important
part, usually, in that it is where most of his activity is
lodged. In the vast majority of courts, volunteers are being
prepared to enter a corrective role. The hoped-for payoff
is that of improved behavior of the offender and a reduced
potential for return to the criminal justice system. Thus a
substantial portion of training time is justified in presenting
such material relating to the helping process of counselling,
interviewing, etc.

It is important in this part of training for volunteers
to have an opportunity to identify those areas where they
anticipate they might have problems, either as a result of
the offender's behavior or because of their own feeling of
inadequacy. Our experience in training volunteers would
suggest that establishing trust, developing communication,
dealing with authority, acceptance, and understanding rank
as the major problems that trainees should and in fact do
anticipate. While these are reality-based concerns, it is
psychologically important for the volunteer to know that his
peers also perceive the challenge in the same way he does.
It is also important for the volunteer to know that many of

his concerns as an "amateur" are the same concerns that
the professional has, and that the problems are very real
for both.

These concerns, being the trainees' inputs, can provide the trainer with starting points for the training program.
For example, if the concern expressed is "how do we develop trust?", a starting question in training might be to ask
the class to think about how much they trust. How did they
learn to trust? Who taught them? Through what experiences? To this the trainer, of course, adds the material
he feels the class must know about the offender's experiences in learning trust and how the process of trust can be
enhanced through the helping process. The methods of providing training will be discussed in later chapters.

In summary, we have in this chapter attempted to
suggest a training regimen that (1) addresses knowledge, attitudes, and skills relevant to the specific training components of (2) crime and delinquency, the criminal justice system and its clientele, problem management, and correction
(3) through a process which moves from general to specific
action-type training. Having done this, we feel it is appropriate to introduce the reader to the following readings
in which current patterns in training are cited as they exist
in 350 volunteer courts, a comprehensive model for training
is proposed, and an existing training outline presently being
used in one court is described.

*   *   *   *

Report I

TOPICS AND TECHNIQUES CURRENTLY COVERED
IN TRAINING COURT VOLUNTEERS

A. Introduction: Purpose

1. This report is the result of a review and analysis
of volunteer training materials in the National Court Volunteer Reference Library, located at the National Information
Center in Boulder, Colorado. Files on approximately 350
volunteer courts were reviewed.

2. Most of the materials reviewed were written out-
lines of volunteer training courses, usually referring to oral

presentations given at such courses, and orientation manuals
or similar written material given to volunteers-in-training.
In addition to lectures and readings, other training media
used by the courts, and frequently also indicated in our topic
headings were: trainee-participation small groups; tours of
facilities or locales; auditing or observation of actual court
and volunteer program operations; role playing; tapes; films;
and assigned outside readings.

   3. The object of the present analysis was to produce
a consensus of the kinds of topics and techniques which have
figured in court volunteer training during the recent renais-
sance of the movement in the 1960's. Please note: reference here is to training of volunteers, not program managers, and primarily volunteers in juvenile court settings, although some of the reviewed material was drawn from and
applied secondarily to adult courts and detention settings.

   4. The principal values of the exercise are: (a) To
remind the trainer of court volunteers, of all the topics and
techniques which have been employed in the past, so that
they may come up for consideration in his own training plan;
(b) To limelight via this enumeration, gaps in the current
court volunteer training structure.

   5. The following limitations of the present analysis
should be noted: (a) The historical fact of usage is only
presumptive evidence that a topic or technique is worthwhile.
Conceivably, some previously incorporated training areas are
ineffectual and should be dropped, and almost certainly many
good training ideas have yet to be tried. Indeed, no attempt
has been made here to evaluate court volunteer training in
terms of volunteer or staff reactions to it, subsequent volunteer effectiveness, etc. (5b) The present list is merely a
baseline of current usage and is intended to encourage inno-
vation rather than restrict it. Surely, many of the most
effective contents and techniques of court volunteer training
fail to figure in this early history because they are yet to
be devised.

   (5c) Some individualities of judgment undoubtedly af-
fected the system of categories into which topical material
was rather lightly organized. Topics typically tend to blend
into one another or overlap; naturally enough since the efforts of scores of courts were never planned in the first
place towards a coherent composite organization. In any
event, enough content is presented so readers may reorganize

categories to taste. For an example of a single court volunteer training program well-conceived to hang together (which, again, the present conglomerate is not), the reader is referred to Report II (following this one). For an example of a single organized written orientation manual, the reader may read our Volunteer Training and Orientation Manual, a copy of which is available for $3.00 from the National Information Center. (5d) In almost all cases, topic headings use the exact words employed by the courts contributing to the composite, and these headings are not always particularly revealing. Elaboration of detailed content under main headings, where such content is available, will be made in future reports in this series.

6. The weight assigned a given training topic or area by the consensus of volunteer courts is roughly indicated by the frequency with which this topic is listed. Note again, however, that least frequently mentioned topics may nevertheless be important in suggesting new ideas, etc.

7. Wherever information was available on the point at which a particular topic occurred in the volunteer training process, this was noted by us, e.g. in the second of six sessions, "early, " "middle, " the "final session, " etc. From this we were able to place topic areas very approximately in chronological order, although it is to be emphasized that there is considerable variation here among courts. (A systematic schema of court volunteer training opportunities is presented in Report IV, Chapter 3.)

B. Topical Analysis of Court Volunteer Training Curricula

1. Welcome

TIME: Usually the very first thing in a volunteer training
        class.
        Welcome and introduction; welcome from judges or
chief probation officer, etc. (Probably most courts do this
in some form at the beginning of the class session.)
        Praise for love and service to the community.

2. Goals of This Training Course

TIME: When it occurs, probably right after the welcome.
        Goals of this Training Course.

3. Historical

TIME: Usually near the very beginning of training sessions.
History of the Juvenile Court; history of the agency;
background of program sponsor's interest in corrections.
History of and description of programs; history of
local volunteer programs.
History of volunteerism nationally; history of court
volunteerism nationally.
(Note: History usually contains naturally, a certain
amount of "program description" material, but that heading,
as a direct description of current programs tends to occur
later in the chronology of training.   See Section 11, "Program Descriptions. ")

4.   Purpose and Goals of Volunteer Programs
(The previous section, "Historical, " often
contains a good deal of this.)

TIME: On the average about 20-25% of the way into pre-
assignment training.
Function and philosophy of the court; introduction and
philosophy; policies; objectives; rational for using volunteers;
volunteer program objectives; program goals; purpose of programs; purpose and goals of program; coordinator discusses
programs; discuss programs; advantages of lay counseling.

5.   Court Procedures: Probation Department Organization
(Relates to following section, "Legal Judicial Matters, "
as the court's expression of them in its own work)

TIME: On the average, tends to be between a quarter and
a third of the way through pre-assignment training.
How the juvenile court works; about the court; court
procedures (2); procedural aspects of juvenile court (2); explanation of juvenile court; explain court set-up; structure of
the court; structure of juvenile home; juvenile process (2);
organization of juvenile court; organization of agency; organization of juvenile department; administrative set-up and staff
functions.
Flow chart; chart of organizational structure; discussion of chart; personnel policies and procedures; understanding the agency and its policies; audit staff meetings;
Referral process; intake procedures; intake and assignment procedures.
What is probation; probation rules; use of records;
understanding psychological reports and terminology;

terminology commonly used around the probation department
(simple but accurate definitions).

Tour of department; tour of agency; tour of juvenile
hall; tour detention home; visit court home.

Mock juvenile court with commentary by lawyers,
social workers and judges; attend actual court session or
juvenile hearing.

6.   Legal Judicial Matters
(See also preceding section)

TIME: Comes on the average, about half way through pre-
assignment training process.

Philosophy of legal system (justice process, sentencing alternatives, pre-sentence investigation); philosophy of
juvenile court system; nature of juvenile court; role of juvenile court; evaluation of prisons; probation and parole.

Legal orientation; juvenile laws and procedures; orientation to legal procedures; Colorado Childrens' Code (4);
legal aspects of family court; panel discussion on family
court.

Juvenile laws as they relate to the policy of court.

What is probation (See "COURT PROCEDURES" section just preceding, which tends to be simply an application
of legal-judicial matters to a particular court.)

7.   Familiarization With Probationer and His
Environment: Theory and Causes of Delinquency

TIME: Varies over a wide range, but tends to average between half and two-thirds through pre-assignment
volunteer training.

Childhood growth and development; personality growth
and development; psychological view of adolescent behavior;
development of adolescence and its problems; (speakers from
various related fields); the child, his characteristics, his
environment.

Cultural patterns of the poor; differences in culture
and behavior.

Understanding adolescents; case presentation, case-
workers discuss specific youth; introduction to deviant behavior (causes, effects, remedies); normal and pre-delinquent
patterns in adolescents; behavioral patterns of childhood and
of delinquent children; the delinquent in contemporary society;
psychological view of delinquency; juvenile delinquency as
seen from the police point of view (delinquency and the police).

Understanding the misdemeanant; the nature of the offender; nature of delinquency; delinquency causes; theories of delinquency; (speakers from related areas or selected courses and lectures).

Specific juvenile problems--educate by problem areas; drugs; drug discussion; the drug issue.

Accompanying P.O. on home visit and/or home investigation; discuss home situation of actual case; discuss family situation.

Presentation of a "classic" juvenile delinquency case; supervised observation of probationers.

A youth panel.

Role-playing.

(Note: Films, cited mainly under "Volunteer Work Methods," section 9, can also be used here for familiarization with the probationer and his environment.)

8.   Community Resources Available to the Volunteer and to the Court

TIME: Tends on the average to be about two-thirds of the way through pre-assignment training.

Role of the court in the community.

Community Resources; How community resources are used to approach community problems; Directory of community services; review of public resources; social services in (local) county; health services in (local) county; psychiatric services.

(Note: Other service resources within the court might also be described here, but are listed under "Program Descriptions," section 11 in the present report.)

Other agencies and how they help; orientation to community agencies; discussion of other agencies.

Relation of the court to outside agencies; relation to other agencies (e.g. role of police); how to deal with outside agencies.

Tour of community centers.

Attend lecture series by professionals in related youth service agencies (as well as describing other services available in the community, these lectures may touch on "Theory and Causes of Delinquency," section 7 preceding).

9.   Volunteer Work Methods and Techniques

(Comes quite naturally off "Volunteer Job Descriptions," section 10; also some relation to "Court Procedures," section 5.)

TIME: Varies quite widely between half and three quarters of the way through pre-assignment training, averaging about two-thirds.

Guidelines; "Do's and Don't's"; Rules-of-Thumb; How-to-do-it; many courts have these, usually in written form, an example being Boulder's "Some Things To Think About in Dealing with Juveniles. " All these "do's and don't's" will later be analyzed separately by the project.

Suggested "Break the Ice" activities, on first meeting your probationer, or in the early stages of the relationship.

Listening and communication; communication; session with current "listener" volunteer.

Interviewing; interviewing concepts; interviewing techniques; audit staff interviews with probationer; volunteer practices interviewing (with staff help).

Introduction to the field of mental health; the helping relationship.

Counseling techniques; detention counseling; listen to therapy tapes; observe staff probation officer counseling a probationer.

Reality therapy.

Behavior modification.

Crisis intervention.

Principles of Casework; basic casework philosophy and skills.

Relationship to child and family; working with parents; workshop on family counseling; visit to home with P.O. to meet family.

Pre-programmed course in interpersonal relations (done in pairs); sensitivity training.

View films (showing people working with probationers, also some familiarization and morale value). The most frequent ones shown thus far in the court volunteer movement's history appear to be "Price of a Life, " "The Revolving Door, " and 'The Dangerous Years, " "The Odds Against, " and 'The Inventions of the Adolescent. " (Please note: in 1970, the National Information Center issued a directory of recommended court volunteer training films.)

Veteran volunteers relate their experiences; experienced volunteers conduct training of new volunteers; review of volunteer experiences working with adolescents; veteran volunteer "guarantors" share experiences with new guarantors.

Role playing.

10.   Volunteer Job Descriptions, Volunteer Responsibilities
      (See also section 11, "Program Descriptions")

TIME: Tends on the average to be about two-thirds of the
        way through pre-assignment training.
General Role of the Volunteer; the volunteer role
towards the child; how to function.
        Job specialization; job descriptions in VISTO; job de-
tails for supervision aide, court aides, investigation assistant, committees and volunteer professionals; describe court
counselor volunteer; role of APO; court expectations of VPO;
the VPO in the Fulton County Juvenile Court; role of the volunteer "listener"; role of the psychiatric consultant intern;
law student volunteer functions; responsibilities of tutors.
(For 155 volunteer job descriptions of the above type, see
the "National Register of Volunteer Jobs in Court Settings, "
available from the National Information Center on Volunteers
in Courts, Boulder County Juvenile Court, Boulder, Colorado.)
        General regulations governing volunteer activity; ob-
ligations of the volunteer (consistency, time investment,
etc.); attendance at volunteer meetings; responsibilities of
the volunteer and the court; hours required, time commitment; summary of volunteer responsibilities.
        Rules for volunteers and reporting; reporting (4); case
presentation; discussion and disposition; frequency and timing
of visits to probationers; the three P's of volunteer work:
Prayer, purpose and preparation.
        (The above blends into "Court Procedures, " section
5, on the one hand and "Volunteer Work Methods, " section
9, on the other.)
        Discuss type of person needed; characteristics of vol-
unteers; qualities needed in the VISTO volunteer.
        Counterpoint: job responsibility of the paid probation
officer (toward the volunteer).

11.   Program Descriptions

TIME: Comes on an average about three-quarters of the
        way through pre-assignment training.
        Program Descriptions; overview of total program; in-
troduction to programs; discussion of programs, proven successful programs (may include non-volunteer as well as volunteer programs); other (non-volunteer) court service programs; court services available.
        Explanation of volunteer programs; how the court uses
volunteers; organization of volunteer programs; review of

programs.

Audit-observe volunteer tutor program (2); observe volunteer APO-DPO meeting; audit high school advisory council meeting; and listen to tapes of volunteer group discussion session with probationers.

("Volunteer Job Descriptions" just preceding relate naturally to Volunteer Program descriptions, when these latter are specified for the individual volunteer.)

12.   Summary of Pre-Assignment Training and Review

Evaluation of Training--open discussion of training; evaluation of training; evaluation; information test of volunteers to see how much they learned and how effective training was.

Evaluation of volunteer--(discussions with him) after training and before assignment; personality testing of volunteer; information and attitude testing of volunteer.

Administration of Oath; presentation of membership cards; "push, pull or get out" (challenge).

Assign according to interests; provide work space.

Introduce Volunteer to staff he'll work with; meet caseworker for assigned probationer; meeting with caseworker; meeting with court coordinator; interview with Youth Director. (Note: many training programs give volunteers some exposure to supervisory staff as faculty, all during pre-assignment training.)

Breakdown into smaller groups after class orientation to discuss specifics.

13.   Ongoing In-service Training (After Work Assignment)

Observe probation officers at work or audit programs in action. (A number of variations of this as previously mentioned.)

Staff-supervised pilot work with children; placement sessions in activity assigned.

Individual work with assigned staff; individual consultations; individual and group meetings on specific programs.

Small group meetings of volunteers; weekly discussion groups; monthly meetings.

Workshops.

Newsletters periodically distributed to volunteers.

Selected University courses or special lectures for volunteers to attend.

14.   Miscellaneous

(Note: The following items are difficult to categorize
and/or locate chronologically in the training process.   They
may nevertheless be fruitful sources of fresh training ideas.)
    Try to get catharsis of volunteer's secret fears, so
they can be brought up for objective discussion and analysis.
    Rewards anticipated.
    Deglamorize corrections.
    Financing of volunteer programs.
    How paid officers see volunteers.
    Paid staff person or senior volunteer discusses infor-
mally and individually with volunteer all orientative aspects
of his job.
    Workshop for supervisory staff on managing volunteer
programs: "Why have volunteers, " "working with volunteers, "
"description of volunteer programs. "

*   *   *   *

Report II

TRAINING THE COURT VOLUNTEER: ONE MODEL
(by James D. Jorgensen)

Introduction

    The training course described below has been designed
specifically for trainees preparing to become volunteer counselors at the juvenile court level.   It has relevance, however, for volunteers who may be preparing to serve in juvenile institutional programs.   With certain modifications it
may lend itself for use in training people to work in adult
courts.   Any training course eventually must address itself
to certain training objectives.   These objectives are based
on certain assumptions on the part of the training designers
regarding the training needs of the people to be trained.
The assumptions on which this training course is designed
are "working assumptions. " They are tentative and subject
to change.   They are based on observations gleaned from
training approximately 2, 000 volunteers preparing to serve
courts dealing with juvenile and young adult offenders.

Assumption I

    Volunteers entering court service for the most part
do not understand the life styles of delinquent youth and are

deficient in understanding the systems which produce delinquency and delinquents. Volunteers do not come from high
delinquency neighborhoods or schools. They generally come
from middle and upper class echelons of the socio-economic
strata. They recognize that delinquents are problems to
society, but they see solutions in changing delinquents to the
exclusion of addressing a "problem system. " The lack of
understanding in this area can be remedied in training which
systematically exposes the trainee to a delinquency producing
system. The trainee could then see delinquency as a social
problem and the delinquent as a victim or "carrier" of the
problem.

Assumption II

The volunteer is deficient in his understanding of how
the problem of juvenile delinquency is managed within our
correctional system, and how the delinquent is dealt with by
society. The citizen participant or lay volunteer although reflecting success, professional and educational achievement,
and concern has not in most cases been exposed to the process of handling delinquents. He has probably not seen juvenile courts in operation, detention homes, jails, training
schools, etc. If he has been exposed to any of the above it
has probably been an isolated experience and not in relation
to understanding a process of problem management.

Assumption III

The volunteer has not thought extensively about delinquency being a means of meeting human needs. Because
delinquency seems bizarre, self-defeating, and alien to the
norms and values of the non-delinquent, any attempts to understand it as purposeful behavior have been met with resistance or at best selective listening on the part of the layman. The citizen who views or hears about deviant behavior
out of context and makes judgments on this basis is being
reinforced in fragmented approaches to understanding the delinquent.

Assumption IV

The trainee does not have adequate perception of
learning as a process and delinquent behavior as learned behavior. Many theories of delinquency are to be found among
volunteers. They are often piecemeal and reflect a popular
theme, a recent book, or public opinion. The "mental

illness" model, "good-bad" model, and "if parents would
shape up" model of explaining delinquents and delinquency
are often expressed in some form by volunteers. However,
to see all behavior, including delinquency, within the framework of learned behavior has not been the experience of
most people in our psychiatrized society. On the contrary
we have gone to extremes in punishing people because they
were bad or "treating" them because they were sick. Only
recently have we begun to talk of re-educating people for living.

Assumption V

        The trainee needs to be made more aware of his po-
tential as a force for change in dealing with delinquency and
delinquents. The volunteer, being a successful person, is
not failure-oriented. He may see the changing of delinquents' behavior in simplistic terms or he may go the other
extreme of looking for things that are not really present.
In short, the volunteer has certain fantasies about himself
in relation to the delinquent. These fantasies must be dealt
with in training in order that the trainee can use himself
constructively to become a change agent.

        Volunteers serving in juvenile courts will benefit from
training which to them is real, as non-theoretical as possible,
and relevant to increasing their understanding of delinquents
and delinquency. The training outlined below is geared to enhance the role performance of volunteers and aid in establishing
a distinct identity for this level of staff as an educator for living. The training content and method will be directed toward
dealing with five major objectives: (1) Preparing the trainee
to see himself in relation to the court and the court within
the total system, (2) Understanding basic human needs, (3)
Becoming aware of learning as a process, (4) Appreciation
of delinquency as learned behavior, and (5) Understanding
the change process and methods of purposefully effective
change.

        In that each class of volunteers represents uniqueness
in terms of levels of understanding, the training can be applied in a differential way to each class. Some material
may be determined to have greater relevance to a particular
class while some material may have little or no relevance
at all. Grouping of trainees in classes will be an important
consideration in terms of developing a level of training which
has meaning for an entire class. Determining the level of

sophistication of volunteers can be achieved by reviewing application forms, contacting personal references, and by conducting personal interviews. These interviews can be utilized for preparation for training and are important in terms of providing the trainee with a reality-based picture of his role in the correctional process and the problem of juvenile delinquency.

Strategy for Achieving Objective No. 1

The major strategy for achieving Objective No. 1 would be training in the form of selected pre-conditioning experiences which would acquaint the trainee with a problem flow which culminates in delinquent behavior.

1. The trainee would:

Visit a high delinquency neighborhood. This visit is intended to give the trainee insights into poverty, blight, and neglect. This visit may be to an urban ghetto, an Indian reservation, or to a rural poverty area. In any case, the purposes of such a visit would be:

A. To provide cultural shock in terms of introduction to different value systems, and

B. To provide opportunities for the trainee to encounter the various social systems affecting youth in high delinquency neighborhoods.

Visits with families of delinquents may be programmed. These visits may be arranged through the cooperation of welfare departments, OEO agencies, churches, private social agencies, probation and parole departments, and obviously through the voluntary consent of the families themselves.

Observation of juvenile officers in police departments, in the performance of their duties would, if made a part of this training program, provide an important dimension of in training in terms of making the trainee aware of the police as an element in the system of delinquency management. The results to be anticipated from such an experience would be:

A. The trainee would develop a better appreciation for different values, life styles, and life forces under which delinquents operate, and

B. Feelings of neutrality toward the delinquent and his physical, social and psychological needs would be reduced.

2. The trainee would attend one or more sessions of a

juvenile court in order to observe the judicial process. Included in this visit would be a meeting with a juvenile judge
and a visit to detention and jail facilities utilized for juveniles. The purposes inherent in such a visit would be to:
  A.   Allow the trainee to observe the judicial process which
       diverts children into a confined status.
  B.   Learn about juvenile law; i. e. , Gault decision and its
       implications for the juvenile court.
  C.   Develop an appreciation for necessary programming at
       this stage of the juvenile correctional process and re-
       late the volunteer to his role at this stage.

       Anticipated results from this experience would be:
  A.   The trainee will become sensitive to the legal nature
       of the problem.
  B.   He will become sensitive to the need for justice for
       delinquent children as well as adults, and further see
       himself as playing an integral role in the judicial dis-
       position of children.
  C.   He will gain appreciation of the meaning of the initial
       experience of confinement to the juvenile.

3.   The trainee would visit one of the high delinquency junior
high schools and/or senior high schools in the state (with
school permission, of course).
       Behind this strategy would be the goals of providing
experience wherein trainees could:
  A.   See first-hand the interaction of students with educa-
       tors.
  B.   Discuss with educators their perceptions of difficult to
       educate students.
  C.   Discuss with students their perceptions of educators
       and the educational process. (Include unsuccessful as
       well as successful students, of course.)
  D.   Observe the processes of education.

       The anticipated results from such an experience would
be that:
  A.   The trainee would become more sensitive to the need
       for education which engages the delinquent youth in
       creative thought and action, and
  B.   He would presumably be helped to see himself as a
       broker and advocate in providing experiences which
       are re-educational in nature.
       This experience would:
  A.   Highlight the secondary preventive role of the volun-
       teer working in a court setting.

B.   Allow the trainee to see an added dimension of the
correctional process.

4.   The trainee would visit a juvenile correctional institution
or a jail or detention facility, where he could observe and
interact with delinquents, institutional personnel and gain insights into institutionalization as a process in handling delinquent children.
The trainee would undergo a session of de-briefing.
It is assumed at this point that the trainee will wish to talk
about what he has seen and heard during these visits.   Although the trainees have each been viewing the same things,
they will not necessarily have perceived the same things.
The trainer who would have accompanied the trainees on
their visits will lead this session for the purposes of:
A.   Providing an experience for the trainee to validate himself in relation to his experiences, and,
B.   To integrate what he perceived with what other trainees have perceived.
The results to be anticipated from this would be that:
A.   The trainee would experience mixed feelings of enthusiasm and dissatisfaction.
B.   The trainee would retain a desire to pursue additional
training sessions.
The above experiences would be considered pre-req-
uisites for admission to further training.   Trainees who have
the benefit of these experiences would enter Phase II--Train-
ing in Understanding Human Needs.

Strategy for Achieving Objective No. 2--Training in Understanding Human Needs

Group discussion would be the major tool utilized in
teaching about basic human needs.   Selected readings, tapes,
games, movies, and role playing would be inserted into the
training program, wherever applicable.   The participation of
juveniles presently on probation as well as ex-offenders as
training aids would add a new dimension of concreteness and
reality to the discussion sessions.

The class leader would personalize this content by
directing the discussion into the area of the trainees' needs.
They would identify needs that they have, the means they
have of satisfying their needs, how they sense the needs of
those around them, how they satisfy the needs of those
around them, etc.   The goal in this procedure is that of
identifying an on-going process of all people; meeting needs

through individual resourcefulness or utilizing other human
resources. The trainee must be helped to recognize that he
is vital in need satisfactions of people with whom he inter-
acts.

When the class leader is satisfied that the class has
begun to personalize the concept of human needs, discussion
is directed to another area with which he is less familiar--
delinquent children. The class can be asked to contrast and
compare the need satisfaction patterns they employ with those
of the delinquent children they have seen. The discussion
leader must at this point employ his skill in making the
trainees aware of the process of need satisfaction. The discussion then can be directed back to the trainees. They
would discuss what they do when they fail to meet their
needs or when they find other people unwilling to meet their
needs. Their behavior is examined and related to and compared with the behavior of delinquent children who cannot
find socially sanctioned ways of meeting their needs.

In the area of human needs: William Glasser's book
Reality Therapy and Schools Without Failure provides rich
material which would be relevant to the trainees' concerns.
A tape by Dr. Glasser which was geared for counselors
would also provide an excellent training aid. The length of
this session may vary from class to class but the training
would not proceed further until the class leader is certain
that the class has become sensitive to the fact that delinquent
behavior is a means for a child to satisfy his needs. Anticipated results from the above training would be:
1.   The class would be sensitized to need satisfaction in
      themselves and each other.
2.   This will provide linkage which will help them under-
      stand need satisfaction in delinquents, that delinquency
      satisfied a need in delinquents.
3.   They will be responsive to the next part of training
      which is The Process of Learning.

Strategy for Achieving Objective No. 3--Training to Understanding The Learning Process

The basic strategy for achieving Objective No. 3
would also utilize the group discussion method. Having become sensitive to seeing behavior as attempts to satisfy
human needs, the class is now ready to move a step toward
seeing how people in the process of satisfying needs undergo
a process of learning. The class would be asked to

personalize learning by discussing how they learn. The class leader may ask each trainee to list something in the performance of their jobs that they do particularly well as well as something they feel they do not do very well. The class may be broken into sub-groups and asked to struggle with how they learned to do something and how they failed to learn.

Having struggled with this, the class would be motivated for additional group discussion and information regarding the learning process. The group leader then might be in a good position to introduce some basic concepts from learning theory. He would particularly emphasize the role of significant others in facilitating or hindering the learning process.

The class, only after having spent adequate time in relating the process of learning to themselves, would move on to learning as it is experienced by delinquent children. This part of training would be facilitated by the discussion of a particular child or case material presented by the trainer. Being able to personalize the issue to a particular subject, the class could be assigned the task of understanding how this child learned to behave in his present manner. If possible, a delinquent child himself may be utilized as a training aid by participating in this part of the training. The inmate or ex-offender would be an integral part of this training phase in that he could provide confirmation or denial regarding some of the trainees pre-conceptions about learning. Such practices as punishment, rewards, etc., could be looked at within the learning framework.

Trainees may be asked to cite certain instances where they dealt with people in ways that facilitated learning and ways that did not. This technique would be implemented by the leadership of the group leader who would begin the process by relating a particular negative as well as a positive incident. The willingness of the group leader to be honest will serve to provide behavior which the class can emulate in honestly looking at their own deficiencies. Anticipated results from the above training would be:
1. The class would see learning as a process in which everyone is engaged.
2. The class would learn that situations can be such that learning can be hindered or facilitated.
3. The class would be prepared to look at delinquency within the learning frame of reference.

4.   They will be motivated to understand behavioral differ-
     ential in terms of learning.

Strategy for Achieving Objective No. 4--Understanding Delinquency as Learned Behavior

    This part of training will encompass a substantial
time period. The strategy must address itself to the tasks
of creating or renewing the trainees' awareness of causal
factors as they relate to the delinquent and thereby leading
into a focus on:
1.   The types of delinquent youth.
2.   The need for a system of identification or classifica-
     tion.
3.   The need for differential re-educative methods and
     techniques keyed to the needs of specific types of de-
     linquents.

    In identifying types of delinquent youth, the class
would be assigned the task of either buzz groups or by themselves categorizing in any way they chose, the kinds of delinquent children they have known. The purpose in this is
to enable the trainees to identify or describe what they have
observed regarding behavior differentials. It is felt to be
important that the class come up with this material by themselves rather than having some typology superimposed by the
training leader. The trainer can translate the class member's inputs into an understandable terminology of categories.

    Once the class has come to some common agreement
regarding types or categories of delinquents, they will be
ready to think of examples of delinquents from their own
communities which reflect this differential. The class leader will lead a discussion which may bring this material even
more into focus as learned behavior. As trainees are cued
to certain children's behavior, they will be more receptive
to understanding the behavior as learned and as behavior
which is an attempt to satisfy basic needs.

    As the class moves from their own understanding to
differences in delinquents, to understanding of differences in
experiences which lead to differences in behavior, they can
be introduced to an organizational frame of reference which
leads to differential strategies in re-education. Such material may well be extracted from the Interpersonal Maturity
Level Classification Scheme as developed by Marguerite War-
ren and the Community Treatment Staff, Community Treatment

Project of the California Youth Authority or the Differential
Treatment Program which is presently in operation at the
Robert F. Kennedy Youth Center in Morgantown, West Vir-
ginia.

The material in either of these systems would lend
itself well to presenting delinquent behavior as learned.
Again, children under the court's jurisdiction who are representative of these different delinquent types may be utilized
as training aids to illustrate development and learning. Anticipated results from this experience:

1. Trainees would be given some authentication regarding
   their own precepts regarding delinquency.
2. They would have an organizational framework to facilitate understanding of delinquency.
3. They would be motivated to learn more about systems
   of intervention and re-education.

Strategy for Achieving Objective No. 5--Understanding the
Change Process

The theory and principles of change underlie the training course.   Basic to the five elements in training is that
people change in the process of meeting their own needs as
well as the needs of others.   They change as they learn.
They change as they fail to learn.   We are interested in the
kind of change related to becoming a socialized human being
who is achieving his self-actualization.   Training is geared
to providing knowledge and skills which allow the cottage
personnel to use themselves in ways which facilitate change
of this type.

Discussion is the primary vehicle for understanding
change.   The class is involved in the task of understanding
changes for better or for worse in their own lives.   They
would through discussion identify changes that they would like
to see in themselves as re-educators of delinquent children.
Identifying and discussing opportunities for changes would also be a part of this phase of training.   The concept must be
developed that we generally are dissatisfied with our own
ability or potential for change.   This dissatisfaction keeps
us continually striving for change within ourselves and changes
in the outside world.   If we cannot find the opportunity to
change and become frustrated as a result, we will transfer
this frustration to the children whom we are supposed to
change.

The class will through discussion come to some agreement about what behavior needs change and what can realistically be changed. The discussion can then be focused on
examples of delinquents or other people known to the trainees
who illustrate change both for the better and for the worse.
These examples can be examined for the process of change
in each instance. The focus of discussion must be on the
factors that produced the change. The class having come
this far and having been oriented to I-level concepts and differential treatment categories, can then be exposed to change
strategies as depicted in this material.

It is recognized, however, that the class will need
more than general change strategies. They will want and
need to develop skills wherein they can become change agents
within change strategies. Role playing, discussion, and
laboratory experiences will be utilized to provide these skills.
Basic principles of counseling will be emphasized. Role
playing with "staged" incidents can be utilized to achieve
maximum involvement. An example of this might be to stage
a particular problem which occurs on probation such as being expelled from school. The problem for the class would
be that of creating out of this incident a learning experience.

Group discussion leading as a technique to create
change will be taught by the example of the trainer. Class
members at this stage of training may be enlisted to lead
the group discussion of trainees. They would be critiqued
by other trainees. This may provide a pool of potential
training. Laboratory sessions where trainees lead group
problem discussion meetings as depicted by Dr. Glasser
would also be a part of training. Other trainees would moni-
tor these sessions and offer feedback. Every trainee should
have a laboratory experience of some type prior to the end
of training.

At this juncture of training, the trainers along with
the class, must decide how and in what areas training will
continue. Options might be that new areas are outlined and
additional training is planned--or the training leader may
find himself in a complementary, consultant, or back-up role
for potential trainers that have emerged out of the class.
An open-ended, fluid arrangement must exist to insure that
training continues and is self-perpetuating. (One track for
continued training, in some courts, would be to move beyond
what every volunteer should know, to concentration on the
trainees' "specialty area" in volunteer work, e. g. , tutor,

foster parent, lay group discussion leader, etc.)

Whatever its content, a model for ongoing training may be based on the continual inputs of class members in the form of questions, concerns, problems, observations, ideas, etc. These inputs are "processed" by the training class which comes up with outputs in the form of solutions, answers, new ideas, new concerns, etc. These outputs become inputs in the form of a feedback loop which continually directs the level and content of training.

Diagram

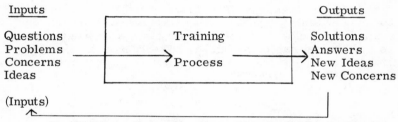

To facilitate the group discussion technique, class size becomes an important consideration. Every trainer may have a number in mind when he thinks of the ideal class size for discussion. Fifteen to 25 people provide a range wherein a group is large enough to warrant the time of a trainer yet small enough to facilitate good discussion. For purposes of in-service training, a group should be large enough to accommodate the usual attrition, yet lend itself to group identity of its members.

*   *   *   *

Report III

REVISED TRAINING OUTLINE

(Outline of training course for volunteer counselors as conducted by University of Denver School of Social Work)

The training sessions are set up on a monthly basis, including three consecutive evening sessions. These sessions begin at 7:30 and last until 10:00, or later. We arrange for a 15-minute break at the mid-point of each session.

Session I, Part I

This features a welcome and introduction by one of the county judges. There is a general orientation to the court, to the program, the background thinking, planning and assumptions underlying the program. At this time there is time for the judge to answer specific questions from the class members. The depth and breadth of this discussion has varied, depending on the particular judge who is giving the presentation.

Session I, Part II

A showing of the movie "The Price of a Life." This is a 25-minute film of a young offender for whom probation is utilized. It rather nicely demonstrates the economy as well as the humaneness of probation. The film is an excellent tool in setting the tone for understanding probation as an alternative to incarceration.

Session I, Part III*

This part of the session is geared toward an understanding of the misdemeanant with particular emphasis on the psychology of the Character Disorder. The following material is covered: character is defined as the set of organized and fixed groups of attitudes developed by social influences operation upon the temperament base. Temperament refers to an original group of individual attitudes existing independently of any social influences. Hans Gerth and C. Wright Mills defined character as a psychic structure formed on a foundation of organic potential. A psychic structure is an integration of perception, emotion and impulse.

Factors in the Formation of Character
   1.   Environment
   2.   Ego (self)
   3.   Super-ego (conscience)
   4.   Ideal models in later life

Etiology of Character Disorder
        Frustration in the satisfaction of the following fundamental needs:

*This part was devised by Professor Alex Zaphiris, University of Denver School of Social Work.

1. Love
2. Security
3. Success
4. Recognition
5. Respect

Early Signs of Character Disorder
1. Resentment
2. Rebelliousness
3. Anti-social behavior
4. Major disturbance during the formative years--history of actual or emotional loss of parents
5. Difficulty expressed in the social field.

General Characteristics
1. Limited motivation to seek help
2. Extreme difficulty
3. Economic, social and physical vulnerability
4. Partial controls
5. No remorse of conscience
6. Calm appearance but sensitive
7. Perpetual state of crisis

Specific Attitudes
1. Impatient for gratification
2. Non-verbal
3. Emotional and physical closeness with their children--separation problems
4. No casual social relationships
5. Spouses of similar condition
6. Sex, money, liquor or food--means to fill their emptiness
7. Financial difficulties
8. Acting out behavior thought of as necessary to their existence
9. Easy going, but when frustrated they become very angry
10. Development of physical symptoms during period of withdrawal from the acting out
11. Provocative, hostile and antagonistic
12. Expectation of rejection
13. Dissatisfaction expressed for the help offered to them

1. Inconsistency of acting out behavior
2. Ambivalent
3. They think in opposites
4. Anxious about "not knowing"

5. Attempt to invade the privacy of others
6. Intellectual controls to deny their feelings
7. "Flight" when tensions occur in their families
8. Feelings of exploitation and expectations from others
    to share the burden of their difficulties
9. Defiant behavior is pleasurable to them

1. Some present mono-symptomatic behavior
2. Some have a competitive orientation and direct their
    energies constructively.

Session 1, Part IV

A showing of the movie "The Revolving Door." This movie
is most relevant to the class in that it deals with the misdemeanant offender. It sensitizes the class to the lack of
programs in jails and the resulting futility of "dead time."
It then proposes some alternative programs, among which is
the Denver County Court Volunteer Probation Counselor Program.

Session II

This entire session is devoted to principles of counseling the
misdemeanant. The session is begun with the class members being asked to write on a piece of paper a brief statement of the main problem that they expect to encounter in
working with the probationer. They are instructed that this
problem may be a result of lack of community resources,
lack of skill on the part of the volunteer, or concern about
the behavior of the probationer. Upon completion of this the
class is broken into task forces of eight to ten people to
identify their concerns, establish patterns or consistencies
among volunteers' concerns, and to return to the class with
no more than three basic problems. These problems or
concerns are shared with the entire class, and at that point
become the class inputs. The material to follow is then,
through lecture-discussion, related to the perceived problems
reflected by the class; the intent is that each problem will
in some way be addressed.

Introduction

Reference is made to the purposeful nature of all behavior. Deviant behavior is contrasted with "normal"

behavior. The history of treatment of socially deviant behavior is pointed up, i.e. punishment of bad people by banishment, maiming, etc. The swing to treatment of what was
considered to be "sick" behavior, and the relative failure of
both approaches. The emerging idea of deviant behavior as
being expected behavior, in view of life experiences, and the
emerging view of treatment as being re-educative and re-
integrative rather than clinical in nature. Use is made of
a case illustration here of a boy who steals a car, is sen-
tenced to an institution later placed on work release and his
consequent sabotaging of this rehabilitation plan. This illustration points up the goal seeking nature of the behavior and
shows how this kind of behavior serves a purpose in terms
of postponement of dealing with the reality of the free world.

Probation is discussed briefly, and the current trend
in the use of the volunteer in corrections is mentioned.
Little application of the use of the volunteer in the U.S.A.,
but extensive use in some European and Asian countries and
in Australia.

Mention is made of the little use of probation with
misdemeanants. Possible reasons for this is that the misdemeanant does not threaten us so much because he is seen
as an ineffective person who does not hurt other people as
much as himself. Make reference at this point to the fact
that 95% of our felons have misdemeanant court records.
Richard Speck of Chicago was in essence a misdemeanant
type.

Considerable time is given at this point in talking
about some of the built-in advantages that the lay counselor
has over the professional probation officer. These advantages are given as follows:
1. The Volunteer has an advantage of not being an "en-
    forcer" type (the offender tends to see probation offi-
    cers in their penalizing role rather than their helping
    role).
2. The Volunteer has the advantage of not being a pro-
    fessional. (The professional is no longer held in such
    high esteem, particularly among poverty groups.)
3. The Volunteer has the advantage (hopefully) of not look-
    ing at people in terms of pathology. (Many profession-
    als are conditioned to dealing with pathology, not
    strengths.)
4. The Volunteer has the advantage of being assigned to
    one person. (The professional deals with caseloads of

100-200 and does become calloused and perhaps more oriented toward record keeping.)
5.   The Volunteer has the advantage of a fresh outlook. (The professional can be handicapped by a closed system and resulting "systems maintenance. ")

The question is raised by the instructor as to what good advantages are if one does not have counseling skill. The question is answered by the instructor that everyone has counseled at some level and has been involved in problem-solving activity.   Our task is to build on these skills in counseling by applying some new knowledge to dealing with a particular kind of person who violates the law.   Emphasis is placed on the fact that there is no magic involved, and no "right" formula.   There may be some wrong approaches but we must be careful before we say something is wrong in that what was considered to be a wrong in traditional counseling years ago may be "right" today.   Stress is placed on the need to be good people rather than pseudo-psychiatrists.

People (ourselves included) have been changed for the better or worse through good or bad relationships.   It is through the use of a relationship that we hope to bring about a favorable change in the misdemeanant.   The impact of a life that is lived devoid of positive relationships is overwhelming.   People who have not been important to other people have no reason to trust the volunteer.   At least there will be reason for them to test his good will and good intentions.   Testing can take many turns.   Considerable time is spent in discussing the manifestations and meaning of testing behavior, testing reality, etc.

Basic Concepts of Counseling:

Listening and Hearing--The differences between listening to a person and actually hearing what he is saying.   Allowing the person to talk because it feels better.   The importance to the offender to be listened to and heard.   Tuning people out.   We do it and so does the offender.   The need to listen for themes in conversations.   What repeats itself may very likely give us clues as to what is bothering the offender.

Empathizing--Being able to feel with another person gives him strength.   To feel like him will make him feel you are as powerless as he is.   We can easily over-identify with the offender if we have had similar experiences and perceive them in the way he does. Being the stronger of the two, the volunteer must maintain control of feelings.

Letting the Offender Get to Know You--Setting an example in terms of behavior. Serving as a new model. Stress is placed here on the experience we have had intimately knowing a good model, and the importance of this to the offender, even though he may be threatened by it. Part of good counseling is being a good teacher. The concept of a corrective experience implies that new models are introduced that can correct old misconceptions. Actions may speak louder than words, and the value of being able to perform a task for the offender is stressed as a means of letting the offender know his counselor.

Showing Respect--Respect is something that most of us take for granted. We overlook that for the offender respect is something he has perhaps not experienced and is consequently unfamiliar with. In this sense, this simple act has tremendous impact in developing a corrective experience.

The question is raised, can we respect someone we don't like? Can we respect someone whose morals run counter to ours? Mention is made of the meaning of what some might consider to be immoral behavior. It is suggested that we as people all have mature and immature sides. We need to speak to the mature part of the person. In this respect we try to deal with a person's present and future rather than his past. To dwell on an unsavory past will only weaken the individual by giving him more opportunity to justify his present functioning on the basis of past deprivation. We may see in the offender's behavior some of the same things we dislike in our own behavior. We may also see the offender manifesting certain behavior that we are struggling to control in ourselves. Perhaps if we recognize this we can keep from over-reacting.

Advice--Advice is a part of counseling but it is not counseling. It is easy to give but there are some safeguards to keep in mind. For advice to be most helpful and meaningful, I would suggest that we look for certain things. (1) Does the person ask for it? (2) Can he take acting without it? (3) Can he use the advice you are giving? The latter is most important because if we advise someone to do something that he finds impossible to do, he will find it difficult to come back and face the counselor and admit his

inadequacy. This sets up an unnecessary block or wedge between the counselor and his charge.

   Holding Out Expectations--As counselors, we can trap
ourselves into thinking that because a person is a failure he
will continue to be a failure. If we feel this in terms of an
attitude we can be sure that the offender will pick up this
feeling and act in the way we expect him to act. The reverse is also true.

   In this area we also discuss the matter of anger. Do
we allow ourselves to express anger and disappointment when
we feel this way toward the offender? I stress the need to
allow expressions of anger and disappointment as one way of
showing concern. I differentiate the differences between losing control of anger and rejecting, or a measured response
of anger and continued acceptance of the individual. I stress
that we should not be using our energy to keep back genuine
feelings. The offender needs to know the counselor has limits to his patience and is not God.

   As a part of discussion in the matter of expectations,
we talk about change occurring in the adult and that we need
to expect and demand change in people even if a pattern may
have been established. We assume that an old dog can be
taught new tricks. People continually mature and mellow.
We need to capitalize on this process. Part of holding out
expectations for the offender is to face him with his own involvement and responsibility in his dilemma. To allow the
offender to perceive himself as someone that "things just
happen to" will only support and encourage further distortion
and lack of self responsibility.

   Causing the Offender to Feel Discomfort--If a person
remains frustrated long enough, he will find a way of adapting to his situation. Having made this adaptation, he may
even become comfortable with it and consider change to be
too much of a risk. It is difficult to bring about discomfort,
but my suggestion is that where you notice an offender's dissatisfaction with his lot in life, move in to exploit it. To
the extent that is possible, attempt to bring about discomfort
in terms of holding out expectations and demands. Get the
person to want something and help him go after it.

   The offender may or may not feel guilt to the extent
we do, but he seems to find different ways of expressing it.
I would hope that to whatever extent possible we try to

promote appropriate guilt feelings in the person. He needs
to handle his guilt in more constructive terms than acting in
such a way as to bring about punishment to alleviate guilt.

Using Appropriate Language--Whose language is used,
mine or the offender's? Stress here that the counselor does
not pick up the offender's vernacular. To use language that
is not a part of us, will likely lead to our being seen as a
phoney. At the same time we should not be so naive as to
leave the impression that we do not understand four-letter
words. A part of the re-educative process is learning new
ways of communicating. I would suggest that there is a
language that we can both use. Stress that we should not use
words that are beyond the offender's comprehension. Speak
simply and directly.

Use of Authority--The authority that the counselor
will find most helpful is the implicit authority of his personal
psychological strength as demonstrated by the fact that he is
a successful person. The counselor has the expertise of
knowing how to get along in this world, whereas the offender
does not. This kind of authority in the long run will serve
you better than the authority to penalize. The authority of
enforcement and penalizing is present, but it rests with the
police and court judges.

Timing--It is very tempting to give immediate solutions to the offender. We should remember, however, that
while we may arrive at a solution to a problem in one way,
this does not mean that another person can understand our
solution. A person who feels obligated to accept a solution
foreign to him may never really identify with it. He may
merely go through the motions.

Persistence--We will probably find the misdemeanant
oriented to failure and expecting failure in himself. Persistence is a key part of counseling in that it conveys to the
misdemeanant that we will not give up on him. This in itself is important when we realize that the misdemeanant expects to be a disappointment.

Using the Crisis--The misdemeanant lives with a crisis much of the time and in fact his whole life is often one
big crisis. He is accustomed to being overcome by crisis
and expects to be defeated. The counselor is in a position
to stand by his charge during a crisis, and may be able to
help the person overcome this situation, and turn habitual

defeat into victory.

Session III, Part I

A short section of Session III deals with Community Resources. A handout lists and describes those health, education, and welfare agencies which are relevant to volunteer
probation counselors as they seek out services for probationers. A professional probation officer in the court elaborates on the handout and discusses agency services by looking
at the problem and then relating agencies which can be of
assistance in solving these problems. Major problems are
listed as employment, training, education, legal, health, alcoholism, and financial.

Session III, Part II

During this ten minute section some procedural and mechani-
cal matters are discussed, i. e. suspended driver's licenses,
enlistment in military services, etc. , as it relates to probationers.

Section III, Part III

The case of Daniel Carter, 22 year old misdemeanant offender, is used as a teaching device. The pre-sentence report is handed out during Session I, and having read it, the
class is broken up into buzz groups to answer these basic
questions about Carter. (1) What are the factors contributing to Mr. Carter's behavior? (2) What evidence is there
that Carter is a proper subject for community treatment
(probation)? (3) What needs to be done to change Mr. Carter's behavior? The class as a whole is then reconvened
and buzz group chairmen form a panel to discuss the case.

Session III, Part IV

Role playing. One of the trainees volunteers to play the role
of Mr. Carter and is interviewed by one of the other trainees in a hypothetical first interview. Through this means
the class is sensitized to the interviewing process. Upon
completion of this there is a critique and rehash.

The class, upon ending this final session, is invited to a formal swearing-in ceremony held at 1:00 PM in County Court, usually on the following day. They are given an oath by one of the judges and indicted into the court as volunteer probation counselors. At this time they are given an identifying lapel pin and a tour of the court and probation offices.

Chapter 3

THE BROADER PROSPECT OF
INFORMAL TRAINING FOR VOLUNTEERS

The preceding chapter has taken us through the process of pre-assignment training. The report which follows looks at eight other opportunities or locales in time, when training can occur. These eight locales are obviously more informal, yet for the alert trainer they are no less opportune than pre-assignment training.

Report IV

TRAINING LOCALES FOR COURT VOLUNTEERS:
NINE OPPORTUNITIES OVER TIME

Purpose of This Chapter

Other chapters in this book will analyze court volunteer training in terms of recommended content and media. The present chapter concentrates on clarifying the number of opportunities we have to reach court volunteers with orientation and training experiences, whatever their content and medium.

This may be an illuminating and broadening exercise for those of us who have thought of training primarily in terms of more traditional classroom modes, e.g., the big formal class convened just before the volunteer begins work. This is indeed a training locale or opportunity; but there are at least eight others, and many of us have no doubt neglected these others, while concentrating on classroom approaches.

Main Dimensions; Explanation of Diagram

Nine training opportunities emerge when the volunteer

COURT VOLUNTEER TRAINING OPPORTUNITIES OVER TIME AND IN GROUPS OR INDIVIDUALLY

process is analyzed, in terms of time and volunteers, as individuals vs. volunteers in groups. Time is presented horizontally on the diagram. This time line extends from the moment of being recruited as a baseline, on through the end of the volunteer's work, in two major time sectors, "prior to beginning work" and "after beginning work--in-service training. " This time dimension enriches our understanding of opportunities for volunteer training in two ways: more training opportunities are perceived, when one thinks of the entire span of volunteer affiliation with the court, likely to be a year or more, rather than just one time. Moreover, the capability of delivering information differentially over time, when the volunteer is ripe for it, is more easily seen. Thus, there are certain things a volunteer is not yet ready to understand before he has work experience, (i. e. , while in time sector I). These things will be wasted on the volunteer, much as an explanation of the intricacies of chess might be wasted on someone who has never actually played the fundamental game. Similarly, in-service training content and approach (sector II) will differ from pre-work training, in taking cognizance of the fact that the volunteer is now somewhat sophisticated through on-the-job experience.

Group vs. individual (vertically on the diagram): we often think of learning as something which occurs in class groups, and indeed, this is frequently the most efficient way in which training is conveyed. Nevertheless, a number of opportunities for training the volunteer as an individual occur as a natural part of the total volunteer work process. Though these locales may not be formally labeled as training and may indeed have other functions as well, clearer awareness of them as training opportunities should lead to a more complete exploitation of them as training opportunities.

Indeed, it seems to us that moderate-sized or smaller courts are going to have to make more use of individual or small group training opportunities. Volunteers trickle in to them, say, one or two a week, and that is all they need. But if they don't put this trickle to work until the next big class is trained, they may have to wait six months or more to use them (and many good volunteers won't wait that long in any event). One alternative is putting volunteers to work as they come in without any training pre-preparation at all and this is obviously disadvantageous in its own right. The solution for smaller or medium-sized courts thus seems to

be more development of effective training for volunteers as
individuals or in small groups, as they are recruited;
later chapters in this book will suggest ways of "individualizing" court volunteer training.

Nine Training-Opportunity Locales

The following opportunities appear as locales in the
accompanying diagram:

Sector I: Prior to Beginning Work

Training Locale 1 (individual): during screening, the
volunteer should be getting a chance to ask questions and
learn about the court, as well as vice versa.

Training Locale 2 (individual): soon after passing
screening, the volunteer can be given reading material preparing him for his work; for example, a volunteer orientation
manual especially prepared by the court and/or a reading
list of interesting and relevant books or pamphlets.

Training Locale 3 (individual or small group): informal natural opportunities for pre-work experience might include tours of jail and court facilities, introductions to key
staff and other volunteers, sitting in on court hearings, sitting in on volunteer or probationer meetings, tours of high
delinquency areas in the community, riding with police on
patrol, etc.

Specially developed materials at the Training Locale
3 stage may include tapes or coordinated slide-tape shows
which the volunteer can listen to or view pretty much by
himself.

Training Locale 4 (group): the traditional training
class, in the relatively formal sense, as many volunteer
courts currently conduct them, with faculty, training aids,
etc. A relatively big class, just before volunteers begin
work.

Training Locale 5 (smaller groups): similar to Locale 4 above, except smaller groups and less formal. Probably doesn't actually occur as often.

Training Locale 6 (individual): at least a few courts
conduct volunteer training simply by letting the volunteer
have a nice long person-to-person chat with an experienced
staff person and/or a veteran volunteer. To this might be
added any of the events described in Locale 3 (simply at a
somewhat later time), especially the tapes and tape-slide
shows the volunteer can hear and see by himself, perhaps

discussing them personally with a staff person afterwards.

Sector II: After Beginning Work: In-Service Training

Training Locale 7 (group): bigger, more formal
class-type meetings, much as described in Locale 4, except
that in Locale 7 they would have to be cognizant of the fact
that the volunteer trainees are no longer beginners. Once
or twice a year might be enough for this type of meeting,
which would probably have a large morale as well as information component.

Training Locale 8 (small group): periodic in-service
training meetings, at, say monthly or bi-monthly intervals
at which small groups of volunteers in similar jobs get together to discuss their "cases," or other job problems,
learning not only from the trainer-type people present, but
also from each other. A number of courts are beginning to
capitalize on this kind of training.

Training Locale 9 (individual): any individual meeting
between the volunteer and his staff supervisor is a prime
opportunity for learning and training, if the supervisor will
only capitalize sufficiently on it.

Conclusion

For the present, the authors' general conclusion is
as follows: we have tended to concentrate our attention too
much on Locale 4 (formal classroom) to the neglect of real
training potential in the other eight locales, with their naturally occurring time-extended options and possibilities, and
their exploitation of small-group, individual and informal
options as well as formal classroom possibilities. Much of
the remainder of this book will concentrate on development
of "the other eight" locales, in a manner realistically con-
sonant with the limited volunteer training resources of most
American courts and institutions.

*   *   *   *

Having presented the nine locales in two time sectors,
let us now examine this scheme in more detail.

Sector I.   Prior to Beginning Work

Training Locale 1--Screening: this is that point in

time when the would-be volunteer offers his services.   At
this point there has been no acceptance on the part of the
court of the citizen's service; only a tacit agreement to pursue the matter more fully.

        This being the case, what should a volunteer program
offer in the way of orientation or training at this juncture?
If, as we said earlier, training should in itself provide a
screening mechanism, what combination of screening-training
should be offered?   This locale is a vital period, because
this segment of training should have within it the potential
both to screen out and screen in.   What stands out then is
the training material which very openly and honestly orients
the citizen to the goals, objectives, and methods of the program.   At this point the volunteer should be faced with the
reality of what the program is all about.   The orientation
here should be geared to deal with and destroy fantasies.
People who are offering their services on the basis of fantasies about the problem, about the people experiencing the
problem, and about themselves as would-be helpers, require
and warrant open, direct, accurate information about what
is really being asked of volunteers.

        In this category we might find, as an example, the
fantasy that the delinquent child's problem can be traced to
poor parental care, which may lead to a second fantasy that
the helper can be a substitute parent, and yet a deeper fantasy that the child will ultimately look to the helper as the
parent and, in fact, accept him as such.   While there may
be instances where the above has actually happened, it obviously would not be the stuff of which volunteer motivation
is built.   People harboring such fantasies must understand
that in spite of inadequate parenting, the court hopes to improve the parent-child relationship, not end it.

        Another possible fantasy might be the ex-convict who
sees his niche in life being that of volunteering, the hidden
agenda being his own self-rehabilitation.   Obviously, courts
would approve of self-help, but would also want to establish
with the would-be volunteer a priority which placed the
helpee first.

        We are not saying that court volunteer programs can-
not utilize ex-offenders or people who volunteer for satisfaction of personal needs.   Courts can and do use them
effectively, but they use them effectively <u>when</u> these individuals <u>know</u> the ground rules and understand completely how the

court anticipates their being used. We owe it to the helper
as well as ultimately the consumer of volunteer services to
make sure this training locale is free from possible misconceptions. To the extent that this is accomplished during
this phase, there obviously will be fewer trainees pursuing
unrealistic and unattainable goals.

Training Locale 2--Individual Pre-Service Orientation:
recognizing that Training Locale 1 has within it the potential
for separating from the program people who are seeking experiences that are not congruent with the goals of the court,
we can assume then that those remaining will be a group of
more reality-oriented helpers.

Keeping in mind also that we still have the concept of
screening foremost in our minds, our procedures still have
screening potential. We are more inclined to see this stage
as a screening in period. For the most part we anticipate
that the trainees at this point will ultimately be helpers.

In the event that the court has written orientation
materials, this is an ideal time to disseminate them. Often
copies of newspaper articles are relevant orientation and
training materials at this juncture. Reprints of magazine
articles which interpret programs are also excellent materials for this group. We hasten to add that these articles
should be lively, relevant, and realistic rather than academic
materials. A volunteer orientation manual may be among
the repertoire of some programs, and this too can be a
part of training content. Bibliographies of recommended
readings could also be productive handout materials. Chapter 15, "Readings," will provide more concrete suggestions
in this area.

The objective at this point is this: having reduced
the group through screening to a more realistic training target, the trainer can induce the group to raise more relevant
questions through the implanting of higher level reading
materials. The levels of reading inherent in the above suggestions have the effect of individualizing the materials to
the wide range of potential trainees.

Training Locale 3--Program Observation and Tours:
the trainee is introduced to a higher level of reality in Locale 3. He moves to a more experiential level of training
wherein he is brought more directly into contact with the
problem, the people experiencing the problem, and the

structure wherein the problem is managed.

This is largely by way of observation, those things
to be observed being jails, detention facilities, court proceedings, introduction to and observation of staff and experienced volunteers, high delinquency neighborhoods, police at
work, etc.   He may also listen to tapes and observe films
or slides.   All of these training methods will be discussed
more in later chapters.

The important part of Locale 3 is that the volunteer,
as he comes closer to the reality of the problem, can utilize
this reality further to test his commitment to pursue the
program further.   If he does not measure up, he still can
feel free to leave the program with no ill results, in that
he has still not come in contact with the offender.   In reality if this scheme is utilized, the volunteer would not be exposed to the offender until just before Training Locale 7 at
which time the screening process should have worked its
will.

Training Locale 4--Formal Pre-Assignment Training:
this has been described in the preceding chapter and we
choose not to reiterate that material here except to emphasize that during this stage a substantial amount of time and
effort will be invested in training.   As training is delivered
here, it takes on a more preparatory note although it should
also provide a means for the trainee to exit from the program with grace and dignity.

Training Locale 5--Small Group Process: where
training is conducted formally in large groups, there is an
obvious need to reduce this impersonality through small
group processes.   This can provide trainees the opportunities
to deal with matters that could not perhaps be handled under
more formal conditions.   Fears can be shared and overcome
in peer situations and also fears that are reality-based can
be admitted to by all concerned.

Small groups are a unique advantage to small courts
who naturally recruit fewer volunteers.   In fact larger
courts may well raise the question of whether it may be
more profitable to have more training sessions with smaller
classes as over and against the large class which is trained
infrequently.

Training Locale 6--Individual Conference: training at

this juncture is closer to the point of no return, in that the
volunteer meets individually with a professional staff member.   This may be for purposes of being introduced to the
professional staff person who may be in charge of assigning
offenders to volunteers, or it may be for the purpose of
direct case assignment.   In any event it provides the last
phase or opportunity for the volunteer to "opt out" as it
were.

The training component at this point may be to discuss a live assignment in terms of its ramifications in order
to determine whether the trainee is ready for assignment.
This may point up certain areas not yet defined in training.

The other possible component may be to get feedback
from the trainee about his experiences and the meaning of
those experiences up to the present.   This could be vital in
terms of the ultimate assignment to the offender.   It sometimes happens, for example, that the volunteer decides that
he really does have feelings about working with a certain
kind of offender.   Training Locale 6 is where these last-
minute adjustments can be made by the court as it considers
the differential use of volunteer manpower.

One court with which the authors are familiar has a
"swearing in" ceremony where the class formally takes an
oath of office before a judge.   Appearing for this ceremony
in a sense certifies the commitment to service, and for
those who are sworn in, their presence in the court provides
an opportunity for individual conferences with the professional
staff.   In another court, the major part of training is comprised of a sit-down session between the volunteer and a
professional staff member.

Sector II.   After Beginning Work: In-Service Training

Training Locale 7:   some courts, after the assignment of their trainees for a direct service role, place the
names of these people on a mailing list for follow-up flyers
or newsletters.   These flyers may be utilized as morale
building communication or they may be for the purpose of
facilitating mass consumption of special announcements, introduction to new community resources, films, speakers,
plays or books.   This flyer provides an excellent device for
in-service information-giving and to some extent can be
thought of as a training tool.

Training Locale 8--Periodic In-Service Training Meetings: after assignment there is a critical need to follow up with in-service training. Chapter 4, "In-Service Training," will deal with this subject in greater detail. Our preliminary experience would suggest that trainers should not expect the kind of attendance at these meetings that was demonstrated earlier if only because it is difficult to get busy people together on a regular ongoing basis.

There should probably be scheduled regular meetings where volunteers can pick and choose times when they can avail themselves of in-service training. The newsletter may be utilized to announce these meetings.

Large in-service meetings have certain advantages in that they offer the trainee opportunities for mass information dissemination or experience sharing. For example a special film or speaker may warrant a large meeting of perhaps all the volunteers.

The small group discussion meeting is obviously the choice when in-service training must address the task of problem solving. The in-service trainer should provide the small group substantial leeway in focusing on the problem to be discussed--letting them establish their own "agenda" as it were. This would include letting them select resource people for their meetings. A basic principle to remember is that people are more likely to involve themselves in meetings that they themselves have had a hand in planning.

Some courts have in-service problem solving meetings held on a regular basis for any volunteer, while still other courts pre-select in-service training classes in advance and schedule them for regular training sessions. One can see some advantages in capitalizing on the "groupness" which usually develops in formal training sessions in Locale 4 by continuing these classes as in-service training units. One must also be prepared for natural attrition which will occur over time.

Training Locale 9--Individual Supervising Conferences: the ongoing direction given by the professional staff members are obvious points of training. The case conference method of training has been used advantageously in the training of professional probation staff and in other social service work. If professional staff are free to consider their supervisory role as having a training dimension, this in itself can perhaps become as important or more important as a locale for training than any of those mentioned up to the present time.

In this context we should mention that a major consideration in offering training at this level is the staff to volunteer ratio. A remedy for heavy volunteer demands on staff time may lie in the possibility of utilizing experienced volunteers as auxiliary resource people who have the capability of providing in-service supervision.

In the not too distant future we may see the computer utilized as a helping agent for the professional and the volunteer in seeking solutions to problems in helping offenders. At this writing there is discussion about the feasibility of having a national data bank with information on known volunteer-offender problem situations and the attempts being made to deal with these problems. We can envision a time when many courts may have access to a terminal where this data can be retrieved. This data could become the meat of inservice training sessions as well as individual conferences.

Chapter 4

IN-SERVICE TRAINING

After having been assigned to a client, the volunteer presents a somewhat different training challenge, one that must be addressed through a good in-service training program. Brief mention was made of this previously; however, it is felt that the subject deserves more detailed treatment here.

The volunteer, prior to assignment, is concerned about entering an arena that is usually quite foreign to him. Training problems at this stage must be geared to helping the volunteer bridge certain unknowns, i.e. life styles, language, values, norms, etc. Volunteers, prior to assignment, often don't know what questions to ask in that they lack the experience to ask them. In other words, the neophyte doesn't really have the experiential hooks on which to hang information. However, after having been faced with the task of being a helping human being, the volunteer becomes a much better candidate for training to assist him in problem solving methods. He now needs more in the way of skills in communication, understanding the meaning of specific behaviors, utilizing community resources, handling authority, and any number of other situational problems.

It is important for the trainer in in-service training to be cognizant of the fact that the volunteer, encountering the client, is now under a new kind of pressure. He is probably for the first time involved in a relationship that has few ground rules. He is dealing with behavior that he doesn't really understand or have a measure of control over. He is reacting and, in many instances, over-reacting. He may be ready to quit, withdraw, project, or diminish the importance of the need for his services. He may be quite angry at the court for placing him in this uncomfortable situation, and as a result attempt to use the in-service sessions as a place to ventilate feelings of frustration or anger. Even people who were quiet in formal training may, under

the pressures of performing, suddenly open up in in-service
training. The critical nature of these sessions is obvious,
and courts and institutions are placing more emphasis on
this phase of training with considerable justification. Crisis
theory tells us that people are more likely to utilize help
when they perceive themselves to be in a state of crisis than
when they do not. The task of helping someone who doesn't
feel he needs help or who outwardly resists help is, needless
to say, a crisis for most of us, particularly when we face
this dilemma for the first time. Formal training, then, does
not find people in the same kind of crisis that we often find
them after assignment.

The small group discussion method of training referred to previously has relevance to providing training for
people in the in-service category. A problem brought into
discussion can be dealt with most economically by the group,
since the problem is one that other group members may have
already experienced or may experience later. In any event,
each member of the group has a vested interest in the problems of another group member and consequently more motivation to involve himself in the in-service training process.
This also builds group cohesiveness and develops the potential
for a growth experience for the volunteer. In this context it
is important to keep volunteers in the same group to the extent that this is possible.

In that we have come to recognize that the group defines reality for the individual, group dynamics become an
important factor in in-service training. Inherent in this is
the ideal size of a training class. Encounter group leaders
seem to prefer groups no larger than 12 to 15 people. Many
classroom teachers state that a class larger than 25 becomes
unwieldy in terms of discussion. Group therapists often feel
that a group larger than eight is disadvantageous if true involvement is to occur. Our opinion is that a class the size
of ten is appropriate for in-service training.

It is obvious that many other factors must go into the
final decision regarding class size, such things as program
demands, room size, frequency of meetings, and the number
of volunteers, to name just a few.

From the standpoint of morale, the individual needs
support in whatever goal he has undertaken. The professional staff, limited as it is in terms of numerical as well as
psychological strength, has only so much to give. The

group, however, because of the nature of group processes, can provide emotional support to the individual member. It can define for him where he is succeeding and where he is not, but as important as anything, it defines the fact that the problem he is experiencing is neither new nor unique. There is solace in the universality of certain experiences!

Thus far we have emphasized the value of in-service training to the volunteer. A word should also be said about the value of this for the court. Every program needs within it feedback mechanisms for purposes of correcting basic errors in assumptions, design, and procedures. The volunteer who is on the line, delivering services, is in a very strategic position to give first hand information about what is happening. Trends and patterns can be spotted, new problems can be identified, and hopefully this can provide new information for use in pre-assignment training sessions. The efficiency of using the group to accomplish this rather than on a one-at-a-time basis is quite obvious.

The unique communication problems generated by a volunteer program have caused some would-be programmers to resist undertaking programs, or to keep programs at such an insignificant level as to lack real import. In-service training can provide the locus where information can be disseminated and also returned in the form of feedback. Where the communication system is overloaded with volunteers telephoning the professional staff over seemingly trivial matters, we might first look to the ongoing in-service training program to see if it is adequate. Professional as well as volunteer staff time is too valuable to be wasted. [See "Incorporating Volunteers in Courts," NICOVIC Frontier Series #1, especially pages 21-24, for a detailed discussion on supervision of volunteers.]

Indeed, we cannot assume because we have in-service training that it will necessarily be successful. Many factors in fact militate against successful in-service training programs. These factors will be discussed below. Suffice it to say here that planning at this phase of training is as necessary as at any other phase. While the material introduced is more problem-oriented, volunteer instigated, and spontaneous, there are still planning requirements that emerge.

Group Composition

The authors' experiences as trainers have caused them
to have some preferences as related to group composition.
How the group is composed, however, may well be dictated
by the number of new recruits entering the court service,
the conditions under which they were oriented and given formal training, as well as other matters unique to a particular
program.

There is obviously some value in bringing together
volunteers who are currently working at the same type of
task. For example volunteers doing counseling are going to
have a great deal of common information to exchange as will
tutors, parent substitutes, etc. Since the frames of reference in terms of setting, clientele, and task are commonal-
ities, it is natural that in-service training could be most
efficient where certain "constants" can be depended upon.

Since all groups experience attrition for one reason
or another, and volunteers are really no different, the matter of replacement is an important consideration. Having
the potential of the regular addition of new members provides the means of renewal and continuation of the group.
It also provides different roles for the individuals in that experienced volunteers can be helpers to neophytes in terms
of sharing experiences and techniques.

Where pre-assignment training has been informal, a
group identity may well have already formed. Often in pre-
assignment training we hear such comments as "Will we
meet together again as a group?" This is a signal that some
important relationships may be forming or may already have
formed. The trainer should be sensitive to this in terms of
its importance for group formation at the in-service level.
Teams may be formed from a large training class which may
provide a nucleus for an in-service training group. These
teams may be formed out of observed relationships or out of
such pragmatic considerations as the proximity of members
to each other geographically. It may well be that volunteers
serving a certain part of a large urban area would find a
commonality in that very fact.

Volunteers of certain ages, such as college students,
may provide criteria for natural groupings as might volunteers working with certain types of offenders, i.e., drug law
violators, joy riders; however we would not wish to suggest

that age in and of itself should be a delimiting factor.

The size of a group for the problem-solving task at hand should not be so large that it prevents discussion, yet so small that it does not provide insurance against the attendance problems facing all groups that meet regularly. A core of 15 members can probably turn out on a regular basis eight to ten people, and this is a good number for problem solving. The availability of professional and other staff, including experienced volunteers, to conduct in-service training is another important consideration. The trainer should be alert to the fact that among volunteers we often have considerable training talent which can be utilized in in-service training.

Frequency of Meetings

To establish a rule of thumb as regards frequency of meetings would be to pin down all that is elusive. Some people like to go to meetings and they would undoubtedly vote for meeting very frequently. Then there are those who are "burned out" from attending meetings on their regular jobs and they resist any kind of meeting.

If there is a rule of thumb, it might be to set definite minimums and leave the maximums up to the group. For example, the court may hold the group to at least a monthly meeting and leave them an option of meeting more frequently within that time period. It should be stated very strongly here that unless meetings produce solutions and meet the needs of individual group members, they will not continue regardless of how much pressure the court exerts to have meetings.

Length of Meetings

Persons who have been victimized by meetings know that Parkinson's Law, if applied, can destroy any meeting and make it personally distasteful for the people in attendance. Parkinson's Law, as applied to meetings, would demand that the meeting last until it is supposed to last (one hour, two hours), regardless of whether there is anything to discuss. Therefore, a rule of thumb might be this: don't apply Parkinson's Law!

The duration of a meeting will never really be a
problem if the trainer is sensitive to group processes. A
good trainer can observe when the group is sharing problems or procrastinating.   He can also feel if individual needs
are being met or not.   When the group is not doing that
which it should be doing, the trainer has a responsiblity to
redirect its efforts or re-examine the process.

Setting

Where group discussion is a hoped-for product in
training, then settings which promote group discussion are
called for.   These settings should be quite informal.   Social
agencies usually have adequate conference rooms.   Colleges
and universities have seminar rooms as do public libraries.
Educational complexes in neighborhood churches often are
under-used facilities.   Courts themselves have excellent
facilities with comfortable chairs and spacious tables in jury
deliberation rooms and judges' chambers.   Finally, homes
and apartments can often provide warm settings where re-
freshments can be served.

Perhaps as important as anything is the climate for
a relaxed atmosphere for group discussion.   This climate
can be set to some extent by the trainer in terms of dress
and demeanor wherever the class happens to be.

Leadership

All of the above mentioned items eventually hinge
upon the person or persons who provide the in-service training leadership.   Again, while there are no firm "musts" or
"must nots, " there are some ideas that have emerged out of
our training experiences which may have value for courts
which are planning in-service training.

Earlier it was mentioned that as important as anything in in-service training is the potential feedback mechanism this provides.   It follows then that if the court or institution is to use the feedback, it must provide trainers
who are in a position to recycle information gleaned from
training sessions in the form of program inputs.   This is
not to say that trainers must be court staff people, but they
would need to be people who are truly knowledgeable in all
facets of the program and have good lines of communication

to the court. Selected experienced volunteers may well be as able to grasp this aspect of the trainer role as would outside resource people.

As will be mentioned in Chapter 16, there is much training talent available from industry and education. We would be remiss if we did not utilize this talent whenever possible, but utilization should be planned with the recognition that training without the trainer having comprehension of the whole can truly be destructive.

Whoever the in-service trainer is, he must be a person knowledgeable in group processes as well as in the operation of the volunteer program. He must be a person who can come through as a resource to the group and be able to control individual and group behavior. He should be chosen carefully and, probably prior to becoming a trainer, he should be trained under the auspices of the court.

Training Methods

It is doubted whether one person can or should try to superimpose his training method on another trainer. To the extent that trainers can adapt and integrate new methods, they will have a more diverse training repertoire. We do not believe that gimmickery alone will stand up well over time. Truly, we will not have good training programs until we understand how people learn, and we will not be able to employ training technology until we understand the learning-teaching principles that undergird the technology.

One reason why meetings of any type often go badly is that they are badly planned, and often, in the name of democratic process, they are allowed to go on aimlessly with little or no goal orientation. We must, then, develop some structure to handle our trainees' problems and concerns.

A way of handling this is to make certain there are opportunities for trainees to make inputs in the form of problems, dilemmas, concerns, etc. However, these problems should be defined in a much more concrete way than simply listing them. They should perhaps be addressed in writing in order that they are very concrete and visible. Once this is done, the trainer has the responsibility of helping the class to priorize these topics in terms of such things as urgency, commonality, and potential for resolution. In

other words the class must be helped to focus on that problem which they feel they want to work on at a given point in
time.   If this is not done, classes, wherever they may be,
tend to randomly and aimlessly expend energy on material
where there is little agreement about the cause and dimensions of the problem.

As one topic emerges as having a high priority, the
training group must be helped to relate to the problem in a
systematic way.   For example the class can be given the
assignment of thinking through how the problem affects all
parties.   The group should come to some agreement as to
the true meaning of the problem to each trainee.   What do
key words mean?   After definition of the problem, the group
can then deal with proposed solutions.   These, too, can be
priorized by the group in terms of feasibility, practicality,
and available resources.   The important thing that should
come out of the meeting is an action component.   The group
should in a sense sanction a course of action on a problem.
The implications are for group members to contract with
each other and the trainer in this regard.

These action plans, when implemented, will have results which of course may provide the training inputs for
another session.   To the extent that group members are involved in helping their peers take action, they will be encouraged to communicate with each other regularly outside
of training sessions.

The importance of structuring problem-solving is that
it forces the group to do more than share common misery.
There is a limit to how long this will go on.   Truly, spontaneity need not be sacrificed, but, on the contrary, we will
find that planning and structuring the process will ultimately
produce more creative people who can truly involve themselves in problem-solving activities in human relations.

An example of a problem solving meeting follows:
The trainer asks the group members to submit individually
a problem each is having working with his offender.   After
waiting five minutes, he writes each problem on the board,
making certain he is conveying to the class the sense of the
problem as it exists to the volunteer.   After all of the problems are written, he and the training group will undoubtedly
notice there is duplication as well as interrelationship among
the problems.   The task then is to priorize, in terms of the
importance to the group, what is to be worked on.   This

should lead to a final problem.   For example, "I am having trouble getting my charge to keep his regular appointments. "

This being the common problem, the trainer should then help the group see the result of such a problem as well as the effect on everyone concerned.   A result might be "the child learns that probation is not to be taken seriously" or "irresponsible behavior is reinforced. "   The effects might be such things as "I feel incompetent as a helper" or "the child feels guilty about not keeping appointments and continuous avoidance. "

These exercises, while seemingly elementary are important in keeping the focus on the problem.   While volunteers do realize that problems do have results and effects, they do not always have the experience of defining them.

The next step after defining the results and effect is to state the objective of the problem solving meeting.   An example of an objective in connection with the above problem might be "to suggest and examine ways and means of causing probationers to keep regular appointments. "   Individuals can then be asked to brainstorm what might be done to bring about such behavior.   Suggestions which might emerge could be "provide incentives for keeping appointments" or "ensure penalties when the probationer fails to keep his appointments, " or "make out appointment notices with a copy for the volunteer and for the probationer. "

The important point in this kind of problem solving is to accept all problem solving ideas at this point in spite of personal preferences.   The class will ultimately rule out unworkable ideas, and their doing so is obviously much more effective than the trainer arbitrarily doing it.

As solutions are proposed, the trainer must help the group priorize these also.   He can do this by asking the group to suggest which of the suggestions can most readily be implemented.   This process forces the group to think not just in theory but in practical terms about how something is to be done.   It also personalizes the process in that the trainer is asking the class members what they think they could do in their situation.   An example of what could come out of such a process might be Mr. Jones, volunteer, saying, "I am going to make certain that every meeting with my probationer has a definite objective or plan. "   The trainer might ask him to say more about this plan or elaborate

on it. This would hopefully lead to greater detail, and, as
this detail emerges, it provides other members of the group
with ideas.   It also provides the trainer with an opportunity
to support the implementation with a request that Mr. Jones
share the outcome of his plan at the next training session.
Thus, new agendas develop for future meetings.   Such content provides a rationale for more sessions and, in fact,
creates new training goals.

Chapter 5

NATURAL PROCESS CONTACTS
AS TRAINING OPPORTUNITIES

Any professional staff member is in a position to provide training for volunteers. Whether an agency follows a
model of using line staff members to coordinate volunteers,
or whether this is done by a liaison person or volunteer coordinator whose job is solely that of volunteer supervision,
a point of contact is potentially a training opportunity.

For the most part, volunteers are supervised through
case conferences on a face-to-face basis or over the telephone. These contacts may last from a few minutes to an
hour, but they all have the potential for high payoff training-
wise, if conceived of and exploited as having training potential.

When the volunteer comes to the staff person for help,
his requests are generally for assistance in (1) dealing with
his own reaction to the offender, (2) dealing with the offender's behavior, and (3) dealing with the offender's environment. If we can sort out the volunteer's requests and in
our minds assign them to these three categories, we will
find that what will emerge is an opportunity to again relate
to the volunteer in terms of his knowledge, attitudes, and
skills.

The model for helping the volunteer solve his problems through the helping relationship as experienced with the
professional staff member can in fact also become the model
for the volunteer in his work with the offender. Some examples of this kind of helping process below will help to illustrate this idea. Suffice to say that the staff member, as
the helping, directing resource person in the case conference, is in a unique position to teach the volunteer how to
be this kind of resource person on a one-to-one basis with
an offender.

It is important, in helping the volunteer to understand the offender's behavior, that he also take from this experience information which has more general training significance. As the volunteer describes the behavior of the offender, it will be helpful if he is asked from time to time such questions as "How do you think John learned to behave that way?" or "What is the effect of John's actions on himself and others?" or "Are John's words consistent with his actions?"

From a training standpoint, the volunteer is moved from simply relating the antics of "his case" to actually setting forth some of his opinions about what is happening. These opinions may have validity or they may not, but they represent some beginning attempt at assessment. The staff member, rather than being the all-knowing authority who interprets behavior, can take these opinions and begin to weigh them with the volunteer. He can begin to ask for supporting data from the volunteer, point out gaps in information, etc.

The propensity for some volunteers to talk a great deal about their experiences, sometimes in random ways, forces the court staff member to bring all this into some structure. Some examples may help us understand this better.

EXAMPLE 1

Volunteer: (After a detailed account of his client's lack of motivation to attend school) "Bill will do anything rather than go to school. I doubt if he would attend if forced to attend at gunpoint. "

Staff: "How do you think Bill learned to skip school?"

V: (Pause) "I suppose it has served a purpose for him. "

S: "What purpose is that?"

V: "It's kept him away from an unpleasant experience. "

S: "Yes?"

V: "I guess you'd say it has kept him from having to experience failure every day. "

S: "I think you're right. It seems that you have established that Bill doesn't want to experience unpleasant things nor does he want to see himself as a failure. That doesn't seem so unusual. "

V: "I hadn't thought of it that way. "

S: "If Bill is telling us he doesn't want to experience failure, I wonder if there is any evidence that he is wanting to succeed at something.... "

The above is an example of the staff person taking a frustration expressed by the volunteer and converting it into a learning experience. Further, through his last statement, he holds out the possibility for action on the part of the volunteer in relation to Bill's possible motivation.

EXAMPLE 2

Volunteer: (Having related how she has lectured her probationer about smoking marijuana) "I felt I had to say what I thought. I told Jane exactly what I would have told my daughter in those circumstances. "
Staff: "What results did you get?"
V: (Pause) "I don't know what you mean. "
S: "How did Jane react?"
V: "She didn't say anything. "
S: "What other reactions did you notice?"
V: "She seemed angry and bored with the whole thing. "
S: "When you lectured Jane, what results did you hope to achieve?"
V: "I never really thought about any results. "
S: "Were you satisfied with the results you got?"
V: "Not really. "
S: "If you were to go through this again, what would you do to get more satisfactory results?"

The above anecdote takes a volunteer from the point of defending what she has done through a process wherein she examines the process of what she has done. She is not criticized but rather is helped to think about her goals and how she can develop new behavior to achieve these goals. She must first of all arrive at the conclusion that what she has done is not satisfactory for her or for Jane. She must learn new approaches, and in fact she is ready to think about alternative courses of action. She has learned something new from this exchange.

EXAMPLE 3

Volunteer: "Jack's neighborhood drags him down. I spend two hours a week, and it's all undone in ten minutes in that neighborhood. He doesn't stand a chance unless he can get out of there. I wish I could find him a foster home or a boys' ranch. "
Staff: "Has Jack asked for this?"
V: "No. "

S: "Have you talked to him about this?"
V̄: "Not yet."
S̄: "What reaction do you think you will get if you do?"
V̄: "I suppose he will resist the idea."
S̄: "Why do you think that?"
V̄: "He would be homesick and all."
S̄: "For what?"
V̄: "Family ... buddies."
S̄: "The neighborhood has some importance to Jack, then?"
V̄: "I guess so. It's hard for me to see why sometimes."
S̄: "Yes, it is hard for you and me to always understand
        what is important to Jack. What do you think Jack
        would do in a foster home?"
V: "Run away, more than likely."
S̄: "I think our discussion has shed some light on Jack and
        his environment. ..."

The above supervisory incident helps the volunteer re-think
a course of action and at the same time re-think what the
meaning of Jack's environment is to him. It is training that
usually cannot be substituted anywhere else in the other
training locales because the subject matter is extremely
personal and the motivation for learning how to relate to the
subject matter is heightened.

Another problem that at times presents itself to the
professional serving the volunteer is the volunteer who is
afraid to commit himself regarding his actions and as a result approaches the conference tight-lipped. An example of
a typical transaction follows.

EXAMPLE 4

Staff: "You haven't said much about you and Bill. I really
        need to know about what is happening." (This sug-
        gests that the volunteer's verbal output should in-
        crease.)
Volunteer: "I haven't said much because I really don't know
        what you think is important."
S: "Tell me some things about you and Bill, and I'll tell
        you if they seem important." (This gives the volun-
        teer no excuse for holding back but "opens up the
        agenda.")
V: "Well, Bill is working fairly regularly now even though
        he doesn't probably like it."
S: "Could you say some more about that?" (An open-ended

question asks for an expansion of the previous statement.)

V: "Well, I pushed him pretty hard about his need to make
a living. He didn't seem too happy about it. "

S: "But you seem to have been successful in what you attempted to do. " (Support for the volunteer's action
suggests approval.)

V: "Yes, but I'm not sure if it's right to force someone
to work. "

S: "Are you wondering if the court thinks it's right?"
(Question attempts to clarify the volunteer's previous
statement.)

V: "Yes, I think that's it, partly. "

S: "I can't give you right or wrong answers on all of these
things, Mr. _____, but I do like the outcome you got
in regard to Bill, and I hope you can share with me
how you are doing without fear of criticism. " (Statement further attempts to dispel fear.)

*   *   *   *

While volunteer management and coordination are the
proper subjects for other books, we cannot avoid the fact
that each contact that the staff person has with the volunteer
is primed for teaching-learning. Case conferences, if
planned well, can be extremely rewarding and productive
training episodes.

We should perhaps spend some time in this chapter
discussing other natural processes in the court-volunteer
pact which allow for training opportunities. Some of these
natural contacts spin off of deliberately planned experiences,
such as tours and observations. These experiences, if allowed to stand alone, may become isolated, forgotten, or
they may be relegated to relative unimportance. However,
if these same experiences can be supplemented with complementary experiences, we will enhance their training value.

For example, a standard part of many training programs are such experiences as observing court proceedings,
visiting detention facilities, jails, and police departments.
If these experiences are followed with group discussion, we
will find that the individual trainee will be exposed not only
to his perception of a court or jail, but also the perceptions
of his peers. If additionally these experiences can be followed by person-to-person contact with the police officers,
offenders, judges who carry out the various roles, as well

as familiarization with the institutions and processes being
observed, we will find that what began as an observation
will be compounded into an "in depth" experience.

Some courts have tapes, slide shows, and movies
which are given to the potential trainee as motivators or
primers. We will be discussing various media later in this
book (chapters 7-15), but at this point it is important for
the reader to be aware that learning is internalized mainly
as experiences are discussed. It follows then that when one-
way messages are the training media (lectures, tapes, films,
slides, etc.), we have a duty as trainers, insofar as possible, to make this a group experience.

An additional natural process contact point occurs
when the volunteer waits in the waiting room to confer with
professional staff. If, during this waiting period, the volunteer has access to an attractive bulletin board, he may take
away valuable information, i. e. openings for jobs, course
announcements for local colleges, etc. (see illustration citing the cost of materials to construct such a bulletin board.)

During the volunteer's tenure with the agency there
are numerous other occasions when professional staff come
together with volunteers, either directly or indirectly. The
newsletter for volunteers, telephone conversations, coffee
hours, and social gatherings where volunteers are honored
are also points of contact. These points of contact are potentially points of teaching-learning opportunity. In fact, no
point of contact is so casual or unimportant that it cannot
be considered for what, broadly speaking, we consider to be
training.

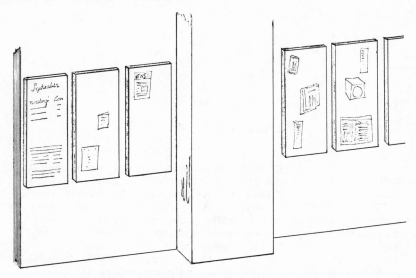

DO-IT-YOURSELF DISPLAY WALL PANELS

Type of Bulletin Board	Frame	Board Material	Other	Total
Chalkboard (or Magnetboard)	$2.73	(metal) $1.68	(paint) 79¢	$5.30
Corkboard	$2.73	$3.03	(masonite) 60¢	$6.36
Composition Board	$2.73	88¢	----	$3.61
Pegboard	$2.73	96¢	(hooks) $1	$4.69
Mirror	$2.73	(optional)	----	$---

1 can Mastic (use wall paneling mastic) to adhere each panel to the canvass (frame) stretchers: $1.50

1 can walnut stain for frames: 49¢

Approximate cost of five do-it-yourself panels: $30.

Chapter 6

TAKE-HOME TRAINING

At the point of assignment to an offender, each volunteer
will be embarking on a distinct kind of helping endeavor. For
this reason training must be devised which is individualized
to the extent that it provides the volunteer with the necessary
knowledge to deal with specific problems. It is obviously
not possible in pre-assignment training to provide material
which will deal with each conceivable problem that each volunteer will later face. We can, however, provide individualized "Take-Home Training" to help volunteers in specific
areas--"learning on demand" in a sense.

For example, it may be inefficient to provide extensive training in the area of alcoholism if few volunteers will
in fact be coping with this kind of behavior. Nevertheless,
for those volunteers who are faced with working with alco-
holics, the need for training which can provide information
on this problem still exists. Readings, tapes, and individualized training packets which can be borrowed and consumed
at the volunteer's need and convenience will prove to be an
important link in the total training program.

Agencies might well consider the adequacy of their
own training programs as resources are made available for
volunteers. It is a fact that as courts have begun to train
volunteers, the training programs have made them much
more aware of staff training needs. It would be economical
if the court library has staff materials, so that they be
utilized as a part of volunteer orientation, too. Vice-versa,
it may well be that the addition of materials for volunteer
consumption will prove to be of mutual benefit to the court
staff as well. Many courts may have to face the embarrass-
ment of operating training programs for volunteers that ex-
cel what is being done in staff training. At this point the
possible spin-off from volunteer programs is an interesting
thought to contemplate. One of the immediate offshoots that

84

has resulted from volunteer programs has been the need to develop training programs for staff to help them utilize and understand volunteers.

Types of Take-Home Training Manuals

Later in this book (Chapter 15) some suggested written manual materials will be presented to the reader. Volunteer orientation manuals can be extremely dull reading if too technical, yet they do make for excellent reference material which may save the volunteer from having to call the staff for answers to a question whenever it arises. Just the economy of a manual from the standpoint of good management is enough to justify it, but beyond this a manual may also serve the dual purpose of providing a tool for training.

Manuals can be extremely helpful if they contain answers to questions. After a while, managers of volunteer programs become well aware of those questions that are asked over and over. These questions can readily be answered in a written training manual in such a manner as to save valuable time later in the program. The appendix to this chapter contains examples of several questions most often asked by volunteers in one court and the answers to these questions.

Books, Pamphlets, and Magazines

Several courts have established excellent pools of reading materials through volunteer contributions or regular volunteer program handouts. Staff and volunteers alike, by pooling subscriptions to magazines, make material available to many people that otherwise may have gone unread. Also, listed below are several books which are in no way exclusive to what is relevant. This listing is done with hesitation and with the realization that such a listing ultimately proves to be outdated and inadequate and invariably omits something that is vital. But here are good volunteer take-home training reading lists actually used in two programs. First, from Columbus, Ohio, for volunteers working with teenage girls in trouble at Friends in Action (thanks to Margaret Hoskins):

Richette, Lisa, The Throwaway Children. (Highly recommended.)

Clarke, John R. , The Importance of Being Imperfect.
(What kind of role model will you make for a troubled girl?
Of special interest in Chapter 8 are the ideas supporting
this quotation: "Children seem to grow best when they have
before their eyes the incentive to grow toward an exciting
and fulfilling world of adult life. ")

Ginott, H. , Between Parent and Teenager. (Could
his approach of giving an individual a real feeling of worth
be applicable to our relationship with our friends?)

Greene, H. , I Never Promised You a Rose Garden.
(Available in paperback. This perceptive account written
about an emotionally ill girl might give clues to how we can
assist our friends in facing reality and also evaluate alternatives and consequences.)

Konopka, G. , The Adolescent Girl in Conflict. (Volunteers working with girls this past year have found this among
the most helpful of suggested resources at their in-service
training meetings.)

Kovar, L. C. , Faces of the Adolescent Girl. (This
author contrasts the girl in search for a relationship with
the more mature persons we all strive to become through
allowing autonomous pursuits and personal relations to en-
rich each other.)

Leonard, G. B. , Education and Ecstasy. (This is a
bonus suggestion of a "mind-stretcher" to help you believe
"every person can delight in learning. " Let this be a challenge for volunteer and friend--to let it happen to both in
whatever relationship develops.)

Marshall, C. , Christy. (Available in paperback. Besides offering a wonderfully human story, this book has a
thread of acceptance interwoven that will help you think about
meeting someone on his own level and moving from there.)

Motley, W. , Knock on Any Door. (This story of a
sensitive boy who dreams of beauty but is driven to crime
has been required reading in Ohio State University juvenile
delinquency prevention courses.)

Sebald, H. , Adolescence: A Sociological Analysis.
(This is by far the most text-bookish approach on our reading list--definitely not for the practical mind unless you
need a cold shower of theory for balance!)

Steere, D. , On Listening to Another. (The first two
chapters only of this book seem especially applicable to what
is involved in learning to really listen as friends.)

Trobisch, W. , I Loved a Girl. (Available in paperback. This book is under consideration for use in sex education courses in high school. Written as an exchange of
letters, it might possibly prove useful for both volunteers

and girls.)

From the "In" Group Delinquency Prevention Project, Santa
Rosa, California, Alan Strachan has a list of the books
they've bought and have on lease to volunteers as part of
their training.   (To save space, we'll leave you to track
down the full citation.)

Hughes, Education in America; P. R. Farnsworth
(ed.), Annual Review of Psychology, 1965; Marx & Hillix,
Systems and Theories in Psychology; Deese, The Psychology
of Learning; Sherif & Sherif, An Outline of Social Psychology; Jersild, The Psychology of Adolescence; Anastasi, Fields
of Applied Psychology; Rogers, On Becoming a Person; Mc-
Curdy, The Personal World; R. W. White, Lives in Progress; Magary & Eichorn, The Exceptional Child; Peters (ed.),
Brett's History of Psychology; Hochberg, Perception; Hyman,
The Nature of Psychological Inquiry; Ellis, Transfer of
Learning; Sanford & Capeldi, Advancing Psychological Sci-
ence (Vol. 1); Aichhorn, Wayward Youth; Crow & Crow,
Child Psychology; Bettelheim, Love is Not Enough; Kemel-
man, Common Sense in Education; Redl & Wineman, Controls
from Within; Holt, How Children Learn; Harris, Emotional
Blocks to Learning; A. S. Neill, Freedom--Not License!;
Bode, Modern Educational Theories; Friendenberg, The Van-
ishing Adolescent; A. S. Neill, Summerhill; Axline, Dibs in
Search of Self; Glover, How to Help Your Teenager Grow
Up; Hart, Summerhill: For and Against; Menninger, The
Crime of Punishment; Tunley, Kids, Crime, and Chaos;
Montessori, The Absorbent Mind; Richette, The Throwaway
Children; Gesell, Ilg, Ames, Youth: The Years from Ten to
Sixteen; Morgan, Introduction to Psychology; Cronbach, Edu-
cational Psychology; Mathewson, Guidance Policy and Prac-
tice; National Institute of Mental Health, "Mental Health Pro-
gram Reports--3"; Scheier, Volunteer Programs in Courts?;
Morris, First Offender; Rissman, Constraint and Variety in
American Education; Teacher and the Taught; Abnormal Psychology; Ginott, Between Parent and Teenager; Redl & Wineman, Children Who Hate.

Popular magazines also contain a great deal that is readable.
For example the section in Time entitled "Behavior" is often
relevant to the volunteer dealing with delinquent and criminal
behavior.

Finally, popular magazines with an audience that is made up primarily of professionals in the behavioral sciences provide much material of use to the volunteer. In this category we would include such magazines as <u>Psychology Today</u> and <u>Trans-Action</u>.

While magazines, journals, and newspapers contain much that is of value for training purposes, these materials will not reach their full potential for training unless the trainer recognizes his need to seek out and extract these materials and get them into the hands of the volunteer in some form.

More selectively there are the professional journals used by the helping professionals. Rather than citing an exhaustive listing here, we would only emphasize that the trainer and the professional staff should see their role as that of being vigilant in looking for consumable volunteer literature in professional journals.

Tapes

It has been our observation that tapes are probably more useful in take-home training than in any other segment of training. There are several reasons for this. Tapes are often of marginal sound quality, and the privacy of the home is conducive to the conditions necessary for concentration when this is the case. Also when people are alone with a tape, they are free to play back certain segments important to the listener. This is not always feasible in a group.

Long tapes tax the patience of listeners, and the individual listening at home has the freedom to stop the tape at any point to take a break, whereas again with the group this may be unsatisfactory. When a tape is featuring one person, there is a particular danger of people becoming bored listening to just one voice.

Finally, tapes address the problems of individual volunteers who need exposure to knowledge regarding specific problems.

A tape library that is at least adequate can be purchased for about $40. We refer the reader to Chapter 8 which lists, with annotation, what we feel are some of the better tapes. It should also be kept in mind that tapes and recording machines are standard equipment in most courts, so the economy of this as a training tool is evident. Courts may even consider the possibility of buying some inexpensive or used equipment for loaning to volunteers. Currently, cassettes can be purchased for as little as $15 per unit. Obviously, a good check-out system is important both for tapes as well as the sound reproduction equipment. A surprising number of people now have tape recording equipment or have access to it.

Ongoing Activities

A trainer should be sensitive to television programs, movies, plays, and lectures as they are available. A regular check on community calendars will often reveal programs which, if called to volunteers' attention, will prove to be useful in terms of training aids. The movie "In Cold Blood, " for example, had much besides entertainment value. It would teach volunteers a great deal about understanding deviant behavior.

In one court volunteer program, not only have the volunteers viewed selected films together, but their probationers have also been included. These sessions have been followed up by discussion periods which have been seen as helpful in terms of training value.

Several "white papers" on crime have been presented by the national TV networks. These programs are often listed a week or less prior to showing, which causes a problem in calling them to the attention of volunteers. However, in small volunteer programs this is not a major obstacle.

Reference was made in the preceding chapter to the internalizing of learning by sharing experiences. This also holds true for take-home training. A tape or a book will have more meaning if, after being consumed, it is discussed with someone. Obviously, a group experience may not be possible in all instances. However when possible, the trainer may want to consider the possible value of bringing together common interest groups for the purpose of pursuing material of common interest. This may well come at the initiation of the volunteer who invites volunteers with common problems to share a TV program, a tape, or the group discussion of a book or magazine. Obviously these kinds of activities will occur with more frequency as they have the sanction of the court itself.

The last item in "take-home training" which we feel
is of value is some type of document which provides the volunteer with philosophical and practical direction. This reading can provide the volunteer with occasional reading which
gives him some grounding in the philosophy of rehabilitation
in correctional settings. It may well be that such a reading
is in fact a synopsis of the content of formal training. In
any event it serves the purpose of rejuvenation of the volunteer when he may not have access to the court staff.

As a sample of such a reading, Report V by Mr.
Jorgensen, "Guides for Volunteers in Correctional Settings, "
follows. Permission to reprint any of this monograph which
may have relevance to an individual volunteer program is
granted.

*   *   *   *

Report V

GUIDES FOR VOLUNTEERS IN CORRECTIONAL SETTINGS

Introduction

When President Kennedy, in January 1961, spoke his
first official words for his constituency, he said, "Ask not
what your country can do for you; ask what you can do for
your country. " The recent great movement in volunteerism
has been both a response and a tribute to President Kennedy.
It has demonstrated that American citizens do care about
social problems and will become involved in their solution.

It should be said, however, that when President Kennedy charged the people of America with this challenge, he
was calling upon a giving of self well entrenched in American society. Americans have always been a volunteering
people. Yet there are differences in volunteerism today
when contrasted with the movement of yesterday. Today we
are faced with problems of greater magnitude than at any
time in our history; such that the present administration is
looking to volunteers to provide solutions to problems that
have defied solutions by the established problem-solving ma-
chinery. Housing and Urban Development Secretary George
Rommney has set as a goal that of enlisting every citizen in

volunteer activity of some type.

As a volunteer member of an ever growing force of
people engaged in correctional work, you have embarked on
a course which will lead you to experience alternate feelings
of frustration, satisfaction, dismay, anger and humor. There
may be times when you will ask yourself, "Why did I ever
let myself in for this kind of experience?" On other occasions, you may experience satisfactions common to many
of us who have worked in corrections professionally; the
satisfaction of helping a person find meaning in his life and
in his world, and the satisfaction of knowing you have helped
an individual re-direct his life toward socially acceptable
goals.

Coming in contact, as you will, with people alienated
from, and in many cases, victimized by our society is an
experience that will sober you and make you count your
blessings. It will give you a new perspective about life as
it is lived in the various segments of our society. It will
provide you with an opportunity to confront first-hand two of
America's most stubborn problems--crime and delinquency.
It will give you cause to question whether our approaches to
the problems are workable.

If crime and delinquency have thrived under old programs, you may take pride in the fact that you are a part
of a new era in corrections. This new era holds the promise that correctional practice can be reshaped as a result of
what has been a knowledge explosion in the social sciences.
You are entering volunteer service at a time when community programs are being pursued with much vigor. Attempts
are being made to utilize the community where the offender
lives as an environment wherein the offender can be controlled and changed.

President Kennedy once said, "One man can make a
difference, and every man should try." It is in this spirit
that this manual is submitted. We believe that your presence in the correctional picture will make a difference to
someone, but in any event, your efforts will provide their
own rewards.

The Problem

Whether you read J. Edgar Hoover's <u>Uniform Crime</u>

Reports, read of crime in newspapers, view it on television,
or become a victim, you are undoubtedly sensitive to the
fact that the country today is more crime conscious than at
any time in the past.   Is crime on the increase as Mr.
Hoover reports, or are we simply more proficient in detect-
ing crime and apprehending criminals?   The answer seems
to be "Yes" in both instances.   The incidence of crime in
relation to population growth has increased but so has our
police technology.   The question of whether we are simply
drawing more water from a well of crime than we formerly
did is circular and somewhat defeating.   What should be of
more concern is what are we doing with those people whom
we draw from the well and inject into the correctional system.

From all indications, what we have been doing with
and for offenders has been spectacularly unsuccessful.   You
may be interested in knowing that the correctional system
of which you are now a member is by and large a study in
failure.   Briefly, we have in the United States spent 80% of
our corrections dollar and 85% of our corrections work force
in lock-up facilities and institutions which too often are associated with failure on the part of the people they were designed to help.   We have only recently begun to establish
new priorities and to seek new solutions.   You are a part
of these new solutions.

The problem is one as old as man himself--the problem of fitting into a dynamic society.   When man cannot
change to fit into society, he often withdraws from that society or if this does not work, he strikes out at society.
The responsibility of any correctional operation is that of
creating changes in society to permit participation on the
part of all its members as well as change in the offender's
view of himself in relation to society.

Past Attempts at Correction

Society has not always faced the problem of correction.   Maiming, banishment, execution, slavery, penal
servitude have all been practiced by man in his attempts to
deal with people who deviate.   Slowly but surely, however,
man has drifted away from the concept of punishment toward
what is today referred to as "re-integration. "   This shift in
thinking has been, for the most part, evolutionary.   As with
all movements, there have been the reformers and revolu-
tionaries who, from time to time, have pricked the conscience

of the people responsible for change.   But rapid change, where present, has been featured by conflict.

If one were to pick a predominant feature of corrections in the United States, it would have to be our inclination to incarcerate offenders rather than work with them in the community.   Our jails and prisons are tributes to America's propensity to do things in a big way--even building correctional institutions!

If Americans have a tendency to do things in a big way, they also have a tendency to find the means to succeed. The ability to put technology to work to solve problems has not, however, been the case in corrections.   The inability to find the means to control crime and rehabilitate criminals while we were solving other problems has frustrated America and, it would seem, has provided much of the impetus to incarcerate and insulate the offender.   If this approach is being questioned now as it seems to be, it is probably the result not of soul searching as much as the inability of institutions to handle the vast numbers of people committed by the judicial system.

A 1967 report by the President's Commission on Law Enforcement and Administration of Justice entitled The Challenge of Crime in a Free Society and the supporting Task Force Reports became landmarks in an inventory of correctional programs.   The report left little doubt that crime control and treatment in the United States has been a disjointed, disorganized effort that must give way to new thoughts and new programs.

Perhaps the real challenge of crime in a free society is whether that society can in the midst of civil unrest and turmoil do the necessary things to bring about a viable system of criminal justice.   We seem to be at the crossroads now.   On the one hand, we are being pulled by forces which would bring to bear more of punishment and incarceration while, on the other hand, we are being pulled by forces which want to expose the problem to search, research, and new courses of action.

The institution of corrections, as with many of our present institutions, is being asked to perform functions for which it was not originally designed.   When new tasks are asked of any organization, concomitant change must also occur in the technology utilized by that organization which

places new demands on the people as well as the structure
within which they operate.

Correctional institutions in the past have had the
tasks of holding and punishing the people who have been
deemed offenders of the law.   It was thought that punishment
would by its aversive nature change offensive behavior.   Thus
a jail or prison through incarceration, detained the offender,
which in itself served as punishment.   This required in the
way of technology, knowledge of prison management, security and control.   In terms of people, it required people who
appreciated this philosophy and who were conscientious about
security and enforcement measures.   In terms of structure
it required a strong physical facility.   The failure of this
model to correct behavior is now well known, yet this model
is still being asked to perform the correctional tasks in relation to many offenders today.

Today the institution of corrections is being asked to
change the behavior of offenders and return them to society
as non-offenders.   In too many instances this task is being
attempted in overcrowded and non-functional structures and
organizations.   The new technology required is superimposed
on personnel that lacks appreciation and understanding of its
goals.   Thus we have a situation where change when it occurs, becomes difficult and at times, violent.

The new task, that of re-integrating offenders into
society, requires decent, honest people such as yourselves,
who can meaningfully enter an offender's life in such a way
as to change his behavior.   That is what this monograph is
about.

What Is Being Corrected?

The question of what is meant by criminal or delinquent behavior has plagued modern man for some time.   If
we cannot agree on the nature of the problem, obviously we
will not agree on correcting it.

Crime and delinquency have been explained by many
theories and to recount them all would not serve any real
purpose.   However, we might say that physical, moral,
psychological and sociological theories have all "had their
day" so far as this behavior is concerned.   It was once felt
that a criminal's physical make-up could account for his

behavior. We still see a remnant of this in the comic strip
"Dick Tracy. "

Today, sociology, psychiatry, psychology, and social
work all have contributions to make in understanding criminal and delinquent behavior. They deal with people within
legal frameworks which vary from jurisdiction to jurisdiction. Delinquency, a legal term, comes from the Latin
word "delinquere"--to fail. This translation has as much
meaning as any, for in reality, the delinquent does reflect
failure--failure on the part of greater society to provide
socially acceptable roles for all its citizens.

Perhaps we might better understand delinquent or
criminal behavior from a couple of examples which depict
this behavior as adjustment as well as a means of achieving
a goal.

The military service, as a part of its training, pre-
scribes certain behavior in the event one becomes a prisoner
of war. It sets out definite expectations that the prisoner
continually harass his captors by planning and attempting to
escape. The rationale for this is that this keeps the enemy
tied up in guarding the captive and thus he is not free to
fight the captive's allies. As a rationale for prescribing a
code of behavior, this is sound. It provides definite role
expectations for the prisoner, but more important, it keeps
his mind busy under oppressive circumstances. In a sense,
it keeps him involved in a mission which gives purpose to
his life and keeps him from losing contact or "going crazy. "

From our knowledge of many offenders, they view their
circumstances in much the same way as the prisoner of war.
They consider the larger society their enemy and there is
an unofficial code which expects and sometimes demands acting out behavior. Thus, the feelings of oppression which
could lead to "becoming crazy" are handled by delinquent or
criminal behavior--which not only prevents insanity from becoming a fact but also provides a measure of status, power,
and meaning.

Let us look at an offender whom I shall call Ronald.
Ronald was a 17-year-old youth who came to a federal institution for delinquent youth for Dyer Act (stealing a car and
taking it across a state line). On the surface, Ronald presented himself as a friendly, somewhat passive youth. He
was liked by staff and by the inmates. He followed the rules

and reaped some of the rewards of the institution in the form
of greater freedom and more privileges.   As his length of
stay progressed, he began to emerge as a candidate for
work-release, a program which allowed him to go into the
community during the day where he was employed in a machine shop and return to the institution at night.   The objectives were to provide him with work skills, good employment habits, and an opportunity to experience community
living.   The episode ended, however, when Ronald one day
managed to smuggle in a hacksaw blade to his friends and
was later found, along with these other inmates, sawing
through the bars of his unit.

How is this self-defeating behavior to be viewed?   Is
it a psychiatric problem?   Is Ronald crazy?   Is he stupid?
Is he accomplishing anything through this behavior?   If so,
what?   These are questions that we all consider as we look
at Ronald and they cannot be answered until we know more
of Ronald in relation to his past and present environment.
Our difficulty in understanding Ronald is compounded by our
natural inclination to look at behavior in terms of our own
motivational system and our own moral schemata.   Until we
can view the behavior from Ronald's perspective, we will
face a puzzle of seemingly bizarre and self-defeating actions
which serve only to keep Ronald in trouble.

Ronald, it should be said, began to learn reactions to
problem situations long before we first met him.   He began
at the age of six when he was removed from the custody of
two ineffective alcoholic parents.   He learned a basic lesson
that adults are not reliable and it is safer if you don't get
too involved with them.   This superficiality was featured in
Ronald's dealings with adults throughout several foster homes
and children's institutions.   He was like many children that
are found along this route.   He simply didn't "put down any
roots. "

The inability or unwillingness to put down roots has
a double edge.   It means that eventually very few people
have vested interests in such a person and the person knows
that few, if any, people really care about his behavior.   Under these conditions, this person, no matter what he does,
is not going to damage anyone's reputation, either his own
or those of significant others.   His reputation is of no concern and there really are no significant others.

This is an important consideration.   For you and for

me to contemplate an illegal act is also to contemplate how this act would reflect on those who are important to us, such as wives, friends, teachers, parents, etc. To steal a car for us would be to hurt the people important to us as well as ourselves. To Ronald, stealing a car is a means of getting from an unpleasant situation to at least an unknown and possibly better situation. The car is transportation and little more.

"But, " you ask, "doesn't this boy realize he will be caught and when he is, he will face federal charges and a criminal record which he will carry the rest of his life?" This question, of course, is asked again out of our frame of reference. We value freedom and an arrest-free record and we assume everyone else does. This, however, is not always the case. Imagine, if you will, living in a sub-culture where jail is accepted as a part of life. As a youth you have probably seen family members go to correctional institutions and jails. You eventually come to the conclusion that this may happen to you. When it does, there is no great surprise. If you serve a ten-day sentence, then later a 30 and then a 60-day sentence, a process is set in motion where jail time is something that can be dealt with just like anything else. A youth exposed to this set of circumstances learns to do time. Jail, then, is no longer a deterrent.

Jail was not a deterrent to Ronald. In fact, it was something for which he had some positive feelings. While he verbalized a wish to be free, he also demonstrated some satisfaction with being confined. He welcomed the concern which was inherent in the discipline of the institution. He also welcomed the fact that decision making in which he had already demonstrated his ineffectiveness was being handled by a higher order, the institutional administrator. This gave Ronald a "rest" from some very taxing demands. When Ronald is viewed in this light, it becomes rather clear that he is aware that work-release is, in fact, a test which, if passed, will lead eventually to release from the institution. If he passes the test, he will be returned to a world in which he has been a failure. To pass or to fail becomes the real question.

In Ronald's case, failure becomes a very reasonable option. It postpones the day when he must face the responsibility of the outside world and it puts him in good with his peers. For anyone who would "risk" his freedom to bring hacksaw blades to his peers must be a good guy. This one

example of one delinquent boy is cited because it demonstrates how behavior becomes reasonable when viewed from
within a set of values.   Until we understand the framework
from which the offender operates, we are left with our own
which more often than not has little relevance to the life of
an offender.   All of which is to say that the behavior with
which we are dealing has purpose and meaning.   Our responsibility is to understand the behavior _first_ and then decide
how we will structure our activities to become a part of the
offender's world.

The Volunteer as a Force for Change

As a volunteer faced with the task of working with offenders, you are perhaps naturally inclined to compare yourself to the professional correctional worker and see yourself
as being deficient by comparison.   While you may lack some
of the formal knowledge of the experienced correctional worker, you possess certain distinct advantages which tend to
compensate for this deficiency.   These advantages deserve
some discussion.

Role Reflection

The professional correctional worker is expected to
behave in certain ways.   He is expected to manage two distinct roles.   He must be the "good guy" in that he must
provide counseling, direction and assistance to the offender
while at the same time acting as the "heavy" who holds out
the prospect of surveillance, investigation, and possible re-
arrest.   It is a tribute to many of the fine, dedicated professionals in corrections that they have managed to handle
both roles.   In many instances, however, despite their efforts, these people are rejected by certain types of offenders
because the offender cannot differentiate between these roles.
What he sees is a contradiction.   His response is to stay
aloof and uninvolved.

The volunteer has a natural advantage in working with
this type of offender because he is being asked to act chiefly
in the role of the guiding, rewarding, directing person.   This
is not to say that the volunteer does not confront the offender
with his behavior or make legitimate demands.   But when he
deals with the offender, he is not burdened with the role of
officialdom which is read into so many correctional, helping

relationships.   When the offender clearly has a positive role
expectation of the helping person as projected by the volunteer, he senses consistency.   This consistency is sadly
needed because in the life of the offender, people have been
most inconsistent.   Perhaps more than any one thing the offender needs to know intimately a stable, reliable person.

Among disadvantaged people where many offenders are
to be found, the word "professional" often has a negative
meaning.   The professional is often viewed as a person who
does a job only because "it's a job to do. "   The pay is considered to be the major motive for performing the job.   It
is not surprising, then, that this kind of person would resent being the problem on which the professional correctional
worker's livelihood is based.   Often are heard the words
"If it wasn't for me, you wouldn't have a job" as the offender vents some of his feelings about being the captive client.

As a volunteer, your motives are obviously not financial.   It is somewhat disarming for an offender to be faced
with someone whose "game" is really one of genuine concern.   He is accustomed to playing the correctional game
with a person who usually under considerable pressure makes
superficial and hurried contacts which reflect the emergency
nature of the encounter.   Your distinct advantage, and one
to be exploited, is that your motives are much more visible.
Offering help under these conditions places upon the offender
a greater responsibility to become involved in a relationship
of truth and genuineness.

Frame of Reference

Those of us who have received our training in the behavioral sciences have, I must admit, often related to what
we have seen as pathology or illness in the offender.   We
have looked for (and often found) symptoms about which we
have read.   Often in this process, we have forgotten about
the person manifesting this behavior.   Most volunteers are
not accustomed to dealing with people in parts, but rather
dealing with them as whole human beings with needs, de-
sires, dreams, and capacities to fulfill expectations.   This
is the kind of person the offender needs to know in order to
grow and develop new perceptions.

Size of Caseload

In the government document, The Challenge of Crime in a Free Society, it was reported that probation and parole caseloads are extremely high. Most of the offenders being supervised were being handled in caseloads of fifty or more. Dealing with large caseloads demands that the professional worker by necessity must be selective about who will get his time. This means that many offenders who need direction will be neglected in favor of those who may need even more help. The volunteer working with relatively few, and in many cases with only one offender, obviously faces a much better ratio in terms of sheer numbers.

Large caseloads do something else to the professional correctional worker. Working daily with failures, people who do not view correctional services as help, poorly motivated and alienated people, creates an atmosphere of defeat which at times leads to indifference. The volunteer who is spending the greater share of his time in success experiences is less conditioned to failure and enters the relationship in a more positive frame of mind. He generally has too much personal investment in his charge to allow failure. In any event, he is an advocate in areas where the professional cannot be.

The advantages discussed above should not be construed as a dismissal of the professional correctional worker. It is rather a plea for recognition of some limits of the professional role and utilization of the volunteer in dealing with the offender where these limits are evident.

Getting Involved--Relationship

Helping anyone to change involves an intangible something known as a "relationship." This word has been bandied about a great deal but its meaning is elusive. If you were to look back at your own life, I would imagine you would identify several people who touched your life in very positive, meaningful ways. They may have been teachers, parents, clergymen, or friends. But because of the quality and depth of their involvement with you, you equate them with certain changes which have occurred in your life. I would imagine you would say that these people had a positive relationship. You would perhaps also recall that these people stood by you during difficult periods, accepted you even when you were

difficult to accept, and, in short, they moved throughout
your life as a strong, constructive force.

The vast majority of offenders have not had the kind
of experience just described and so often taken for granted.
In contrast, they have experienced people touching their lives
in destructive ways. Rather than giving, they have seen
these people take. Where the offender has sought people to
lean on, he has found people who were too unstable to lean
on. In short, he has come to know needy, deficient people
unable to fulfill the adult roles society expects of them.
From these negative relationships, the offender has learned
that involvement will be painful. It is from this experience
that the offender is conditioned to deal with a helping person.
His approach is often one of resistance to involvement or he
becomes involved in much the same way as a child with
childlike expectations and demands. Establishing a good relationship with this kind of person is taxing, often frustrating,
but crucial for any help which will bring about change.

Getting Involved--Showing Respect

The idea of showing respect seems to the reader to
be very elementary to the helping process, I am sure. Perhaps it seems elementary because it is something that we
as reasonably successful people come to expect and even
demand. Generally if we are not afforded the kind of respect we think we are due, we do something about it. We
may complain, confront or demand, but we do not usually
accept second-rate treatment.

The offender does not generally expect respect. He
is by now accustomed to being in the way. He has probably
been getting very little real respect in school, home, or in
his employment situation. He may well not be accustomed
to respect and may need to learn new responses to people
who respect him as a human being. It stands to reason
then that if a person is to learn self-respect, he must be
respected. You may well be the first person to provide this
very basic experience.

But, can we truly respect someone who behaves in
ways that are contrary to our moral system? It is easy to
say, "I accept you and respect you, " but accepting and respecting people who behave in ways which deviate from our
accepted norms is not all that easy when put to the test.

As a volunteer working with people who behave in anti-social
ways, it becomes extremely important for you to be aware
of some of your own hang-ups.   All of us, if we were to be
candid, would probably admit that there is part of us that we
like about ourselves and we tend to project that facet as much
as possible.   We would also admit that there is a part of us
that we may not like very much and we are inclined to isolate or hide this part of ourselves.   This may be an immature facet or it may be anti-social.

The offender with whom we are involved often reminds
us of the very immaturity or anti-social tendencies we dislike in ourselves.   Our response to the offender for remind-
ing us of our fallibility can be one of anger unless we are
aware of and have some insights into our own feelings.   As
a volunteer, you should be frank to admit when you are unable to deal with certain behavior.   It may well be that an
early realization of this will save you and the offender from
a deteriorating situation later.

Getting Involved--Listening and Hearing

Reluctance to talk may be one of the characteristics
of the offender.   There is good reason for this.   Many people are reluctant to talk because they have realized that no
one will listen to them or hear what they are saying.   They
realize finally that communicating by words is not effective.
Such a person needs to be dealt with with patience.   He has
to be convinced that he will be listened to and that once listened to, you have heard him.   Thus, it is important that
you reflect back to the offender your understanding of his
message.   This will provide him with a realization that you
are trying to tune him in rather than tune him out.

Allowing a person to talk helps him in other ways.
In your own life, I am sure you can recall where talking
about a problem has made it more clear and more manage-
able.   To get a problem "out on the table" makes it more
visible and puts one in a better position to deal with it.   So
often in our day-to-day contacts, we see people talking at
each other.   They may look at each other in the process of
a conversation, but one is compelled to say that this looking
serves only to provide one communicator with a signal to
start talking--that signal being that the other communicator
has stopped.   This kind of exchange does not provide meaningful communication.   Rather it becomes a way of avoiding

real interchange. It becomes important in hearing people that we listen for repeated themes as well as for material that is avoided.

I remember a very unattractive young girl whom I saw on the day she was referred to a juvenile court for "incorrigibility. " As with many girls referred for this offense, she had been sexually promiscuous. As I listened to her words which, in essence said, "Daddy loves me more than the other children" and "I have six boy friends, all of whom want to marry me, " I heard quite another set of messages which were, "Daddy doesn't care about me" and "boys like me for my body. "

A good listener is generally in demand anywhere, but particularly in a helping situation. People do generally wish to talk about themselves if someone will only listen and evidence that they care.

The Helping Process

Being Accessible. Making oneself available to the offender is actually much more than being physically present. It is demonstrating your willingness to let the offender know you as a human being. There has been a reluctance on the part of many correctional workers to become involved with the people they are supposed to help. Behind this reluctance has been a fear that if one became involved, he would be "conned" or in other ways become disappointed. There is presently a different view emerging regarding involvement which maintains that the offender not having learned how to become involved must learn this, among other things, if he is to find his way in the world. As a helper, obviously you must teach him how to become involved by being a good model.

Letting the offender know you as a person starts by your setting an example, in terms of behavior. Just as we have learned from examples of authority figures in our lives, so must the offender. The impact of a correctional experience is having new human models injected into the life of the offender in such a way as to allow him to interact with these models.

Professional correctional workers have been reluctant to do things for the offender, the rationale being if we do

things for the offender, he will do nothing for himself. This
has also come under considerable scrutiny. We do things
for people for whom we have deep concern and this becomes
a way of letting them see us as human beings. We sometimes forget that in corrections we find many immobilized
people who are unable to take action in their own behalf.
They may need someone to pick up a telephone to make a
contact or they may see in the offer of concrete help an indication of real interest. The offender is tired of words.
He is much more impressed with action. He has too often
seen people fail to follow through on what they said they
would do. As a volunteer, it is assumed that you have a
vital interest in the offender. Let this come through naturally and you will find that the offender in time will pick up
these signals and respond to you.

Empathizing. A difficulty which many helpers face is
that of being unable to put one's self in the position of a person facing difficulties in adapting to society's demands.
Added to this is the tendency to be overcome by the offender's situation once we begin to feel with him and recognize
his problem. Our task as the helping person is to develop
the capacity to feel with him, yet remain in a position with
respect to the problem so as to be able to view it and deal
with it.

All of us have experienced certain hurts throughout
our lives and it is difficult for us to avoid over-identification
when we see other people experiencing similar hurts. All
of this is to say that knowledge of ourselves is an important
factor in helping. We must continually keep in mind that
when the helper offers help, he must be psychologically
stronger than the person being helped. If he is not, he will
be dismissed very quickly.

Communication. In order to effectively communicate
with an individual, we are faced with finding ways of getting
that individual to listen to what we are communicating, understanding the messages we are sending, and taking appropriate action upon receipt of the message. When the
communicants come from different segments of our society,
as is often the case with the correctional client and the volunteer, we can anticipate that there may be communications
problems.

Two mistakes are often made by the helping person.
One is to attempt to speak a language with which the

offender is familiar. The other is to speak over the head
of the offender. Both of these deserve some discussion.

I have heard it said by neophytes in correctional work
that "... if you're going to help these people, you have to
get down on their level and talk their language." The problem that presents itself here, however, is that one does not
easily go to another level and speak another language without
being considered false. To attempt to use a sub-cultural
language when you are not familiar with it is to invite disaster. It is important that the language used is simple and
clear. There is a common language that can be understood
by everyone in our society. To attempt to converse in a
sub-cultural language is to suggest that the offender cannot
converse except in certain circles. This delays re-integration rather than enhances it.

The tendency to speak over the head of the offender
is best illustrated by an experience I once had while visiting
a boys' correctional facility. A youth approached me on the
sidewalk and asked if I could help him. I said I would try
and asked the youth what he wanted. "Tell me the meaning
of 'reluctantly'," he said. I replied "Reluctantly means that
someone did something against their wishes. They really
didn't want to do it, but they did it anyway." Satisfied, the
boy began to leave, but curiosity made me ask, "Why did
you want to know the meaning of that word?" His reply was,
"My caseworker just told me my parole had been approved
by the parole board--reluctantly."

The lesson to be learned from the above example is
that we cannot assume that because one acts as if he understands, that he really does. The youth just cited sought me
out, a safe object whom he didn't know nor did he expect to
know in the future. It didn't matter to him that I was aware
of his ignorance, but he didn't want his caseworker to presume that he was ignorant. Thus he let his caseworker assume that he understood something that was in reality not
understood at all. If we were to tell someone, for example,
that we thought he had done a good job, we could say to
him, "You performed that task in an exemplary manner,"
or we could say, "Right on," or we could say simply, "You
did a good job." The latter would be understood by everyone and would be preferable.

Causing the Offender to Feel Discomfort. The offender, like many other people who have been disengaged

from the greater society, must find a way to cope with this
fact.   This coping often takes the form of becoming content
with a life style which is anti-social or asocial.   This requires that a purposeful effort be made by the volunteer to
bring about discomfort on the part of the offender.

This phenomenon of becoming content with a life that
is fraught with problems does not happen easily nor is it
arrived at quickly.   Perhaps the best example can be drawn
from another group of disengaged citizens who receive public
assistance or "welfare." The miracle of our age is that we
have seen people being paid monthly welfare checks based on
out-dated cost of living indices--these checks being slashed
at times to as low as 70% of what is considered needed.
And yet these people somehow do not die!   What seems to
happen is that faced with the prospect of a bleak future, it
is possible for the human mind and body to enter into some
kind of mold and create some semblance of life within that
mold.   Once this decision has been made, it is a difficult
one to reverse.   Many offenders follow this same basic pattern.   They assume jail will continue to be a factor in their
lives and that they will never truly fit into society.   Nevertheless, life must go on.   Life then becomes a matter of
building your life, not on future expectations but rather on
what is possible here and now.

One of the first steps in creating discomfort is that
of holding out expectations and demands.   The offender really
expects and demands very little of himself.   He expects
others to do likewise.   However, when someone approaches
him with expectations and certain demands, he is left with
the uncomfortable feeling that he must be viewed as being
capable of carrying out these expectations.   This in itself
creates discomfort.   He can, of course, fail to measure up
to the expectations, but this is not a real alternative if the
person holding out the expectation persists.   A common response on the part of all of us is to fashion our behavior to
fit the roles set out for us.

Persistence is a key word in dealing with the offender.   It means very simply that the person who is the helper
must outlast, be more stubborn, or simply refuse to accept
failure on the part of the offender.   The attitude that must
be conveyed is that the offender can overcome adversity and
undertake responsibility.   Offenders have been past masters
in convincing others to give up on them, and they will expect you to follow this pattern also.   We can trap ourselves

into thinking that because we encounter offenders who have behaved in a self-defeating pattern for a number of years, they will always do so regardless of what we do. The fact of the matter is, however, that offenders just like the rest of us, mature, change, and stabilize. If we as workers or helpers do not convey an expectation that change can occur, there is probably no one else in the offender's life who will.

It should be noted that many offenders who have a distorted notion of how they can control their own lives come to the conclusion that they indeed do not or cannot control their lives. They project on others the blame for their own irresponsible behavior. The person who presents such behavior must be faced with the reality of the choices that he has in directing his life. When an individual has lived a life thinking he has no choices, suddenly to find that he can make choices is often an amazing discovery. To discover that one's behavior determines how others react to him is a shock to the offender but a very necessary one.

In attempting to counsel and direct offenders, we are more inclined to try to soften our approach rather than confront the offender with reality. Time, being of the essence, requires that we cut through some of this resistance, but just as important is the fact that a person who is allowed to go on thinking dishonestly is actually being supported in the kind of behavior which leads to arrest and re-arrest.

A question that is asked by many volunteers is "What should I do if I become angry with the offender to whom I am assigned?" Obviously, when we hold out expectations and demands, we also lay ourselves open to disappointment and anger when our expectations are not met. When we invest ourselves deeply in a person, we expect to see some return on our investment. This is only natural. It is also very natural that we should be honest with the offender when we are angry or disappointed in him. To attempt to conceal real anger would actually be dishonest. When we care about someone, we express anger when their behavior is such that it doesn't serve their best interest. Rather than try to conceal anger, it will serve the relationship much better if the volunteer admits openly to his anger, expresses it, and proceeds from there. This will serve to clear the air.

A major consideration, however, in dealing with anger is that we as helpers demonstrate the maturity to

recover from this emotion and resume the relationship. To
the offender, who has been the recipient of much anger, it
is a natural assumption that anger is equated with rejection.
To correct this misapprehension, the offender must be taught
that rejection need not follow anger. If this lesson can be
taught, it is the basis for a corrective experience.

Hostility or anger may also be expressed by the offender. Being confined in the sense of having definite responsibilities to another person who expects change will, in
all likelihood, trigger some direct or indirect hostile feelings. It is important for the volunteer to realize that much
of the anger expressed by the offender actually masks fear--
fear of not measuring up, fear of someone getting too close,
and fear of change. If the volunteer can react to the fear
rather than the anger, he will be much less intimidated and
thus able to withstand the anger. The life of the offender
has been filled with anger which is usually responded to with
anger. The badly needed experience as far as the offender
is concerned is to witness and experience alternatives to
anger. He needs to know people who can "keep their own
cool" or regain it.

Using the Crisis. In corrections, we deal with a
crisis-prone group of people. We find as a group, people
who tend to be in a crisis more often than not, and who in
many instances, precipitate the very crisis which causes
them so much pain and discomfort. If we were to look for
the reasons why one group of people should be in a continual
state of crisis where more often than not they are being
overcome by the crisis, while another group finds through
crises the experiences which lead to growth and maturity,
we would undoubtedly find that the former group has faced
crises pretty much alone, while the latter group has faced
crises with models who taught responses to crisis which, as
we know, set the groundwork for directing our own lives.

Crisis serves a real purpose in the lives of inadequate people. If one is faced daily with thoughts of how insignificant one is, how inadequate one is to life's demands,
and how little self-worth one has, then dealing with a crisis
serves to get the mind off these intolerable thoughts. To do
combat with some outer force even though resigned to being
overcome, serves to provide activity which diverts one from
the hopeless day-to-day contemplation of self-worthlessness.

Helping the person during the crisis is vital. A

person is most mobilized to take action in crises. For the volunteer, the opportunity exists for this action to be directed constructively. The person who has faced crises alone needs to have someone stand by him through this period; again, for the reason that he needs to learn new responses. The old adage "nothing succeeds like success" is very relevant in understanding people in crisis. The challenge for the volunteer is that of programming for the first successful experience.

Changing the pattern of people in crisis has been noted when they experience a role change. We have, I am sure, noted that many ex-offenders have been effective in designing programs to help other offenders. To help rather than be helped is a significant difference; one that places the offender in a role with different expectations. This writer has seen many people on the receiving end of help who, when asked to alleviate someone else's pain re-defined their own self-image. The volunteer might ask himself from time to time, "Can I find a way to help this offender help someone else?" If the answer becomes "Yes," this is a milestone in development.

Using Authority. We are all inclined when we think of the concept of authority to think perhaps more in terms of negative or aversive actions which direct people into behavior which is conformist or socially acceptable. We are less inclined to look at authority as a positive entity. In correctional work, authority stands as a major tool of the correcting agent. How it is used will determine whether correction actually occurs.

As a volunteer, the authority you will find most helpful is the implicit authority of your personal psychological strength as evidenced by the fact that you are a successful person. If nothing else, you possess the expertise of knowing how to get along in this world without breaking the law. This authority is vital to the helping relationship. Beyond this expertise is the authority to reward and commend. These two are powerful factors in the helping relationship. Too often rewards and compliments which we take for granted elude the offender. He is thus forced to operate without really having defined for himself what is perceived as good.

The enforcement aspect of authority need not be emphasized unduly. As a volunteer, you are really not being asked to be an enforcer. The power of society to enforce

will continue to be obvious whether you are working with the
offender in the institution or in the community. He is aware
of the contingencies of being an offender. The volunteer
should emphasize what must eventually govern the lives of
all of us, that is, the ability to gain from society and contribute to society in somewhat equal measure.

Giving Advice. As we view offenders' attempts to relate themselves to the world and we see them doing it badly,
we are tempted to tell them how to do it better. Giving advice in itself is not bad, but advice that is given with no
consideration for a person's ability to perceive and carry
out the advice is likely to be ignored.

Three things should be considered in giving advice:

(1) The request: does the offender ask for advice? The
     point to be made here is that advice given upon re-
     quest may be received and acted upon better than ad-
     vice given without a request.
(2) The need for advice: some people are simply im-
     mobilized--too immobilized to ask for any kind of
     help. They are "hung up on dead center" as it were.
     Such people may need help in the form of advice. If
     so, test their willingness to listen and give them the
     benefit of a suggested plan of action.
(3) The ability to use advice: obviously if we advise peo-
     ple to take a course of action they do not understand,
     they will not know the rationale for the action and
     will resist taking the action. Much as the high school
     freshman may look over the shoulder of his fellow
     algebra student for a correct answer; he gets the
     answer but he never understands the rationale for the
     answer. The result is he fails algebra.

Conclusion

There are no magic solutions to be found in changing
offenders into non-offenders. There are no "right" answers.
The above material is suggested to guide you. It in no way
is suggested as a "counseling cookbook. "

Helping the offender is a process. The process is
usually uneven. The goal of help is that of bringing the offender to the point where he will participate in a world in
which he has not previously participated. He learns to do

this, with your help, by perceiving himself as a better person and the world as a less hostile world. He also learns, through your example, that the immediate gratification of impulses to which he has become accustomed, can be controlled or at least postponed. He learns that there are other ways of obtaining satisfaction than acting on impulse. This learning or corrective experience provides the groundwork for perceiving and responding to a world that is real rather than one that is distorted.

*   *   *   *

APPENDIX TO CHAPTER 6

Over a period of time several procedural questions have come up regarding the rights and duties of probationers under the supervision of the _____ Court. Below are some of the most often asked questions and the answers.

(1) Q   Can probation be granted for more than a
          year?
     A   No. The statutory limit for probation for a
          misdemeanant is one year. We have had the
          experience, however, of probationers committing
          new offenses which can lead to a new probationary
          period.

(2) Q   Can probation terms be reduced?
     A   Yes, although this is generally not encouraged
          in that it is felt that a period of one year is
          not a particularly long period in which to ac-
          complish probation goals. If you think that the
          length of probation should be reduced, talk it
          over with one of the court staff. He will take
          the necessary steps to shorten the probation
          period if it is deemed advisable.

(3) Q   Can probationers leave the community while on
          probation?
     A   Yes, if it is in the interest of the probationer
          to move, he may receive permission to do so.
          As a volunteer probation counselor, your as-
          sessment of the situation would be the chief
          determining factor in granting permission.
          Temporary or emergency trips out of the com-
          munity are also permissible.

(4) Q   Can probationers enter the military service
        while on probation?

    A   While under civil restraint, the probationer
        cannot enter military service.   Probation is
        considered civil restraint.   However, if you
        think that military service would be to the pro-
        bationer's advantage and if there is a good in-
        dication that he can qualify mentally and physi-
        cally for military service, he could be con-
        sidered for discharge from probation.   It is
        important to assess this situation carefully
        however, usually if a person is having trouble
        with authority in civilian life, he can be ex-
        pected to take this same attitude with him into
        a military situation.

(5) Q   What if the probationer doesn't keep his ap-
        pointments?

    A   He has signed a probation agreement agreeing
        to see you once weekly.   If you think you need
        the authority of the court to reinforce this or-
        der, feel free to be in touch with the court
        staff member who assigned you the case.   He
        will try to help you.

(6) Q   What about driving restrictions?

    A   Since many of our probationers come from
        Traffic Court, we deal with many people whose
        driver's licenses have been suspended.   The
        loss of mobility caused by losing a license is
        a severe hardship in that it limits access to
        certain areas of employment and means that the
        probationer must rely on the public transporta-
        tion system.   In some instances the Motor
        Vehicle Division will issue special driving per-
        mits for use during certain hours of employ-
        ment.   This would only be done after a hear-
        ing.   It must be remembered that the Motor
        Vehicle Division sees its responsibility as that
        of keeping bad drivers off the road rather than
        making concessions to traffic offenders.   In
        some instances you can best help the probation-
        er by forcing him to face up to the fact that
        he cannot and/or should not drive.

(7) Q   Where is the best place to meet my probationer?

    A   This is your decision.   There may be times

when meeting the probationer at his or her
home would be advantageous. You may want
to see the probationer's environment. Sometimes a neutral environment is best. If you
think the authority of the court needs to be reinforced, meeting in one of the court offices
can be arranged. Maybe a restaurant over a
cup of coffee would be disarming and helpful.

(8) Q What if the probationer asks for money?

A You were not recruited as a volunteer counselor to lend money but rather to give of your
time. Lending money can stand in the way of
a good relationship and is certainly discouraged. There are agencies and resources at
your disposal which can render financial assistance.

(9) Q What will the probationer know about me?

A Actually very little. The court staff member
will probably have told the probationer your
name and occupation. Whatever else you
choose to tell the probationer is up to you.

(10) Q Do you encourage probationers to keep in contact with the volunteer after probation is over?

A In many cases this happens. We feel this is
usually a positive action.

(11) Q What about visiting our probationers in jail?

A This is permissible and is certainly encouraged. If being in jail is viewed by the probationer as a crisis it gives you an opportunity
to see him during a critical period. A letter
of introduction can be obtained from the Probation Office.

(12) Q Am I legally responsible for the acts of my
probationer?

A Definitely not.

(13) Q What do I do if I go on vacation or on a business trip for an extended period of time?

A Our volunteers are busy people and we expect
that they will be out of town at times. We
certainly don't want your volunteer duties to
change your life style. Your probationer can

be supervised during your absence and if you
are to be away for longer than two weeks, in-
struct your probationer to contact the court
staff.

(14) Q Are expenses incurred during volunteer service
        tax deductible?
     A Any "out of the pocket" expenses are deductible.
        Mileage expenses are deductible at a rate of
        five cents per mile.

(15) Q What are the rules of probation?
     A They are very simple. The probationer is
        expected to obey all laws, federal, state, and
        local. He is expected to maintain regular
        contact with his probation counselor. The
        rules of probation are geared to avoid the "do
        nots." If the probationer obeys all laws, ob-
        viously he is doing what we are all expected
        to do.

(16) Q How do I report on the probationer?
     A Feel free to call the Probation Office anytime
        to report progress, lack of progress or ask
        for help. Written reports should be submitted
        once monthly by the 5th of each month. Re-
        port forms are provided for your convenience
        although you may wish to send a letter.

(17) Q Are there instances where a volunteer works
        with more than one probationer at a time?
     A Seldom, although this could be arranged de-
        pending on the circumstances.

(18) Q Are volunteers encouraged to "re-enlist" and
        work an additional year with a second proba-
        tioner?
     A Nine out of ten volunteers indicate their desire
        to continue with a second probationer. If the
        volunteer is so inclined the Probation Depart-
        ment would be happy to make a second assign-
        ment. We hope you will keep us advised of
        new addresses, telephone numbers, etc., so
        we can keep your file active.

III: MEDIA OR MODALITIES OF TRAINING AT ANY
      TRAINING CONTACT POINT

Chapter 7

INTRODUCTION--BASIC CONCEPTS

In Part II of this book we discussed formal and informal opportunities for orientation and training during the
time that the volunteer is in contact with the court, from
beginning to end of service. We have mentioned in passing
the various media that could be used, but we have not gone
into detail regarding the rationale and procedures for the
use of these media. This is what we hope to accomplish in
this chapter.

When we think of the tools at our disposal during
training, we generally think of (1) audio tapes, (2) slide
shows, (3) films, (4) television, (5) tours, visits, and observation experiences, (6) lectures and panels, and (7) trainee participation. In this Part III we will discuss all of
these.

In addition to discussing the above, we wish to share
with the reader our thoughts in regard to producing training
material such as slides, films, and tapes. We also want to
provide an annotated list of some of the training aids that
currently exist that may have relevance for correctional volunteer training.

The authors as well as the staff of the National Court
Volunteer Training Project spent literally hundreds of hours
viewing films and slide shows and listening to tapes, in order to arrive at the current listings in this book. We pe-
rused tape and film catalogs, arriving at what we believe are
probably the adequate to excellent materials. Those materials deleted from our listings were in some cases very outdated or in other cases extremely bad. In still other cases
we eliminated material which, while of good quality, was
more appropriate for recruiting or public relations.

115

There are some general principles that we might suggest before embarking on the discussion of training media.
First, it is unwise to weight training heavily with any one
medium. The reader can realize from his own experience
that listening to tapes or watching films have certain time
limits. We reach saturation points beyond which we cannot
receive and process information efficiently when presented
through the same media. However, as we provide a change
of pace and alternate our means of delivery, we give the
trainee a respite from an experience that otherwise may potentially be deadening.

Secondly, and consistent with our statement in the beginning of the book, we should utilize our media to achieve
the goals of moving the trainee from abstract to more real
or concrete material and from theoretical understanding to
an application of theory in terms of being a helping person.
Trainers of volunteers should consider the consequences of
weighting training too heavily with abstract concepts. To do
so is to invite potentially helpful people to become disen-
chanted with programs and consider leaving. Volunteers en-
list to do things and our training should be designed to facilitate action. The challenge to the trainer is to develop
the means to present abstract or technical material in practical, understandable ways.

A practical matter which the reader may raise is that
of the expense of films, slides, tapes, etc. We recognize
that smaller courts do not always have budgets that allow
for the purchase of these training tools. It is suggested
that one of the ways of addressing this problem is to think
of cooperative ventures among several courts where perhaps
regional libraries can be established. Even more preferable
would be state libraries developed by state LEAA offices,
or where state volunteer coordinators exist, these offices can
take on the task of servicing local training programs with
training aids. The state of Georgia already has such a library for its volunteer programs in probation and parole.

The following chapters were written at a time when
we have only begun to understand how to creatively use various media for training. Since we have only scratched the
surface of this important area, we would be remiss if we
did not urge the reader to think well beyond these rather
fragmentary ideas. Indeed, in training the volunteer, "the
medium is the message," and we hope many will use the
materials presented here as a platform from which they will

go on to produce more sophisticated training aids for volunteers.

Chapter 8

AUDIO TAPES FOR TRAINING

The advantages of tapes as a take-home training device have already been mentioned. They can be individualized to the specific training needs of volunteers and can be
programmed to fit his individual time schedule. Because
there is an abundance of sound reproduction equipment in
homes, tapes are convenient training aids. They are also
relatively inexpensive to procure and produce. Tapes are,
in fact, training "packages" which have utility for the individual listener as well as the group.

Audio tapes are for listening. Like radio, they demand that the listener create his own mental pictures. To
the extent that the audio material allows the listener to create his own relevance in visual pictures, it serves as excellent training material. Thus tapes serve as excellent media
to depict group interaction and conversations. They have
less training value when the objective is to convey abstract
ideas or subject matter.

Because there are experts in certain areas who have
information crucial to the operation of certain programs,
audio tapes do provide a means wherein there is created a
repository for lecture-type messages. These messages can
be stored over long periods of time and delivered at the desire of the trainer.

We should not consider audio tapes as purveyors of
complete and self-contained training messages, but rather as
triggers or catalysts for discussion. This means that the
trainer must extract from the tapes the major teaching points.
This can most effectively be done through pre-listening.

When tapes are utilized for delivering lectures, the
trainer should consider what alternatives there are for getting this information to the trainee. Can the material on
tape be better presented in written form? Can the tape itself

be transcribed and put into written form? Does the speaker
have the ability to hold the listener's attention? For how
long? These questions can only be answered through the
trainer's listening to the tapes prior to exposing a class to
them. This is not to say that a tape that does not hold the
interest of the trainer will necessarily lose the interest of
the trainee. What it may suggest, however, is that the
trainer may need to listen again for what in the tape is
causing him to lose interest. If it is a monotonous voice,
then this may have the same impact on the class. If it is
that the tape contains information which is not new to the
trainer, he cannot necessarily surmise that this is the case
with the class.

Speakers whose voices are monotonous will not hold
a listener's attention. Some people can speak on tape and
through inflection hold the listener's attention, while others
will almost immediately disengage the listener.

Generally, when tapes are being used for purposes of
presenting a lecture, the trainer should be sensitive to how
well the message is holding the attention of the class. A
change of pace can be effected by limiting the time a class
is asked to listen to a tape through interjecting discussion
periods between listening periods. Suffice it to say a lecture on tape is valuable from a training standpoint only if it
is a truly superior production in regard to content, interest,
and mode of production.

We should not however confine ourselves to thinking
of tapes as something that someone else has made for our
consumption. Rather we should also think of tapes as something we as trainers may produce for our own use.

Case material can often be presented in a live fashion
through the use of tapes. In particular, process can be
examined in detail when tapes are used. The use of a tape
in conjunction with role playing has been tried out by the
senior author by recording a role playing session, then re-
playing the session, stopping the tape at critical junctures
to ask the principal role players why they said what they did
and asking the class what they might have said under similar
conditions. This provides immediate feedback for the entire
class and captures process while it is still fresh and alive.
This feedback can then serve the purpose of helping the
trainee hear how he is coming across and as a consequence
make any desired change.

Audio tapes can also be used to provide the trainer with feedback on the training session. A playback of a complete training session, or parts thereof, can be productive in terms of helping the trainer listen from a consumer's point of view to what is being presented. Modification of training, of course, should then follow.

In regard to the production of tapes, we cannot stress enough the crucial need for good equipment and proper acoustics. If content is one half of a good tape, technical quality constitutes the other half. Tapes present enough problems in terms of teaching devices without adding the problem of poor sound quality in production and reproduction. Large groups will probably have difficulty hearing even a well produced tape because raising the volume in reproduction creates additional noise.

The directory of tapes for training volunteers which follows speaks in more detail to the matter of producing tapes of good technical quality.

*   *   *   *

Report VI

DIRECTORY OF TAPES FOR TRAINING
COURT VOLUNTEERS (1971)

I. Introduction: Purpose and Background

We estimate 2000 courts use volunteers today. Of these, we believe at least 1999 would like to do a better job orienting and training their volunteers. Staff want more training, better training; so do volunteers. The problem is that the court is not a college; staff has neither the time nor experience to be fully effective as trainers of volunteers. One avenue of solution is to provide court volunteer training materials which are (1) pre-fabricated, "canned," already prepared for use and re-use by the trainer, (2) readily and inexpensively procurable, (3) realistic and interesting, and (4) which strike a common core curriculum of reasonable relevance to court volunteers anywhere. The purpose of the present report is to provide a preliminary guide to audio tapes which can be used to orient and train court volunteers. It is thus primarily for staff trainers of volunteers, in making their volunteer training selections; it is not directly for volunteers themselves.

Our criteria for selecting tapes were (1) realism, (2) relevance to court volunteer knowledge needs, (3) readily and inexpensively procurable. In addition, audio tapes as training aids can always have the following special advantages: (4) they can reproduce the highest quality presentations or the most specialized materials which the average court could not easily be able to procure for itself "in person," e.g., Mr. Johnson to lecture on any given night or Dr. Smith to talk to your volunteers; an alcoholic or a runaway girl talking emotionally about their experiences, etc.; (5) tapes can, of course, be used over and over again, without absorbing staff time and effort for a special work-up each time a volunteer training session is contemplated; (6) this automatically repeatable characteristic of tapes also leads to increased flexibility in capitalizing on various informal opportunities for orienting and training court volunteers (see Report IV).

Virtually the only limit is the trainer's imagination in exploiting such opportunities. Thus, training tapes can be used not only (a) in larger formal training sessions, but also (b) in more informal small-group sessions, either pre-service or in-service. Finally, (c) volunteers as individuals can listen to the tapes, play them in the next office, or even take them home. (Perhaps, using cassette rigs now available at about $15 each, your court could keep four to five loaned out to your volunteers for pre-service or in-service "take-home training." Why not?) Another fruitful fallout for imaginative use might be to have the volunteer applicant make some realistic tapes to listen to as part of a self-screening process.

The training intention of these tapes "spills over" not only into screening, as above; many of the tapes may also be useful in recruiting volunteers or in general community education.

Along with all these potential advantages, two limitations should also be emphasized. First, the tapes reviewed in this report are of necessity quite general, and may miss the mark quite substantially when it comes to the special or unique characteristics of your court, your community, your probationers or parolees. Therefore, consider them mainly as a good departure point to prime the pump for eventual production of your own tapes. Maybe your tapes will incorporate portions of the general tapes; maybe not. They could

include your own veteran volunteers talking about their experiences, your own staff lecturing, your own probationers,
a tape of a particularly "hot" volunteer in-service training
session, etc.

Secondly, whether general or individualized to your
court, audio tapes should not be considered a complete self-
contained training unit. More than that, they should be used
to stimulate questions, act as a catalyst for further discussion. Some competent leader has to be there to field the
questions, guide the discussions, after the tape. Remember,
a large part of the tape's training value is not in what it is,
but in what it leads to after you turn off the tape. It's a
trigger for training.

Audio tape differs from film, slides, and written
material as a medium, but it often covers the same kind of
content in this different medium. For example, a number
of the tapes reviewed here are essentially case studies.
Thus, content-wise, they belong with our written case study
compendium (Report XII, Chapter 15). Other tapes are essentially lectures by outstanding experts and might thus fit
in as, in some sense, substitutes for live lecturers at various points in your volunteer orientation curriculum (Report
I), or as re-emphasizers of volunteer "Thou Shalts and Thou
Shalt Nots" (Report XI, Chapter 15), etc.

A total of 36 tapes are reviewed here and recommended for various areas of volunteer orientation and training. Yet, this should be considered only a beginning, and
we most eagerly welcome your suggestions as to additional
tapes which ought to be added. If you can, please send us
an actual copy of your proposed tape for review, after which
we are in an excellent position to place it in a national tape
library.

II.   Training Tape Directory and Review

The 36 tapes are reviewed in four sections:

A.   "Volunteers Helping Offenders, " eight tapes prepared or procured by the National Information Center, especially and specifically for orientation and training of court
volunteers.
B.   "The NCAT Review" is the result of Professor
Jorgensen's scanning of a catalog of 12, 000 tapes, the

largest collection in the world, then listening to the most
likely prospects for adaptability to court volunteer training.
Result: 15 tapes.

      C. "Children's Charter, " tapes were produced orig-
inally for corrections personnel generally and for broad community orientation, rather than for volunteers specifically.
This particular series, called "The Child's View, " is reviewed
by Professor Jorgensen specifically for applicability to court
volunteer training. Seven tapes were reviewed, five of
which seem quite applicable.

      D. "Berkshire Farm, " a situation similar to Chil-
dren's Charter. Professor Jorgensen reviewed all six tapes
and recommended two as having some particular relevance
to court volunteer orientation and training.

      Section III of this report, following, provides details
on how to procure tapes.

II. A. "Volunteers Helping Offenders"

      This series was especially prepared for orientation
and training of court volunteers. This is the only series
specifically so designed, of which we are aware at this time.
These eight tapes have been placed in the library of the
National Center for Audio Tapes, henceforth referred to as
NCAT.

**** 1.   Volunteers Helping Offenders: <u>Shelley</u> (1970)
        <u>Duration</u>: 18 minutes <u>Speed</u>: <u>3-3/4</u> <u>NCAT Order</u>
        <u># 0751-01</u>

      By Dr. Ernest Shelley, with an introduction by Dr.
Ivan H. Scheier, Director of the National Information Center
on Volunteers in Courts. Dr. Shelley, a psychologist, has
worked with volunteers since the 1950's when he used them
as lay group counselors in adult prisons in Michigan. Since
1967 he has been developing volunteer programs in probation
at Ingham County Court, East Lansing, Michigan. This particular tape is from a talk at the Third National Court Volunteer Management Institute in Boulder, Colorado, January,
1970. Thus, though a most eloquent talk, volunteers should
be prepared for the fact that it was aimed primarily at volunteer program leaders rather than volunteers themselves.

      Dr. Shelley speaks of volunteerism in America today.
He speaks not on a personal level to a single new court volunteer, but on an historical level to the concept of

volunteerism, and how it relates both to our American heritage and to twentieth century problems. The theme is: we're getting back to personal participation in solving community problems. Volunteerism is moving America back to the healthy attitudes of the early days when people in a community joined resources to get the job done. The movement today proves that the idea of people tackling a common problem and working together personally to solve it is still a viable solution for America. Those in the movement are all exploring to make this kind of active citizen participation an ever more effective solution.

Second, volunteerism is making a direct contribution to America's greatest problem, the "desensitization of the twentieth century." It is combatting the problem of callousness and impersonalization by demonstrating that people still do care. Volunteers are speaking directly to this malaise in the country. And maybe someday the resurgence of volunteerism today will be looked back on as the turning point, when America began to be saved. Third, volunteerism is a way of saving one's own soul. The volunteer, by caring and experiencing a meaningful personal relationship, is helping himself better to deal with his own twentieth century problems--alienation and inadequacy.

In summary, volunteerism is not merely salvaging individual lives, but salvaging them with a method that says America is still good, and people are still interested in demonstrating the traditional democratic way of life. This tape is most appropriate as an excellent general philosophical background and perspective for the new volunteer, and as a stimulation of morale for the volunteer about to begin work with a probationer. It is an eloquent discussion of volunteerism in general, and might have good use also as a means of recruiting volunteers from the community. More citizens should be made aware of the concept of volunteerism, and how it is helping us all.

**** 2.   Volunteers Helping Offenders: Scheier (1970)
           Duration: 16 minutes   Speed: 3-3/4   NCAT
           Order # 0751-02

By Dr. Ivan H. Scheier, Director, National Information Center on Volunteers in Courts, Hall of Justice, Division 3, Boulder, Colorado. Dr. Scheier is in touch with about 2000 courts using volunteers across the country. He knows, therefore, that different courts often tend to have different problems, different approaches, and different philosophies. In this tape he avoids stating any overly specific goals, points of view, or methods for the court volunteer. Rather, his tape is directed to the court volunteer in general. The tape also contains personal suggestions for the volunteer, presented by Dr. Scheier, a court volunteer himself for eight years. His advice, in the form of an informal conversation, should be reassurance-with-realism for anyone about to begin work with an offender.

He discusses some common myths about court volunteer work; for example: expecting quick miracles and easy solutions in your work; expecting visible results all at once; expecting thanks from your probationer. Also, you should learn from your probationer, as well as vice versa. You must listen, and when you do talk, be sensitive. Get involved in activities with your probationer. Be a good model of decent behavior, and to do this you must be yourself and be honest.

Finally, to be a good court volunteer you must understand the aims of your court--listen and you will learn what your own court wants. And, very important, you must always use your head along with your heart--you must make use of methods, insights and techniques. Use know-how along with concern. Though court volunteer work is challenging and often frustrating, remember, "it is better to light one candle than to curse the darkness, " and every candle counts. Dr. Scheier's discussion is essentially what he would like to say to the new court volunteer, if he had a chance for a personal chat with them before they began their work.

**** 3.   Volunteers Helping Offenders: Leenhouts (1970)
           Duration: 17 minutes   Speed: 3-3/4   NCAT
           Order # 0751-03

By Judge Keith Leenhouts, with an introduction by Dr. Ivan H. Scheier. Addressing the new court volunteer, Judge Leenhouts, currently Director of Volunteers in Probation, Inc. , 200 Washington Square Plaza, Royal Oak, Michigan, sees the role of the volunteer as primarily a friend to the probationer. In this tape he explains how a mature, sophisticated volunteer can establish this friendship and thus experience one of the greatest pleasures. He assumes the

volunteer is a strong and capable inspirational personality to
the probationer, and as such, able to bring about a complete
attitude change in a troubled probationer. As an inspirational personality, the volunteer must appeal to the probationer
on a human level; he must not lecture or punish, but must
show concern and affection.

The procedure for the volunteer is as follows: the
volunteer must listen to his probationer, despite abuse he
will receive at first. This may well be the first time an
adult ever listened to the probationer. Listening doesn't
mean the volunteer necessarily approves of all the probationer's actions, and in fact he should not, but he must show
he is accepting him. As he continues to show affection by
listening, and as the probationer learns the volunteer is not
being paid, the feeling of friendship will develop. After three
or four months, the probationer will call upon the volunteer
in a time of crisis. This will provide the volunteer with the
opportunity of performing an act of friendship to cement their
relationship, hopefully, for a long time. And here we see
that the friendship should ideally last beyond the time of
probation. A volunteer should be guided by the single question: "What would one friend do for another friend?" As
he continually asks this question, he will find the solutions
to the problems that might arise with his probationer.

It is suggested that this tape be used as a guide for
an ideal volunteer-probationer relationship. In using this
tape, some questions should be asked and discussed. A few
might be: How hard would it be to fulfill the role of inspirational personality as Judge Leenhouts describes him?
How much change should a volunteer expect to see in his
probationer, and how quickly? How realistic is this change
in terms of the relationship? What problems or incidents
might arise in establishing the friendship? What should be
the aims of the volunteer?

**** 4.   Volunteers Helping Offenders: Jorgensen [short]
          1970
          Duration: 17 minutes   Speed: 3-3/4   NCAT
          Order # 0751-04
          (Do not confuse with the longer tape by Jorgensen,
          **** 8.)

By Professor Jorgensen, with an introduction by Dr.
Scheier. Professor Jorgensen, who has trained 5000 court

volunteers at Denver County and other courts, talks to the
new court volunteer and sees the volunteer-probationer relationship as a helping relationship, directed to the corrective experience. The offender must learn to perceive and
respond to a real world rather than the world as he has
distorted it. The volunteer, then, is in a special position
to help the offender bring about a change in his perception.
The volunteer should understand the advantages of his position, and why they are advantages.

First, the role expectation of the volunteer is quite
straightforward: he is to be the guiding, rewarding person.
His motives, since he is working for no pay, are more
visible, and it is easier for him to become involved in a
relationship. The second advantage is that the volunteer is
not so trained in pathology and illness as the professional,
and can thus react with the offender on a more personal
level; the offender must have this really human contact in
order to grow and develop new perceptions. Also, the volunteer will work with only a few, usually one, offender, so
he will have a better chance than the professional who
usually has fifty cases or more. Most important, the volunteer is usually a successful person in other endeavors,
and will thus bring a fresh attitude which can influence the
offender in a more positive way.

The establishment of a strong positive relationship is
important for the offender to grow and change, and Professor
Jorgensen gives the volunteer a number of concepts to keep
in mind when working to establish such a relationship with
his probationer. These concepts are realistically stated,
and will help the volunteer understand some of the problems
he might encounter, especially with an offender of different
background and value system. It is vital the volunteer
keep in mind that, especially at first, he will be tested by
his probationer who is not primed to accept help. This
tape is useful as a beginning aid for the volunteer as well
as a continual help throughout contact with the probationer.
It might be useful for the beginning volunteer to listen to the
tape with an experienced volunteer to discuss these concepts
and discover where the most difficulty might lie.

**** 5.   Volunteers Helping Offenders: "Interview-Outer-
           view" (1970)
           Duration: 15 minutes   Speed: 3-3/4   NCAT
           Order # 0751-05

By Kathleen and Matthew Wells and David and Kathy Hoffman, with an introduction by Dr. Scheier. This tape is of an actual training session for volunteer probation officers. The training technique used is role-playing: two would-be volunteers assume the roles of volunteer and probationer. They must learn the skills of communication, since no relationship can develop, nor can future rehabilitation take place without good communication. The narrator introduces the two trainee-participants and explains that they will be meeting for the first time. This first (role play) meeting will set the stage for further meetings and thus is important for future communication.

The first role play encounter is not very successful, and is interrupted by the narrator for discussion. The two participants explain the difficulties they had and criticize each other. The listener can supplement the discussion with his own observations. Some points are: the volunteer did not listen to the probationer, she was preaching; she made no real attempt at understanding, especially since she was faced with a different moral system. The two participants ("volunteer" and "probationer"), after discussing their initial mistakes, go on to try again a role play of a first meeting. This time they are much more successful, and really seem to have learned from their discussion. They become much closer and much less antagonistic.

This tape is a training aid either to be used as a starting point for future discussions or a model for courts to set up their own role-playing volunteer training sessions. Technically, however, it is sometimes difficult to understand. It should be listened to several times, preferably while watching the written script, and then there should be no trouble. (The script, available from the National Information Center, contains an excellent study guide and methods to approach discussion of this tape.) It is felt there are many excellent directions to go with this material, including slides.

**** 6.   Volunteers Helping Offenders: Attention Homes
           (1970)
           Duration: 40 minutes   Speed: 3-3/4 NCAT
           Order # 0751-06

This is a tape about Attention Homes, Inc., Boulder, Colorado. These are primarily volunteer-supported group foster homes where children can go instead of going to jail.

The tape is a discussion by various people involved with the
Homes--the Boulder County Juvenile Judge, the President of
the Board of Directors of Attention, Inc., a houseparent, a
housekeeper, a member of the Board of Directors since its
founding, and the editor of the Home's newsletter.

Some of the questions they discuss are: How did Attention Homes get started? What is the relation between Attention Homes and the court? What kind of philosophy helped
bring about Attention Homes? How are the houses financed?
What are the costs? How is fund raising handled? What
goes on at the home? Why do houseparents take the job?
What rules do they set up? What type of training do they
get? Why are kids there? What type of rehabilitation is
there for the children? How do the Homes get along with
their neighbors? How does it work with girls and boys living in the same house?

Many aspects of Attention Homes, Inc. are covered
here, although most emphasis is on the organizational side,
and thus the tape would be excellent for people wanting to
start an Attention Home in their own community. It might
also be good for getting the community involved in an Attention Home project. The tape is good technically, easy to
listen to, long but holds interest. (For further and latest
information on Attention Homes in Boulder and across the
country, and how to set them up, write to Mrs. Susan
Boulding, Attention Homes, Inc., P. O. Box 907, Boulder,
Colo.)

**** 7.   Volunteers Helping Offenders: Dr. Erb (1970)
          Duration: 75 minutes   Speed: 3-3/4   NCAT
          Order # 0751-07

By Dr. David Erb, a psychiatrist at the University
of Delaware, with an introduction by Dr. Scheier. This
tape is actually used as a training aid for the Partners
volunteer program in Denver, Colorado. On it, Dr. Erb
provides the listener with a clear picture of the adolescent--
his problems, his struggles, his emotions and needs. First,
he takes the question "Who am I?" that the adolescent in his
period of transition will ask, and examines it in relation to
these aspects of his identity: the adolescent's body, his
parents, his peer groups, his feelings and emotions, adults
other than his parents, and his sexuality. The tape discusses
these relationships thoroughly and suggests how the court

volunteer might fit into each one.   The relationship between
the volunteer and adolescent is an important one, and the
volunteer must be careful not to hurt the adolescent by encouraging his dependence on him, nor should he use him in
any way to do his work.   The speaker points out that many
middle class volunteers will be working with lower class
adolescents and will encounter very different value systems.
So it is important for the volunteer not to force one or the
other on the adolescent, but try and understand and talk
about the differences.   And finally the tape explains some
things the volunteer needs to be in his relationship with an
adolescent.   He must make an effort to grow and learn along
with him; he must show he is human and not try to appear
superhuman; he must assume responsibility for the relationship, and set the limits; he must let himself be tested; and
especially he should be sensitive to the adolescent.

The tape clearly illustrates the exciting and challenging experience of working with an adolescent, and how the
court volunteer or any adult can provide real impact for his
growth in a genuine and real way.   It is highly recommended
for any adult working with adolescents, such as parents,
teachers, and even adolescents themselves might learn from
discussing it.   It is full of excellent observations and keen
sensitivity.   Technically it is good.

**** 8.   Volunteers Helping Offenders: Jorgensen [long]
           (1970)
           Duration: 60 minutes   Speed: 3-3/4   NCAT
           Order # 0751-08

"Guides For Volunteers in Correctional Settings, " by
Professor Jorgensen.   (Distinct from the short Jorgensen
tape which was reviewed previously, no. **** 4.)   We feel
this tape has particular value as a training aid for new volunteers, and we suggest the playing of the tape be distributed over two or three sessions.   It may also be used in
orientation sessions for correctional workers.   The tape provides a frame of reference for understanding deviant behavior
with particular emphasis on principles of counselling.   It is
meant to be general enough to cover volunteer activities with
juveniles and adults in institutions as well as in community
(probation or parole) programs.   It includes some history
of volunteerism, some case material, insights into the correctional process, and some clear and pertinent guidelines
for the volunteer as an aid to the helping process with

offenders. Though distinct from the shorter Jorgensen tape,
it is in many respects a more formal elaboration of its basic points, so if you find the shorter tape valuable, this longer one may be even more so.

II. B. "The NCAT Review"

Professor Jorgensen scanned titles and descriptions
for some 12,000 tapes in the National Center for Audio
Tapes (NCAT) 1970-72 Catalog, the largest collection of
tapes in the world. After this preliminary scanning, Professor Jorgensen listened to the better prospects and eventually came out with 15 recommended court volunteer orientation tapes, which are described below. Thus, while none of
the tapes were originally made specifically for court volunteer
training, they are a highly select group considered relevant
to this purpose by an experienced reviewer.

Again, let it be said that Section III of this report,
following, gives ordering information (not from the National
Information Center on Volunteers in Courts); that section will
also make more sense of the various code numbers identifying the tapes. Professor Jorgensen has organized his re-
views according to topic categories in the NCAT catalog.

[EDUCATION]
CHILD STUDY   (HQ796 C55)   1961

Order #0029-08   Delinquency and   15 minutes
                      Adjustment
    A discussion between a sociologist and psychologist
regarding causes of delinquency as well as a discussion of
early signs of delinquency. This tape is very elementary,
basic, and general. It would provide a basis for class discussion. A volunteer training program could utilize this
tape as a supplement to other training aids.

Order #0029-30   Problems of   15 minutes
                      Adolescence
    This tape represents a rather realistic discussion of
physical, psychological, and social facets of adolescence.
A three-way discussion among three professionals gives the
listener some excellent insights into the adolescent and his
world. This tape would probably facilitate discussion in a
training session.

[LANGUAGE AND LITERATURE]
COMMUNICATION AND SPEECH   (P 90 C64)   1961

Order #0032-05   The Psychology of   30 minutes
                      Human Interaction
        An excellent tape which is one of a 13-part series on
communication.   The listener is introduced to concepts of
roles, groups, self-concepts, functional and dysfunctional
human interactions, reality perceptions, etc.   These concepts are depicted in real life situations through role-playing.
A simple concrete presentation which would be relevant to
the volunteer as a helper, particularly in in-service training.

[SOCIAL STUDIES]
SOCIOLOGY
     The Glue Sniffers   (Rc568 G4 G48)

Order #0624-01   The Glue Sniffers   55 minutes
        This tape is recommended for use with volunteers
who are working with youth who might manifest the problem
of glue sniffing or related drug abuse.   The length of the
tape may be too long to maintain good attention span, but the
sound quality is good, and the content provides the listener
with an excellent insight into the problem itself, as well as
the life of the child who sniffs glue.

PSYCHOLOGY   (BF 121 P78)   1968

Order #0438-20   Rational Attitudes   15 minutes
                      Toward Crime   (Barnes)
        A 15-minute tape lecture by Harry Barnes, noted
criminologist, regarding the present status of our policy regarding crime and criminals, with proposals for change.
This tape would be useful for training volunteers, particularly in developing a better understanding of the criminal justice
system from police to parole.

Order #0438-52   Child in Delinquency   15 minutes
                                                    (Paul Hohn)
        An excellent 15-minute lecture by a juvenile court
probation officer.   The lecture deals with the juvenile court
as a change agent, delinquency as behavior, and juvenile
delinquents as human beings, attempting to meet their needs.
The citing of case examples makes this tape come to life.
It would be an excellent tape for orientation of volunteers to
the juvenile court and the correctional process.

CASE HISTORIES   (HV9103 C38)   1961

Order # 0025-01   The Story of Andy   19 minutes
     Andy is a 33-year-old man, still living a marginal
life, who discusses very frankly and openly his early delinquent behavior.   He traces an early history of separation
from his parents, drinking, fighting, stealing, eventually
rape, and subsequent incarceration.   The interview is rather
dramatic and emotional in that Andy is unable to discuss his
situation without tears.   The tape would provide an excellent
insight into the life of the aggressive delinquent.   It would
have value as an orientation device as well as value for in-
service training.

Order # 0025-02   The Story of Anthony   11 minutes
     Anthony is a 16-year-old boy who lived in an orphan-
age from age four until age twelve when he joined his mother
and step-father.   He does not have a juvenile record, except
that he was questioned by the police for possessing $200
which he claims he found.   This tape has training value in
that it reflects a view of the world as held by an urban 16-
year-old who is exposed to the current problems of youth.
And Anthony is still a "preventive" case.

Order # 0025-03   The Story of Bill   12 minutes
     Bill is a 16-year-old boy who was placed on probation
for involvement in an auto theft.   He discusses his reasons
for dropping out of school, his view of police, race problems, and his hopes for the future.   The tape has training
value in terms of exposing the volunteer to a delinquent
"type."   The hopelessness and dim future of the adolescent
in the core city is well depicted in this tape.

Order # 0025-04   The Story of Bob   12 minutes
     This tape is one of the least effective in this series
of case histories.   Bob is a 16-year-old high school dropout
who has recently completed an eleven month stay at a boys'
training school.   He is unemployed.   Bob's inarticulateness
forces the listener to question a great deal, which has the
effect of diluting the material.   The training value in this
tape is probably in its use in comparing Bob with other
youths in the series.   A discussion on how to communicate
with nonverbal children might usefully emanate from this
tape.

Order # 0025-05   The Story of Don   12 minutes
     Don reflects the expectable attitude of a youth of 18

who has in his time, experienced family dysfunction as a result of his father's death, mother's mental illness, and subsequent poverty. He has quit school and is unemployed. He
has been on probation for robbing and has experienced jail
and detention. His outlook on life is bleak. He is not unlike many young people in this situation. For training purposes this tape could best be used to depict the multi-problem family as it attempts to cope with stress.

Order #0025-06   The Story of Jerry   9 minutes
        Jerry is a bored 16-year-old probationer who has
quit school. He has been involved in petty theft. His
world is rather basic, and his thought processes are uncom-
plicated. Training value of this tape is somewhat limited
except for purposes of comparison.

Order #0025-07   The Story of Joe   14 minutes
        Joe is a 16-year-old articulate youth who has been on
the fringe of delinquent behavior but has no juvenile record.
He attends a vocational school and is planning a future. He
discusses the importance of heroes, role models, and group
forces in the lives of young people. His sensitivity to motives and interpersonal relations gives the tape added importance for training purposes.

Order #0025-08   The Story of Mary   11 minutes
        Mary is a bright, articulate 15-year-old who tells a
story of acting-out behavior related to the alcoholism of her
father and the subsequent breakup of the family. The tape
reflects the ability of a young person to cope with stress,
adapt and become reoriented to the demands of living. This
being the only tape related to a female in the present series
adds special training value. (Note: the Children's Charter
tapes in the following section and series do have much more
case material on girls.)

Order #0025-09   The Story of Nick   9 minutes
        At the time of this interview Nick is 20 and recently
returned from military service. He looks back at a broken
home, a break-in at age 13, gang wars, and two commitments
to juvenile institutions. He is now preparing to enter college. The particular value of this tape is the insight it provides into gang activity and the forces operating on a black
youth in a core city.

II. C. Children's Charter "Child's View" Series

The seven tapes in this "Child's View" series were not produced by the National Information Center on Volunteers in Courts. Also they are not in the NCAT library. The fine organization which produced these seven tapes describes itself as follows: "Children's Charter of the Courts of Michigan, Inc., is a non-profit organization whose purpose is to improve judicial services to children. Presently its basic financial support is furnished by The W. K. Kellogg Foundation. The 'Child's View' project was financed by The Field Foundation, Inc. Children's Charter headquarters are located at 1121 Knollwood, Kalamazoo, Michigan 49007. "

The background and relevance of this series, as presented in the Children's Charter brochure for these seven tapes, is as follows:

"INTERESTED IN CHILDREN?"

"As teacher, student, policeman, probation officer, judge, parent, guidance counselor, correctional officer--in fact if you work with children in any way--you will find all seven of the taped 'Child's View' programs valuable in understanding youth's problems and attitudes. Although the emphasis of each differs, as will be described, each one will assist everyone concerned with children better to understand them. These taped aids to understanding youth were developed under a grant from the Field Foundation, Inc.

"In all, 271 teenagers known to the Juvenile Courts in Michigan, for reasons of delinquency or neglect, were interviewed to get their reactions to the ways of, and the people in, authority. From its inception, the project has received nationwide attention and commendation. The taped programs, running just under one half hour each, feature the actual voices and opinions, unrehearsed and unprompted, of the teenagers interviewed. Included with each tape is a printed instruction sheet suggesting the best ways to utilize the tape, a transcript of the tape itself, and a discussion aid to assist your group in getting the most value from the taped information.

"'Child's View' can help anyone who truly wants to do a better job in relating to youth. It can help you understand their thinking, their attitudes, their likes and dislikes--and it expresses these ideas with dramatic impact that can only

be achieved by the voices of the youngsters themselves.
They are invaluable for use in university classes at the un-
dergraduate or graduate level, and for in-service training. "

As the brochure quoted above indicates, the tapes
were not specifically directed to court volunteers, but were
rather directed generally to correctional personnel and concerned community people.   Volunteers are in both those ball
parks, however, and Professor Jorgensen's summary indicates the degree to which this is true for each tape.

Generally, in that they present the child's view of the
major people and factors conditioning his delinquency, these
are particularly valuable for the naive volunteer, who may
concentrate too much on what his own views are, and lack
insight into how the child sees things.   This is a fatal in-
sensitivity for building a good volunteer-probationer relationship.   Tapes 3 through 7 are relatively more relevant to
volunteer training; numbers 1 and 2 relatively less so.   All
are approximately 30 minutes long.   Note again: these tapes
are not available directly from the National Information Center on Volunteers in Courts.   Complete ordering information
for them is in Section III, C of this report.

1.   The Child's View of the Law Enforcing Officer

Assorted interviews with children who have been apprehended by the police reveal a variety of responses varying from respect to intense dislike.   However, the interviewees show considerable insight into the dilemma of the
police as well as understanding of the law enforcement task.
Training value for volunteers: These interviews
would have some training value for volunteers.   They provide some insight into juveniles' responses to authority as
represented by the police.   They would undoubtedly be of interest to people working in the law enforcement field.

2.   The Child's View of the Judge and the Court
Hearing

Ten children who have been through a juvenile court
hearing are interviewed.   Their responses to judges, procedures of the court, and the rationale for the procedures, are
varied.
Training value for volunteers: This tape has limitations in terms of training value for volunteers.   It would undoubtedly be of interest to judges and professional court

personnel, however.

3. The Child's View of the Probation Officer

Twenty-two children are interviewed regarding their views of the probation officer. These children possess considerable insight into the necessities of an authoritative helping relationship. They discuss inconsistencies on the part of various officers and place the process of probation within the perspective of "the consumer."

Training value for volunteers: Because most volunteers will be acting as a probation counselor or in some capacity in relation to the probation process, this tape is valuable for volunteer training. While the children's comments are directed to the paid professional probation officer, they are relevant to the volunteer working with children in the community, insofar as the two roles do overlap in court work. Moreover, this will help the volunteer prepare for the child's discussing his view of the probation officer with him, as children often do with their volunteers.

4. The Child's View of Detention

This tape is comprised of 17 interviews with children who have experienced confinement in juvenile detention. Differential responses on the part of these youth provide rather fascinating listening. A general dislike of detention was expressed; however, a need for detention was agreed upon by a majority of the interviewees.

Training value for volunteers: This tape would be very beneficial to the volunteer specifically serving children in detention facilities. It would also have some general relevance to volunteers working with delinquent children. A basic training focus would be to discuss the purpose and use of detention facilities. Sound reproduction is somewhat uneven which makes the accompanying written transcription very necessary.

5. The Child's View of His Home Conditions

A series of ten interviews with children who discuss various family situations and their reactions to these situations. Alcoholism, divorce, promiscuity, etc., on the part of parents are seen through the eyes of the child.

Training value for volunteers: The tape is accompanied by a transcript and a discussion guide which facilitates the use of the tape for training. Volunteers would be better

informed about families of juveniles coming before the courts
as a result of hearing this tape.   The volunteer who doesn't
understand multi-problem families would definitely be confronted with the reality of family dysfunction through hearing
this tape, and our impression is that many, if not most,
juvenile court volunteers end up squarely in the middle of
family problems, whether this is intended or not.   They had
best be prepared for it.

6.   The Story of a Delinquent Girl

This interview with a delinquent girl would provide
"cultural shock" to most volunteers.   A confused parental
situation, early marriage, pregnancy, childbirth, and ongoing turmoil provide a very clear picture of extreme deprivation in the life of this youngster.
Training value for volunteers might be in the areas
of (1) interviewing techniques, (2) understanding a child's reactions to stress, (3) the meaning of flight as a way of a
child's handling of problems, (4) impulsiveness.   This tape
should produce excellent discussion.   The written transcript
and study guide which accompany the tape facilitate its use
for volunteer training.

7.   The Story of the Neglected Boy

An interview with a 14-year-old boy who discusses
the family experience leading up to his being declared a
neglected child.   As in other tapes in this series, a step-
parent situation, alcoholism, parental ineffectiveness contribute to a deteriorating family situation.   Placement in foster
care follows.
Training value for volunteers: This tape has potential
for (1) helping the volunteer understand the difference between
a neglected child and a delinquent child, (2) understanding
the place of the foster home in child care, (3) understanding
the meaning of placement to a child, and (4) the significance
of the absent parent.   Accompanying written transcript and
study guide serve as valuable adjuncts to training.

II.   D.   "Berkshire Farm" Tapes

The title of this series is "A Step Toward Professionalism: A Dynamic Method for Training Child Care Workers. "   The tapes were prepared by the Berkshire Farm Institute for Research and Training, and are distributed by the

Center for Mass Communication of Columbia University Press
(1967). The series is composed of six tapes, two lessons
on each tape, for a total of 12 lessons on six tapes. The
series is designed to train child care workers for juvenile
correctional institutions. The problems depicted are within
an institutional frame of reference. As such they would have
more relevance for volunteers preparing for institutions than
volunteers working in probation.

The lessons vary from 15 to 30 minutes each in
length, average a little more than 20 minutes each. Each
tape is thus twice as long--e.g., about 45 minutes.

Tapes		Lessons
Tape 1 - - -	(1)	The Child Care Worker
	(2)	Working with the Aggressive Youngster
Tape 2 - - -	(3)	Working with the Passive and Withdrawn Youngster
	(4)	Working with the Group
Tape 3 - - -	(5)	Cottage Programming and Activities
	(6)	Discipline and Punishment
Tape 4 - - -	(7)	Child Care Worker and Supervision
	(8)	Visiting Parent
Tape 5 - - -	(9)	Working with Prejudice
	(10)	Sex Problems in the Institution
Tape 6 - - -	(11)	Child Care Worker and Professional Staff
	(12)	Summary

Each lesson includes written discussion questions.
The format for each lesson is that of a problem vignette
which is acted out by a delinquent youth and a child care
worker. However, the vignettes are not particularly well
acted out and they provide examples of "how not to be a
good child care worker." In reviewing this series, Professor Jorgensen's conclusion was that Lessons 1, 2, and 3
(i.e., on Tapes 1 and 2) seem to be most relevant for volunteer training in that the principles depicted would have application in working with children in the community as well
as in an institution. Also, after Tapes 1-2 (Lessons 1, 2,
and 3), one tends to get into a bit of repetition of some
material.

III.   Ordering Information

     The National Information Center on Volunteers in
Courts (NICOVIC) has produced some of these tapes, reviewed
all of them, and assembled them in the present directory.
However, NICOVIC does not stock any of these tapes for
rental or sale.   To our knowledge, none of these tapes can
be procured on a trial or a rental basis.   They must be
purchased outright.   Usually this is no hardship since tape
prices are rather low.   Indeed, a court can acquire a quite
varied and comprehensive audio library for volunteer orientation for something like $30 to $50 total.   In ordering be as
specific and complete as possible in identifying the tape(s)
desired.   Better to over-identify the tape than under-identify,
so give all relevant titles, numbers, etc.

     Ordering: II A   "Volunteers Helping Offenders"
          and II B   "The NCAT Review"

     All tapes in both these sections (23 tapes in all) are
ordered from the National Center for Audio Tapes (NCAT),
University of Colorado, Stadium Building, Boulder, Colorado
80302.   We quote from their catalog:

    "When ordering tapes, fill out the order blank or a
    reasonable facsimile of the order blank (which follows),
    and mail along with your check or purchase order (in-
    clude P.O. number) to the:
          National Center for Audio Tapes
          University of Colorado
          Stadium Building, Room 319
          Boulder, Colorado 80302
          Telephone 303/443-2211, x 7341

    "When compiling orders for tape recordings listed in
    this catalog, please note the following procedures:
    "1.   Specify the exact and complete title of the individual
    program desired, even though it is listed under a series
    heading.   (Orders cannot be filled simply by designating
    the series title* unless the entire series is ordered.)
    Each individual title listed on the order must have the

---

*In Section A, the series title is "Volunteers Helping Of-
fenders"; in Section II B it is the title top left of the review.

running time associated with it in the catalog. This
running time must be included when designating the title
of the tape program desired. The stock number for individual program titles immediately preceding the tape
title should be included. (This is "Order #" on all re-
views in Sections II A and II B.)
"2. Audio tapes will be provided as follows: (a) All
open reel tapes will be duplicated at 3-3/4 Ips on 7
inch reels. All Cassettes duplicated at 1-7/8 Ips. (b)
All open reel tapes are duplicated on a full-track configuration. All Cassettes are half-track. (c) All tapes
are duplicated on first quality Polyester tape 1/4 inch
wide, or Cassette width. (d) All tapes will be duplicated on magnetic tape provided by the National Center
for Audio Tapes. NCAT cannot accept tapes supplied
by the customer. (e) Except where otherwise noted,
prices are based on individual program titles and their
individual running time. (An individual title refers to
separate titles within a series and not a complete series. Prices are effective as of July 1, 1969.) Prices
given below now include the cost of postage and insurance for orders shipped within the U. S. boundaries.
Foreign countries will be charged for the postage involved.
"Note: Orders must be accompanied by purchase order
with purchase order number or check enclosed.
"Prices for Open Reel Tapes
$2. 40 for each individual title, running time 0 - 16
minutes.
$3. 10 for each individual title, running time 16 - 35
minutes.
$3. 95 for each individual title, running time 35 - 50
minutes.
$4. 50 for each individual title, running time 50 - 75
minutes.
"Prices for Cassettes
$2. 90 for each individual title, running time 0 - 16
minutes.
$3. 60 for each individual title, running time 16 - 35
minutes.
$4. 45 for each individual title, running time 35 - 50
minutes.
$5. 00 for each individual title, running time 50 - 75
minutes. "

(Editor's note: Thus, most of the tapes reviewed here are
available for four dollars or less per tape, and many for

$3.10 or less. Quantity discounts give even better prices
and we quote further from NCAT):

> "The following quantity discounts apply to the fees listed
> in the 1970-72 catalog:

"REELS	(as noted above) 1st Copy	Next 4 [in multiples of 5]
15 min.	2.40	1.50 ea.
30 min.	3.10	2.00 ea.
45 min.	3.95	2.50 ea.
60 min.	4.50	3.25 ea.

> "To receive the quantity discounts, orders must be 5
> copies of a given (single) program or in multiples of 5.
> Odd numbers of copies (i.e., not evenly divisible by 5)
> will be charged at the individual (first copy) rate. Dis-
> counts apply to copies of single programs.

"CASSETTES	1st Copy	Next 3 [in multiples of 4]
15 min.	2.90	1.80 ea.
30 min.	3.60	2.30 ea.
45 min.	4.45	2.80 ea.
60 min.	5.00	3.55 ea.

> "To receive the quantity discount, orders must be 4
> copies of a given (single) program or in multiples of 4.
> Odd numbers of copies (i.e., not evenly divisible by 4)
> will be charged at the individual (first copy) rate. Dis-
> counts apply to copies of single programs."

For maximum convenience, on pages 144-145 is the
recommended Order Form to be used in ordering from
NCAT (all tapes reviewed in Section II A and II B).

Ordering: II C Children's Charter "Child's View"

These are all the tapes described in Section II C.
Children's Charter ordering information is reproduced below:

> "Because Children's Charter's main purpose is to im-
> prove services to children, we are anxious that this
> valuable material be made available to any and all who
> desire to hear it. Therefore we are offering the pro-
> grams at cost. We cannot offer free trials. Order any
> one for $10.00, or all seven for the package price of
> $65.00. Extra copies of the printed transcript for group
> participants are also available at $1.00 each.
> "Please enclose check or money order to cover payment

in full.   Use the convenient order form to request tapes. "

CHILDREN'S CHARTER of the Courts of Michigan, Inc.
1121 Knollwood, Kalamazoo, Michigan 49007
Please send indicated number of copies of the following
taped programs.   Enclosed is $_____ in full payment.
It is understood that materials will be shipped postpaid.
(Michigan residents include 4% sales tax.)

NUMBER   NAME
_____   The Child's View of the Law Enforcing
                Officer
_____   The Child's View of the Judge and the
                Court Hearing
_____   The Child's View of the Probation Officer
_____   The Child's View of Detention
_____   The Child's View of His Home Conditions
_____   The Story of a Delinquent Girl
_____   The Story of a Neglected Boy
                All seven for $65.00

NAME_____
STREET_____
CITY_____STATE_____ZIP_____

Ordering: II D "Berkshire Farm" Tapes

The complete "Step Toward Professionalism" Series,
as described in Section II D, six tapes, 12 lessons, tape
speed 3-3/4, can be ordered for $75.00 from Columbia
University Press, Center for Mass Communication, 440
West 110th Street, New York, New York 10025.   They also
have a free catalog with further information on the tapes.
Arrangements may be possible to purchase only two of the
six tapes, the first two, but such arrangements must be
worked out directly with the distributor at the above address.
If you do attempt to order anything less than the total series, be sure to identify the tapes clearly by lesson number,
primarily (e. g. , Lessons 1 and 2), and only secondarily by
tape number.

IV.   Care of Tapes and Preparation for Use

Obviously, the best tape in the world is no good if
played on poor or poorly maintained equipment.   And the

It is suggested that customers use this form as a master from which copies can be made using heavy white paper.

PART IV

TO: NATIONAL CENTER FOR AUDIO TAPES
BUREAU OF AUDIOVISUAL INSTRUCTION
STADIUM BUILDING, ROOM 319
UNIVERSITY OF COLORADO
BOULDER, COLORADO 80302

* ORDER FORM

SEND TAPES TO:

SEND INVOICE TO:

CHARGES ARE SHOWN BELOW FOR INDICATED PROGRAM LENGTH AND INCLUDES DUPLICATION OF PRO-
GRAM(S), TAPE, REEL, BOX WITH LABEL, OR CASSETTE, AND POSTAGE.

Price — Open 7 Inch Reel

RUNNING TIME: 1 to 16 Minutes .... $2.40   RUNNING TIME: 36 to 50 Minutes $3.95
                17 to 35 Minutes .... $3.10   51 to 65 Minutes $4.50

Price — Cassettes

RUNNING TIME: 1 to 16 Minutes .... $2.90   RUNNING TIME: 36 to 50 Minutes $4.45
                17 to 35 Minutes .... $3.60   51 to 65 Minutes $5.00

POSTAGE WILL BE PREPAID FROM BOULDER, COLORADO AND IS BASED ON 1968 RATES. (ADDITIONAL POSTAGE CHARGES, DUE TO INCREASED RATES, SPECIAL HANDLING OR FOR FOREIGN SHIPMENTS, WILL BE ADDED). SHIPMENTS WILL BE FOURTH CLASS RATES.

DATE NEEDED: _____

PURCHASE ORDER ENCLOSED☐   PURCHASE ORDER NUMBER _____   CHECK ENCLOSED☐

SUBMIT CHECK OR PURCHASE ORDER TO ELIMINATE UNNECESSARY DELAY IN PROCESSING.

ORDER # Please List Program Desired by Stock Number, Individual Title & Running Time.

STOCK #	PROGRAM TITLE	OPEN REEL	CASSETTE	RUNNING TIME	COST

best equipment in the world may not project sound as well
as you think in the back of the room. Be sure to test volume and ask about that before people settle down to listen.
Obviously, too, you as a trainer shouldn't be hearing the
tape for the first time at the same time your volunteers do.
You should listen to it first, check it out for technical and
content quality, get at least a little ahead of your students
in understanding its implications, a few good discussion
openers, etc.

As for care of tapes and equipment, the University
of Colorado and the National Center for Audio Tapes under
the supervision of their director and the Educational Media
Program Coordinator, have developed guidelines for audio
tape libraries under a USOE grant. Included in these guidelines are recommendations and procedures for: (1) Equipment; (2) Maintenance; (3) Tape Specifications; (4) Storage;
(5) General information such as tape splicing, editing of
tape, maintenance techniques, tape libraries, and references
for some audio tape libraries other than NCAT and institutions utilizing audio tapes for instruction. To secure a copy
of these guidelines, send a check or purchase order for
$1.00 to the National Center for Audio Tapes, University of
Colorado, Room 319, Stadium Building, Boulder, Colorado
80302.

V.   Non-Concluding Remarks

This has been only a start. There are probably many
other volunteer-valuable tapes we don't know of (so please
tell us), and there will be even more in the near future, including the ones you make, individually tailored to your own
court volunteer program. If you want to be in on a wider
array of possibilities even now, you might find some our review missed in the 1970-72 NCAT Catalog, available for
$4.50 per copy from NCAT, University of Colorado, Stadium
Building, Boulder, Colorado 80302.

You might also keep in touch with the Westinghouse
Learning Corporation, 100 Park Avenue, New York City
10017, concerning the learning directory they are preparing
in all media, involving the widest possible range of learning
topics. The Berkshire Farm for Boys distribute a series
themselves, to radio stations, which deals with juvenile delinquency generally and includes interviews with children in
trouble with the law. They are $4.00 per tape. This is in

addition to the series of tapes reviewed in Section II D of this Report, and for further information on the series, you should write to Mr. Philip Kaminstein, Audio Communication Center, Berkshire Farm for Boys, Institute for Training and Research, Inc., Canaan, New York 12029. The series is called "Listen to Their Voices," recorded at 7 1/2 inches per second, full track, running for about 25 minutes each.

Mr. Kaminstein can send you a catalog describing this rich reservoir of audio case material for young people in trouble, ages 12 to 20, including interviews made in diagnostic centers, institutions, detention homes, juvenile courts, police stations, community centers, group homes, etc. There are at least 20-25 such tapes, offered at a cost of $4.00 each.

Berkshire Farms has also just completed another series called "Youth Turns On" which will also be distributed by Columbia University Press, Center for Mass Communication, 440 West 110th Street, New York 10025. This series deals specifically with drug abuse and is aimed at the high school student, though it may also have some value for volunteers, we believe. There are 12 tapes in the set, each tape is 15 minutes in length, and the purpose is to stimulate discussion in the classroom. No charge has been fixed yet, but we are advised that, as of August, 1970, the Center for Mass Communication was in the process of preparing descriptive material on this series.

Chapter 9

SLIDE SHOWS

Some Potential Advantages

Along with audio tapes, films, and television, training slide shows give you a standard, repeatable presentation.
Once you have the show, you can run it again and again until it gets outdated (probably at least a few years) without
having to re-prepare something new each time. And slides
can be added or deleted so that the show can be updated at
intervals.

Potentially, at least, slide shows have multi-media
impact, both visual and auditory, and they can be far better
than either alone. For the same reason they have at least
some of the realism and visual drama of the film medium,
and far more than lectures or panels.

At the same time they tend to be far less expensive
than films. Purchase-wise a film might cost anywhere from
$100 to $200, while a slide show might cost from $10 to
$30. Most often slide shows aren't available for rental (the
rental cost is too close to purchase), but where they are,
there is not so much difference between slide show and film
rental fees ($10 to $15), although, remember, a good film
is likely to be far more powerful than an equally good slide
show.

Suppose you decide to produce your own. We'll have
more to say about that below, but from the standpoint of expenses, it's approximately one-tenth the cost of the film. A
real cheapie slide show with lots of unpaid contributed service, etc., might be produced for as little as $100, while
the equivalent economy film would be about $1,000. The
fully funded professionally produced slide show, on the other
hand, might well have a price tag of $3,000; the film,
similarly produced, $30,000.

A potential advantage of slide shows over other training aids is their capacity for individualization to your community and agency.   (You can substitute a picture of your
courthouse, your judge, your volunteers, your main street,
etc.)

For all these reasons, slide shows can be a good
medium to mix in with all your other training media.

Hazards and Cautions

The principal hazard is that slide shows must be
viewed in the dark, and the poorly produced slide show does
everything further to encourage sleep.

A related hazard.   Something in the American experience, possibly due to the ease with which slide shows of
last summer's vacation can be inflicted on helpless guests
for an evening, has encouraged the notion that there is nothing to producing a good slide show.   Actually, nothing could
be further from the truth.   It is very difficult to produce a
good slide show, far harder than it looks, which is why
there are so many poor slide shows available for loan, rental, or purchase, and the tortured experience of the hapless
guest is transferred to the training class.   Please try to
keep these points in mind whether you borrow, rent, or
purchase.

1.   Brevity.   Most slide shows are far too long.
Ten minutes of zippy presentation is plenty, remembering
always that you're trying more to stimulate and catalyze
discussion than have a finished, self-contained, and complete
training message.   And because of this, Mr. Trainer, be
sure you're primed and organized for productive discussion
following the slide show.   We recommend producing a study
guide right along with the show.   In any case, don't let the
slide show just hang there.   Be ready to move in with productive discussion.

2.   Selection of visual content.   Most slide show pro-
ducers seem to feel that four or five consecutive views of
the court house, or of main street, or of the volunteer coordinator's profile are utterly fascinating.   Most viewers
do not seem to agree.   Select visuals carefully, for sharp-
ness, drama, and non-repetitive hard-hittingness.   You can
even vary from photographs to cartoons, etc.

3. Preparing visual content. Even though you may
have excellent ideas as to content, don't assume that anyone
who can more or less point a camera will produce technically
good photos for you. It isn't so. Try to get people with
real professional expertise in photography.

4. The role of the visuals. Many slide shows make
the mistake of creating the words first, then tacking on the
visuals as more or less an afterthought. But if you can
take out the slides and still get the message just from the
audio, or script, you've failed to capitalize on the visuals.
They should lead in carrying the message; let the script or
audio follow along.

5. But give careful attention to the script, too.
Have your best reader read it if taped (a good idea). Again,
professional expertise should be involved if at all possible.

6. What all the above means is that before purchasing a slide show, or at least before showing it to your
trainees, review it carefully. If you decide to produce a
slide show of your own, don't underestimate the task, the
budget, or the need for professional audio-visual expertise.
The Center's slide shows, described in the readings attached
here, had to economize on these commodities by virtue of a
very low budget--and the results show. Hennepin County's
effort will budget substantially for such help ($3,000 per
show), and we expect their results will show it. Materials
are easily $100-150, and that's just the beginning. Also,
don't underestimate how long it takes to produce a good
show: it can easily run to six months.

7. The best slide show in the world can be ruined
by poor equipment and preparation. First, be sure you
have good projection, audio, etc. equipment (this can be expensive), good seating, audibility, etc. Also, if you read
the script aloud, have an inconspicuous reading light available (pencil beam) and in any case, try to place the slide
operator and/or reader so that they won't distract from the
audience's line of sight to the screen.

Above all, dry run the whole procedure first, far
enough ahead of time so errors can be corrected, but not
so far ahead that gremlins can get back into the equipment
before show time. In 1936, in South Podunk, it is reported
that a slide show went off okay without having had a dry run
of this type preceding it. But that's the only instance we

know of in all recorded history.

Along that line, you can try to standardize your best
performance by taping your best reader, and linking it all
up with a tape-cassette rig (could run $450 to $500). We've
even heard of taking a video tape film of your best presentation and then showing only "the film of the slide show" for
best standard presentation.   But that might be expensive,
too.   If you do tape, appropriate music can add a great deal
to the slides.

Potentials

Obviously, we are far from overwhelmingly enthusi-
astic about the training value of run-of-the-mill slide shows.
Well-produced ones, yes, but there you are getting close to
the rental cost of films, which have far more potential, and
even in the purchase range films are within hailing distance
of slide shows.

But still, the good slide show is good, and with imagination can be better.   For example, Denver Red Cross
uses two projectors for sync flashing of really impactful
pictures and music.   We suggest you write them for more
on this truly compelling technique, which we believe is more
dramatic than most films (Jim Williams, Mile High Chapter,
American Red Cross, 170 Steele Street, Denver, Colorado
80203).

What's Available or Coming?

We've been talking here about volunteer orientation
or training slide shows.   Sometimes, these shows also have
volunteer recruiting or sheer documentary relevance, also.
But the reverse is not the case.   Shows produced primarily
to document, sell, or promote a program usually do not
have any particular volunteer training value.   They're proba-
bly easier to produce, too, and some good ones exist.   For
further information you can write to Mr. Philip Carlson,
Coordinator, Illinois Information Center on Volunteers in
Courts, P. O. Box 3264, Peoria, Illinois 61614; Mr. Bob
Moffitt, Director, Partners Program, 817 17th Street,
Suite 424, Denver, Colorado 80202; Lane County Juvenile
Court, 2411 Centennial Blvd. , Eugene, Oregon 97401; or
Bill Wilcken, Black Hawk County Court House, Waterloo, Iowa.

The National Court Volunteer Training Project (NCVTP)
produced three slide shows in 1970-71 specifically for training of court volunteers.   These are presently available for
purchase as indicated in the attached readings.   While these
readings give some idea of script content and study points,
the Project unfortunately cannot lend out or rent the slides
themselves for review prior to purchase because the cost of
handling and mailing for review approaches the cost of purchase.

"Hear Ye, Hear Ye" is for the neophyte court volunteer, attempting to raise and satirize common anxieties of
beginning volunteers.   "Nobody's Child" is for the foster
parent volunteers, and, for all volunteers, stresses the importance of the volunteer's perceptions and preconceptions of
the juvenile offender.   "The Open Ear" is for the lay group
discussion leader volunteer and makes some general points
on communication with juvenile offenders, too.   The attached
three-part Report provides details on each of these shows,
plus procurement information.

Hennepin County Court, Minnesota, has just completed
three more court volunteer training slide shows.   As noted
previously, they have a good budget for this.   Moreover,
this is a highly talented group which, profiting from the
earlier project's experiences, has some excellent shows.
One of them, not incidentally, is on volunteer-staff relations
and is thus useful for staff orientation to volunteers, as well
as for volunteer orientation.   These shows are unique in that
they were produced by volunteers for the training of volunteers.   The technique of synchronizing audio with slides has
been perfected to the point that these slide shows are totally
automated in a compact unit which sells for approximately
$400. 00.   This unit can be set up in a room, lobby, or any
public place, and it can also be used as a recruiting device.
For the latest information on availability of these shows,
write Mr. John Stoeckel, Department of Court Services,
Hennepin County, 22 Court House, Minneapolis, Minnesota
55415.

For the latest information on availability of any other
volunteer training slide shows, write the National Information
Center.

*   *   *   *

Report VII [in 3 parts]

"HEAR YE, HEAR YE"

This is the first in a series of slide shows to be
prepared by the National Court Volunteer Training Project.
The purpose is to provide realistic, re-usable, and stimu-
lating training aids for the orientation of court volunteers
who work directly with probationers.   The first show is designed to be near the very first orientation presentation made
to the volunteer.   He's been recruited and screened, but he
probably hasn't been assigned a probationer as yet.   Though
very likely a mature, successful, alert person, he's also
extremely naive about corrections, the court, probation, and
probationers.

"Hear Ye Hear Ye" therefore attempts to bring out in
the open the common misconceptions of neophyte court volunteers.   Then, it contradicts them, sometimes to the point
of caricature.   It is thus squarely in the tradition of court
volunteer training--to replace fantasy with reality.   But no
one claims this show completes the training job.   In fact,
it is designed to be followed by other slide shows, films,
lectures, etc., providing far more specific information and
guidance for the volunteer.   But first, we've got to get rid
of some common hang-up illusions, and that's the purpose
of "Hear Ye Hear Ye."   Running time: 8-10 minutes.

Narrator's and Projectionist's Script

Notes: A suggested pause is indicated in the script by
----------, or by placing following script on the next line.
Actual script is in regular type; slide descriptions or our
directions are underlined.   Be sure to allow viewers plenty
of time to see the slides.

(Room in Darkness, Screen is Dark)
Hear Ye, Hear Ye, Hear Ye!
Court volunteer programs are now in session.
(Three raps of gavel)
Slide 1.   Signatory slide, about 15 seconds
          Welcome.   We'd like you to meet some of the folks
          you'll be working with.
Slide 2.   Judge, Staff, Crowd of Volunteers
          That's the judge.

Right behind him in the second line is his regular
professional staff.
That crowd behind the judge and his staff are volunteers like yourselves.
Now, how'd you like to meet a typical probationer?

Slide 3.   Probationer as Dracula (scary music if you have it)
It's not him, though that's what some people seem to
think.

Slide 4.   Probationer as angel (cathedral or angelic music)
It's not her either.   The victimized angel is just as
unrealistic as the dangerous Dracula image.
This is more like him (or her).

Slide 5.   Ordinary crowd of teenagers with one surrounded
adult, hardly noticeable off in corner.
Pretty ordinary looking crew isn't it?   You could
easily pass these kids on the street without labeling
them delinquents, and plenty of kids who look like
your picture of a delinquent aren't.
Appearances can be deceiving.
By the way, did you notice something a little different
there in one part of the picture?

Slide 6.   Slide 5 with a circle limelighting the adult
That's a regular probation officer in the bad old days
before volunteers: surrounded by the kids he's sup-
posed to work with.
Doing his best but overwhelmed.
He's lucky if he knows the names of the kids.

Slide 7.   Slide 6 but with all the kids' faces blank
So much for trying to do something with a huge face-
less mass.
When you help as a volunteer, though, it gets more
like this.

Slide 8.   One-to-one pairs, adults with kids
Though it isn't quite like this.

Slide 9.   A crowd of adults overbearing on one small kid
Still.   You're part of a team as a court volunteer.
You're not alone.   Some good people have preceded
you in this court.   Many thousand more volunteers
are at work today in two thousand courts across the
country. ----------And, we haven't lost a volunteer
yet.

Slide 10.   A lonely grave (funeral march music)
We've lost a few kids though.

Slide 11.   Collage of kids in jail (may flash on, then leave
in dark, sound of crying, flash on again, if you
want to try that).
But with your help as a volunteer, we're not losing

quite so many these days.
Slide 12.   Slide 11 with half of the cells empty.
Research shows that the use of court volunteers means
fewer kids in jail, and at the same time a reduction
in juvenile anger and anti-social impulses.   Fewer
crimes against the community.
Slide 13.   Slide of juvenile acting-out offenses (sound of
glass breaking)
Fewer crimes of children against themselves, too.
Slide 14.   Collage, crimes against themselves (sound of
adolescent crying)
The evidence is also overwhelming that court volun-
teer programs will be warmly welcomed by your com-
munity.
Your fellow citizens will appreciate your good work.
Slide 15.   Collage of editorial, "yea volunteers," etc. (sound
of applause, fades)
But it isn't all roses.   Success with your probationer
isn't easy; it isn't fast; and it isn't consistent.
Look for lots of ups and downs.
Sometimes it's like a roller coaster in a high wind.
Or the stock market; some days your stock's up,
sometimes it's down.
Slide 16.   Up-and-down graph with smiles and scowls
Hang in there, don't sell out.
And remember, you'll have help and support from
regular and senior staff.
Slide 17.   Volunteer with group in office
Keep them in the picture so they can help you.   Co-
operate.   It's a team effort and we need the whole
team.   And like we said, research shows that your
court volunteer service can have real positive impact
on the probationer and for the community.
And, by the way, it doesn't do you any harm either.
Slide 18.   Satisfied volunteer with kid
If you take your volunteer work seriously, you'll learn
and grow right along with your probationer.
(Flash next slide on quickly)
Slide 19.   Slide 18 exactly but volunteer and kid are much
bigger, and closer too.
So, like we said, welcome.
Slide 20.   (From here on, slides move quite rapidly in and
out)
Exact repeat of slide 2, Judge, Staff and volunteers
We're glad to have you with us.
Slide 21.   Slide 2, but now showing volunteer coming in, in
the foreground and being greeted by the Judge

Slide 22. <u>Volunteer takes position with other volunteers</u>
            And good luck with the good work.
Slide 23. <u>Repeat of Slide 1, Signatory Slide</u>
            We'll be seeing you.
            And thanks.

<u>Study Guide to "Hear Ye, Hear Ye"</u>

        The greatest value in a training aid such as this may
lie not in what it is, but in what it <u>leads to</u>: the discussion
it stimulates. Here are a few suggested lead-ins for a discussion leader, after the show. (Incidentally, they might
also be given as a written test--see Report XV--as well as
in a discussion.)

"We saw several 'images' of the probationer, including 'the
dangerous dracula' and 'the victimized angel!'" What's your
own image and prediction at this point, as to what your
probationer (or probationers in general) will be like?

"Do you think you'll be in any actual physical danger from
your probationer? Are there dangers of any other kind you
foresee at this time?"

"What do kids get put in jail for around here, or on probation?"

"Who is hurt by the main types of crime we have, and how,
etc. ?" (May lead in to causes of offenses.)

"As of now, what do you want to accomplish with your probationer? What is it you want your work with him to do for
him or change for the better?"

"How long do you think it might take to accomplish this?
Optimistically? Pessimistically?" (Try to develop need
for patience, preparation for frustrating setbacks).

"What do you think your work with your probationer might
do for <u>you</u>?"

"Will this likely include thanks from the probationer? From
his parents? From his friends?"

"What are typical caseloads for professional staff in this
court?" (That is, how many probationers and/or volunteers

is each paid staff person responsible for?)

Continue to pursue this with questions like, "How many phone calls a day does he get?" "How much paper work?" "How many meetings?" The objects are to develop understanding by the volunteer of why his phone call to staff may not be returned immediately, or his request or office visit dealt with immediately, and to reinforce his feeling of being needed to alleviate this short-staff situation.

In presenting the slide show it is very desirable that the narrator have reading light concentrated enough for his own use which would not however interfere with the darkness of the room. Secondly, his position in the room should not be such as to attract attention to himself personally, rather than the presentations on the screen. Thirdly, it is vastly preferable to have automated slide-showing equipment arranged in such a way so that the narrator can move to the next slide automatically, e.g., by pressing a button according to his own immediate feeling for appropriate timing. If the narrator himself cannot do this a second person should be available to do it in a non-distracting way according to the cues of the narrator. Be sure to practice your narration and projection procedures so you have them down smoothly before presenting the show for training to volunteers.

Ordering "Hear Ye, Hear Ye"

National Information Center on Volunteers in Courts
Suite 717, The Colorado Building
Boulder, Colorado 80302
(Prices as of December, 1971.)
Set of 5 scripts at $.50 per set
Slides and Script at $12.00
Slides, Tape, Script at $15.00
Make check payable to: The National Information Center

*   *   *   *

Report VII [2nd of 3 parts]

"NOBODY'S CHILD" SLIDE SHOW*

"Nobody's Child" is a slide show designed specifically
for court foster parents but applicable to volunteers in general. Though developed as an orientation-training tool, it can
easily be used for recruiting. Volunteers, as a rule, have
little time to spend on written materials, and it is felt visual
and audio training aids, so long as they are not too complicated for the non-expert, can relieve some of the burden of
lengthy written materials. This slide show is simply enough
designed that a new volunteer can see it on his own, with
little supervision, or the volunteer trainer can show it to a
group.

"Nobody's Child" points out some typical attitudes new
volunteers have--especially those pertaining to children and
their new job. It further presents several obstacles foster
parents will encounter in dealing with a foster child, as well
as places that can help with support and information. The
show consists of 51 numbered slides, with a running time of
12 minutes. An audio tape, designed to accompany the slide
show, is also available. The following script is a word-for-
word account of the tape, so it can be read aloud if a tape
recorder is not available. However the tape supplies background music and is professionally done. It is recommended
for use if at all possible. It is intended that this manual is
for the use of the volunteer trainer. To obtain maximum
benefit of the tape-slide presentation as a training aid, we
would stress it is most important that the trainer should
practice the operation several times before the first showing,
so as to synchronize the correct slide with the corresponding
audio message.

Narrator's and Projectionist's Script

[Note: again, narration is in regular type, slide descriptions
or directions are underlined.]

Slides 1-7.   Introductory and credit slides.   Background
               music, 45 seconds

*Written and directed by Judith A. Berry; original narration
and audio by K. G. Prather; original art by Mountain Studio.

There are many varieties of volunteers. They all
come to the court to give of their time and talent, but the
volunteer foster parent has the most demanding job of all.
They are the 24 hour a day volunteers. They are the people
who give all their time and talents for a period ranging from
weeks to years. To a child thrust into a strange world
without a home and unwanted, a good foster parent is one
of the best things that can happen.

But, like all of us, volunteer foster parents have different perspectives of children depending upon their different
personalities.

Slide 8. Rose-colored glasses--1

Some volunteers see today's children through rose-
colored glasses. They say: "These are nice children.
They aren't disturbed at all. They're persecuted. All they
need is a little love. "

Slide 9. Rose-colored glasses--2

These volunteers blame the court, blame the parents,
blame the community, the schools, the peer group influence.

If this volunteer is you, come join us in the real
world where children do have problems resulting from a
combination of elements including themselves sometimes.
If you don't realize this, you will fail, because you are fail-
ing to face the real issues, because you don't know how, or
maybe because you are afraid.

Slide 10. Glasses with blinders--1

Other types of volunteers view children with blinders
on their glasses. Through their blinders they say: "These
are mean kids. Never will amount to any good. They have
more opportunity than when I was a kid. What these kids
need is ...

Slide 11. Glasses with blinders--2

"... a good belt in the mouth and a few good strap-
pings. "

Correct application of discipline is necessary but it
is not the whole story. Take off those blinders and let's
see that there is more to developing healthy personalities
than harsh, unreasonable discipline. With such rigid attitudes you can't expect much constructive change in a child.

Slide 12. Smoked lens glasses--1

The third type of volunteer wears glasses with smoked
lenses. This is the gloomy volunteer. To him the whole
world looks dark and children are doomed to a destiny--be-
yond help. These volunteers say: "You can't change these
kids. They'll resist all efforts of help, they'll rebel. "

Slide 13. Smoked lens glasses--2

This volunteer sees responsibility as restricted only

to physical things.   'I'll feed them, house them, and clothe
them, but I don't expect change or improvement. " This volunteer foster parent gets exactly what he expects--nothing.
He fails more than anyone, because he fails to try.

If your world looks gloomy, try to look more for the
positive things and try to help to develop the child's talents.
The response can be amazing.

Slide 14.   Clear prescription lenses--1

Then you will be an effective realistic volunteer who
looks at today's children through prescription lenses.   Vision
is perfect.   There is no distortion.

He sees the problems of children.   He sees their
hurts, insecurity, need for love and attention.   He sees too
that they are suspicious of anyone trying to help.

Slide 15.   Clear prescription lenses--2

This volunteer foster parent sees not only the problems and frustrations of the child, he also sees potential
for achievement and the good in children.   He is positive
about change.

This volunteer is a realist.   The outlook is hopeful.

Slide 16.   Math symbols for job description

The role of foster parent is a demanding one.   To
your regular role of parent ...

Slide 17.   Math symbol, addition

... add the role of counselor, doctor, psychologist,
arbitrator, mother, father, disciplinarian ...

Slide 18.   Math symbol, division

... divide all those things by a troubled child ...

Slide 19.   Math symbol, multiply

... and your duties multiply in every direction.   You
become intermediary between the child and the court.   Mediator with other volunteers who may be working with your
foster child, and intermediary between the child and his own
natural parents.

Slide 20.   Math symbol, equal

Equaling a 24 hour vigil.

Slide 21.   Begin series of qualities

You must have a high degree of frustration tolerance.

Slide 22.   Series continues

You must have a sense of ingenuity.

Slide 23.   Series continues

You must be flexible.

Slide 24.   Series continues

You should be willing to learn.

Series 25.   Series continues

You can certainly use a sense of humor.

Slide 26.   Series continues
You must have a fondness for children.
Slide 27.   Series continues
You've got to believe in yourself as a change agent
and in the child as able to be changed.
Slide 28.   Boy with parents--honeymoon
No matter how well prepared for your new job you
are, the initial "honeymoon period"--the early period of
wine and roses ...
Slide 29.   Above scene shattered
... will end, hopefully with no large crisis, and that
is where the hard work begins, with ...
Slide 30.   Picture being put together--communication
... communication, understanding, honesty, putting it
all together again.
Slide 31.   Natural parents and foster parents with child
There will be crises besides the end of the honeymoon period.   Dealing with the natural parents is one of
these.   Just remember that you can't and shouldn't want to
replace the child's own parents or break the bond that exists.
The child may be returned to these parents at some future
time, and you must help prepare him for this.
Slide 32.   Natural and foster children together
Bringing a foster child into your home can create
problems between your own natural children and the foster
child: competition, repression, jealousy, feelings of not
being wanted.   The natural children should be aware of the
situation and accept it before a foster child is accepted into
the home, and then the family should work together as a
unit to help the new child adjust.
Natural children can be a great asset to a foster
child if they are guided in the right direction.
But don't let all the problems get you down before
you get started.   There are many sources of help and the
court is at the top of the list.
Slide 33.   Begin series of sources of help from the court
The court can provide confidential data on the child
to help you in understanding him better.
Slide 34.   Series continues
They can give you the benefit of their professional
experience.
Slide 35.   Series continues
Court in-service volunteer meetings give you a place
to discuss common problems and solutions among other vol-
unteers like yourself.
Slide 36.   Series continues
Perhaps the court can provide other volunteers to

help with your foster child in specific areas, as tutors, big brothers, group discussion leaders, professional resource people, etc.
Slide 37. Series continues
      The court can help you in dealing with the child's own natural parents.
          Music begins.
      There will be setbacks and disadvantages whether your foster child is six or 16, but the rewards far outweigh any disadvantages.
Slides 38-50. Series of 13 photographs shown at regular
               intervals. Background music, 2 minutes.
    No narration.
Slide 51. The end.
    No narration.

Study Guide to "Nobody's Child"

      The following remarks are to help generate discussion. You can use your own or adapt the following to your specific requirements, if you wish.

      1. There were four types of foster parents presented (rose colored glasses, glasses with blinders, smoked lens glasses, and clear prescription lens). Can you think of any others? Can these types be effective with certain children?
      2. How can you prepare yourself for the "honeymoon" period? How can the court help?
      3. Besides the court, are there agencies in your community that can give help with your child? List and discuss their services.
      4. What specific help can the court be? What services do they provide?
      5. Discuss the role of a foster parent regarding (a) natural parents; (b) the foster child; (c) the natural siblings in the home (same age - opposite sex, very young siblings).
      6. Discuss the legal issues of being and becoming a foster parent.
      7. Where do foster children referrals originate (agency), and what are your obligations to that agency (court, welfare, private)?
      8. Is routine reporting required? Is it necessary?

      Remote topics: what about single foster parents?
Retired foster parents? How many foster children in one home?

Ordering "Nobody's Child"

National Information Center on Volunteers in Courts
Suite 717, The Colorado Building
Boulder, Colorado 80302
(Prices as of December, 1971)
set of 5 scripts at $.50 per set
slides, tape, script at $20.00

*　　　　　*　　　　　*　　　　　*

Report VII [3rd of 3 parts]

(C) "THE OPEN EAR" SLIDE SHOW*

Narrator's and Projectionist's Script

[Note: narrator's voice (or otherwise specified) is in regular type; slide descriptions or directions are underlined.]

[no slide] First 30 seconds in darkness with sound of tape of women prisoners at Colorado State Penitentiary directed to girls probationer group:
(Woman prisoner): You girls wanted to know something about our life in here.... Well, I'll tell you there isn't much of anything in here. You get up to bells and you go to sleep to bells and you just watch the clocks and you just think and gossip, and you work maybe a couple of hours out of the day, and the rest of the time is your own. And most of the time you're just sitting there feeling sorry for yourself and blaming other people for being in here, and actually all the blame is upon yourself.
Slide 1. Music--guitar and singing group. HEW and Boulder Juvenile Court Credits
Slide 2. Music--guitar and singing group. Title and Director Credits
Slide 3. Music--guitar and singing group. Other credits
Slides 4-9. Jail scenes to be changed about every three seconds for each slide.

*Written and directed by Ursula Davies; original narrator, K. G. Prathan; original graphics, Gloria Kroeger; original music, Wintercricket Group and Grant Gray on guitar; original audio, Paul Corey; original "Linda," Julie Johnson. Number of slides, 80; running time, 18 minutes.

(Narrator): These are scenes from inside a prison. What events lead up to a boy or girl teenager being jailed behind these doors?

Slides 10-21.   Slides of girl looking at and stealing jewelry, with alternate slide of jail #5. Slides to be changed about every 3 seconds. Background of silence. 10: girl smiling looking at jewelry counter; 11: jail #5; 12: girl backview looking at jewelry; 13: jail #5; 14: girl's face close-up "Are they looking at me?"; 15: jail #5; 16: close-up of girl's hand pushing jewelry into handbag; 17: jail #5; 18: girl longview "Did they see me?"; 19: jail #5; 20: girl walking through store door into street; 21: jail #5.

Slide 22.   Courtroom scene with Linda and judge, distance view.
When teenagers come to the attention of the court for committing minor offences, what can we do to keep them from committing more serious crimes? A teenager experiments between fantasy and reality. How can we encourage them to develop a sense of reality and responsibility? They are searching for an identity. When a teenager is put on probation, what does this mean?

Slide 23.   Graphic--Juvenile Probation Department sign
Different courts set different rules, and some courts have rehabilitative programs for the teenager who is put on "probation." Many such programs use volunteers out of the community to work with the teenager.

Slide 24.   Background music. Linda standing, leaning against tree.
Linda has been put on probation by the court for stealing jewelry. Her father is a successful business executive who spends a great deal of time travelling on business; her mother is a part-owner of a beauty salon.

Slide 25.   Linda sitting, looking at a magazine.
They both say they allow Linda a more than liberal allowance and cannot understand why she stole the jewelry.

Slide 26.   Courtroom scene with judge and Linda, close-up.
At Linda's court hearing the judge put Linda on probation for a year, and ordered her to attend a weekly group discussion meeting led by two women volunteers --who are not necessarily professionals themselves-- from the community.

Slide 27. <u>Two group leaders and group in relaxed scene.</u>
Why two? Generally it is better to have two group
leaders; group members get used to, and develop confidence in, two persons, so if one wants a vacation
or cannot make one meeting, there is the other to
carry on the continuity.

Slide 28. <u>Two adult leaders and a few girls sitting, two</u>
<u>others coming through the door to join the group.</u>
During the first 15 minutes or so, there is usually
superficial talk before getting down to serious discussion. We have had between seven and nine members in a group, and we find this number gives the
best chance for an easy interchange of talk and also
covers the occasional absence.

Slide 29. <u>Leaders and girls sitting formally.</u>
At the first meeting, or when a new girl joins the
group, it is a good idea to have the leaders explain
something about themselves as volunteers, that they
are unpaid and not court professionals and to say
how they came to be volunteers.

Slide 30. <u>Close-up of one of the leaders speaking to group,</u>
<u>still formal.</u>
Then go on to say that the meetings are an experiment into seeing if sharing problems, hopes and disappointments can do some good. This helps to put
the new member more at ease.

Slide 31. <u>Same group, more relaxed-looking.</u>
We feel there should be a few basic rules, as it
were, in all group discussions. Such as "confidentiality." Each person should understand and accept
that things said within the group meetings should not
be discussed outside.

Slide 32. <u>Relaxed group.</u>
The group members should realize that the leaders
visit the probation officer and each week send in reports covering the general trend of the discussions.
The leaders, however, should always be sensitive to
the group rule of confidentiality, and see that the group
members understand this contact is as a mediator
with the Court and not in any way as an informant.
Of course, some extreme situations do arise when,
for the well-being of the probationer, the leaders
should perhaps disclose certain issues discussed in
the meetings. This subject of confidentiality between
the probationer, the volunteer, and the probation officer is dealt with in different ways by different
courts, but it is extremely important that an

understanding is reached--which is appropriate to
your own court--before the start of the group discussion meetings.

Slide 33.   One leader "preaching" and group members hanging their heads.
The leaders should be "listeners, " and play the role
of the "sounding board"; remember that most juveniles have been talked "at" for most of their lives.

Slide 34.   Rearranged group.
Griping sessions are frequent and they have their own
value.   When they are running their course, the leader could briefly turn the discussion into a more constructive channel by asking what alternatives are
open.   Silences have their value, too; if a long silence
develops, it is usually good to leave it to a group
member to break it.

Slide 35.   Blue grass music.   Group and leaders on a country hike.
A good way to build inter-dependence and confidence
within the group is to have an occasional outdoor
activity.   This could be a vigorous-type hike if it is
possible to get into a country environment.

Slide 36.   Blue grass music.   View of a museum.
If in a big built-up city, visit a natural science museum or have a handball or swimming party.

Slide 37.   Blue grass music.   Group in "slum clearance. "
Other suggestions are a visit to a hospital, or a
working-visit to a group of VISTA volunteers in a
city-slum setting.

Slide 38.   Blue grass music concluding.   Indoor "discussion"
group.
This visit could be followed by a carefully planned
probing discussion at the next group meeting which
may prove helpful to the members to be realistic
about their own problems and fears.

Slides 39-41.   Slides to be changed about every 3 seconds.
39: distant shot of broken house; 40: money-
lending signs; 41: fire in slum area.
It would show them that maybe their own problems,
fears and frustration are perhaps minor, compared
to other people's.   Again, a constructive solution-
seeking discussion could develop.

Slide 42.   Group in sitting-room setting, relaxed.
The leaders should be flexible, and have secure and
stable personalities.   During the first sessions--be-
fore the group members have put confidence in their
leaders--they may be hostile, which is usual in

persons who are having problems.
Slide 43. Girls being "hostile" to leader.
The members are testing out their leaders. The
leaders should remember that after several sessions,
some members may appear extremely critical of the
group process. This usually means that they are
struggling, and they are finally being faced with reality, and they don't like what they see. The leaders
should make use of such occasions by throwing the
situation back to the other group members for handling and general discussion.
Slide 44. Group, one girl speaking into microphone.
An idea that has been tried out as an experiment in
communication was a tape exchange. A girls' group
made a taped conversation directed towards a group
of women prisoners in the State Penitentiary.
Slides 45-47. Slides to be shown during excerpt of girls'
tape directed to women prisoners. Duration:
1 minute, 40 seconds. 45: girl speaking
into microphone; 46: another girl speaking
into microphone; 47: close-up of girl speaking into microphone.
(1st girl probationer): Well, we thought maybe you'd
be interested to know why some of us are on probation. Myself, I've been caught at about two or three
drinking parties when I was under age, and I took
my mom's car one time without permission--I didn't
have a driver's license ...
(2nd girl): And I was put on probation for mainly the
same things, the parties, and out after curfew and
vagrancy and truancy from school.
(3rd girl): The first question I'd like to ask is about
your family life before, you know, you got into any
trouble at all. And I was wondering if you thought
that if your family life would have been different, if
it would have prevented some of the mistakes you
made--that got you in trouble later on with the law.
(4th girl): And I'd like to ask you if you feel that
when you get out of the penitentiary, will you change
your way of life or will you go back and do what you
did before. And also I'd like to know if any of you
were on probation in your teens before you got sent
up.
(1st girl): Another thing I'd like to talk about is
that I know some of us weren't accepted by some of
the other kids around school and around our town that
we live in, and I know that my sister and I kind of

struck out at these people and I think we rebelled
against society and that's what got us into trouble.
And I was wondering if maybe any of you were the
same way, you know, if you were rebelling against
not being accepted, or being accepted too much and
having too much responsibility.

(Narrator):   Then the women prisoners replied.

Slides 48-56.   Slides to be shown during excerpt of women
prisoners' tape.   Duration: 3 minutes, 15
seconds.   48:   jail slide; 49: girls' group
listening intently; 50: jail slide; 51: jail slide;
52: close-up of girls listening; 53: jail slide;
54: jail slide; 55: group listening; 56: jail
slide.

(1st woman prisoner):   I think that you probably all
know the meaning of loyalty.   You can use it correctly in a sentence, but it wouldn't hurt to talk to
someone that you have respect for, someone whose
opinion you really value, and ask then what really is
loyalty.   How much do you owe to the "in crowd,"
to the bunch out there, to be accepted, and how much
do you really owe to yourself and to what you're going to be in the future.

(2nd woman):   My name is P. and I'm here for aggravated robbery, and my age is 17 years old.   The
reason I am telling you my age is because I feel that
I started out just like you ... some of the girls that
have been in juvenile hall.   I was on probation before
and I've been also on parole from Morrison.   I was
on probation for sniffing glue and drinking and violation of probation--that's why I went to Morrison.
And I thought I was big and bad when I was doing all
these things.

(3rd woman):   Right now you all are resenting sometimes what your parents tell you to do and that they
are trying to bring a little order into your life and
help you grow up the right way.   But you keep doing
as you please.   Well, one thing--when you get down
here, after you've been here for a while, you might
think, "Well, gee, I know they really worried about
me.   I know how much heartache and grief I've
caused them and when I get out, I'll, ah, I'll make
it all up to them."   And then you're sitting in your
room some morning and the matron comes in and
says "I've got some bad news for you.   Your mother
died last night or your father died last night."   So
what do you do?   You just sit back.   You can't even--

nine out of ten times you can't even go to the funeral.
And all those good thoughts you was having and seeing how they might have been right after all, well,
that's sort of shot to hell. There's really not much
left you can do then.
(4th woman): This is J. And you girls were talking
about going to drinking parties and staying out after
curfew and everything. And if these are the kinds of
parties where you do a lot of heavy petting or you go
--to put it bluntly--all the way and have sexual intercourse, one of these days, if you're messing around
with a lot of different guys, or maybe just one that's
been messing around with somebody else, you're gonna
end up with syphilis or gonorrhea, and from that you
can go on to being a prostitute on the streets, because I know, I've been that route. And a lot of
these guys, they'll give you that line about you're
really fine and everything else, but all they want you
to do is get out on the streets and make them some
money.
    And you think you're a big wheel, ditching school
and everything, but if you ever want to be anything
after you get out of high school, without being a drop
out or a "kick out, " you'd better finish school or
else you'll just be slinging hash in a restaurant or a
truck stop or working in some bar or else be on the
street.
    I know what I would have thought if somebody,
when I was on probation, had asked me to sit down
and make a tape like this. I would have thought well,
I'll do it just so I can keep my doggone probation.
And I wouldn't listen to a damn word anybody said.
But I hope some of this sinks in to some of you, or
you're going to be up here and you're going to be in
the same position some of us are, and you aren't
gonna be so big and brave.
Slide 57.   Probation officer and one leader talking in P.O. 's
             office.
(Narrator): An important point to be remembered is
that the volunteer must give feedback, by phone or
written report, to the probation officer, and vice versa. In this way the probation officer has some knowledge of what is happening and in return can give support and advice to the volunteer.
Slide 58.   Volunteer close-up looking in filing cabinet.
It also enables the volunteer to receive facts and prevents the possibility of the probationer manipulating

the volunteer with hard-luck stories.   The volunteer
should also have access to all probation office files.

Slide 59.   Background music.   Animated group.
One technique that has been used very successfully in
the group sessions is role playing.   Different members in the group themselves play different roles, say
of a probationer, a probation officer, a policeman, a
mother.   The group then plays out a hypothetical
scene, say of a girl being apprehended by a policeman for shoplifting, and being interviewed with her
mother by a probation officer.   This enactment helps
each group member to gain insight, and experience
situations from the point of view other than that of
their own.

Slide 60.   Background music.   Living room with group members putting on coats.
In a meaningful group experience it is hoped the members have eventually learned constructive ways of
handling their own feelings of anger, frustration,
guilt, shame, etc.   These are all natural emotions
which they must learn that everybody experiences.

Slide 61.   Background music.   Girl earnestly talking to volunteer.
It is essential also to learn how to deal with these
emotions in a socially acceptable way, and how to
counterbalance them with logical reasoning.

Slide 62.   Continued background music.   Group leaving house.
The group experience can be said to be an outside
life experience in a nutshell, where one can learn to
accept people with all their limitations and their mistakes.

Slide 63.   Continued background music.   Group leaving, long
view.
One of the values of group interaction for a teenager
is that he or she can learn to "talk out" strong emotional feelings instead of using their fists or other
destructive--frequently self-destructive--ways to relieve their frustrations.
Silence.
So, is it going to be this ... ?

Slides 64-69.   Jail slides flashed quickly, say one every 3
seconds.   No narration.

Slides 70-72.   70: boy/girl group working on construction;
71: river scene; 72: construction scene.   To
be shown every 4 seconds.
Or this?   Remember we are all involved.

Slides 73-74.   Each slide of 4 brochures: "Community Vol-
                unteers as Discussion Group Leaders for Ju-
                venile Probationers"; "Tape Exchange and
                Court Probation"; "Using Volunteers in Court
                Settings"; Volunteer Programs in Courts. "
        The brochures "Community Volunteers as Discussion
        Group Leaders for Juvenile Probationers" and "Tape
        Exchange and Court Probationers" deal specifically
        with the group discussion situation.
Slide 75.   First two brochures with graphic: obtainable from
            National Information Center on Volunteers in
            Courts, Suite 717, The Colorado Building, Boulder,
            Colorado 80302.
        These, together with other written material on setting
        up court volunteer programs, can be obtained from
        the National Information Center on Volunteers in
        Courts, Boulder County Juvenile Court, Boulder,
        Colorado 80302.
Slide 76.   Second two brochures with graphic: prices and
            address of U. S. Government Printing Office.
        The two manuals, "Using Volunteers in Court Settings, "
        price $1. 00 per copy, and "Volunteer Programs in
        Courts, " price $1. 25 per copy, can be obtained di-
        rect from the Superintendent of Documents, U. S.
        Government Printing Office, Washington, D. C. 20402.
Slide 77.   Courtroom scene with judge and Linda, distance
            view.
        One of the pioneers in the use of volunteers as group
        discussion leaders is Dr. Ernest Shelley, at present
        Chief Psychologist of Ingham County Probate Court,
        Lansing, Michigan 48933.
Slide 78.   Courtroom scene with judge and Linda, close-up,
            same as slide #26.
        Dr. Shelley is an acknowledged authority in this field,
        and we strongly recommend that volunteer program
        coordinators contact him.
Slide 79.   Background music.   Same as slide #1: HEW and
            Boulder Juvenile Court credits.
Slide 80.   Background music.   Title with "The End. "

Ordering "The Open Ear"

            National Information Center on Volunteers in Courts
                    Suite 717, The Colorado Building
                    Boulder, Colorado 80302

(Prices as of December, 1971)
    set of 5 scripts at $.50 per set
    Slides, Tape, Script at $25.00
Make Check payable to: The National Information Center
    Please note: Please check with the Center before
ordering. As of 1973 this slide show may go on limited
distribution.

Chapter 10

FILMS

In this chapter we will describe those films that we
feel have the greatest utility in court volunteer training.
The films described were selected from among hundreds of
films which by description seemed to have training relevance.
The relative few that emerged attest to the fact that there
are in reality few films that are good enough for training.
Many good documentaries exist that do not serve a real
training purpose, we might add.   They may serve for recruiting or as motivators, however.

Many of the films, although only a few years old,
were already out of date.   Clothing styles, automobiles,
language, and issues were no longer up to date; such is the
pace of social change.   Thus we submit the films below,
cognizant of the fact that they too may soon lose their real
significance.

Whether the films a few years hence are significant,
the medium of films as a training tool is not likely to change
so quickly.   Thus this chapter will also serve the purpose
of sharing with the reader some of the observations we have
made about the use of films in volunteer training.

Films have many advantages in training.   They serve
the multi-purpose of relating to knowledge, attitudes, and
skills.   They depict reality.   They can convey a sense of
the process of corrections.   They present compact messages
and hold the attention of the class, if they are good.   A
poor film squanders the natural advantages of the medium.

Films provide a good change of pace from other media.   They serve as a catalyst for discussion.   They entertain while they inform.   Yet many trainers do not make full
use of films.   They rely too much on the film as a complete self-contained message.   A trainer should of course
preview each of the films he uses for the purpose of

extracting its possibilities for later learning and discussion.
To show a film without introduction or follow-up discussion
is to lose a moment where the class may well have become
primed for discussion.

Prior to showing a film, it is desirable to tell very
briefly what the film is about, how long it is, and generally
what the training objective is. For example in introducing
the film, "The Revolving Door," we note that the film is
about 30 minutes long, and it is about the lower courts,
jails, and the misery of people being processed by these institutions. We note that the film shows some of the worst
of our programs as well as the best. Importantly, it suggests directions for change. We call attention to the photography, the looks on people's faces and we ask the class to
be thinking about the following question: "What do the defendants in this film think of themselves?" This technique
gives the viewer an assignment in a sense. In addition to
entertainment, he has been pre-programmed to extract certain learning points from the film.

After the film has been shown, the trainer can get
feedback from the class as to the meaning of the film to
them. He can then ask the basic question again: "What do
the defendants in this film think of themselves?" When the
responses are made, he can ask the class members to give
the data on which their opinions are based. This has the
effect of informing the rest of the class what individual members saw. In many instances we find that individuals do not
see the same thing in a film. A few minutes given to discussion will have the effect of giving depth as well as breadth
to the viewing experience.

In showing films, the trainer should be certain that,
if there is a study guide which accompanies the film, this
is utilized by the trainer in extracting the teaching points in
the film. These guides can provide a framework for introducing the film as well as for the discussion that follows
the showing. The reader is directed to the reading, "A
Second Chance," at the end of this chapter which is a good
example of a film study guide for one 25-minute film.

We would like to caution the trainer about some of the
considerations in using films as training devices. First, in
terms of length, it is probably not practical to order films
that are much longer than 30 minutes. People who are tired
(and most volunteers are trained at night) seem to lose

interest in any one thing that goes beyond 30 minutes, and
that includes films. Added to this is the fact that mixing
up the media serves an important function of diversifying
training. Also since time is usually essential in training,
the trainer has to move on to cover the necessary material.

In regard to age, as we have already noted, films
after five or six years take on the appearance of having been
of another era. This is not a uniform thing, but, in a surprising number of the films we viewed, the six-year-old ones
telegraphed something that wasn't authentic to the present
day viewer. When styles, language, and issues depicted in
a film are no longer relevant, the film often takes on a
dimension of comedy. This can be entertaining, but not
necessarily of value for training. It is a good policy to obtain a copy of the film for review before purchase for the
reasons cited above.

Another obvious matter regarding films is the kind of
equipment used. Breakdowns in films or projectors serve
only to destroy continuity of thought and mood, and this can
be at least partially alleviated by using good equipment.
Courts sometimes have projectors and screens of good quality. Much of the newer equipment can be operated with a
minimum of preparation, but this minimum preparation is
vital to a smooth training session. If the trainer is to be
the projectionist, he definitely should be "checked out" on
the equipment being used. A partial "dry run" of the machine prior to the class may be in order. Such things as
seating arrangements, room ventilation, and screen-projector
alignment should be handled prior to the beginning of the
session.

A word about commercial movies. Hollywood has
made many full-length features that have much to say to the
court volunteer. How these films might be used in time-
limited training is not clear. However, one might for example consider showing a film such as In Cold Blood as an
in-service training film. Rebel Without a Cause, Joe, and
others too numerous to mention, if used in the context of a
particular problem, could likely serve to enhance training.

A valuable national catalog of current films of this
type is INSCAPE, available from the Center for the Study of
Crime, Delinquency, and Corrections, Southern Illinois University, Carbondale, Illinois.

        We would also suggest that the trainer either consult
with the film librarian or examine the catalog of his local
college or university film library for the possible acquisition
of television documentaries which may have been converted
to 16 mm film.   This has been done with the NBC News
White Paper Report, "This Child is Rated X." Many other
documentaries on criminal justice may be available, and
may be obtainable through the local outlet of the particular
network which produced the program.

        "A Preliminary Film Guide for Training Court Volun-
teers," which follows, will categorize the better existing
films in terms of their training value.   This film guide was
current as of mid-1970, but new films are anticipated, of
course.   Readers are urged to keep abreast of developments
in the <u>Volunteer Courts Newsletter</u>, published by the National
Information Center on Volunteers in Courts, Boulder, Colorado.

        We found after reviewing several films that many if
not most films become quite dated after 5 or 6 years, and
technically and stylistically, the newer the film, generally
speaking, the better.   We strongly advise caution in considering any film which is more than five or six years old.
The films are arranged roughly in order from highest to
lowest rated, first the direct-rated films, then the Barker-
Durning films.   Included at the end of this collection is an
alphabetical list of films reviewed and rejected as having
no training or orientation value, or because they were outdated.

        We will continue to review films and update the col-
lection--therefore readers' suggestions and recommendations
are welcome and appreciated.   We particularly want to learn
of new films with potential training value to volunteers in
courts.   The following films were evaluated by our reviewers
and considered not to have substantial training value for
court volunteers.   Most of them are excellent films for other
purposes, or were at one time excellent films but are now
inevitably outdated.   The Image Changers, Look Further
Than Tomorrow, Make Way for Youth, On the Outside Again,
One to One, Three Steps to Start, To Touch a Child, What
About Juvenile Delinquency, Who's Delinquent, Youth and the
Law, and Big Help for Small Offenders.

*   *   *   *

Report VIII

A PRELIMINARY FILM GUIDE
FOR TRAINING COURT VOLUNTEERS

Edited by Judith Berry*

Preface

    This film guide draws upon two film review studies.
In 1968, Dr. Gordon Barker and Mr. Hunter Durning made
a review of films for a project sponsored by the Youth Services of the state of Colorado. Their purpose was to screen
training films for paid workers rather than volunteers but
some of their observations are applicable for volunteer orientation as well. The Barker-Durning films are asterisked
at the top of each sheet. In 1969-70 our own study was to
review films for training court volunteers. In six separate
screenings, a total of 49 people, most of them highly experienced in court volunteer programs, rated the films specifically for their training value for court volunteers. A systematic evaluation form was used for this purpose. All the
films fall short in one way or another but some are quite
good for training-orientation purposes. These films reviewed by the National Information Center have a plus (+)
rating comparable to those on the Barker-Durning films and
in addition have a numeric rating ranging from 0 (low value
film) to 5 (high). These latter numbers were computed from
a scale each reviewer marked regarding "Training Value to
Volunteers in Courts." Films reviewed by both groups will
have both sign and numeric ratings, in which sign ratings
range from a potential low of "---" to a high of "+++."

---

*Associate Director (formerly Research Assistant), the National Information
Center on Volunteers in Courts, Boulder County Juvenile Court, Boulder,
Colorado 80302. With appreciation to the following film raters: Ron Acker-
man, Dr. Gordon Barker, Judith Berry, Margaret Brooks, Bob Brumberger,
Jean Cahlan, Charles Cameron, Mary Carroll, Peggy Cullen, Ursula Davies,
Georgiana Dillon, Dr. Jackson Dillon, Cal Dodge, Hunter Durning, William
Fain, Eleanor Flanders, Charles Gavin, Frances Gilfoil, Jackie Gossard,
Robert Hamm, Harriett Harris, Judy Hawkes, Thomas Hewes, Kathy Hoff-
man, Stan Hogsett, Jim Holliday, Judge Horace B. Holmes, Frank Jacobucci,
Ray Johnson, Jim Jorgensen, Emma Lerma, Charlotte Lefler, Eleanor Mc-
Kinley, Elaine Maness, Ruth Mangan, Gloria Mayfield, Bob Moffitt, F. P.
Morgan, June Morrison, Amalia Nelson, Spencer Nelson, David Purdy, Don
Rogers, Dr. Ivan Scheier, Dorothy Silverman, Judge Glenn Swanson, Lionel
Todman, Kathleen Wells, Jim Williams, Melinda Wolf, Sharon Woody. (Nat-
urally not all raters rated each film; the number of raters averaged about
ten per film.)

In addition to training-orientation films, we have included juvenile orientation films dealing with the problems of drugs and
dropouts. [Ordering information may have changed since 1970.]

The Dangerous Years   30 min., 1968, B & W   + +   4.0
    Rent (no charge):   Purchase ($25?):
       Kemper Insurance Co.   Same
    Mutual Insurance Bldg.
    4750 Sheridan Road
    Chicago, Illinois 60640
       Attn. John Lavino, Jr., Nat'l Advertising Supervisor
Content: Shows inadequacies of prison and detention facil-
    ities. Describes attempts at progressive reforms.
    Shows good scenes of group discussions, incentive pro-
    grams. Gives true-to-life picture of overworked proba-
    tion officer. Probationers talk about themselves. Great
    view of problems with rehabilitation.
Technical: Excellent technically. Not a how-to-do-it film,
    but gives background and leaves off where the volunteer
    picks up. Shows need for volunteers.
Recommended Use: Orientation for tutors, assistant proba-
    tion officers, new volunteers, and juvenile volunteers.
    This film is currently in use for juvenile court volunteer
    training.

The Odds Against   30 min., 1968, B & W   + +   4.0
    Rent (no charge):   Purchase (??):
       American Foundation   Same
    Institute of Corrections
    1532 Philadelphia National Bank Bldg.
    Philadelphia, Penn. 19107
Content: A case study of John J. Mitchell, 22, who has
    evolved a "life of crime." Illustrates his numerous of-
    fenses. Shows the inadequacy of the present criminal
    justice system for actually rehabilitating this prisoner.
    Indicates innovative channels, so that he could spend his
    time productively, and so re-enter society with a chance
    of going straight. Emphasis on the detention facilities
    and their inadequacy. Discusses and illustrates proba-
    tion as an alternative to imprisonment.
Technical: Excellent treatment of its main theme, namely,
    the inadequacy of the present correctional system. Very
    good treatment of time sequence in the life of John J.
    Mitchell. Very good format. Very good photography.
    Point: prisons and jails are outmoded in concept and
    physical facilities.
Recommended Use: Adult volunteers and detention volunteers.

Conveys sense of frustration lack of attention has created in the history of an adult probationer.

Homeless Child   28 min., 1968 or 69, color   + +   3.5
  Rent (no charge):   Purchase ($125):
    Family and Children's Ser-   Hollywood Film En-
    vices   prises, Inc.
    Foster Home Licensing Div.   6060 Sunset Blvd.
    3856 W. Santa Barbara Ave.   Hollywood, Calif.
    Los Angeles, Calif. 90008   90028
Content: In the United States every year, there are a quar-
    ter of a million children who become homeless. Who
    are they ... where do they come from ... does anyone
    care about these children? The film tells the story of
    children who have been deprived of parental love. It is
    a documentation of case histories of homeless children
    and the community's efforts to find homes and parental
    love for them through the foster parent's program. Il-
    lustrates useful techniques for foster parents.
Technical: This realistic and emotion filled film is designed
    to make a direct appeal to prospective foster parents. It
    is a graphic and heart-warming portrayal of how the
    Child Welfare Services brings together the children in
    need and the people who care.
Recommended Use: Excellent training for foster parents or
    adoptive parents. Also for child placement agencies.
    Too specific for other volunteers.

Store Front   35 min., 1967 approx., B & W   + +   3.4
  Rent (no charge):   Purchase Source:
    Modern Talking Picture Service,
    Inc.
    1212 Avenue of the Americas
    New York, N.Y. 10036
Content: Goes through training and orientation of "new ca-
    reer" social workers who themselves come from low in-
    come areas in large cities. Their assignment is to
    establish Store-front centers in ghetto areas. Takes
    them through role playing, group discussion, field ex-
    periences and other training techniques. Shows failure
    experiences also.
Technical: Up to date. Shows training techniques. Real
    people in real situations--not staged. Very good photog-
    raphy.
Recommended Use: Social workers, especially in ghetto
    areas. For staff and trainers in urban areas. Urban
    volunteers and adult volunteer in urban area. Definitely

an urban emphasis, and as much use for a trainer as
trainee.

The Invisible Child   30 min., 1969, color   + +   3.4
  Rent (free loan):
    Association Films, Inc.
    1621 Dragon St.
    Dallas, Texas 75207
Content: Is a documentary on the causes, treatment, and
    prevention of juvenile delinquency as told and seen from
    the viewpoint of those most closely involved ... the
    750,000 troubled boys and girls who annually pass through
    our juvenile courts, and the millions more who go un-
    noticed, unguided, and unseen.
Technical: Geared to big cities and institutions, very little
    on probation. Might be better for recruiting than train-
    ing. Excessive narration in part. Interviews with chil-
    dren are realistic and very good. Technically good.
Recommended Use: Orientation for new volunteers. Re-
    cruiting. Juvenile volunteers in city and institution.

The Price of A Life   30 min., 1968, B & W   + +   3.1
  Rent (no charge):   Purchase Source:
    American Foundation   Same
    Institute of Corrections
    1532 Philadelphia National Bank Bldg.
    Philadelphia, Pennsylvania 19107
Content: How to deal with the case of an older, angry de-
    linquent boy, from the perspective of a probation officer
    and his daily pattern. Illustrates the outlook and proce-
    dure of the probation officer. Narrated from the proba-
    tion officer's point of view. Illustrates how he works
    with Eddie. How he tries to reach him, understand him,
    guide and counsel him, and encourage him when the go-
    ing is rough. How he seeks to reunite Eddie with his
    wife, and get Eddie into a secure job. How set-backs
    are bound to occur, but can be dealt with.
Technical: An excellent presentation, in terms of format,
    theme, photography, realism of the characters, and
    message it drives home. Very current. Very realistic.
    Excellent treatment of time sequence. Excellent por-
    trayal of the emotional problems and set-backs, and re-
    coveries. Very good illustration of how the probation
    system can work.
Recommended Use: Training of probation volunteer. Good
    for group discussion. Has been used extensively in
    training court volunteers in Denver and elsewhere. But

note that the probationer depicted is definitely older than
the average juvenile.

The Revolving Door   30 min. , 1968, B & W   + +   3. 3
Rent (no charge):   Purchase (? ?):
    American Foundation   Same
    Institute of Corrections
    1532 Philadelphia National Bank Bldg.
    Philadelphia, Penn. 19107
Content: How the minor offender is dealt with in today's
    correctional system. Alcoholics, vagrants, prostitutes,
    delinquents. Theme: the revolving door of crime and
    punishment. Jails and prisons are schools for crime,
    and are bound to lead the offender right back. Nar-
    rated. Inadequacies of lower courts. Lack of informa-
    tion. Inadequacies of probation. Production line jus-
    tice. Jail conditions. Some illustration of the alterna-
    tives. Diagnostic clinic. Probation. Work release,
    group counselling.
Technical: Excellent narrator. Excellent, vivid and con-
    vincing photography. Illustration of jail conditions might
    serve as deterrent. Excellent treatment of the need for
    improvement throughout the correctional system. Shows
    alternatives to incarceration.
Recommended Use: New volunteers or institutional volun-
    teers. Good for group discussion. Has been used for
    orienting volunteers working with adult probationers.

You're No Good   28 min. , 1965, B & W   +   3. 1
Rent ($5-6):   Purchase (? ?):
    check college film libraries in
    your area. The following have
    the film: Audio-visual dept. of
    Wyoming University, Laramie 82070
    Colorado University, Boulder 80302
    Brigham Young University, Provo, Utah 84601
Content: A film of youth, and the impulses of youth that
    sometimes clash with society's need for circumspection,
    law, and order. The youth is Eddie and his mistake was
    to "borrow" a motorcycle parked in front of a bike sales
    store. He takes his girl for a spin and then the law
    steps in. When he hides out, a social worker persuades
    him to give up while he still has a chance to get off with
    a warning.
Technical: Made in Toronto, the film is a commentary on a
    society that often offers youth little purpose or sense of
    accomplishment. It is better for recruiting than training.

Very artfully done. Series of day dream flashbacks to
give clue to child's mind is used but tends to confuse
some viewers.
Recommended Use: Juvenile staff or juvenile volunteers--
new volunteers.

LSD = Insight or Insanity   28 min. , 1968, color   + + +
Rent: Purchase: ($300)
??   Bailey Films
perhaps college film   6509 De Longpre
libraries   Avenue
                                              Hollywood, Calif.
                                              90028
Content: Discusses LSD in context of adolescents' unending
search for self-expression. Taking drugs as a means
of proving yourself to others. Presents expert medical
research and opinion regarding the motivation and consequences of taking the drug. Realistically discusses
what is known and not known about LSD. Illustrates
potential dangers of congenital defects, chromosome
damage, and bad effects on experimental animals. Nar-
rated in part by Sal Mineo.
Technical: Very up to date in terms of style, jargon, behavior. Excellent presentation, skillful use of color and
photography. Illustrates the psychological, emotional,
and physiological aspects of use of the drug. Clear and
lucid discussion by competent medical persons on the
dangers. Excellent for high school audiences.
Recommended Use: Specific concentration on orientation of
volunteers to drug problems of youth.

The Seekers   31 min. , 1967, color   + + +
Rent (? ?):   Purchase (? ?):
New York State Narcotic   Same
Control Comm.
Executive Plaza South
Stuyvesant Plaza
Albany, New York 12203
Content: An encounter group discussion group in a variety
of settings. Group dedicated to helping others stop the
use, or never get involved in drugs. Drug use is
viewed as symptomatic of other problems. A way to
get around dealing honestly with your real problems.
Presents various motivations for use in adolescence,
e. g. , friends, influences, show you can do it, be a
man, etc. Emphasis on why they all eventually stopped
using and the kind of life it led them to, even though it

wasn't what they intended.   Sincere presentation.   Convincing.

Technical: Total presentation in terms of discussion group in candid, informal setting.   Argumentation is convincing.   By adolescents who come across as real figures. Their individual histories are very realistic.   Good focus on hippies--their use of drugs and their underlying rationale is probed.

Recommended Use: Good for drug orientation.

Phoebe: Story of Premarital Pregnancy   + +
                       29 min. , 1965, B&W
   Rent (? ?):   Purchase ($175):
   McGraw-Hill Text Films   Same
   330 West 42nd Street
   New York, N. Y. 10036

Content: A middle-class teenage girl is portrayed in a dramatic sequence in which she attempts to deal with the emotional burden and responsibility of this awareness of her own pre-marital pregnancy.   Illustrates her own feelings of sickness, irritability, and mental conflict, as she struggles with problems of deciding how and who to confide in.   Her relationship with her father and her reluctance to tell him.   The false happiness and security they share.   No narration.

Technical: Superbly produced.   Extensive and effective use of flashback technique for depicting how the problem came about.   Excellent portrayal of the emotional burden carried by this unwed mother-to-be.   No narration.   Excellent use of dialogue (limited), photography, and music. Very current in its presentation, and somewhat middle class in orientation.   Strength is in realistic presentation of the realities and emotional aspects of premarital pregnancy.

Recommended Use: Good group discussion device.   For volunteers working with girls.

Portrait of a Disadvantaged Child--Tommy Knight   + +
                       16 min. , 1965, B&W
   Rent (? ?):   Purchase ($125):
   McGraw-Hill Text Films   Same
   330 West 42nd Street
   New York, New York

Content: Film accurately portrays a Negro boy in a slum area and indicates how fatigue and other home-related problems affect his school performance.   A semi-documentary film.   Shows the typical day in his life, with

hunger and lack of sleep prevalent.   Has an angry mother
who works.   Indicates where the problems begin, and
where the blame lies.   Emphasizes that much patience
is needed.   Good illustration of the failure of the school
system.
Technical: Well acted and good photography.   Excellent format.   Stresses the need to understand the behavior of
children from areas and conditions like those portrayed.
Very good narration, and commentary on the disadvantaged child.   Good illustration of the contributing factors.
Recommended Use: Where volunteers need to be familiarized
with Negro boy probationer in ghetto area.

No Reason To Stay: A Dropout Looks At Education   + +
                    28 min. , 1966, B & W
Rent: Purchase ($167.50):
Encyclopaedia Britannica   Same
Education Corp.
425 No. Michigan Ave.
Chicago, Ill. 60611
Content: Case study of one student.   How rigidity of system, subject matter, dullness of presentation contribute
to drop out incentive.   Presentation of the void that the
dropout enters.   Case of Christopher, high school student.   The elements in the school system which encourage him to drop out.   Includes relationship with his
girl.   Very candid about sex.   He presents good argumentation in the terms that are current today.   Good illustration of parental conflict, domineering mother, etc.
Technical: Excellent presentation.   Use of flashbacks and
other superimposed sequences.   Not a documentary, but
use of Hollywood format.   Excellent in portraying Christopher's relation with the significant people in his life.
Does not explicitly say "do not be a dropout, " but does
show the very real problems that result.
Recommended Use: Orientation to school problems.

Hide and Seek   15 min. , ??, B & W   + +
Rent: Purchase ($150):
Center for Mass Communication   Same
Columbia University
New York, New York
Content: This film begins with a talented middle-class boy
who has gotten hooked on drugs.   A series of flashbacks
as to how it all came about.   Drives a flashy sportscar.
Indicates the relationship of the boy, an older teenager,
to his father.   Father dies, and boy feels anguish at

having left home and gotten into the rut he is in. Theme:
no way to beat the drug habit. Shows how much you
lose by getting involved.
Technical: Good color presentation. Excellent photography.
Moderately well acted. Excellent portrayal of the lone-
liness that accompanies the drug habit. Portrayal of all
the hang-ups of being hooked. How the self-concept de-
teriorates. Excellent format.
Recommended Use: Where familiarization is desired specifically in the drug area.

From Runaway to Hippie   18 min., 1968, color   ++
   Rent (??):   Purchase (??):
   Association Films   Same
   25358 Cypress Avenue
   Hayward, Calif. 94544
Content: The migration of hippies to Haight Ashbury. A
two-part series shown on Huntley-Brinkley. Stresses
that the hippie movement is much more than dope, drugs,
etc. Shows actual communal glue parties in progress--
hallucinations, crashing, anguish. Follows teenagers
from Dallas to Haight. Discusses the relationship between dope and protesting. Good photographic portrayal
of Haight. Shows Drop City in Colorado. Role of mass
media today.
Technical: Excellent candid photography of the hippie phenomenon. Gives some feeling of the helplessness of the
situation. Powerful sense of "bad trips." Excellent
narration, although somewhat judgmental. Concerned
about reducing the hippie movement to drug use alone.
Recommended Use: Where familiarization is desired particularly in the drug area.

The Hard Way [America's Crisis Series]   +
                55 min., 1965, B & W
   Rent ($9.15):   Purchase ($200):
   Indiana University   Same
   NET
Content: Today we have a new kind of poor. Therefore,
traditional solutions are outmoded, and patchwork. Discusses the relationship of poverty to education. Basic
questions of priorities raised for an affluent society.
Interview with Dr. S. M. Miller. Need to define poverty
realistically. Problem of inequality. Emphasizes the
dropout, and the problem he faces. Film is oriented
toward lower class, and lower middle class. Basic
problem is the unavailability of jobs. Education is the key.

Technical: Excellent photography of poor people and their
living areas. A semi-documentary film. An excellent
attempt to understand the deeper nature of poverty.
Basic issues presented. Strong factual basis for discussion.
Recommended Use: Might be useful where lower class probationers are involved, and/or big cities.

Nobody Waved Goodby   80 min., 1964, B & W   +
   Rent (??):   Purchase (??):
      Western Cinema Guild, Inc.   Same
      244 Kearny St.
      San Francisco, Calif. 94108
Content: How teenage boy revolts against family with middle-
class values. Gets on probation. Shows relationship
with girl friend. Wants to drop out and run away.
Struggle for identity in system which stifles his identity.
Emphasizes sense of immediacy and reality of the situation. Current language and dialogue. Won numerous
awards.
Technical: Less convincing to the adolescents themselves.
More of interest to parents, teachers, counsellors. Excellent production in what it does. Ends with sense of
futility of what all this rebellion leads to, together with
the very real feelings that underlie the conflict and rebellion.
Recommended Use: Good for discussion.

*   *   *   *

Report IX

"A SECOND CHANCE":
A JUVENILE COURT VOLUNTEER ORIENTATION FILM

Introduction

        Perhaps 15 films have partial relevance to orientation
of court volunteers: "The Dangerous Years, " "The Odds
Against, " "The Invisible Child, " "The Price of a Life, "
"The Revolving Door, " and a few others (all reviewed and
rated in Report VIII). However, "A Second Chance" is the
first film designed specifically for orientation and training of
juvenile court volunteers: 16 mm, color, sound, 25 minutes
following a volunteer through his ups and downs with a 16-
year-old juvenile boy. "A Second Chance" is realistic,

hard-nosed, and rather gripping, we think. Though it will
scarcely appeal to those who think of court volunteer programs in terms of instant solutions, it will lead in well to
productive discussion between the trainer and his volunteers.
Each film comes with a written study guide for the volunteer
trainer.

First released in November, 1970, the film was made
possible by a grant from the Youth Development and Delinquency Prevention Administration, Social and Rehabilitation
Service of the Department of Health, Education, and Welfare,
and was produced by SPENFILM, Inc., 2920 Pearl Street,
Boulder, Colorado 80302. The film can be purchased as
well as rented, and latest information as to this is available
from the National Information Center on Volunteers in
Courts.

While the film is designed focally for orientation of
volunteers who work one-to-one with juvenile offenders, extension is possible to young adult offenders and non-court
agency volunteers working preventatively with potential offenders. Another dimension of extension is from first orientation of volunteers to recruiting and even screening, by
selecting out those viewers who realize themselves to be
unsuited after seeing the film's realistic approach to court-
volunteerism-as-it-really-is. The film may also have some
use for general public education regarding the problems of
juvenile delinquency and juvenile courts, and finally, it may
even have some value for training of juvenile court paid
staff. "A Second Chance" tries for realism rather than
glamor or the easy miracle-cure solution. The problems
seen are typical ones which court volunteers actually encounter on the job. The volunteer in the film does make
mistakes; he is not perfect, though he also does some things
right, too, including learning from his mistakes.

The following guide (included with all copies of the
film) points up for suggested discussion the mistakes,
strengths, and other areas of significance, for use of the
trainer of volunteers, to help get the ball rolling on discussion after viewing the film. Indeed, the film should be seen
primarily as a catalyst to productive discussion between
trainer and volunteers, rather than as a self-contained complete set of "answers." In addition to discussion, the film
can lead to role plays, or rather role re-plays of some of
the film situations. We feel that the film is useful for in-
service as well as pre-assignment training of volunteers;

that is, it has something to say to all but the most sophisticated volunteer.

Some Discussion Possibilities, Scene by Scene

[Note: Undoubtedly many other discussion possibilities exist beyond these listed, and the trainer will do well to be flexible in letting discussion gravitate toward areas of concern for his particular volunteer trainees.]

SCENE I: This scene shows Tom (the boy in trouble) committing the offense of joy-riding: stealing a car from a used-car lot. A friend is with him. The major purpose is to set the scene but there are some discussion possibilities:

1. Common offenses for which boys get in trouble in your community. Ditto, extending to girls, younger vs. older probationers, etc.
2. Note that boy is with another boy. Proportion of offenses committed in company vs. solo.
3. Fact that key was left in car might trigger some discussion of community responsibility (temptation of new car, key in new car, etc.) for juvenile crime.
4. Outside possibility: maybe the lyrics of the accompanying music, "Why Can't Somebody Smile at Me," might provoke some discussion.

SCENE II: Tom is before the juvenile judge in the court for sentencing. With him are his mother and his professional probation officer, Walter. Again, a major purpose is to set the scene, but there are discussion possibilities.

1. Sentencing and court procedures related to juveniles: How is your court similar or different from the pictured one? Even more basic, the meaning and purpose of probation, etc.
2. Only the boy's mother is there. Theme of father's failure of responsibility.
3. Perhaps notice: mother is kind of broken up; boy is succeeding fairly well in keeping up an impassive, tough exterior.
4. Note this about the judge: he informs the boy and his mother clearly, from the first, that a volunteer will be involved, and just as clearly throws the weight of his office behind the support of the

volunteer in his role. How does your court support
the work of volunteers, back them up? What role
does it expect them to fulfill, etc.? Secondly, note
that just because he has a volunteer program doesn't
mean a judge is wishy-washy. This judge is firm
as well as kind. Possible lead-in to discussion of
judge's role in relation to a volunteer program, how
he must protect the community as well as support
the volunteer.

SCENE III: (following movie credits): This scene is
a sound stage, a "limbo" set. All the main movie characters reflect on the roles they will play in the movie. The
actors in their roles are: Martin, the volunteer; Walter,
the professional probation officer; Tom, the boy in trouble;
Tom's father; his mother; his shop teacher. Along with setting roles, this scene also begins to stimulate discussion on
the following kinds of points.

1. The volunteer's early easy overconfidence begins to
    be reality-tested by the boy (brutally), the probation
    officer, and the other characters. Instead of naive
    underestimation of the job, we get a more sober
    humility. Probe for your volunteers' own estimates
    of the difficulty of their job, as they foresee it or
    have found it.
2. Major theme: The volunteer must also work with
    the important people surrounding the juvenile, e.g.,
    parents, school, court, and must pay attention to
    them as important factors in the boy's rehabilitation.
    He must cooperate with them, not compete or anta-
    gonize. Dangers of overidentifying with the child,
    etc.
3. In regard to the paid probation officer, note: (a)
    What he says about why he needs volunteers' help.
    Discuss the ways in which volunteers help, why
    they're needed at your court. (b) Though he needs
    volunteers' help, the probation officer is the boss.
    Who's the boss of your volunteers in your program,
    what are the lines of authority, communication,
    etc.? (c) Possibly, the image of the probation offi-
    cer. The movie depicts a younger, "new breed"
    professional.

SCENE IV: The probation officer and the volunteer
arrive at Tom's home for their first visit. Martin is very
nervous, the mother very distraught, the father very rude

and uncooperative, and Tom appears "cool." Martin ar-
ranges his next meeting with Tom.

General Discussion Points:
1. The insight that the family of the boy may be contributing to his problem and must be worked with in
   some way.
2. The tension of the first meeting; the volunteer is
   tense and a little scared. Talk about this, get
   ready for it.
3. The fact that the volunteer should not expect overt
   thanks from anyone, boy, father, etc., and may instead find indifference and actual hostility.
4. The professional's being there with the volunteer,
   and what it means when his support is withdrawn
   (too soon) and he leaves the volunteer on his own
   (prematurely?).

More Specific Points:
1. Father: Apparent indifference--TV blaring, doesn't
   look at the volunteer or probation officer. Attitude
   varying between truculence and futility. Still, he's
   trying to give a "good" impression in his way:
   "We make that kid study." Father's inconsistency
   when confronted with "facts" from boy; note this is
   a lie. When later we find the child lying, remember, we caught his father at it first. Note also
   conflicts between (1) father and volunteer, and (2)
   father and boy. What are fathers of other delinquents like?
2. The Boy: Indifferent, sullen, or actively hostile--
   could possibly be scared underneath? (Don't expect
   overt gratitude, etc.) What he looks like.... Baseline his unreactivity here with the fact that he does
   begin talking to the volunteer later.... Conflict
   with the father.... Focus shot on auto magazine--
   his natural interests are important--later we'll see
   the volunteer capitalize on that.... Possible de-
   glamorization of the whole volunteer job--boy is in
   the bathroom, etc.
3. Mother: What is she like? Weak? Overwhelmed,
   but trying to keep up the appearance of good man-
   ners? She doesn't know the volunteer's name--he's
   not as important as he may think, at least right now
   at the beginning.
4. Volunteer: Tense, awkward, scared.... Is he right
   to fade out fast after the probation officer leaves...?

His conflict with the father--even this early he does
"stand up" to him on the matter of the first meeting.... What about his setting the first meeting in
front of the court? Lead into discussion of best
places to meet.

Other Possible Discussion Points:
1. What the home looks like; what other delinquents'
   homes look like. Someone might notice that the volunteer's car is a whole lot more expensive than the
   probation officer's (working for someone who makes
   less; possible tension there).

    SCENE V: Martin is in a telephone booth talking to
Tom's father. Tom has not shown up for the meeting and
Mr. Peterson (the father) is apparently being uncooperative.
Martin appeals for the father's help. Note these points.

1. The boy's unreliability--don't expect much of him,
   especially at first.... Possible motivations for it--
   actually maybe he didn't "forget".... Sub-theme
   that he is possibly using the volunteer as an excuse
   to get out of the house.... Whole theme that juvenile may be testing the volunteer--just to see what
   he will do.
2. Whether or not volunteer happens to approve of father, he does need his help in working with the boy:
   "I can't do it alone."
3. More subtly, someone might notice that since the
   volunteer does indeed find the boy in the next scene,
   the father must indeed have helped him at least to
   the extent of telling him where the boy might be....
   Also, comments on the kinds of places delinquent
   boys (girls) naturally like to be.

    SCENE VI: Tom is playing a shooting game in a pin-
ball joint. Martin appears and Tom makes an excuse for
missing the meeting. They have a coke and talk about Tom's
offense and their relationship. The volunteer begins to look
a little good in this scene.

1. Perseverance: He does come after Tom, rather
   than going home discouraged, etc., and at the end
   of the meeting in this scene, he does persevere in
   setting up another meeting (in a less threatening setting than the court). What else might he have done
   besides this? As the boy notes, he might have

"called the cops. " What about that (Martin's explanation) and other possible courses when the boy
defaults on his promises?

2. Belief: The volunteer believes the kid's story. ...
   Child's reaction to this. ... Baseline for later believing too much (and in response to this, perhaps
   the boy starts telling him things, the first of which
   are lame excuses: "I forgot. " "I meant to return
   the car. ") Is the boy testing the limits of the volunteer's belief... ? Caring enough to try to get the
   volunteer "on his side?"

3. Authority-Friendship: The volunteer says he's a
   friend, wants to keep the child out of jail (volunteer
   role definition discussion), and in fact he didn't call
   the police. But he does call upon the court's backing, in a sense: "You must meet with me or go to
   jail. " Your volunteers' reactions to possible need
   for forcing the child into accepting the relation with
   them?

4. Support for the court: The volunteer, though a
   friend, is also reinforcing the judge's admonitions
   on the seriousness of the situation, and in this respect is supporting the court. But how about when
   he says he won't report the boy's lapse to the
   court? And the boy's intent reaction to that? Lead
   into the whole issue of integrating friendship with
   reporting offenses; how your court does it; clarifi-
   cation of volunteer's responsibilities here.

5. Somewhat more subtle issues: Volunteer tries a
   small joke (you don't have to be serious all the
   time), but it went over like a lead balloon with the
   kid--apparently your humor isn't necessarily his,
   sub-cultural distance, etc. ... Volunteer does work
   with the boy in his "natural habitat" at the slot machine joint, rather than try to drag him back to
   "neutral ground, " his own home ground, or the court
   as meeting place. But the next meeting place he
   sets ("walk in the woods") is still pretty much his
   own choice of meeting places.

   SCENE VII: Tom and Martin are walking through the
woods, hiking and talking. Martin does most of the talking
--preaching--and Tom straggles along behind not paying
much attention until Martin starts listening to him. Note
these discussion themes.

1. Volunteer starts by talking at the boy, lecturing,

preaching ("try harder"), and the boy tunes out.
But when the volunteer begins listening, the boy
really opens up (which in a way is a good measure
of the volunteer's progress since the early unreactivity and hostility of the boy). They look more
natural, less strained, walking together, too.

2. The boy's deep sense of futility, inadequacy, and
discouragement, and acceptance of failure as his
norm. ("I'm not good enough ... I'm dumb ... the
outfield moved in ... I can't get a job ... No teacher takes an interest in me...." etc.) To what extent is this likely to be typical in a delinquent boy,
even underneath the bluster and anger, and/or what
other causations and expressions might there be in
delinquent boys? How are delinquent girls different?
The volunteer tries to be supportive at this point;
when the boy says, "I'm dumb," Martin disagrees.
Yet his "try harder" prescription does look glaringly
oversimplified and naive in contrast to the deep-
seated pattern of futility in the boy's life. Note,
too, in this respect, the inkling of a vicious cycle
in the boy's life: when he tries to get a job, his
previous "troublemaker" tag at school comes back
to haunt and defeat his efforts to remove himself
from the troublemaker category.

3. The school theme first alluded to in the home scene
("We make that kid study") recurs here: Martin
keeps asking about school. Is he right to do that,
believing it's a crucial arena for the boy? Lead-in
to discussion of most important environmental factors influencing juveniles.

4. Possible point: This scene is filmed in an activity
setting out of doors. What recreational activities,
indoors and out of doors, are available in your community, and what is their particular value in working with a youngster?

SCENE VIII: Tom and Martin are looking at the en-
gine of a car. Martin is very ignorant about cars, and
Tom gets to take the lead in the conversation as an "expert."
Tom tells Martin a persecution story about his shop class.

1. The volunteer is now beginning to work from where
the boy "is at," perhaps the one potentially positive
interest he's discovered thus far in the boy:
cars.... Whole issue of working from and through
juvenile's natural interests, instead of yours....

Also (vs. the boy's basic inferiority feelings), the volunteer found something the boy is good at: cars.... Also, he's letting the boy teach him, as a clear contrast to his previous superior-lecture stance. At least symbolically, the point could be that the volunteer can and should be willing to learn through his volunteer experience, rather than assuming that he's pretty perfect and inspirational to begin with and the boy has to do all the learning.

2. A second major theme continues and accentuates the early theme of believing the boy. His testing the limits of the volunteer's belief, and his trying to get the volunteer "on his side" at any cost are all involved here. Note that the boy's actual lying (remember his father?) may be trying to get the volunteer's sympathy, trying to get him to side with him against his "natural enemies," represented here by the shop teacher. (Discuss the boy's different concept of friendship.) Also, with his "cooked up" story of how he's the victim of unjustified persecution, school continues as a focal trouble area.

SCENE IX: Martin goes to the school to talk to the boy's shop teacher, following up the boy's story in the previous scene. The shop teacher has a very different view of what actually happened, and the volunteer also lets slip the fact that he's from the court. Martin and Tom confront each other after the shop teacher's revelation, in a scene filled with anger, and finally both sadness and humility.

Just getting the boy to talk was a step in the right direction, but it wasn't enough. Talk can include lies. The whole area of belief and reality-testing keys this scene. The volunteer follows through on what the boy told him in the previous scene, and begins to try to work actively with the perceived trouble spots in the boy's environment. So far, so good--let this not be forgotten in the ensuing disaster. But apparently the volunteer has been too uncritically willing to take the boy's story entirely at face value; in his advocacy, too willing to believe all. The shop teacher sets him right on the true facts of the case [we assume true from the movie, though it is possible to start a line of inference from the assumption the shop teacher isn't right either]. The shop teacher's "You don't know Tom very well, do you?" is a cutting point, in

realizing that other people have insights on the boy,
too, sometimes from longer experience than the volunteer. And again the point: don't let your natural
sympathy for the boy overwhelm your common sense
feeling for factuality.
Assuming the shop teacher was in fact correct,
we see the volunteer going on to make mistake after
mistake.   First, he blurts that he's from the court.
(Discuss the whole issue of confidentiality, identifying boys as delinquents, actual senses in which the
volunteer is affiliated with the court or not, etc.)
He then goes back and essentially lies to the boy
about the above.   To the boy's question, he says,
"I told him I was your friend, " which is true, but
not the whole truth, since he also did in fact let
slip to the teacher that he was from the court.
(Discussion: Responsibility of the volunteer to tell
the boy the truth, the whole truth, and nothing but
the truth, irrespective of problems in relationship,
etc.)   Finally, the volunteer at first pitches his
whole confrontation with the boy on the fact that he,
the volunteer, was embarrassed, made a fool of,
could have gotten in trouble, etc. , totally overlook-
ing what the situation might have meant in ego-
bruising to the boy, etc.   Actually, he's being quite
self-centered and ego-oriented here.
The volunteer's anger is responded to by the boy's
anger.   Though you're trying to help the boy, you
can't expect him to lick your hand for it, all the
time.   Delinquents do get angry at people who are
trying to help them (though the boy certainly didn't
expect to get the kind of help he got in this scene,
and maybe that's one problem)....   The boy's anger
and rejection obviously hurts the volunteer ... and
we get some further insights into the boy: he's not
accustomed to attempts at real friendship and simply
doesn't know how to handle it; he's puzzled at the
unfamiliarity of it, and quickly goes from puzzle-
ment to anger--"I didn't ask for your help. "
At the end, a badly shaken up and humble volunteer nevertheless says something most insightful:
"You owe improvement to yourself, not to me. "
Sidelights: The boy's curse words and the indicated word on the work bench are good shock testing for volunteers who are too easily shockable and
refuse to believe or constructively respond in any
way to the fact that delinquents do express

themselves in that way and do other things shocking
to middle-class mores.

SCENE X: Tom and friends break into the shop and
bust things up. Largely, the scene sets the stage dramatically for the denouement in the next scene. But there are
a few at least indicative discussion themes: variety of juvenile offenses--a car stealer can also bust up shops, etc.,
one boy may perform several of them, and a boy who com-
mits an offense once may well do so again, etc.... Again,
the boy's special hostility toward school as the scene of his
failure, and for Tom personally and specifically, the scene
of his recent shaming in front of the volunteer (a guy he
now wants to impress, as his way of showing friendship?)....
Also, perhaps the significance of the nature and locale of a
delinquent's offense or pattern of offenses in helping to diag-
nose his central hangups and failures.... And once more,
most juvenile offenses are not committed by "loners."

SCENE XI: Second "limbo" scene. There are three
other juvenile delinquents, different from Tom, giving their
views of the movie so far. All juveniles are different and
Tom is only one example. There is a female volunteer
there, too, and she objects to Martin's approach to his job.
Martin, the volunteer, tells the other five main characters
that he is quitting his volunteer work because he failed.
Tom and Walter point out the things he did right and wrong.
It appears he wasn't a total failure. The probation officer
explains to Martin that when the film resumes there is one
more scene and Martin will have to decide if he will continue working with Tom and give himself a second chance.

The first part of this scene attempts to make us
aware of the great variety and individuality of juvenile offenders, their backgrounds, personalities,
etc. Stress in discussion that every offender won't
be just like Tom, and there is therefore no pat formula, etc. The variety of volunteers is also indicated; the other one in this scene is younger and a
girl (college age), suggesting the differences possible
in a discussion of "who can be a volunteer, what
are the qualifications," etc. The strong crack at
the volunteer as a "do-gooder" might also elicit
comment and discussion.

The second part of the scene is set dramatically
by the volunteer's announcement that he is quitting.
A review of his failures follows, including some new

ones too, such as giving up too quickly and easily.
Formerly stated faults are analyzed a bit more,
such as being too gullible, lecturing vs. listening,
etc. One quite new dimension here is that the <u>vol-
unteer joins via self</u>-criticism. We get a glimpse
<u>of his doubts and anxiet</u>ies: 'I'm a bungler ... you
should let a professional do it. " (Let volunteers in
discussion let <u>their</u> hair down, too; also discuss
special issues <u>such</u> as what indeed can professionals
do that volunteers can't and vice versa.)
     Then there is a new turn. Led supportively by
the probation officer (value of professional support
for volunteers) and also by the boy himself, the
group begins looking at the more positive side of
the volunteer's performance. Yes, he lectured, but
he later began to listen, too. ... He bungled, but
at least he tried. ... And he <u>cared</u> ("You came after me instead of calling the <u>cops</u>"; "you were wrong
about the shop thing, but at least you came to my
defense"), even if he was too gullible, etc.
     The volunteer joins here and says indeed he did
think he and the boy had something going there during their talk at the shop. The boy says yes, and
then for the second time in the film, the spotlight
turns on the boy rather than the volunteer, with
several points: he doesn't know how to say thanks
... he can't figure out why the volunteer has been
nice to him--hardly anyone else ever was ... he
can't change, at least not right away. ... All of
these are insights to ponder and discuss on the part
of a volunteer, too, in attempting to understand the
sometimes (by his own standards) puzzling reactions
he gets from delinquent children. <u>Underlying point:
try to see things from the probatione</u>r's viewpoint,
<u>too</u> (even though seeing through his eyes isn't neces-
sarily agreeing or condoning).
     Particularly worth pondering for any volunteer is
Tom's remark that his busting into the shop was not
anything <u>personal</u> against the volunteer. Too many
volunteers <u>do take</u> their probationer's infractions as
a <u>personal</u> affront.
     At this point the probation officer poses the pivotal
question to the volunteer. While in the first scenes
he was so unimportant key people had trouble getting his name right, now he has become <u>the</u> important person in Tom's life (a measure of progress in
itself, in spite of his "bungling"). Tom is in jail,

and whether that is "his final scene" depends a
great deal on the volunteer (the point that this volunteer thing can become a real responsibility for
another person's life). The probation officer urges
the volunteer to give it another try. He says you
shouldn't expect to succeed all the time with all
kids (discuss that), but at least you can try (an interesting and somewhat ironic reprise of the volunteer himself, lecturing the boy to "try harder").
So, says the probation officer: give yourself a second chance as a volunteer, just as probation itself
was a second chance for the boy. (Again, importance of the probation officer as a supporter, not a
competitor, at crucial times.)
   The scene closes as the volunteer tries to decide
whether he'll quit or try again, with flashbacks reviewing his past with the boy.

   SCENE XII: We see Tom in jail, then walking out to
where the volunteer is waiting, and they walk off together.
Though largely a dramatic finale, there are discussable nuggets here, too. Note especially: (1) the volunteer did decide to persevere, which is good, and (2) this can mean the
difference between the boy's staying in jail or getting another
chance. (3) Yet, while that disaster was averted, we still
don't know how ultimately it is going to turn out. Though
the volunteer is still trying, there could well be future setbacks. Discuss this: A volunteer may never know for sure
whether he's succeeded or failed. It takes a long time; all
he knows is it probably would have been worse if he hadn't
tried. The scene may also lead to discussion of what juvenile jails are like. (What about your jail or detention facilities?)

   Loan and purchase arrangements for this film are
now handled exclusively by the National Audio Visual Center,
General Services Administration, Washington, D. C., 20409.
When requesting the film, cite it by full title, "A Second
Chance," and note that it is a Youth Development and Delinquency Prevention Administration (YD/DPA) release. At
present, purchase price is in the $95-100 range, and wait-
ing time at least four to six weeks. [Demand for loan and
rental has made these uncertain at present.]

Chapter 11

TELEVISION AND VIDEO TAPE
FOR TRAINING VOLUNTEERS

The medium of television holds great promise for training purposes. However, in the area of training court volunteers, these promises have not been realized as yet. With the exception of some use of video tapes, most courts have not really found the way to utilize this medium. This chapter will attempt to suggest some avenues for the use of commercial television, educational television, closed circuit, and video tapes for the training of volunteers preparing for court service.

Commercial Television

With interest high as it is regarding crime and delinquency, the national television networks have devoted a considerable amount of time to the subject during the past few years. These programs have a considerable amount of material of training value. In some programs the correctional system and the courts themselves have been scrutinized. Some of these programs have been discussed in Chapter 10.

These programs would have an additional training dimension if they could be edited for content, if the viewers were preconditioned to view the programs from a court volunteer frame of reference, and if presented within the context of an organized training effort. Similar television programs which have examined the problems of crime and delinquency with more of a regional or local flavor might also contain ready-made information of considerable value to trainers of volunteers.

In communities where there are network outlets, there would undoubtedly be material in the television station's library that could be previewed for purposes of selecting

199

training materials. Conceivably these programs could be
shown over closed-circuit television or educational television
to an audience of trainees, or, as was discussed in the previous chapter, they could be shown on a 16 mm projector if
they have been converted to film. The side benefit of this
approach would be that many people would view this material
who would not necessarily be volunteers, but would be better
informed as a result of having viewed the program. Indeed,
this could have the effect of interesting more people in volunteering. One other possibility growing out of such an approach would be to announce on the education TV station a
series of programs for training court volunteers, and solicit
applications from people who have viewed the series. Such
a program could achieve the multiple objectives of public information and education, volunteer recruiting, and volunteer
training.

Indeed, as this book goes to press, idea has become
actuality in Seattle, Washington, where a "telecourse" for
volunteers and volunteer program leadership is about to be
offered regularly.

Educational Television

Nearly every state is now a part of National Educational Television. State universities and colleges as well as
private higher education are in the broadcasting business.
In some of our urban areas, the public schools are operating
educational television stations. There is no lack of personnel or equipment for training through educational television.
Almost every volunteer is a television viewer.

Under such a set of circumstances, it would seem
quite possible that the facilities of such a broadcasting complex could be used for training volunteers. The studios
themselves might be the locus for training using closed circuit equipment, or some of the regular program time could
be designated for this purpose. All that we said about the
relevance of commercial programs on crime and delinquency
might be repeated in relation to educational television. The
libraries of these stations might also be examined for training materials.

In that educational stations are non-profit, non-com-
mercial ventures, supported by tax monies, their role of
public education is perhaps more naturally congruent with

the training programs of volunteer courts and correctional
agencies.

Closed Circuit Television

Classrooms in higher education facilities as well as
in intermediate schools are increasingly utilizing closed circuit television as a teaching device. Much of the money
which went to education during the Sixties went for the purpose of purchasing this kind of equipment. Educators have
praised this kind of medium for its efficiency in serving
large numbers of students, the potential for storage of lessons, and as a device for providing feedback to teachers who
view themselves as they teach. These classrooms may well
become the locus for volunteer training. The local school
person most familiar with the equipment may become an associate volunteer trainer.

Video Tapes

Entire training sessions or parts of sessions can
readily be stored on video tape with the obvious potential
for later showing to individuals or to entire classes. Make-
up sessions can be nicely handled through this method.
Lectures, role playing, and group discussion all lend themselves well to video taping. A few courts with which we
are familiar video tape the role-playing sessions and play
them back for the class for discussion purposes.

Judge Paul Fowler in Portsmouth, Ohio provides an
example of a court volunteer program which utilizes video
tape for training professional staff as well as volunteers.
Judge Fowler has stored on video tape a variety of training
materials which he can selectively use in group or in individual training.

What we noted earlier as the advantages of audio
tapes could apply to video tapes as well. Obviously, video
tapes provide the additional advantage of viewing while listening. It offers the disadvantage of being more expensive.

The use of video tape is especially helpful in the
training of volunteers who are being prepared to do substantial interviewing. Volunteer counselors all interview, to
be sure, but many courts have been preparing volunteers to

do very specific interviewing of an intake or diagnostic nature.   In these instances video tape can be most effective in
providing immediate and accurate feedback on the interviewer's progress.

One model which we have utilized is as follows:
through the use of role playing the class members are given
an assignment of creating for themselves an offender role
which they believe might be consistent with their personality.   Having done this they are interviewed by each other.
Other trainees in the class are given specific assignments
such as monitoring facial expressions, voice inflections, use
of words, body posture, etc.   When the interview is completed, it is critiqued by the class through their providing
feedback on what their observations were in these areas.
This is followed by another level of feedback, namely the
playback of the video tape of the session.

The use of video tape in this way is a powerful way
of confirming the feedback that has been provided by the
trainees' critiques.   To carry this even further, video tape
can be utilized to help the trainee correct his mistakes and
improve his performance by having him identify areas where
he needs improvement and then doing a follow-up role play
interview where he can see if he has achieved his objectives.

We can envision a basic core training program of
video tapes which might have relevance to any court volunteer program with the proper supplementation from the local
trainer.   This in fact may ultimately be a less expensive
way of training volunteers in that it would not require pulling
together a lot of resource people at regular intervals.

The above discussion obviously could apply to the
training of volunteers per se, not just court volunteers.
Just as we as a society really have not yet used television
in its optimum creativeness for entertainment purposes, we
have also failed to maximize its use in teaching.   In fact,
we have really only skimmed the surface of its real possibilities.   As the use of television and video tape for teaching
is developed, its use for training will emerge, and with it
the use for training volunteers.   At this time, we would
urge the reader to do an inventory on the educational television and video tape resources in his community and further
consider how much of this potential can be realized in volunteer training.

Chapter 12

TOURS, VISITS, AND OBSERVATIONAL EXPERIENCES

We pointed out, in an earlier chapter in our proposed
training model, that training must replace fantasy with reality. We have also emphasized the need for training which
ultimately can provide the trainee with reality-oriented approaches instead of abstractions. As we discussed the use
of observational experiences such as tours and visits, we
stressed this factor as well as the use of such experiences
as prerequisites for additional training. Thus we see a
multi-purpose in providing observational experiences: (1)
badly needed public education to citizens whether they choose
to remain in the program or not; (2) a screening device for
people who may not wish to proceed with an application once
they have taken part in this more realistic and immediate
stage of training; and (3) a solid groundwork for further
training. In this chapter we hope to detail some of the observational experiences which can be programmed. Most of
the observational experiences we will be discussing can be
carried out with relatively little expense and only minor inconvenience.

Tours of Court Facilities

This type of experience can be effected quite easily
with a little organizing and advance notice. There is an obvious need for volunteers to attach names and faces to titles,
and for staff to come to know volunteers and vice versa.
The court probation office, detention facilities, and the court-
rooms are all places that volunteers should see physically,
but they should also visit the people who work in these locales. Thus, it is helpful in planning such tours if a period
of time can be set aside for a person-to-person type meeting, where people can proceed beyond introductions to a
deeper level of interaction.

Interaction is really the objective of such a tour, and the reader is cautioned about the tendency for tours to become unnatural, over-prepared ceremonies where at certain stations the tour stops, while a short presentation is given regarding the duties of a certain staff member. A tour leader must intervene to make certain there is interaction. He can elicit questions from the group and make certain these questions are answered.

Observation of Court Hearings

While present at the court, it is advantageous if the trainees can be allowed to sit in on some type of court proceedings. The court docket should be consulted ahead of time so the class can be exposed to those proceedings which have the most training value. Such business as arraignments or detention hearings are particularly useful from a training standpoint because a number of people are processed during such sessions, and trainees get a rather valid sample of a day's court transactions in terms of the human problems being considered. Trials and hearings on petitions can be time consuming, and while definitely presenting good training material, they do not always fit into the trainer's schedule. Such matters, unless seen from beginning to end, are often of questionable value as learning experiences.

A second dimension of observing a court experience, if possible, is to have the training class meet with the judge who presided over the session. Even a short session during a recess can maximize this experience for the trainees. The judge can give a rationale for the decisions he made during the session, answer questions and generally provide information about this stage of the judicial process.

Attendance at Meetings of Court Staff

While having the training class on the premises of the court, the trainer can plan for volunteers to sit in on staff meetings when relevant material is being discussed. Some guidelines which should be cited here may be obvious but we state them nevertheless! Some staff may object to having volunteers sit in on their proceedings. Some may object for reasons of confidentiality or because they feel visitors inhibit their input. Interpretation to the staff prior to such visits may serve to pave the way for more receptiveness on the part of staff. There is obviously little training value in having a volunteer observe a staff meeting that is stifled due to his presence. It should be added that objections to volunteers' being at certain meetings is definitely justified. Staff meetings where staff problems are being aired might be an example.

Perhaps the type of staff meeting of most benefit for training volunteers is the staffing of cases prior to making recommendations for disposition. Not all probation staffs operate from a group decision-making model, but where this is the case, the authors have been impressed with the potential of such meetings for conveying the rationale for decisions and for helping volunteers see into the lives of offenders with a higher degree of perception.

Another type of observational experience of this type might be attendance at an in-service training session of working volunteers or case conferences between staff and volunteers. Again, we find this kind of experience meaningful in terms of the reality of the trainees' identification with the volunteer in action. In some instances, trainees can observe an individual volunteer in action. In several other courts volunteers are given "tag along" training by accompanying a professional probation officer in the performance of his duties. Obviously some volunteers as well as some professional staff members may object to being observed in the performance of their duties, and these objections should be respected.

Tours of High Delinquency Neighborhoods

Beyond the locale of the court are the neighborhoods where large segments of the delinquent population reside. It is important for the volunteer to see these neighborhoods beyond their surface manifestations. He should meet the people who live there, visit their schools, churches, community centers, and social agencies.

Volunteers coming as they do from largely middle-class neighborhoods do not really appreciate how a disadvantaged segment of the population comes to the point of being disadvantaged, and how disadvantaged people in a sense are "locked in" to their neighborhoods. This is a "cultural shock" type of experience and one that a large number of volunteers have never had.

Living as we do in a time when many segments of our
population feel alienated from the larger segment, there can
be resentment upon the felt intrusion of middle class people
into these neighborhoods. Thus every effort must be made
to keep such experiences from becoming "tourist outings. "
It would be a good idea to have one of the existing agencies
in the neighborhood plan and deliver this experience. For
example, a community center or settlement house indigenous
to the neighborhood can provide much better data about their
neighborhood than someone from outside. This also can
have the effect of giving local sanction to the volunteers'
presence in the community.

The trainer may find that the use of offenders or ex-
offenders who are indigenous to the neighborhood being observed are invaluable in providing reality for such tours.

Observation of Police

Some communities have had ride-along programs
where citizens can accompany police officers in the performance of their duties. These programs have for the most
part been police sponsored, with the objective of improving
public relations between the police and the community. Some
courts have capitalized on such programs to provide another
observational type of experience for volunteers.

However, we would caution the trainer who is considering such training that he had best make sure that such experiences are absolutely voluntary. We know of no city that
insures its citizens while they are with on-duty police officers. We would also ask the trainer to think through the
objective of such an experience. It should be stressed that,
at least in most courts, the volunteer is not being asked to
perform a police function, and such training should be clearly
labeled for what it is in order that a police role not emerge
for the volunteer.

Tours of Jails or Holding Facilities

The jail is an integral part of the judicial system, if
not always one of its bright spots. Juveniles in many communities are held in jail in the absence of detention facilities. The jail is also the holding facility for adult defendants awaiting trial and serves as the punishing agent for both

misdemeanants and felons. Thus the jail, in spite of its
negative connotation, cannot be overlooked and the experience
of visiting a jail can definitely be of training value. Indeed,
many jails are looking to volunteer programs to provide them
with natural links to the community.

The conditions that prevail in many of our jails cause
another "cultural shock" experience for the trainees. Jails
are toured by a relatively small percentage of our population, and we can assume that few volunteers have had such
an experience. Jail tours can be very effective in dramatiz-
ing the urgency of the need for community programs in corrections as an alternative to jail due to the visible lack of
any programs in most jails.

We know of one judge who has provided volunteers
the experience of remaining in a locked cell for a short
period of time to get the feel of such an environment. The
authors can neither recommend for or against such a procedure, not having had the opportunity to assess the training
value of such an experience.

Tours of Correctional Institutions

Although there are some institutions that do not welcome visitors, by and large tours of correctional institutions
are reasonably frequent. While providing this type of tour
may be difficult due to transportation expenses and other in-
conveniences, where possible it does provide an experience
with training value. Much that we have said about jails
above applies to correctional institutions. Such visits serve
to point up the fact that community programs also have failures and such failure often means institutionalization. As
a motivation for volunteers to participate in community programs which are alternatives to institutionalization, such
visits can have high payoff. In the past few years many institutions have initiated volunteer programs themselves.

Tours of Community Health, Education, and Welfare Agencies

Obviously, not all community social agencies can be
visited, but most courts have identified a core of agencies
that have special relevance to offenders. Since the volunteer
will often be placed in the role of advocate-broker for his
client, direct knowledge of certain agencies beyond that in

written descriptive material may be advantageous. Our
thought here is that agencies which provide direct services
such as Synanon, or other agencies related to the drug problem, AA facilities, health centers, welfare and rehabilitation
agencies, and schools, etc. provide the trainee with settings
where process can be observed. They also provide opportunities where potential clients can meet volunteers. Often
"rap sessions" can be generated through such visits.

Visits to Youth Hostels

        While tours in the formal sense are not recommended
as regards youth hangouts for the obvious reasons that they
would fly in the face of any kind of spontaneous interaction,
trainees should be encouraged to make it a point to talk to
youth where the youth are comfortable. Too many people
are disturbed by youth of the "Now Generation" and the "Age
of Aquarius" who wear long hair, dress unconventionally, or
perhaps talk in subcultural symbolisms. This concern often
leads to avoidance. Yet, the vast majority of youth are not
reluctant to talk with people from all walks of life. These
sessions can be extremely productive for the reason that
many of our youth are extremely bright and articulate. They
are honest and direct, and they have definite ideas about
many things, including the criminal justice system. We all
need to learn from our youth, but particularly people in
youth-serving roles must be willing to learn from them.
Most importantly they need to understand how young people
perceive the world, for therein lies much of the explanation
for their behavior. If any one of the above experiences
were to be recommended with extremely high priority, rap
sessions with young people would be high on our list.

        In instances where face to face meetings cannot be
facilitated, trainers may want to entertain the idea of tape
exchanges. This procedure is well established at the Boulder
County Juvenile Court and has been described in a generally
available publication. ["Tape Exchange and Court Probation, "
currently available from the National Information Center on
Volunteers in Courts, Suite 717, The Colorado Building,
Boulder, Colorado 80302, $1 a copy.] Rap sessions between
volunteers and members of adult offender self-help groups also
present opportunities for volunteer training.

        As we have suggested with all training experiences
the observational ones we have discussed in this

chapter should not be considered entities in themselves, but rather additional food for discussion and group interaction. We cannot overemphasize the need, time consuming as it is, for people to talk about what they have experienced. We said previously that the trainee needs to "validate" himself in relation to his experiences. What we mean by this is that volunteers, like all of us, after experiencing something must then integrate what this means personally. A training program, wherever it is, must have within it the potential to help the trainee accomplish this.

The potential of observational experiences for training is virtually unlimited. The outer limits are the trainer's imagination. We would hope that the imaginative trainer would develop more in-depth experiential training in that we know that participation in experiences provides a dimension beyond just listening and observing.

Chapter 13

LECTURES AND PANEL PRESENTATIONS

Lectures

Most of us in our educational experiences have been exposed to the lecture method of teaching, if not over-exposed; thus out of habit we tend to over-produce this kind of medium. But there is definitely a trend away from lecture as a way of teaching. There is increasing evidence that people will sit only so long and listen to one person before they lose interest in what is being said. And if the lecture is to be questioned as to its suitability for high school and college students, it definitely must be questioned at the level of teaching correctional volunteers.

The message of this book has been to find new, creative, and exciting methods of training volunteers, and, moreover, methods which conform to their special affinity for realism and relevance. A lecture can be exciting; however, far too many are not. We are not advocating the wholesale discarding of lectures as a tool for training, but rather we are suggesting that the trainer be discriminating as to their use. The lecture, if properly applied, still has something to be said for it.

Lectures are most often utilized when we are training a large group. Many training facilities have been designed more for speakers or lecturers than for group processes. In that sense we are sometimes trapped by our architecture into a lecture motif. This fact should be considered when seeking out training facilities.

A lecture is one way of initially implanting basic information. This information can be further processed by the use of question-answer periods during and/or after the lecture. A teacher delivering a lecture has a responsibility to elaborate on certain points previously identified by the trainer and should be willing to do so. We would advocate that

when lecturers are employed by trainers, they first of all
be willing to listen to the trainer's concepts of what is
needed and secondly agree to a question-answer-discussion
period.

Lecture material can also be brought to life through
the creative use of real life situations. If a class is really
to glean the meaning of an abstract point, we owe it to those
trainees with the least conceptual ability to provide examples
which depict our concepts. These case examples must be
couched in such a way as to protect confidentiality, but they
are extremely necessary if we are to internalize the learning
experience for our class. We are all inclined to relate
more closely to material that is exemplified by the human
experience. Since courts and correctional institutions deal
daily with the human experience, we do not lack for examples!

In choosing lecturers, it is important that the trainer
sample the lecturer's wares beforehand if possible, with a
view to determining how the lecture material would be understood by volunteers. Many a brilliant university professor
has "bombed out" when in front of the wrong audience because he has presented material that was too theoretical or
academic. Volunteers, we must remember, tend to be active participators in life, and want experiences that give
them a piece of life rather than academe.

It is frustrating for any of us to sit in an audience
listening to something that we do not understand or that we
consider irrelevant. Our inclination, when we have a
choice, is to leave such an unpleasant situation. It is even
more frustrating to listen to a message you don't understand
when you are further left with the feeling that the material
is nevertheless vital to your future performance as a helper.
The volunteer may well surmise, "If this is what they want
me to do, I had best get out of the program before I am in
over my head." If this happens, we may find that training
has served to screen out a potentially helpful volunteer for
the wrong reasons.

Training volunteers, as we often do, after working
hours, we find that people are tired and not ready to sit
for extended periods of time as listeners. Thus we would
suggest limiting lectures to 25-30 minutes at a stretch, providing changes of pace with such media as films, tapes, or
group interaction. We also believe the lecturer should try

to keep the atmosphere as informal as possible, inviting
questions and interruptions during and after the lectures.

It should also be kept in mind that lectures can be
made more palatable through the proper use of a blackboard
or flip chart. Supplementing lectures with visual aids has
the effect of providing the proper "mix" which in turn holds
the attention of the trainee during lectures.

What material lends itself to a lecture? Generally
descriptions of programs, explanations of policies, orientation of classes to community resources, and orientation to
understanding of behavior. In the case of the above we
should then get lecturers who have the expertise in the area
we are discussing. If court policies are being explained,
then the chief probation officer or presiding judge might be
the resource. Community resources might be explained by
a member of a community planning council. A human behavior lecture might be provided by a psychologist or psychiatrist. The court staff itself provides a pool of people
who use community resources and who deal with deviant behavior, and they present an important advantage to the trainer because they are already in the program and are paid
personnel. They also need to be involved in the volunteer
training programs since that involvement in training has
implications for their involvement in the program at later
stages.

An example of the significance of involving court staff
as lecturers is the skeptical staff member who feels threatened by the presence of volunteers in the court. Placed in
the role of expert providing training, the skeptic finds less
reason to be threatened because he discovers through direct
experience that he has knowledge upon which the volunteer
is by necessity dependent. He is then freed to become an
ally of the program, because he has been given the opportunity for a stake in its success.

Veteran volunteers provide another important pool of
lecture people. They are generally people who have something to say that the trainees want to hear, for they have
experienced something that the trainees expect to experience.
Volunteer lecturers generally present informal descriptive
anecdotes and are willing and anxious to answer questions
and discuss their experiences with the volunteers. Their
presence also has a reassuring quality for the class in that
their presence is living proof that a volunteer not only

survived the experience, but what's more is here to tell
about it! Time-limiting these guests is quite necessary in
that volunteers, just like anyone else, have a tendency to
find the podium to their liking.

Another group that can serve an important function
as lecturers are the people we refer to as clients, ex-cli-
ents, ex-offenders, etc. In a Salt Lake City training program ex-offenders are participating in training along with
volunteers. This is purely an experimental venture to see
what this kind of "mix" will produce in terms of interaction.
They present some challenges to the trainer, however, because among these people we often find some with more
medium than message, and they do not always have all that
much expertise. Being an ex-offender does not necessarily
mean that one understands crime and delinquency or how to
be a helping person. An interview with the individual prior
to bringing him into a training role will usually satisfy the
trainer as to his real ability to add significant information
to the class.

Panel Presentations

The trainer should give serious thought to the use of
panelists as an alternative to lectures. A panel presents
the class with a differential in terms of expertise, personality, and appearance, and presents the very necessary change
of pace we have been emphasizing in volunteer training.
Panelists provide the obvious advantage of complementing
each other and also provide several training roles for court
staff members that the trainer wishes to utilize. Panelists
also can be selected so as to present conflicting opinions on
issues which can be of considerable training value for volunteers. An example might be to have a panel of social
worker, judge, police officer, and student discuss "Why Delinquency?" Panels where there are divergent views provide
the ingredient of creative conflict, an ingredient that helps
to sharpen issues.

One of the dangers in the use of the panel is having
too many members. This of necessity places the last panelist to appear at a disadvantage in that the class may have
become bored by the time of his presentation. It also
forces the panel members to rush and feel pushed. If we
are inclined to limit the time of a panelist to ten minutes
and we utilize six panel members, we have already

consumed an hour. If panelists go over their time limit, a common occurrence, over an hour has expired. By the time necessary discussion has been added, we can see that easily two hours may have been used.

From a procedural standpoint, then, we believe that limiting the panel to no more than four people is good operating procedure. Further, we advocate that panelists be held by the trainer to definite time limits. Recognizing that these time limits may be exceeded, the trainer may find that it is necessary to allow an hour for four people with ten minute presentations. We believe, too, that time utilized for panel dialogue and panel-class dialogue is vital for making the panel a viable medium for training. This becomes a prime responsibility for the trainer.

In conclusion, we would like to suggest to the reader that lecturers or panelists will serve the needs of the trainer only as they are utilized to achieve training goals compatible with this medium and as they have sufficient expertise and speaking skills to hold the class members' interest.

Chapter 14

TRAINEE PARTICIPATION: ROLE PLAYING, ETC.

In this chapter we are focusing on role playing as a
major method of involving the trainee in "doing." As the
reader has surmised by now, we have stressed trainee participation in all facets of training, whether this participation
consists of discussing a film, exchanging ideas with other
trainees, or being involved in determining training content.
In short, we have stressed the importance of involving the
trainee directly whenever this is feasible.

The old adage, "A picture is worth a thousand words,"
provides the rationale for the use of role playing in training.
People playing roles present a visual picture to the class
that is of much more value than a thousand words when what
we are attempting to relate to are attitudes and skills.

Secondly, role playing, if properly conducted, allows
the trainee to be involved directly in the learning process.
This kind of participation is increasingly recognized as having high training value, particularly in short-term training
sessions where time is of the essence. Learning by being
involved brings the learner closer to the experience of doing. It helps the participant examine his feelings and attitudes and at the same time also allows the observer to approximate the conditions under which he will render his services. Role playing also provides an opportunity for the
class not only to observe the helping process, but also to
think about how this process might have been enhanced.
Role playing is participation, and volunteers are by definition
participators.

There has been a great deal of interest in various
kinds of encounters in human relations training. Psycho-
drama or sociodrama, encounter and growth experiences of
various types have been utilized for some time now in sensitivity training. The authors are well aware of some of
the criticisms of such groups, and we do not disagree with

some of them in that the faddishness that has emerged from
such training has probably been harmful in many instances.
Therefore, the role playing that we advocate is geared to the
specific purpose of improving helping skills and attitudes.
We hope this chapter will provide the reader with some
guidelines in using this medium for training.   A well planned
role-playing session has within it the potential for experi-
ential-type learning that can be a valuable and memorable
experience.   It need not be destructive.

When to Use Role Playing

        Role playing is not a panacea.   We do not advocate
this method where the goal of training is to supply such information as basic knowledge about programs or knowledge
regarding the criminal justice system.   Where role playing
is a useful training tool is at the point in training where
we are attempting to sensitize volunteers to a helping process and for the application of previously gained knowledge
of any relevance to concrete human situations.   In such
cases, we can sensitize people by asking them to approximate the conditions for which we are preparing them.   Role
playing can also be a technique to get people past some of
the fears they have about anticipated encounters with offenders by conducting these encounters, albeit in a controlled
and artificial setting, and then discussing the experience in
a protected setting.

Selecting the Role Players

        Critics of role playing will contend that some people
are in fact too brittle to be placed in front of a group to
display their inner feelings.   The resultant guilt over having
done so, according to the critics, will produce a destructive
aftermath over which the trainer will have no control.   This
criticism is sometimes valid, and precautions should be taken
to protect people who need it.   This protection will only
come from experienced trainers who know how to manage
role playing sessions.

        As was stated at the beginning of our book, however,
the people who are being screened into our programs are
highly successful people who do not generally present severe
psychological problems.   They represent, as a group, a
part of the population that has attained a high degree of

mental health and is operating at a high level on the hierarchy of needs. The number of people in training who should not be involved in role playing is rather insignificant in reality, and even they can participate vicariously.

Our procedure in selecting role players is that of asking for "volunteers" among your volunteers first of all. Since we are training volunteers, the act of volunteering for role playing is really not an unrealistic expectation, and in any training class we have rarely in fact failed to obtain participants through this method.

In instances where the trainer is unable to elicit volunteer participation in role playing, the following suggestions are submitted: (1) The trainer can demonstrate the role playing technique by playing one of the roles. (2) Set the stage by presenting a relatively simple, uncharged situation to be role played. (3) Ask the trainees to propose a hypothetical situation to be role played.

Once one has a pool of volunteers, the trainer can, through the group interview process, eliminate the individuals about whom he has doubts as to the personal value of the experience. He can do this in a very positive way by saying, at the time he is soliciting the volunteers, that not all of them will be used, but he wishes to choose those who seem to fit the training needs vis-à-vis age, personality, etc. This group interview can even be conducted during a coffee break by asking the volunteer role players to remain a few minutes to discuss their possible use in training.

Preparing the Role Players

It is a good idea to acknowledge the courage the volunteers have demonstrated by volunteering as role-playing participants. They should be given a basic idea of what the goal of the role-playing session is and the approximate time limit involved. They should be given to understand that there is no "right" outcome, but that what they do in the session will be discussed with a view to constructive criticism.

When assigning the players' roles, it is important that they be asked whether they can feel themselves in the role, and whether they have questions about the role or the basic premise under which the role play is being conducted.

We would caution the trainer not to rehearse role playing or
to give too much detail regarding the situation.   To be sure,
the basic premise of the encounter should be stated, i. e.,
"this is a first interview situation of a probationer and his
counselor, and they are meeting in the probation office, having been introduced by a professional probation officer, " or
"this is a fifth session and the probationer has not shown up
for his two previous appointments. "   Note, however, that to
give too much detail militates against spontaneity.   The actors should be asked to do what they feel they would do under
the stated conditions as naturally as it is possible for them
to do so.   Report X(B) at the end of this chapter provides
the reader with several hypothetical role playing situations.

Selecting the Role-Playing Premise

        Any problem that occurs in a correctional situation
that would be relevant to a volunteer is a possible role-play
premise.   Many trainers may not feel particularly competent
to handle spontaneous situations, but if they do, a premise
might be to ask the principal participants to think about a
particular offender-type role and situation they would like to
depict and use this as the role-play premise.

        A standard role-play situation one of the authors used
in training for several months was that of a 35-year-old
bricklayer with a drinking problem who is brought into court
on a charge of beating his wife.   The role play included in
some cases lawyers, who defended and prosecuted, as well
as a judge who did the sentencing.   Following sentencing to
probation, the role play included a first interview between a
volunteer probation counselor and the probationer.   In this
instance the author played the role of the defendant while one
of the class members acted as the volunteer counselor.

        Where the trainer wishes to have a more structured
role-playing format, the use of prepared pre-sentence material as a basis for role playing may be more satisfactory
because teaching points can be better thought out in advance.
Two sample pre-sentence reports are included in Report
X(A) at the end of this chapter, the Daniel Carter Case and
the Dora Alias Case.   They have been utilized successfully
by the senior author repeatedly.   However, if "live" material is being used, caution must be exercised in reproducing
the material so that names, dates, and places are changed.
In small communities it would probably be inadvisable to use

material depicting the problem of people from that community. But a creative trainer can also create his own presentence report from elements of actual cases. This has the advantage of insuring confidentiality, and it allows for the producing of the teaching points the trainer feels to be most important.

In using pre-sentence reports for role playing, we advise the trainer that an excellent preparation for this process can be effected by breaking the class into small groups for a half-hour or 45 minutes to address themselves to various questions which reading the pre-sentence report raises. Such questions are (1) what basic lessons has the offender learned? (2) What problems would you anticipate in working with this person? (3) What are the goals of probation with this client? After struggling with these questions, the class is better primed to see the offender in the pre-sentence report "come to life" in the role play situation.

Preparing the Class

Some time should be given to preparing the class to observe the role-playing session. Even a large class can make effective use of this experience if properly conditioned. Individual class members, depending upon the goal, can be asked to imagine as much as possible that they are sitting in the chair of the role player(s). If, for example, the goal is to sensitize the class to how the offender feels, ask them to imagine that they are sitting in his chair. If the goal is preparing the class to function as a helper or counselor, they can be asked to imagine that they are in that chair, and they can be further asked to think about what their responses would have been in each exchange.

Classes can be helped to understand the principals in the role-playing session if they are in a position to ask these people questions about themselves. One technique of doing this which often has the effect of pointing up the hidden agendas of the principals is this: prior to the encounter ask one of the two role players to leave the room so that the instructor and the class can elicit some of the feelings, attitudes, and expectations of the person remaining; then this second person can be dismissed to leave the room, the first asked to return, and the process repeated (and similarly, of course, with three or more role players); the class is then in a much better position to see how each of the individuals

is "programmed" prior to performing and how they carry out
these programs.

Questions which can help the class better understand
the feelings of the role players might be like these: "What
kind of person do you think the probation counselor (offender) will be?" "What behavior do you expect from the probationer?" "What goals do you have in mind in this meeting
with the probationer?" When such questions are answered,
the class is somewhat aware of the "agendas" of each role
player, even though the role players themselves are not
aware of each other's agenda.

The Encounter

When possible, role playing is best accomplished
when there is a small group in a fairly small room.   Some
individuals have a difficult time projecting their voices, and,
in fact, many of the roles played are roles of subdued or
withdrawn people.   The role players should be placed where
their voices can best be directed to the class.   Ideally, we
like to place the actors in the center of a room with the
class in a circle.

Generally, we find that the encounter proceeds without
prompting and ends in a natural way without outside direction.   In instances where the role playing seems to be un-
productive (i.e., the "counselor" role player talks too much),
the trainer may find it profitable to re-enter briefly to ask
the class to provide some feedback.   As an example the
trainer may say, "Let's stop at this point to see what the
observers think."   It is best, however, if the encounter can
be allowed to find its own level and proceed until the players
themselves end it.

Time is a consideration, however, and the trainer
needs to be aware of the reaction of the participants as well
as the class for clues as to how or when the staging should
be terminated.

Managing Feedback

The ultimate value of role playing as a training device
is in getting feedback from the class and the instructor, as
well as the participants.   This calls upon the exercise of

good judgment on the part of the trainer in making certain
that the participants, when criticized, are not unfairly at-
tacked. Thus the trainer must often assume the role of defender by managing the feedback and interpreting it. If the
role-play participants are faced with criticism without these
safeguards, the danger always exists that they will become
defensive and resistant.

One technique for meaningful feedback is to set very
strict ground rules for the class to react to the participants.
We ask them first of all to report on what they particularly
like about what the actors did, what they felt was handled
well, and what they found they responded to most positively.
The reason for this is that the participant gets an opportunity to hear the positive things first, the theory being that an
individual can tolerate negative criticism better if he has
first been given an opportunity to hear the positives. It also
forces the class to think of their criticisms in terms of
positives as well as negatives. Often we find that we are
most prone to react to what was negative rather than positive.

After eliciting the positive material, the class is
asked to relate to what they feel are areas that could be
improved. The phrasing of this is important. Rather than
saying, "What was wrong or bad?", we can say, "What
might have been a better approach?" and "Why?" If the
above safeguards are exercised, the trainer will find that he
will have structured the situation to maximize the chances
of the encounter's being a positive and productive learning experience. Again, the participants should be thanked openly
for their courage in participating and dealing with the criticisms of their performance.

Beyond this, the class, once having provided direct
feedback, should be asked to relate what they learned from
the role playing. This in a sense correlates, for the individuals in the class, some things they may not have thought
about, and again it has the effect of internalizing the experience. A good learning experience, particularly where the
trainee may have made many mistakes in the role-play situation, is to ask him to repeat the process with the benefit
of this feedback.

Where the trainer's goal is to provide a role-playing
experience for each trainee, a slightly different methodology
can be employed. As an example, in one court where our

objective was specifically to train volunteers to conduct interviews and write pre-sentence reports for a court diagnostic clinic, we first of all asked each participant to create an offender role in his own mind that he could see himself playing. (This request was made early in training in order that the participants had time to create a viable character.) Having developed the characters, the participants paired off. One trainee was given the task of interviewing the other. When this interview was completed, the person being interviewed provided feedback by relating what he felt had been done well and relating what he felt could have been improved. The individuals then reversed their roles and repeated the process, after which they each wrote a pre-sentence report on the basis of what they had gleaned from the interview, on both sides of the fence, so to speak.

A trainer should not be in the position of being unwilling to do something that he is asking the trainees to do. There is real training value in the trainer's being a participant in role playing. The justification for this is that by example the instructor can help to loosen up reluctant trainees, and that by example he can teach skills in helping processes. In the feedback segment he can talk readily about what he did and his reason for doing it. The trainer also is, hopefully, more able to deal with criticism without being demoralized, and the time-saving facet of using the instructor in this way has something to be said for it.

Managing the role playing is not something to be done by the neophyte trainer. It requires skill in making rapid assessments about the process, how to intervene, and what teaching points to extract. It requires an outgoing, spontaneous person who can by example elicit demonstrative behaviors from trainees. The trainer in this setting must be confident about what he is doing. We would suggest that anyone embarking on plans to conduct role playing do so only after having worked with another trainer under actual training conditions. Ideally, having co-trainers is advantageous in that this allows one trainer to "spell" the other, and it also provides better coverage of the ongoing process.

*   *   *   *

Report X [in 2 parts]

(A) TWO ROLE-PLAY PREMISES:
THE DANIEL CARTER CASE, AND THE DORIA ALIAS CASE

DEPARTMENT OF PROBATION SERVICES
DENVER COUNTY COURT

Defendant: Daniel Carter   Age: 22
Charges: Concealed Weapon   Sex: Male
Address: 1348 Pearl St.   Judge: Sanchez
                    Dob: 7-24-46
                    Docket: #53728
                    Date of Report: 8-6-68

Offense:
Mr. Daniel Carter is a 22-year-old single Caucasian male
who has pled guilty to a charge of carrying a concealed
weapon.   He is represented by the Public Defender's Office
and has been encouraged to apply for probation.

The official version of the offense as stated in the formal
complaint signed by Officer Dines is "Subject was walking on
the 1200 block of Washington St. shouting obscenities at two
youths in a 1962 Chevrolet parked on the street.   When approached by officers, he started to run north but apparently
decided to stop upon Officer Baker's insistence.   When
searched he was found to be carrying a switchblade knife.
Subject was arrested and booked. "

The defendant's explanation of the incident is that he was
spotted by two acquaintances; Bill Kenney and Steve Price.
He and Price had been in a disagreement two weeks prior
over a sum of money which the defendant is alleged to have
borrowed.   Defendant states he promised to repay the money
but because of no job has been unable to do so.   Price, he
says, will not listen to reason and was threatening to get it
out of him one way or another.   Carter can give no reason
for carrying a knife.   He denies any intent to use it or any
need for a weapon for self-defense.

Prior Record:
The defendant admits to several arrests during the past four
years.   Official police records reveal he was arrested for
a drunk and disturbance in 1964 and fined $25. 00.   In 1965
he had a drunk arrest and a Driving Under the Influence

arrest within a three month period. He was fined $50.00 on the drunk charge and served ten days in County Jail on the DUI. In 1966, he was arrested and released on a burglary charge. He was held for brandishing a weapon in that same year although no disposition is noted.

In Jan., 1967, the defendant was convicted of burglary and placed under supervision of the Denver District Court. He was supervised until June, 1968, by Mr. Baird who reports that Mr. Carter reported regularly and conformed to the probation rules. He maintained steady employment as a gas station attendant during the probation period.

As a juvenile the defendant was in Denver Juvenile Court for truancy on several occasions. He was handled unofficially until age 17 when he was placed on probation for breaking and entering. His adjustment on probation was considered satisfactory although the supervising officer notes that the boy had a bad family situation.

Family:
Mr. Carter is a lifelong resident of Denver. He is the fourth of eight children of William and Dora [Eastman] Carter, ages 42 and 40 respectively. The family situation has been unstable from the beginning of the parents' marriage, which was necessitated by Mrs. Carter's pregnancy. When the defendant was ten, his father left the home and apparently began living with another woman in Albuquerque, New Mexico. His present whereabouts are unknown. He was a very unstable person who drank heavily, was abusive, and chased other women. He had a poor employment record and was arrested several times on drunk charges.

The mother attempted to work for a short time when Mr. Carter left the family but was unable to work and care for the younger children. She applied for ADC and has been on welfare ever since. She is considered by the Welfare Department to be a sincere but defeated woman who has little control over her children. Two of the other children have juvenile court records.

Daniel seems to follow a pattern of living in and out of the home. He has tried to move out and live independently, but comes home when he cannot pay the room rent.

Employment:
Presently Daniel is unemployed. His last employment was at

Ace Box Co. operating a cutting machine at $1.75 per hour but he left over a disagreement with the foreman over his inability to produce. He had worked there three months. Prior employment has been irregular and periods of unemployment seem to prevail over periods of employment. His longest job (1-1/2 years) was as a gas station attendant. Daniel said he liked this job because he was around cars, but he was fired when he did not show up to open up the station one morning. He is vague about his future employment goals but says he once wanted to be a mechanic.

Education:
This youth dropped out of school in the ninth grade at Morey Jr. High School. He had no particular reason except that he was not getting anything out of it and teachers were getting tired of him so he quit. He thinks now it would have been a good idea to stay in school but he is too old to go back, he believes.

He is uncertain about future training or education. He once thought about getting some Army schooling. This is out, he thinks, because he understands he failed the Army entrance tests.

Health:
The defendant apparently is in good health now. He was hospitalized at age ten for pneumonia. The District Court probation report states that he was treated for gonorrhea during a 1966 jail sentence.

Habits:
Mr. Carter admits to getting drunk once a month. He smokes tobacco and says he has tried smoking pot but does not want to continue. He denies using narcotics. He says he does not date very much but "lays up" with women when he feels like it. He does not plan to marry.

Psychiatric Report:
This young man was examined and found to be logical in his thinking. He is not psychotic and expresses little outward anxiety. He sees no reason to change. I would have some concern about this man drinking and carrying a weapon.

Diagnostic Procedure Findings:
This youth has a poor self-concept, little anxiety and seems not to profit much from experience. He sees himself as weak and foolish. He is hedonistic.

Summary:
This young man lacks education, skills and motivation to develop a different life style.   There is some indication that
he is beginning to think of himself in anti-social terms in
that being anti-social is better than being inadequate.   The
one positive force still in operation is Mr. Carter's dislike
of jail.   His past responses to probation may be considered
a strength also.

Corrective Recommendation:
Probation is recommended although it is felt that a suspended
jail sentence may be necessary to keep Mr. Carter motivated toward achieving the goals of probation.

> Respectfully submitted
> James Justice
> Probation Counselor

Report X [1st part cont.]

THE DORA ALIAS CASE

DENVER COUNTY COURT
DEPARTMENT OF PROBATION SERVICES

Name: Dora Alias   Address: 8915 So. Clayton
AKA:
Phone No.: 935-7480   Age: 18   Probation No.: 8984
     Hearing Date: 6/27/68
DOB: 12/1/49   Sex: F   Jailed: Bond: DPD/DL No.:
Employed: Yes ☐   No ☐   Wage:
     Employment Length:

Complaint No(s):
Charge(s):   Possession of implements for use of narcotics
Div.: General Sessions   Judge: Caruso   Court: 191-J
Plea: Guilty   Def. Atty.:   Filing Date:

Disposition: Jail Sentence (Length)_____
Fine (Amt.)_____ Cond. Suspension (Length)_____
Prob. (Length)_____   Special Prob. Cond._____

Dora Alias   DC#1234   Docket 88741   Ct. Rm.   6/27/68

Offense: Dora was arrested at approximately 2:40 P.M.,

April 13, 1968, at Republic Drugs, 1600 Tremont, where
she was attempting to fill a stolen and forged prescription
for methedrine.   At the time of her apprehension, she was
found to be in possession of several hypodermic needles and
other implements for drug use.   She entered a plea of not
guilty and trial was set for June 27, 1968.   She remained in
jail three days until cash bond was posted by family friends.
At her court appearance, she entered a guilty plea to the
implement charge.   Dora readily admits the use of various
drugs and hallucinogenics and states that the needles and
other implements were property for this purpose.   She admits knowing that the prescription she was attempting to fill
had been stolen and was forged, but she will not reveal any
information regarding its origin other than that it came from
a friend.

Previous Offenses: None.

Family: Dora was born December 1, 1949, in Dallas, Texas, the second of three children born to Mr. and Mrs.
Alias.   At the time of her birth, her father was in the Air
Force and assigned to Shepard Air Force Base.   Throughout
the interview, she was confused about time, but it is be-
lieved the family remained in Wichita Falls for about nine
years after which time her father left the Air Force and
the family moved to Tennessee, where they remained until
coming to the Denver area in 1959.   The father entered an
Episcopal Seminary in April 1968 in Wisconsin.   Before this
he was employed as a watchmaker.   The father is an overly
rigid, strict individual who views his daughter as a sinner
and one beyond hope of change.   The mother, on the contrary, is an overly permissive, ineffectual woman who has
been totally dominated by the father.   Dora has encountered
serious conflicts with the father since she was nine years
old, and there has been a long period of rebellion against
him on Dora's part.   Dora's 20-year-old brother, John, is
a music student at Denver University, and he continues to
live in the parental home.

Also in the rented home at 8915 S. Clayton is Dora's 16-
year-old brother, Bob.   She has been influential in involving
this younger brother in the use of drugs, and the father is
particularly concerned about the younger child's future behavior should this close relationship between him and Dora
continue.   This in part is one reason why the father approves of Dora's being out of the home.   This young girl has
been using assorted forms of drugs and narcotics for at

least two years and from time to time, the father has had
her committed through the family physician to Mt. Airy
Mental Hospital in Denver to at least temporarily stop drug
usage. During the past two years, she has been primarily
dependent on hippie friends for her basic needs. This has
resulted in considerable mobility in and about the Denver
area. At the time of her arrest, she was staying at 096
Sherman, but at this time, she lives with a group of male
and female hippies on South Clayton. She has no desire to
return to her parents' home, even during the absence of her
father. Shortly after being released from jail, May 1, 1968,
Dora went to San Francisco, California, remaining approximately one month. She returned to Denver voluntarily a
few days preceding her scheduled court appearance on this
charge.

Employment: None.

Education: Dora last attended school at Central High School
in January 1968. Her academic achievement was very poor,
as was her attendance. She failed the 11th grade and was
repeating these classes at the time of her last enrollment.
She was not involved in any extra-curricular activities at
school.

Health: Dora does not report any serious illnesses or in-
juries, but it is apparent from observation that she is seriously underweight as a result of poor eating habits and the
effects of drugs. The interview was quite difficult as she
does not appear to have completely recovered from recent
drug usages. Her speech was slurred and on occasions, in-
coherent. There were inappropriate gestures and bursts of
laughter. She complained numerous times that her speech
could not keep up with her mind, attributing this on one occasion to the use of "speed. "

In February 1968 Dora was committed to Mt. Airy Hospital,
by the family physician, and was then placed on a 90-day
hold-and-treat order at Fort Logan Mental Health Center.
An interview with her psychiatric social worker, Miss M.,
disclosed much of the above social information. Dora is on
out-patient treatment and is supposed to be attending weekly
sessions which she has failed to do since her arrest. However, prior to this, she kept appointments regularly, obtaining transportation either through friends or public transportation. During her commitment at Fort Logan, she was a
serious challenge as she was able to have friends bring her

various drugs, and on one occasion, it resulted in her boy friend being arrested for introducing methedrine into the hospital. Dora was not considered schizophrenic nor in need of hospitalization. However, out-patient care was considered warranted, and will be continued although recognizing prognosis is guarded.

Religion: Undoubtedly representing additional rebellion against her father, Dora professes a cult of the Buddhist faith. She describes at length nine stages of life and rather proudly reported attainment of the eighth stage. She purports existence in the form of a cat during the seventh stage, but is unable to describe any previous stages. With amusement, Dora related discussing her religious beliefs with her father which would infuriate him.

Diagnostic Procedure Findings: She seems expansive and somewhat hypomanic on the tests. Depressive elements seem feared and guarded against but perceived as inevitable with mood swings. She seems to try hard to avoid thought of the future. A simple, happy existence with a minimum of pain and suffering seems her goal.

Impressions: This 18-year-old girl, attired in full hippie regalia, has rebelled against her strict, prudish, unyielding father in every form available. In doing so, she has become thoroughly aligned with the hippie element resulting in drug usage, sexual promiscuity, mobility and anti-social behavior. Her native ability permits her to rationalize her behavior through pseudo intellectualization. There presently is no evidence of motivation for behavior change. While her present existence is obviously self-destructive, Dora does present some strengths: i.e., returning from California in time to appear in Court, maintaining appointments at Fort Logan before the instant offense, and native ability. The aspect of cause-effect looms from the gross inconsistency between parental figures.

Psychiatric Evaluation: Dora appears not to have recovered from her methedrine psychosis. She is confused about time and somewhat as to place. Her speech is rapid and distorted. She complained that she couldn't keep up with her mind. Her affect was at times silly and inappropriate. Her relationships appear superficial and self-serving.

E. W. Brown, M. D.

Corrective Recommendations: A jail sentence would seem to
be the means of achieving the immediate goal of allowing the
defendant to withdraw from the effects of drug usage. Supervision would also be useful, providing the defendant with an
opportunity to correct her behavior if she so chooses.   A
penalty and probation supervision is recommended.   It is
expected that the defendant will be very difficult to supervise.

> Respectfully submitted,
> Robert Trujillo, Director
> By: A. O. Buswell
> Probation Officer

*   *   *   *

Report X [2nd of 2 parts]

(B) SOME TYPICAL ROLE-PLAY PREMISES*

Missing Money

Situation: Volunteer.   There was a ten dollar bill on
the table when I was called out, I was almost sure.   It's
gone now.   Maybe the boy took it.   He might have, you
know.   What do I do?   Ignore it?   Challenge him?   Ask him
if he might have borrowed it?

Situation: Youth.   Here comes that volunteer.   I wonder if he knows he left that ten dollar bill on the table.
What the hell, he'll never miss it.   What will I do if he
acts like he thinks I took it?

— — — — — — — — —

The Missed Meeting

Situation: Youth.   I wonder what he'll say after I cut
on him last week, but I had better things to do.

*Our appreciation for these actually used ideas to Dan Logan
of the Y-Pals Program in Kansas City.   Further in-service
situation role play ideas can easily be developed from the
"Casebook for Court Volunteers" presented in the next chapter.

Situation: Volunteer. My youth failed to show up last week when he was supposed to. What do I do? -- Challenge him? Ignore? Simply say I missed him?

- - - - - - - - - -

"Grass"

Situation: Youth. My volunteer has learned I have marijuana. What shall I do? Run out? Admit it--so what? Deny it?

Situation: Volunteer. I have accidentally found out my youth has marijuana. What do I do? Tell him I am obligated to report and urge him to "turn himself in?" Just report it to the authorities? This is not my problem? Ignore the whole matter? This is not my role?

- - - - - - - - - -

First Encounter

Situation: Volunteer. Fifteen year old youth is being introduced to me. He is slovenly acting, sloppily dressed. What kind of first impression do I want to make? Do I move toward him eagerly? Tentatively? What do I say? Is my language calculated to make him comfortable?

Situation: Youth. I am meeting the Volunteer for the first time. I am cautious. What kind of guy is this? Why is he doing this? For me? Himself? The Law? Guess I'll just wait him out--at least at first.

- - - - - - - - - -

Testing Out

Situation: Youth. I wonder if this guy is for real? Maybe he is a phoney like the others before him? I'm going to find out. I'll give him a hard time to see what he does.

Situation: Volunteer. My youth is acting belligerent toward me. He doesn't like any of my suggestions. He gets rude and makes comments like--"What's in this for you, anyway? What are you, some kind of fink?" What do I do? Get tough? Show "understanding?" Ignore?

Chapter 15

READINGS

Introduction

The written word may lack much of the drama and immediacy of films, tapes, or role plays, but it has its unique advantages, too. Mainly, it can be preserved for ready reference as needed. (You can't just turn the film on again whenever you need it.) It can be taken home, taken out, wherever the volunteer goes. Readings have much in common with other training media, including their most common mis-usages: readings can be technical, dull, theoretical, irrelevant, or poorly produced, just like films and tapes. Please remember, your volunteers came to be relevant. So make your readings relevant. Above all, make your readings readable. For convenience, we have divided this chapter into three sections: I. Volunteer Orientation Manual; II. Other Court-Prepared Readings; III. Outside Readings. Following these sections are two reports, XI and XII, containing exemplary readings for volunteers.

I. The Volunteer Orientation Manual

Most courts now have manuals for their volunteers. The manual should concentrate on "What every good volunteer should know," leaving the elaboration and particularization to other readings and other media. The manual should be put in the volunteer's hands either at screening-acceptance or during volunteer pre-assignment training. Desirable characteristics of a volunteer orientation manual are that it be:

1. Readable, interesting, relevant, informative, without being technical or jargonistic;
2. Well-indexed for reference, and a reasonable organization behind that index--don't just slap together

232

materials in some order or other;
    3. Locally relevant (<u>adapt</u> and individualize to your
program any national materials you may happen upon);
    4. Concise--40-50 pages is probably maximum;
    5. Given to the volunteer to keep, if at all possible
(there's a morale as well as an information function here);
    6. As physically attractive as possible, personalized
with volunteer's name, court seal, etc., on cover, etc.
(it may still cost not more than $1 a copy, if produced in
quantities of 100 or more--a few extra dollars here is really
worth it);
    7. Handy to carry around (Memphis has a pocket-
sized one)--other physical features might be pouches in back,
supply of blank pages for taking notes, etc. (in general,
give a lot of thought to format, making it relevant to what
you want the manual to do, e.g., looseleaf if there'll be
frequent additions, etc.); and
    8. Revised frequently, or at least sections thereof,
updating names, etc.

    Common components of a correctional volunteer ori-
entation manual are (not necessarily in the following order,
and by no means necessarily including all of these in any
one agency's manual):

    1. Introduction.
          a. Welcoming letter or message from judge
or senior staff officer and/or leading volunteer. May be
personally signed.
          b. <u>Good</u> index, table of contents.

    2. Something about the court.
          a. History, basic mission of court.
          b. History of volunteer programs at court,
their philosophy and purpose, how they fit in the overall
picture of probation. Take through to current status of programs, and don't neglect mention of <u>non</u>-volunteer programs
and efforts, to give the volunteer the <u>total</u> context in which
his efforts take place.
          c. Brief description of currently existing vol-
unteer programs in the agency (if there are more than one).
Also other non-volunteer resources in the agency (e.g.,
diagnostic files, professional consultants, facilities, etc.).
          d. Identification and introduction of key lead-
ership (judge, staff, leadership volunteers), who they are,
what they do, when and where they are available (office
hours, address, telephone number, etc.). This can help

get communication off on the right track. You might even
have a section at the end in which you (or the volunteer) fill
in the specific name, address, and telephone number of each
volunteer's individual supervisor(s).
          e. Administrative organization and judicial-
probation process. Use <u>clear</u> organization and flow charts
wherever possible.

    3. Something about the client.
          a. Status and identification (age range, pri-
mary types of offenses in your locality), rights of client, etc.
          b. Court procedures, in regard to typical
probation rules (you may fill in blanks specifically for each
volunteer with his individual case).
          c. Digest of laws and ordinances pertaining
to offenders in your state. Make this <u>clear</u>, in laymen's
terms. (See also 4 b iii below.)

    4. Something about volunteer's job.
          a. The general roles and obligations of the
volunteer. The court's expectations, as explicitly as possible
as to confidentiality, time investment, minimum length of
service, reporting, conduct, other responsibilities to court
and to client, etc.
          b. Techniques and strategies
              i. Aphorisms, "Thou Shalt and Thou
Shalt Not" (Report XI, this chapter), is an example of these.
              ii. Counseling, etc., strategies for the
volunteer, as given in Chapter 6, which see.
              iii. Case studies (Report XII, e.g., in
this chapter).
              iv. Community resource directory, and
how to get the use of these resources.

    5. Appendix, or back of Orientation Manual.
          a. Clear definitions of key terminology used
at the court. Very important.
          b. Possibly, a map showing court and other
key locations, if a large city.
          c. Possibly, an honor roll of past and cur-
rent volunteers.
          d. Possibly, a filled-in form sheet with basic
identification information on volunteer's individual client.
          e. Possibly--if orientation manual is "what
every good volunteer should know" and there are a variety
of specific individual jobs beyond that, e.g., tutor, foster
parent, office worker--a brief work-up on this volunteer's

specific job.

In addition to noting the specimens of the types of materials frequently represented in volunteer orientation manuals, attached here as reports XI and XII, the reader might also want to see what an intact manual looks like when it's all put together. At present such an example of a complete manual, "The Boulder County Juvenile Court Orientation Manual," is available for two dollars by writing the National Information Center.

II.   Other Court-Prepared Readings

The court may have other special readings prepared and available on loan to volunteers, as needed. These are for elaboration or special information, but probably are too long for full inclusion in the volunteer orientation manual. Thus, for example, case studies about volunteers working with probationers make excellent training material, and a few can be included in any volunteer orientation manual. But in addition, the volunteer might want to leaf through a longer casebook to find case situations more similar to his own, in which case the court could have on hand a "Casebook for Court Volunteers" (Report XII).

Again while the senior author's "Guides for Volunteers in Correctional Settings" (Report V, Chapter 6) could be incorporated in an orientation manual, there is much to be said for making it available to volunteers as a separate item.   Much the same could be said for a piece by Eva Schindler-Rainman called "Communicating with Today's Teenagers: An Exercise Between Generations." This is, in fact, reprinted and distributed by the State of Washington (write Jim DeBlasio, Washington State OEO, Hotel Olympian, Legion and Washington Streets, Olympia, Washington 98501).

Finally, the agency's own newsletter for volunteers can be a lively communicator and entertainer and still be an extremely effective ongoing training medium.   While we have not given much space to local volunteer program newsletters as training vehicles, we do wish to stress their effectiveness in this role.   The good ones are highly readable, yet contain most of the content components recommended throughout this book, e.g., brief "case studies" from the volunteers, a question-and-answer column, notices as to significant movies, lectures, etc. in town, reminders of volunteer in-service

training events, and articles on typical client problems (jobs,
drugs, etc.) and on available community resources.

III. Outside Readings

      Much that is readable and relevant will not be formal-
ly or deliberately designed for volunteer orientation by the
court or anyone else, but rather part of the reading matter
in general circulation. The alert volunteer coordinator can
identify these and either recommend or actually assign them
as readings to his volunteers. At least one program actually has volunteers write book reports.

      The advantages here is very similar to that of com-
mercial films used as training vehicles (see Chapter 10):
these are readings which have to compete for interest on the
open market; they cannot count on a captive classroom audience. So they usually are better written and more interesting than formal educational materials. In any case, a few
correctional agencies are building libraries of take-home
training readings for their volunteers, duly noting their
availability, new accessions, etc., in the volunteer newsletter, the bulletin board, etc. Outside readings can include
pamphlets and brochures, magazines, and books.

      It's up to the volunteer trainer and his volunteers to
be alert to pamphlets, to identify training-relevant publications by national organizations such as the PTA, churches,
service clubs, the federal government (especially HEW and
LEAA), the Children's Division of the American Humane
Society, and many others. Once identified, these pamphlets
can usually be procured in quantity at modest cost or sometimes without charge.

      Almost any national magazine might have a relevant
article in any given issue: Time, Newsweek, Life, Look,
Readers' Digest, Playboy, etc. Again, the volunteer trainer
should check them out, or perhaps even better, a volun-
teer(s) can be assigned to keep a continuous scan on them,
so that good and relevant articles can be brought to the attention of all volunteers, placed in the volunteer library, etc.
The same may be true of daily newspapers, although one
must be wary of some sensationalism and superficiality in
all but the best dailies. But even these kinds of articles
can be a basis for critique and discussion.

Beyond this there are a few laymen's periodicals which are meaty and likely to be regularly relevant, and the correctional agency might consider purchasing subscriptions for its volunteers.   Among these are <u>Psychology Today</u> and <u>Trans-Action</u>.   But, unless your unpaid workers happen to be, say, graduate student interns, we do not generally favor <u>technical</u> journals for the education of volunteers.

The considerations for books are similar: relevance, along with natural gripping interest and current topicality. It also helps if the books are available in paperback, relatively inexpensively, though of course this isn't a reason for excluding an otherwise worthwhile reading.   It is desirable but by no means necessary that the entire book be relevant. It's possible to suggest reading only a section.

Many correctional volunteer agencies (and/or libraries) have reading lists suggested for volunteers, and the list may extend to 50 or 75 titles, with a lot of relatively "specialized" books, e. g. , a book about a runaway girl for a volunteer whose charge is in fact runaway-prone.

While we could present here a list of up to 200 titles which have been suggested as take-home training by one agency or another, we see no point in doing so.   First of all because it is generally best for each agency to "discover" its own list; it's fun and it's more likely to produce <u>locally</u> relevant readings.   Second of all, topicality is one of the special fresh features of outside readings, and any list prepared today might well be somewhat stale by the time this book is published.   Nevertheless, mainly by way of illustration, a few of the kinds of books one hears about frequently on such volunteer take-home training lists in 1971 were presented in Chapter 6.

In regard to the specimen volunteer orientation materials given here as reports XI and XII, the following points should be noted: permission to reproduce for your own use in whole or in part can be considered as given, although acknowledgment of source would be appreciated; we strongly recommend, however, that you select and adapt these materials to local needs and conditions, rather than simply reproducing them as they are here.

Much that is in good readings can be absorbed at the volunteer's own pace and need, and we have no intent to advocate babysitting the volunteer learning-wise.   It is

nevertheless true, generally, that readings can take better
effect when the volunteer has a chance to discuss them with
others--his supervisor, his in-service training group, etc.
Try to see that he has an opportunity to do so, and indeed
to suggest readings for himself and others in the first place.

*   *   *   *

Report XI

THOU SHALT AND THOU SHALT NOT:
GUIDELINES FOR VOLUNTEERS

Introduction

        There are no simple "right" answers in dealing with
probationers; no cut and dried solutions. The volunteer
must be able to attach fresh solutions to old problems, and
the following should be considered only general guidelines to
help get the volunteer started on the road to rehabilitation:
a long and bumpy road indeed.

        The following "nuggets, " aphorisms and felicitous
phrases were collected from the National Information Center's
files of volunteer orientation material used by courts across
the nation, including juvenile, adult, probation, parole, and
detention, as well as independent volunteer agencies. This
accounts for some variety and occasional contradiction,
though a pretty substantial consensus emerges among courts
on the "do's and don'ts" they give their volunteers. [Our
reference library is composed of data on over 2, 000 courts
and volunteer organizations across the U. S. and several foreign countries.]

        Categorization is very general and many categories
overlap and reiterate each other. Our apologies for this
very general grouping. It is hoped that your court will select those aphorisms most applicable to you for use as training aids or as ideas to formulate new ones. But it is up to
the program leader to take this compendium and select from
it the particular points and phrases he wants in his guidelines for volunteers. They will rarely be exactly the same
set from court to court. This collection does not tell you
how to put them together, but Section Two of it, "Some
Things to Think About in Working with Juveniles, " is a
sample to demonstrate the compilation process. It is taken

from the Boulder County Juvenile Court's current volunteer
orientation manual.

The versatility of these "nuggets" should be noted.
Not only are they useful as simple written "do's and don'ts, "
but they can also be used as ideas for role-play situations,
lecture points, group discussion topics at in-service training, ideas for training aids, etc. You may also use them
on bulletin boards, displays, as "Take One" pamphlets, or
include them in volunteer newsletters. The only limit is
training needs and your imagination. Thus, as an added
dash for an orientation meeting, you could even insert each
guideline in a fortune cookie!

The incompleteness of this compilation should be
noted. There is much more to be said, from what courts
have already said and from what you find newly needed for
your court. We invite you to send us new guidelines plus
good phrasing of points already made. The value of this is
not just covering old points in the same old ways, but in
finding ways to phrase them with special vividness and re-
memberability.

SECTION ONE: EXCERPTS FROM ACROSS THE NATION

I. Communication Skills: Listening, Talking, Advice

Communication is one of the keys to developing a
good working relationship with your probationer. Most courts
list some guidelines for volunteers in regard to communication skills--both listening and talking. Here are some
quotes. (Note: dashes separate quotes from different courts
on the topic.)

First; do listen. Listening, not talking, is the key here.

Be prepared to listen and to understand what your
child says. Maybe it's easier for you to do most of the
talking, even to "preach, " but chances are the child has
had plenty of this before and hasn't responded to it.
What he very likely hasn't had is an adult who will hear
him out, really listen to what he has to say. What the
child has to say may shock you, in its difference from
your own set of values and standards; try therefore to
think of it in terms of its causes, objectively, without
either judging or condoning.
- - - - - - - -

One of the child's important problems, remember, is communication with adults; not because they haven't "talked at" him, but because they haven't listened to him enough.   Therefore, too much talking on your part is more likely to break communication than enhance it.

- - - - - - - -

Create rapport so that intimate problems can be discussed.   Don't talk too much--listen.

- - - - - - - -

If you feel a good lecture coming on, keep still and listen.   I suppose that talking too much is a common shortcoming of teachers, probation officers and parents. We have an over-riding urge to set the child right with our "vocal pearls of wisdom. "   We feel that they just naturally will accept what we say and do it.   If it were that simple, rearing children would be an easy task. We too often rely on exhortations and even threats to get the behavior that we want.

Lecturing and exhorting have a place in good teaching but they must be used sparingly.   Leading the child into a friendly conversation and encouraging him to discuss his problems and plans probably will bring more lasting results.   There is a very thin line of demarcation between lecturing and nagging.   The volunteer probation officer must be a good listener.

Second, listen discriminately.   How to listen is an art.

Listening and hearing--the differences are important between listening to a person and actually hearing what he is saying ... allowing the person to talk because it feels better ... the importance to the offender to be listened to and heard.   Tuning people out ... we do it and so does the offender....   The need to listen for themes in conversations ... what repeats itself may very likely give us clues as to what is bothering the offender.

- - - - - - - -

Still, don't be a naive all-believing listener.   Check the facts whenever you can; see how well what the youngster tells you accords with reality.   When it doesn't, it is frequently good to let him know you know this, kindly but firmly, i. e. , "reality test" for him. As he comes to know that you expect accuracy (within his means to achieve it), maybe he'll get in the habit of producing it more often, and very likely he'll respect you the more because you expect it.

- - - - - - - -

Be a discerning listener. Listening doesn't mean
you have to believe everything you hear. Some of these
kids are pretty skilled manipulators, and have come to
believe that stretching the facts a bit is an effective life
style (they may not even know they do it). Much of this,
too, will just be letting off steam, getting things off
their chest, and within limits, this is a good thing.

- - - - - - - -

Concentrate on the emotions--the music is much more
important than the words. You should try to understand
the underlying feelings and not be overly concerned about
the actual words. As we all know, words can be used
to hide feelings.... Another way of emphasizing this
point is: "It isn't so much what is said, as how it is
said." Also be listening carefully for the feelings; you
can ascertain then what is really important to the client.

- - - - - - - -

Listening and the defining of problems--the most basic
technique employed by the counselor is listening. This
may seem like a very simple thing to do, but, in reality, it is not as simple as it might appear at first
glance. There is a great tendency in all of us as human
beings to want to "stick our two cents in" prematurely.
There is also a great tendency to pass judgment and
moralize. As human beings we may simply fail to
register what we do not wish to hear, or we may dis-
tort the meaning because it touches on something we are
sensitive about. For all of these reasons, as well as
others, it is important for the volunteer counselor to
develop an attitude of patient, objective listening. Remember you are listening for the music and that you are
trying to understand the emotional situation of your client. The comments that you make or the questions that
you ask ought to be primarily for the purpose of eliciting
pertinent data. As the client talks and you listen, you
are trying to understand and define in your own mind
what his problems are. When you are clear as to what
the problems are, you then convey it to the client so
that he should understand what his problems are. Then,
when there is a clear definition of the problems, a cooperative effort between you and the client can be made
to solve them.

I might also state here that listening serves a good
general purpose of catharsis; that is, allowing the client
to verbalize and express pent-up emotion. It might take
considerable, astute listening and questioning in order to
ascertain what the problems are because clients frequently

hide it from themselves because these problems are
painful.

Although listening is very important, there will be
times when talking is necessary.   How to talk becomes important then.   Following are some courts' guidelines for talking.

Respecting the privacy of the juvenile - be cautious
and judicious about asking probing personal questions,
especially early in the relationship.   The response may
be only resentment, until such time as the relationship
can support discussion of personal material.   (Nor
should you assume the youngster wants to hear you discuss your personal life in lieu of his.)
          - - - - - - - -
Don't discuss yourself and your family unless asked.
If you are asked personal questions, however, you should
answer them honestly, even if this is difficult.
          - - - - - - - -
Don't probe into the personal lives or histories of the
children or into reasons why a child is in detention.
Don't ask personal questions, such as last names, where
they are from, parents' names, what school attended,
etc., but do listen and feel free to ask about interests,
hobbies, and what they like to do.
          - - - - - - - -
Use simple language--since the educational and cultural level of the volunteer is apt to be higher than that
of the probationer, it is very important that you use
simple, non-technical language so that you can effectively
communicate with the probationer.   It is obvious that no
matter how astute your observations and how well you
are able to formulate the problems of the probationer,
it will be to no avail if you "talk over his head. "
          - - - - - - - -
Do ... talk on his level.   Don't ... talk above the
probationer and parolee's ability to comprehend and effectively communicate with you.
          - - - - - - - -
You can talk about your participation in the programs
offered and how a child receives help through them.
You might tell of the contrast in a youngster's behavior
as you see him benefitting and perhaps growing emotionally as a result of the help and care he receives here.
You might explain, for example, how a girl without adequate clothing was afforded an opportunity to make some

garments through the sewing program. You can further
in the community the appreciation and support of the
work being done here for children by expressing and
emphasizing the good experiences that children have.
The goals and standards of the Juvenile Department and
its detention facility are high and this can and should be
communicated to the public.

Advice may sometimes be a prime part of what you
say, when you talk. Where, when, and how to give advice
is a very sensitive area, however. Here's what some
courts tell their volunteers about it; volunteers should be
forewarned about giving advice injudiciously.

Advice is a part of counseling but it is not all of it.
It is easy to give but there are some safeguards to
keep in mind. For advice to be most helpful and meaningful, I would suggest that we look for certain things.
(1) Does the person ask for it? (2) Can he take action
without it? (3) Can he use the advice you are giving?
The latter is most important because if we advise someone to do something that he finds impossible to do, he
will find it difficult to come back and face the volunteer
and admit his inadequacy. This sets up an unnecessary
block or wedge between the counselor and his charge.
- - - - - - - -
Advice--it is sometimes helpful to give clients advice, particularly when dealing with younger ones who
have not had the same experience in living as the counselor has had. There also may be times when your objectivity will be very useful in terms of solving a problem that the client is too close to himself. There is a
word of caution here, however, and that is to understand the problem fully and particularly from the client's
point of view. Advice often goes astray if it is given
from the volunteer's point of view rather than the client's. In other words, given a certain situation, you
might solve it in a certain way which would be very
good for you; however, this same type of solution for
the probationer might not be good at all and might not
be in his best interest. It is, therefore, important to
sympathize with your probationer and give advice from
his point of view.

II. Handling of Information: Confidentiality, Reporting

In working with probationers, volunteers will pick up
much confidential information.   Each court should specify
clearly how it wants this issue handled; it needn't be the
same from court to court and probably won't be.   Here's
what some courts tell their volunteers on this issue.

Be discreet.   Respect and safeguard the rights of
children and parents served, to absolute privacy in their
contacts with the department; keep in strict confidence
all information obtained in performance of duty.

- - - - - - - -

Never betray a confidence, even to the court, without
permission from the person who has talked confidentially
to you.   Remember that you are being tested by a mother
(or other client) who cannot quite believe that she has
finally found a friend in whom she can put complete
trust.

- - - - - - - -

You are to keep in strict confidence all personal information regarding your probationer.

- - - - - - - -

Do not break the confidence of the youngster except
with his consent or knowledge.   One of the prime marks
of a volunteer worker is respect for confidential information given by the client.   The fact that the client is
a child is no excuse for gossip.   If the information given
to the worker has to be passed on to the court, the
child will understand and most likely he will give his
consent.   Careless divulging of confidential information
will quickly erode the child's confidence in the worker.

- - - - - - - -

Respect confidentiality at all times.   Anything you
learn or do in relation to the juvenile offender or his
family is not under any circumstances to be divulged to
anyone except duly authorized court people, supervising
your work.

- - - - - - - -

Maintaining confidentiality in regard to the child is an
absolute must that cannot be stressed strongly enough.
Never reveal the identity of any child you meet here.
Do not discuss the cases outside of the department.   If
you know or recognize any of the children, assure them
that you will keep it confidential.   You will be questioned
about the children and pressed for details regarding their
cases.   Since one of your duties as a volunteer is to

represent the department in the community, you will
want to strictly adhere to the department's policy of
protecting the identity of the children detained.

- - - - - - - -

A volunteer may not release information to radio,
press, T. V., or other news media without specific au-
thorization given by the administration of the department.

- - - - - - - -

Respect confidentiality utterly and completely. Whatever you know or surmise about a youngster is under
no circumstances to be divulged or discussed with anyone but a person fully authorized by the court to receive
this information. Not even the fact that he is a juvenile
offender should be disclosed. This stricture is absolute.
Violations are not only highly unethical, they are, if
discovered, as they frequently are, the surest way to
destroy a relationship with the juvenile.

Reporting violations is a very important issue to make
clear with new volunteers. Some courts have strict rules
to follow which may be quite opposite to or at least condition
the rules of confidentiality, as stated by other courts.

Report violations. Confidentiality does not include
keeping known violations a secret from the juvenile officer in charge of the youngster. However easy and
"nice" it may seem to do so, in the long run, sweeping
such things under the rug does the child a disservice,
i. e., he continues to think he can always "get away with
it, " and you, by sacrificing everything to win his friendship, will end up by losing his respect--by being a
"tool" he can do anything with. Report all violations,
promptly. In general, whenever you have the slightest
doubt as to what your legal or law enforcement obligations are, you should check with a supervisory person
in the court. Do this immediately, before taking any
action which might be seriously wrong or even illegal.

- - - - - - - -

You are responsible for immediately informing the
director of any incident which could have a negative effect on your relationship with your probationer.

(Many courts take a softer attitude on the necessity of a volunteer reporting anything but major violations.)

III.   Qualifications and Qualities: What kind of person should
you try to be as a volunteer?

       Some courts have guidelines on dress, language, and
behavior in general.   These guidelines are combined here as
"being a good model. "

       Clothing should be neat.   The way a volunteer looks
is an example to the children, and an attractive appearance is always appreciated by them.   Conservative
clothing will keep both you and the children at ease.
       - - - - - - - -
       Dress--neatly and casually--going easy on the make-
up.
       - - - - - - - -
       Be a good behavior model for the child.   One of the
best things you can do is to become, in your own behavior, a good model for the youngster.   If your own
dress, language and behavior is not of a good standard,
you can scarcely expect it from your probationer.
Chances are he has had enough "bad models" already;
give him a good one.
       There is another respect in which it is especially im-
portant that your own conduct be above reproach while
working for the court; in that you represent the court
and your behavior reflects on the court at all times.
You may justifiably consider a few hours volunteer work
in the court as but a portion of your life; mainly you
may be a college student, a housewife or a businessman.
Others do not make that distinction so readily.   To them
you are a court person, and expected fully to meet the
high standards the court itself expects of others (much
the same thing as community expectations of teachers
and ministers).   If you do not do this, the court will
come in for heavy criticism to which it is very vulnerable, perhaps more so than you yourself are.   This is
not a hypothetical situation; it has happened, and quite
painfully, in a few cases.   Before accepting court volunteer work, you must decide to live up to this special
condition.   If you don't feel you can, no harm is done,
provided it is stated clearly to us beforehand.
       - - - - - - - -
       Identification--if one is to be effective, particularly
with younger clients, it is important that you set a good
example in much the same way as a parent would to
their children.   There is a great tendency for the probationer to identify with the volunteer; that is, he may

assume the mannerisms and even the way of thinking of
the volunteer. You thus have a big responsibility to
conduct yourself in the most honorable, conscientious,
sincere way you can.

- - - - - - - -

Letting the offender get to know you--setting an example in terms of behavior. Serving as a new model.
Stress is placed here on the experience we have had intimately knowing a good model, and the importance of
this to the offender, even though he may be threatened
by it. Part of good counseling is being a good teacher.
The concept of a corrective experience implies that new
models are introduced that can correct old misconceptions.

- - - - - - - -

Actions may speak louder than words, and the value
of being able to perform a task for the offender is
stressed as a means of letting the offender know his
volunteer.

Besides being generally a good model, courts often
ask more specific qualities of a volunteer. Some courts
list these qualities separately while others prefer to combine them into one single guideline. Here are some volunteer qualifications in a "nutshell."

Qualifications of the volunteer--the most important
single qualification is to be a good human being in the
best sense of that term. This includes the basic virtues
of honesty, integrity, fairness, objectivity, kindness and
understanding. Obviously, if we are to establish rapport and to gain the client's respect, we must demonstrate these kinds of qualities to him. It is not enough
just to tell him that we want to help; we must conduct
ourselves in such a manner as to make this obvious to
him.

- - - - - - - -

Personality: the volunteer must have good judgment,
sympathy, resilience, and the ability to deal with all
kinds of people.

- - - - - - - -

Be supportive, encouraging, friendly, but also firm.
Whatever role and obligation you have, as the youngster's "conscience," to oppose and report infractions,
you can still be supportive, encouraging, friendly, to the
limit possible. Indeed, respect and friendship will be
far more solid with both if the child knows that at the

same time as you appreciate and respond to efforts at
self-improvement, you will be firm, honest, and objective in disapproving where this is warranted.

Following by category are some volunteer qualities
courts feel important enough to list separately.

Persistence.

We will probably find the misdemeanant oriented to
failure and expecting failure in himself. Persistence is
a key part of counseling in that it conveys to the misdemeanant that we will not give up on him. This in itself is important when we realize that the misdemeanant
expects to be a disappointment.
                  - - - - - - - -
The volunteer should be persistent and aggressive in
a healthy way--be able to go out toward people.

Patience.

Remember that children change and grow by spurts.
A graph of change will likely show an upward trend with
some valleys of retrogression and some plateaus showing
little change. Rehabilitation is a slow process in most
instances. Occasionally we see a youngster who seems
to change his direction all at once. But this is not the
pattern. Consistent and persistent care, guidance and
control over a period of time may bring some evidence
of success.
                  - - - - - - - -
Don't expect overnight miracles. When things have
been going wrong for years and years with a child, they
don't get corrected in a few weeks or months. Indeed,
the positive impact of your work may not have decisive
effects till long after you've stopped working with a
youngster; you may never even see them. It takes time.
Even if slow progress is visible, there will be frequent
setbacks.
                  - - - - - - - -
Be ready for such setbacks, with patience and the
ability to deal with your own disappointment and heartbreak. That does not mean you can't show anger-under-
control as a normal human would respond to "bad" behavior. But do not vent your frustration and anger on
the child; it's a very easy trap to fall into, even unconsciously. Although we all like to achieve success with

a child, remember he does not owe it to us; he owes it
only to himself.

- - - - - - - -

Exercise patience, wisdom, and understanding. Sometimes positive results do not appear on the surface until
a much later time.

Consistency.

Be kind and consistent in your attitude toward each.
Avoid favoritism towards one child and rejection of
another.

- - - - - - - -

Present your ideas clearly, firmly, simply. Always
mean what you say, and be consistent. Never make a
promise or proposal unless you've thought it through
first, and are fully prepared to back it up. The juvenile will test you, "call your bluff," and see if you will
in fact consistently deliver as promised, either as rewards or in backing up the limits you set. Be serious
about the limits when he tests you, and the rewards
when you've promised them and he has delivered. All
this is an important part of his learning to trust you
(which will come slowly in any case).

Empathy.

Empathy--this refers to an attitude of attempting to
put yourself in the probationer's place. In essence, you
are trying to imagine how the probationer must feel in
the situation he is in by trying to imagine how you might
feel if you were in such a situation. In that way you
can begin to understand your probationer.

- - - - - - - -

Being able to feel with another person gives him
strength, but to feel like him will make him feel you
are as powerless as he is. We can easily over-identify
with the offender if we have had similar experiences
and perceive them in the way he does. Being the stronger of the two, the volunteer must maintain control of
feelings.

- - - - - - - -

Provide empathy. Don't provide sympathy.

Friendliness.

Try to learn first names and call the youngsters by

name as much as possible. This is a small thing, but
in calling by name you communicate friendliness and
warmth. (Volunteers in detention)

- - - - - - - -

Give your home number to your probationer. This
is most important as a gesture of trust and friendship.

- - - - - - - -

Give attention and affection. The child you're working with may never have known really sustained attention
and affection, and (at least at first) he may not know
how to handle it in a normal way, i. e. , he may tend
just to grab it up hungrily without giving in return.

- - - - - - - -

Attempt to persuade rather than try to force or in-
timidate the child. Don't be discouraged by setbacks or
disappointments in the relationship.

- - - - - - - -

Promote a genuine friendship based on respect and
understanding of the youngster. Some seem to feel that
friendship with the youngster is a threat to the worker's
authority. Others voice the opinion that the relationship
should be strictly professional. If the latter means objectivity, non-involvement and remoteness, we must
stop and review relationships and responsibilities in the
juvenile court setting.

- - - - - - - -

Above all, be honest and sincere and don't force
yourself to show affection or attention if you genuinely
don't feel it. Don't impose yourself on a child, but do
be friendly, kind and pleasant, thereby making yourself
receptive for a relationship.

Honesty--Trust.

Do be frank and truthful in your relationship. Don't
be untruthful or unrealistic with the child.

- - - - - - - -

Build on trust even though you are crossed up occasionally. Many of the youngsters interviewed in "The
Child's View of the Court" project stated that the thing
that got them down was not to be trusted. One boy
said, "I let my probation officer down and I felt pretty
bad. He got me another break and I'm not about to let
him down again. " Trust can be a bridge to self respect
and responsibility.

- - - - - - - -

When asked to comment upon a finished product, give

an honest answer. Praise the work and the child if you
can, but if it is a sloppy job, the child can tell, so
don't smooth it over. Suggest it would only take a few
minutes to re-sew a dart, for example, and the girl
would be much happier with it.

- - - - - - - -

Display a genuine interest in the youngster and his
family. Unless you have a genuine interest, you cannot
display it. When you are assigned a youth with whom
you are to work, do you get a lift? Are you anxious
to get acquainted with him and share his problems? Do
you look forward to an appointment with him--or is it
an unpleasant task? There is nothing more trying than
to be a volunteer or probation officer without a real interest in youth. Of course, it follows that you develop
an interest in his family if you are interested in him.

- - - - - - - -

Promises must not be made lightly. If you cannot
make good on a promise, give an explanation. Keeping
promises is tangible evidence of the volunteer's honesty
and his respect for the youngster. Occasionally the
volunteer will find it impossible to make good on a
promise. An explanation that is reasonable will probably
satisfy the child if the disappointment is not repeated
too often.

- - - - - - - -

Don't let the kid down even in apparently small things,
like showing up for appointments, and being on time.
If you don't show responsibility as a model for him, you
cannot expect him to learn it for himself.

Respect.

If you make an appointment, keep it. If this is not
possible, call or send a note to explain why you cannot
be at her home at the time she expects you.

- - - - - - - -

Be on time and faithful to your obligation. Don't be
undependable or late for your appointments.

- - - - - - - -

Be as punctual with the child as you expect him to
be. Children deserve this courtesy just the same as
adults do. It is evidence that we have respect for them.

- - - - - - - -

Show respect--something that most of us take for
granted. We overlook that for the offender respect is
something he has perhaps not experienced and is

consequently unfamiliar with.   In this sense, this simple
act has tremendous impact in developing a corrective
experience.
    The question raised - can we respect someone we
don't like?   Can we respect someone whose morals run
counter to ours?   Mention is made of the meaning of
what some might consider to be immoral behavior.   It
is suggested that we as people all have mature and immature sides.   We need to speak to the mature part of
the person.   In this respect we try to deal with a person's present and future rather than his past.   To dwell
on an unsavory past will only weaken the individual by
giving him more opportunity to justify his present functioning on the basis of past deprivation.   We may see
in the offender's behavior some of the same things we
dislike in our own behavior.   We may also see the offender manifesting certain behavior we are struggling to
control in ourselves.   Perhaps if we recognize this, we
can keep from over-reacting.
- - - - - - - -
    Show respect for the probationer - I mean to respect
his individuality and his basic rights as a fellow human
being.   It means to view him with the dignity that another
human being in trouble deserves.   There is no room for
narrow prejudices, provincialism or haughtiness.   Basically, you must like the person in order to do an effective job.   If you dislike a probationer and cannot resolve
this within yourself, it is best not to work with him.

IV.   What to Expect and Not to Expect

Don't expect thanks for displays of affection.

    For one thing, don't expect explicit thanks and grati-
tude either from the child or his parents.   Even if the
child feels it, he may not know how to express and communicate it, may actually be embarrassed by it.   In
fact, puzzled by what your role is, and angry at being
on probation, the child may frequently focus his resentment on you, and this will be hard to take when you
know you're only trying to help him.   But though your
work is not rewarded by specific "thank you's, " it is in
the long run appreciated, probably more than you or we
shall ever know.
- - - - - - - -
    Don't expect thanks or a show of appreciation.   If you

need to have an outward sign of appreciation you may
often be disappointed in this work as so many of the
children are not able to demonstrate or verbalize their
thanks even if they feel it. We must be mature enough
and have sufficient feelings of security and adequacy to
be able to give without expecting anything in return.

Expect the best.

As a part of discussion in the matter of expectations,
we talk about change occurring in the adult and that we
need to expect and demand change in people even if a
pattern may have been established. We assume that an
old dog can be taught new tricks. People continually
mature and mellow. We need to capitalize on this process.

- - - - - - - -

Even in discussing with the youngster possible or unproven violations, be honest and firm when you disapprove. This is not inconsistent with being supportive
and friendly, whenever possible. After all, if you don't
stand for something in his eyes, there are very few
others who will.

Accept situations and people as they are.

The volunteer must not be too rigid or too easily
shocked at the problems she finds, or she can't be
helpful to the child or his family.

- - - - - - - -

I might also add here that your probationer is apt to
come from a different socio-economic group from your
own, and here again, it is important that you do not try
to foist your values onto him. They may serve you
well but be useless to him, and if he tried to adopt
them, it would only lead to more difficulty for him.
Your aim should be to attempt to have the client develop
his own potentialities to the fullest.

- - - - - - - -

Don't pre-judge, particularly at first. Keep an open
mind on the probationer especially when first getting to
know him. Avoid forming fixed and premature opinions
until you've done a lot of discerning listening, and
gathered all the background information you can.

- - - - - - - -

Always accept the family at the level at which you
find it, remembering that there are many cultures other

than your own. Do not criticize, even by implication,
family patterns, housekeeping standards, the children,
or the presence of boy friends or girl friends.

- - - - - - - -

Accept the youngster as he is and do not allow his
behavior or environment to affect your respect for him
as a human being. We cannot allow our prejudices to
obscure our evaluation of the youngster as a person.
Of course, we cannot condone his misbehavior, but we
must make it apparent that we see his good traits too.
Many of the youngsters who commit delinquent acts have
a low estimate of their worth. As one girl said in an
interview, "I ran away from the Detention Home and
they caught me. But I wasn't worth running after."

- - - - - - - -

Believe that human beings can change their behavior
patterns. Unless we accept this idea the whole concept
of rehabilitation is meaningless.

- - - - - - - -

Holding out expectations - as volunteers, we can trap
ourselves into thinking that because a person is a failure
he will continue to be a failure. If we feel this in
terms of an attitude, we can be sure that the offender
will pick up this feeling and act in the way we expect
him to act. The reverse is also true.

- - - - - - - -

Expect the best from youngsters, but do not be unduly
upset if you get the worst. The volunteer must have an
optimistic viewpoint with youngsters. This optimism
may rub off on the youngster and help him to develop a
better feeling about himself. Chances are great that he
will make mistakes and we must encourage him to try
again. Old habits cannot be changed overnight. Many
new starts must be made. Our faith in the youngster
can become the greatest motivation for him to improve.

V.   Strategies and Situations

Attention and Encouragement.

Give sincere interest and attention to them as individuals and try to respond to the interests and needs of the
child rather than to what you personally like or dislike
in their behavior.

- - - - - - - -

Do praise the child for even small accomplishments.

Don't criticize. Offer suggestions.

- - - - - - - -

    Do encourage initiative and creativity. Don't discour-
age trivial efforts.

- - - - - - - -

    Always identify some of the youngster's good points
and emphasize them. When he knows that you recognize
his good traits, he is more receptive of your criticism.
Not many people are persuaded by a blunt statement that
"you are wrong. " Such an approach only sets their defenses. After all, we are concerned with selling the
youngster on the merits of sound ethical conduct as a
way of life. It is doubtful that we can impose those
standards. But we can sell them if we follow sound
principles. One of those sound principles is to identify
the youngster's good points before we get to the criticisms.

- - - - - - - -

    Do recognize the child's capabilities, either limited
or above average. Don't resent the child's initial attitude toward you.

Hostility, anger, and fear.

    The matter of anger: do we allow ourselves to ex-
press anger and disappointment when we feel this way
toward the offender? I stress the need to allow expressions of anger and disappointment as one way of showing
concern. I differentiate the difference between losing
control of anger and rejecting, or a measured response
of anger with continued acceptance of the individual. I
stress that we should not be using our energy to keep
back genuine feelings. The offender needs to know the
volunteer has limits to his patience and is not God.

- - - - - - - -

    Hostility--when confronted with a hostile child, don't
force conversation upon him; move on to others who
may be eager to visit with you. Never respond to hostility with anger as this simply reinforces the child's behavior and begets more hostility.

- - - - - - - -

    Don't be afraid of the children. You will find that
even though most have serious problems, when you meet
them here in the group work situation, they are very
much like any other teenagers.

- - - - - - - -

    Using the crisis--the misdemeanant lives with a crisis

much of the time and in fact his whole life is often one
big crisis. He is accustomed to being overcome by
crisis and expects to be defeated. The volunteer is in
a position to stand by his charge during a crisis, and
may be able to help the person overcome this situation
and turn habitual defeat into victory.

- - - - - - - -

Swearing--if a child curses, tests, makes cutting remarks or attempts to agitate you, above all try not to
fall into the trap of responding in a hostile, sarcastic,
or anxious manner. Don't act shocked. Retain your
composure, ignore it, and chances are the child will
feel no further reason to irritate you. If swearing or
such is done repeatedly, you can call it to the attention
of the houseparent and he will deal with the situation.

- - - - - - - -

Do accept the individual as he is. Don't compare his
values with yours. Because of his background and environment, his sense of values may be vastly different
from yours.

- - - - - - - -

Accept the children as human beings with problems
and as individuals who are no better or worse than any
of us. Accept them as they are rather than as you
would like them to be. Assume a non-judgmental attitude toward the children so that you will be able to give
the acceptance they so badly need. Everyone needs acceptance in order to grow, whether it be you or me or
your child or mine. This need is no different in the
children here and must be met by those of us who come
into contact with them.

Aspirations for the Probationer.

Timing--it is very tempting to give immediate solutions to the offender. We should remember, however,
that while we may arrive at a solution to a problem in
one way, this may still mean that another person who
feels obligated to accept a solution foreign to him may
never really identify with it. He may merely go through
the motions.

- - - - - - - -

Don't rush it, but as the relationship develops you
can encourage the youngster to think about himself, his
actions, goals, etc., and from that knowledge plan together more constructive activities from which he'll derive a measure of self-respect and success. Many of

our youngsters have previously done almost no careful
thinking about themselves in any planful, forward-looking
way.   They seem almost to run away from self-awareness.

- - - - - - - -

Set up realistic goals--as you begin to understand
your client and his problems you should begin thinking
of realistic solutions.   These should be presented as
tentative suggestions rather than as affirmative com-
mands.   The emphasis also must be on the realities of
the situation, his capabilities and his inadequacies.   The
reality possibilities will obviously depend on his external
situation.

- - - - - - - -

Help the youngster to develop a dream or goal.   Life
without direction or goals can become monotonous, meaningless, and confusing.   On the other hand, a goal can
motivate, bring hope and interest to one's daily activities.   Even an unrealistic goal is better than none.
Half the fun is planning and working toward accomplish-
ment.   Many times the unreachable and the unaccom-
plished serves its purpose very well.   The volunteer
probation officer must encourage the youngster to give
thought to the future.   The youngster must set his own
goals, however unrealistic they are.   There is plenty
of time for them to introduce realism.   Youth, because
of their enthusiasm and optimism, are apt to do quite a
bit of dreaming.   Encourage them to dream.   Even
though we never reach the top of the mountain, every
step up the path broadens our horizon.

- - - - - - - -

Since it is unrealistic to expect to change a youngster's entire behavior, attitudes, and environment immediately, we should concentrate on one or two basic
problems of each youngster and work toward a solution
with him.   The youngster's problems may be very complex and an attempt to solve all of them at once may be
frustrating and discouraging to all concerned.   On the
other hand, success in one or two areas should bring
satisfaction and encouragement.   Children as well as
adults need to be successful at something.

- - - - - - - -

Causing the offender to feel discomfort - if a person
remains frustrated long enough, he will find a way of
adapting to his situation.   Having made this adaptation,
he may even become comfortable with it and consider
change to be too much of a risk.   It is difficult to bring

about discomfort, but my suggestion is that where you
notice an offender's dissatisfaction with his lot in life,
move in to exploit it. To the extent that is possible attempt to bring about discomfort in terms of holding out
expectations and demands. Get the person to want something and help him go after it. The offender may or
may not feel guilt to the extent we do, but he seems to
find different ways of expressing it. I would hope that
to whatever extent possible we try to promote appropriate guilt feelings in the person. He needs to handle his
guilt in more constructive terms than acting in such a
way as to bring about punishment to alleviate guilt.

VI. Authority of the Court

A volunteer should be very clear about the court and
his relationship to it. Keeping in contact with the officer
in charge is very important. Some quotations from courts
in this area follow:

For those working directly with juveniles and especially those in APO and DPO volunteer programs, it is essential that court orders concerning juveniles be understood and complied with. Most of us fully appreciate
the counseling and rehabilitation aspects of our work
and there is no intent to minimize these here. On the
other hand, it must be understood that in court work
with adjudicated delinquents, this counseling and rehabilitation action must take place within a necessary framework of the juvenile's compliance with the requirements
of law and his probationary rules.
- - - - - - - -
You, as a volunteer, are responsible for meeting
your probationer's staff counselor for consultation on a
bi-monthly basis.
- - - - - - - -
Notify supervisors of any pending court appearances
of your probationer or parolee. Don't appear in court
on behalf of the probationer without the knowledge and
concurrence of supervisors.
- - - - - - - -
Houseparents will supply us with any information they
feel we should know about a child if unusual behavior is
anticipated.
- - - - - - - -
Advise the court as much as you can, but it must be

obvious to the child that the disposition is determined
by the judge. It is very important that the child and
his parents understand the relationship between themselves, the volunteer court workers and the judge. It
seems logical that the judge should take responsibility
for the basic decisions of the court. It seems reasonable that the judge will depend on the volunteer probation officer to interpret the child and his family to the
court and even make some recommendations to the court
when he so requests. But it should be evident to the
child that the judge has made his decision after considering carefully the information received from all reliable sources. This puts the probation officer in the
position of the representative of both the court and the
child. Some youngsters interviewed in "The Child's
View of the Court" project stated that the probation officer defended them in the hearing. This surely puts
the probation officer in a favorable position with the
youngster.

- - - - - - - -

Never attempt to interpret court procedures or policies to family members.

- - - - - - - -

Notify the staff probation officer if you are to be out
of the city for any extended period of time. Explain
that you will be away and will get in touch with them
when you return.

- - - - - - - -

Keep in contact not only with the child, but with the
juvenile department. The APO, tutor, or other volunteer worker reports you fill out on each contact with the
child are extremely important in keeping the juvenile
officer in charge of the child fully advised as to the
child's progress with you and the other volunteers working with him. Please file and return these reports fully
and promptly. It's crucial. Also come in and see us
as frequently as you can, with your ideas, reports, suggestions, and problems. We're here to help too, and
the staff juvenile officer in overall charge of your youngster is the one person who has all the threads in his
hands since he alone receives reports from all volunteers and agencies working with that child.

VII.   Use of Authority and Discipline by Volunteers

The volunteer's use of authority in dealing with probationers varies widely from court to court. Here's what
some courts have to say about this to their volunteers.

Establish a friendly working relationship with the person with whom you are working. Don't exercise or use
authority--this is vested in the probation and parole
supervisor.

- - - - - - - -

Be a friend and companion. Don't be another authority figure in the child's life.

- - - - - - - -

Encourage obedience to the parent or guardian. Don't
encourage the child to question the parents' authority.

- - - - - - - -

Discipline, authority and supervision--don't ever discipline a child or give one child responsibility for supervising another. If a child overwhelms you in terms of
his acting out or behavior problems, confer with the
houseparents, but never threaten a child with "I'll get
the houseparent. " Volunteers are not responsible for
supervision of the children; the houseparents are. We
do not have the authority to discipline or the ability to
deal with difficult behavior problems. Volunteers are
never left alone with the youngster as there are always
houseparents on duty.

- - - - - - - -

Don't over-identify with children by behaving as they
do or by joining them on their level. Find a meeting
ground where you can relate to them while maintaining
a friendly adult attitude. In relating to them on the level
of a peer, you may think you are really "in, " but this
isn't a good relationship. The children should aspire to
our level, rather than our resorting to theirs.

- - - - - - - -

Encourage school attendance. Don't criticize teachers
or schools.

- - - - - - - -

Remember that youngsters respect discipline if it is
reasonable and is invoked by a person who they know
respects them. Discipline and control are a part of the
process of the rehabilitation of a wayward youngster.
Since the juvenile court complements, or substitutes for
the family, it must initiate control and discipline, since
these are prime functions of the family. In the family,

discipline is proof of the affection of the parents for the
child. There are some who believe that discipline, to
be effective, should be accompanied by toughness, harsh-
ness, sarcasm, and anger. Probably it is more effective in the long run to invoke penalties with kindness
and dignity. There is a good deal of wisdom in the old
cliche, "It hurts me more than it does you. "

- - - - - - - -

Use of authority - the authority that the volunteer
counselor will find most helpful is the implicit authority of his personal psychological strength as demonstrated by the fact that he is a successful person. The
counselor has the expertise of knowing how to get along
in this world, whereas the offender does not. This kind
of authority in the long run will serve you better than
the authority to penalize. The authority of enforcement
and penalizing is present, but it rests with the police
and court judges.

- - - - - - - -

Identify a real need of the youngster and attempt to
satisfy it early in the association. Such action serves
to convince the youngster that the volunteer officer is
more than an authority figure. It is proof of the officer's desire to help the youngster. Of course, this
strengthens the authority of the officer.

VIII.   Volunteer Commitment to the Court and the Probationer

A volunteer must know what commitment is expected
of him prior to starting work for the court. This varies
from place to place but is an important guideline to know.
Most courts don't handle this point as a rule or guideline,
but one does so in this way:

Commitment - a volunteer must be willing to be involved in the program for a period of one year, devot-
ing at least two hours each week to the assigned case.

Then there is the commitment to the probationer--regularity
is the password here.

Keep in contact with the child. Rome wasn't built in
a day, nor is a child's life rebuilt in a day. Whatever
your volunteer job, be prepared to invest some time
with the child. We recommend at least one visit a
week as a minimum. Occasional contacts are unlikely

to make the kind of impression we need.

- - - - - - - -

See the youngster regularly and often. Most youngsters who are adjudicated delinquents expect something
to happen when the court takes over. Though a few want
to be left alone, a great majority value the contacts with
the volunteer probation officer if they sense that he really
wants to help them. In fact, the restrictions imposed
and the activities suggested are evidence that he is interested in them. The successful contact must offer
positive help and some satisfaction to the youngster. If
it can be raised from the level of jailer versus criminal,
to that of friend meets friend, success is bound to follow.

- - - - - - - -

You are responsible for meeting your probationer for
a minimum of three hours a week, each week. If you
are unable to meet your probationer (for reasons of illness, emergency, etc.), you are to contact your probationer by phone or letter. Volunteers who leave for
vacation during their nine month obligation will also continue contacts, through the period they are away, by letters and phone calls. Regular meetings will be resumed
upon return.

- - - - - - - -

Make yourself available to the child.

- - - - - - - -

Always make daytime calls at times convenient both
to yourself and the family.

IX.   Knowing Your Job, Your Probationer, Your Community

Know your job. A volunteer should be very clear on
his specific job. He must be willing to work within the system. Here's what some courts say to volunteers about it.

Know your job. Much of the above depends on what
volunteer job you have. Group discussion leaders have
"privileged communication" with probationers, for example. APO's and DPO's do not, and must report most
violations. Be sure you discuss with a juvenile officer
or chief volunteer and understand thoroughly your particular volunteer role, before beginning work. Know its
possibilities and its limits. In general, your volunteer
initiatives are encouraged but do not expand your role,
e. g. from tutor to APO, or APO to tutor, even

unofficially, until you consult thoroughly with a regular
staff person. This includes extras like taking the youngster on a trip with your family, etc.

Know your probationer and his world. Knowing your
job, knowing the community you will work in, and knowing
all you can about the probationer are key things to arm yourself with prior to the first meeting.

Familiarize yourself with the range of services in the
court and community from which your child might benefit. Do not hesitate to suggest to us that they be added,
if you think it appropriate.
- - - - - - - -
Attempt to differentiate between a withdrawn and a
hostile child. A withdrawn child can use your attention.
- - - - - - - -
Know your youngster; get all the information you can
on him. Some volunteers prefer to form their initial
opinions solely by direct contact with a child and not by
previous study of the extensive files we have on him.
Others prefer to study these files first, but at some
point you will want to take advantage of the enormous
stores of information in the youngster's file at the probation department. You'll need all the background you
can get on the whole child, and you'll be missing vital
parts of it if you don't study this resource file. It contains home and school investigation reports, continuous
evaluative comments and reports by regular staff and
volunteers, personality, attitude, aptitude, school
achievement, optometric and audiological test results,
and basic papers describing the child's family background, record of previous offenses, legal status as an
adjudicated delinquent, etc. This file, and other information resources at the court are to be studied only at
the court; they cannot be taken out except in very rare
cases with clear and explicit special permission from
regular staff.

Work with family and friends of the probationer. In
the role of the volunteer it is inevitable that the relationship
extends beyond the probationer to the family and peer group.
A volunteer can easily get caught in the middle. Several
courts warn against being "caught between." Others give
clues for establishing working relationships with the family
and peers.

Case background--sometimes a child will need to tell
you the details of his case in an attempt to get your
support. Don't be drawn into giving an opinion on the
facts related to persons involved. (You might say that
you can understand why he might feel a certain way,
agreeing, disagreeing, or having an opinion.)

- - - - - - - -

The volunteer is the representative of the court.
When the court intervenes in the life of a youngster, it
becomes a partner of the family and in many cases, a
substitute for the family. The juvenile code states,
"Each child coming within the jurisdiction of the court
shall receive such care, guidance and control, preferably in his own home, as will be conducive to the child's
welfare and the best interests of the state and that when
such child is removed from control of his parents, the
court shall secure for him care as nearly as possible
equivalent to the care which should have been given to
him by them. "
Since we know that the prime purpose of the family
is to help the youngster develop a respect for himself
through friendship and affection, it seems illogical that
the court and the probation officer hold themselves aloof
from a genuine friendship with the youngster. In many
cases the main thing the youngster needs is a friend
who really cares.

- - - - - - - -

To attempt to help the child without reference to his
family is to disregard the genesis of his attitudes, habits,
and values, and to disregard one of your fundamental
purposes, namely, to help the youngster to become an
efficient member of the family unit.

- - - - - - - -

Recognize the teenager's close ties with his peers.
The volunteer probation officer must constantly be aware
of the intensity of teenage friendships. It is not uncom-
mon for a youth to run the risk of disgracing his family
in order to save face with teenage friends. An attack
on his friends is a direct attack on the child. Many
times it is very important to break such friendships. In
these cases it is better to say that both are good kids,
but that they are not good for one another. To bawl a
youngster out in the presence of his friends is fatal.
You surely will set his defenses and invite discourteous
behavior. If reprimands are necessary, they will be
done more effectively in private.

- - - - - - - -

Encourage the family relationship.   Don't attempt to
usurp parental authority.
- - - - - - - -
If there is an alcoholic in the child's family, help the
child to understand that the alcoholic has a very serious
illness.   An understanding of the situation may help the
child to have a little more patience and kindliness with
the afflicted parent.   Surely patience and kindness are a
good substitute for bitterness.
- - - - - - - -
Avoid being "caught in the middle. " You can be a
liaison between the child and his world, but be careful
not to get "caught" between the child and his parents,
the child and his teachers, the child and the court, especially as an intercessor in some way used by the child
against his parents, or vice versa.   Frequently, this
happens when you succumb to the temptation to be liked
by the child at all costs, to be a "nice guy" no matter
what.   It can easily happen here that the child will then
"use" you in the conflict with authority which is often
his control problem.
Relations with the child's parents are a particularly
sensitive area.   Move with care here and inform yourself as fully as possible early in the relationship by discussions with the juvenile officer in charge of the child,
etc.   In general, remember that though your own relationship with the child is naturally foremost in your
mind, he has other important relationships as well: to
his parents, peers, teachers, etc.   Give some careful
thought and attention to these too.
- - - - - - - -
Remember that a child may love an immoral and dis-
solute parent dearly.   This situation calls for delicacy
and careful consideration.   The child is torn between
his love for the parent and the realization that the parent's conduct is unacceptable to him and society.   It
seems reasonable that we spare the child the anguish of
giving evidence against the parent.   The volunteer worker may help by sympathy and understanding of the child's
dilemma.
- - - - - - - -
Close acquaintance with his family is paramount.   It
is a courtesy if nothing more.   It is very important the
court try to work with and through the family.   If the
family is bypassed by the court, it can easily become
alienated from the court and its purposes.   But if the
family understands that the court's primary purpose is

to help the child, it can give support to the court and
gain a good deal of understanding of the child in the
process. The intervention of the court is in itself a
threat to the family. Neutralizing this feeling calls for
care and consideration of the family's rights and prerog-
atives. In the first instance the court can well afford
to assume that the family is anxious that its child behave properly. Probably the support of the family can
best be gained through respectful and courteous treatment. The use of authority to gain the cooperation of
the family should be the last resort.

When to help or not to help. Some courts deem it
necessary to advise their volunteers about providing physical
help to their probationer and his family.

Feel free to provide used clothing or household items
that are needed if these things can be donated by yourself or your friends without cost to you.
- - - - - - - -
Use your car for the transportation of family members in emergencies only. You must decide what constitutes an emergency. Do not provide free taxi service.
- - - - - - - -
Never give money to any member of the family. This
is most important.
- - - - - - - -
Help them solve financial problems for themselves,
but don't lend money.

SECTION TWO: HOW ONE COURT DOES IT

You can't use all of the foregoing in your own set of
aphorisms, just a selection from among them, plus your own
additions. Here is an example of one set that one juvenile
court probation department has used successfully. Note
especially a certain continuity or flow between one aphorism
and another. This you have to do for yourself, blending together the aphorisms you choose into more of a continuous
readable unit. (Taken from the Boulder Juvenile Court
"Volunteer Orientation Manual. ")

"We realize fully that working with juveniles cannot
be reduced to 'cookbook' form. Much will always be left to
your own good judgment. Every case has much of the
unique in it and can't be handled exclusively in terms of
general rules.

"As a general rule, our juvenile probation staff feels
that respect is the keystone in working with a juvenile offender. Your ultimate goal, counseling, is not possible until
he respects and trusts you as a person. He will never respect you until he realizes that he cannot 'con' you and that
you will not 'con' him. He has very probably learned that
he can in many respects 'con' most of the people like yourself that he has come into contact with (school, parents,
employers, etc.). You must be different. You must be
honest. Never make a promise or a threat that you cannot
back up. When he realizes that this situation is really 'for
real,' then you will begin to make some progress. Within
this general framework here are some guidelines well worth
your thinking about as points of departure around which to
build and organize your own personal experiences working
with juveniles.

"1. Keep in contact with the child. Rome wasn't
built in a day nor is a child's life rebuilt in a day. Whatever your volunteer job, be prepared to invest some time
with the child. We recommend at least one visit a week as
a minimum. Occasional contacts are unlikely to make the
kind of impression we need.

"Keep in contact not only with the child but with the
juvenile department. The APO, tutor, or other reports you
fill out on each contact with the child are extremely important in keeping the Juvenile Officer in charge of the child
fully advised as to the child's progress with you and the other volunteers working with him. Please file and return
these reports fully and promptly. It's crucial.

"Also come in and see us as frequently as you can,
with your ideas, reports, suggestions and problems. We're
here to help, too, and the Juvenile Officer in overall charge
of your youngster is the one person who has all threads in
his hands since he alone receives reports from all volunteers
and agencies working with that child.

"2. Patience: Don't expect overnight miracles.
When things have been going wrong for years and years with
a child, they don't get corrected in a few weeks or months.
Indeed, the positive impact of your work may not have decisive effects till long after you've stopped working with a
youngster; you may never even see them.

"It takes time. Even if slow progress is visible,

there will be frequent setbacks.

"3. <u>Be ready for such setbacks</u>; with patience and
the ability to deal with your own disappointment and heartbreak. That does not mean you can't show anger-under-
control as a normal human would respond to 'bad' behavior.
But do not vent your frustration and anger on the child; it's
a very easy trap to fall into, even unconsciously. Although
we all like to achieve success with a child, remember he
does not <u>owe</u> it to us; he owes it only to himself.

"4. <u>Give attention and affection.</u> The child you're
working with may never have known really sustained attention
and affection, and (at least at first) he may not know how
to handle it in a normal way, i.e., he may tend just to slop
it up hungrily without giving in return.

"For one thing, <u>don't expect explicit thanks and grati-
tude</u> either from the child or his parents. Even if the child
feels it, he may not know how to express and communicate
it, may actually be embarrassed by it. In fact, puzzled by
what your role is, and angry at being on probation, the
child may frequently focus his resentment on you, and this
will be hard to take when you know you're only trying to
help him.

"But though your work is not rewarded by specific
thank-you's, it is in the long run appreciated, probably more
than you or we shall ever know.

"5. <u>Be prepared to listen and to understand</u> what
your child says. Maybe it's easier for you to do most of
the talking, even to 'preach,' but chances are the child has
had plenty of this before and hasn't responded to it. What
he very likely <u>hasn't</u> had is an adult who will hear him out,
really listen to what he has to say. What the child has to
say may shock you, in its difference from your own set of
values and standards; try therefore to think of it in terms
of its causes, objectively, without either judging or condoning.

'One of the child's important problems, remember,
is communication with adults; not because they haven't
'talked at' him, but because they haven't listened to him
enough. Therefore, <u>too much talking on your part</u> is more
likely to break communication than enhance it.

"6. Be a discerning listener. Listening doesn't mean you have to believe everything you hear. Some of these kids are pretty skilled manipulators, and have come to believe that stretching the facts a bit is an effective life style (they may not even know they do it). Much of this, too, will be just letting off steam, getting things off their chest, and within limits, this is a good thing.

"Still, don't be a naive all-believing listener. Check the facts whenever you can; see how well what the youngster tells you accords with reality. When it doesn't, it is frequently good to let him know you know this, kindly but firmly, i. e., "reality test" for him. As he comes to know that you expect accuracy (within his means to achieve it), maybe he'll get in the habit of producing it more often, and very likely he'll respect you the more because you expect it.

"7. Don't pre-judge, particularly at first. Keep an open mind on the probationer especially when first getting to know him. Avoid forming fixed and premature opinions, until you've done a lot of discerning listening, and gathered all the background information you can.

"8. Know your youngster; get all the information you can on him. Some volunteers prefer to form their initial opinions solely by direct contact with a child and not by previous study of the extensive files we have on him. Others prefer to study these files first, but at some point you will want to take advantage of the enormous stores of information in the youngster's files at the probation department. You'll need all the background you can get on the whole child, and you'll be missing vital parts of it if you don't study this resource file. It contains home and school investigation reports, continuous evaluative comments and reports by regular staff and volunteers, personality, attitude, aptitude, school achievement, optimetric and audiological test results, and basic papers describing the child's family background, record of previous offenses, legal status as an adjudicated delinquent, etc. This file, and other information resources at the Court are to be studied only at the Court; they cannot be taken out except in very rare cases with clear and explicit special permission from regular staff.

"As a related point, familiarize yourself with the range of services in the Court and community, from which your child might benefit. Do not hesitate to suggest to us that they be added, if you think it appropriate.

"9. Respect confidentiality, utterly and completely. Whatever you know or surmise about a youngster is under no circumstances to be divulged to or discussed with anyone but a person fully authorized by the Court to receive this information. Not even the fact that he is a juvenile offender should be disclosed.

"This stricture is absolute. Violations are not only highly unethical; they are the surest way to destroy a relationship with the juvenile, if discovered, as they frequently are.

"As a related point--respecting the privacy of the juvenile--be cautious and judicious about asking probing-personal questions, especially early in the relationship. The response may be only resentment, until such time as the relationship can support discussion of personal material. (Nor should you assume the youngster wants to hear you discuss your personal life in lieu of his.)

"10. Don't rush it, but as the relationship develops you can encourage the youngster to think about himself, his actions, goals, etc. and from that knowledge plan together, more constructive activities from which he'll derive a measure to self-respect and success. Many of our youngsters have previously done almost no careful thinking about themselves in any planful, forward-looking way. They seem almost to run away from self-awareness.

"11. Report violations. Confidentiality does not include keeping known violations a secret from the Juvenile Officer in charge of the youngster.

"However easy and 'nice' it may seem to do so, in the long run, sweeping such things under the rug does the child a disservice, i. e., he continues to think he can always 'get away with it,' and you, by sacrificing everything to win his friendship, will end up by losing his respect--by being a 'tool' he can do anything with. Report all violations, promptly. In general, whenever you have the slightest doubt as to what your legal or law enforcement obligations are, you should check with a supervisory person in the Court. Do this immediately, before taking any action which might be seriously wrong or even illegal.

"Even in discussing with the youngster possible or unproven violations, be honest and firm when you disapprove;

this is not inconsistent with being supportive and friendly, whenever possible. After all, if you don't stand for something in his eyes, there are very few others who will.

"12. Know your job. Much of the above depends on what volunteer job you have. Group Discussion Leaders have 'privileged communication' with probationers, for example; Volunteer Probation Officers don't, and must report violations.

"Be sure you discuss with a juvenile officer or chief volunteer and understand thoroughly your particular volunteer role, before beginning work. Know its possibilities and its limits.

"In general, your volunteer initiatives are encouraged, but do not expand your role, e.g., from tutor to VPO, or VPO to tutor, even unofficially, until you consult thoroughly with a regular staff person. This includes extras, of course, like taking the youngster on a trip with your family, etc.

"13. Be supportive, encouraging, friendly, but also firm. Whatever role and obligation you have, as the youngster's 'conscience,' to oppose and report infractions, you can still be supportive, encouraging, friendly, to the limit possible. Indeed, respect and friendship will be far more solid with both if the child knows that at the same time as you appreciate and respond to efforts at self-improvement, you will be firm, honest, and objective in disapproving where this is warranted.

"14. Present your ideas clearly, firmly, simply. Always mean what you say, and be consistent. Never make a promise or proposal unless you've thought it through first, and are fully prepared to back it up. The juvenile will test you, 'call your bluff' and see if you will in fact consistently deliver as promised, either as rewards or in backing up the limits you set. Be serious about the limits when he tests you, and the rewards when you've promised them and he has delivered. All this is an important part of his learning to trust you (which will come slowly in any case).

"Don't let the kid down even in apparently small things, like showing up for appointments, and being on time. If you don't show responsibility as a model for him, you cannot expect him to learn it for himself.

"15. Be a good behavior model for the child. One

of the best things you can do is to become, in your own behavior, a good model for the youngster. If your own dress,
language and behavior are not of a good standard, you can
scarcely expect it from your probationer. Chances are he
has had enough 'bad models' already; give him a good one.

"There is another respect in which it is especially
important that your own conduct be above reproach while
working for the Court, in that you represent the Court and
your behavior reflects on the Court at all times. You may
justifiably consider a few hours volunteer work in the Court
as but a portion of your life; mainly, you may be a college
student, a housewife or a businessman. Others do not make
that distinction so readily. To them you are a Court person, and expected fully to meet the high standards the Court
itself expects of others (much the same thing as community
expectations of teachers and ministers). If you do not do
this, the Court will come in for heavy criticism to which it
is very vulnerable, perhaps more so than you yourself are.
This is not a hypothetical situation; it has happened, and
quite painfully, in a few cases. Before accepting Court volunteer work, you must decide to live up to this special condition. If you don't feel you can, no harm is done, provided it is stated clearly to us beforehand.

"16. Avoid being 'caught in the middle.' You can
be a liaison between the child and his world, but be careful
not to get 'caught' between the child and his parents, the
child and his teachers, the child and the Court, especially
as an intercessor is some way used by the child against his
parents, or vice versa. Frequently, this happens when you
succumb to the temptation to be liked by the child at all
costs, to be a 'nice guy' no matter what. It can easily happen here that the child will then 'use' you in the conflict
with authority which is often his control problem.

"Your relations with the child's parents are a particularly sensitive area. Move with care here and inform
yourself as fully as possible early in the relationship, by
discussion with the Juvenile Officer in charge of the child,
etc.

"In general, remember that though your own relationship with the child is naturally foremost in your mind, he
has other important relationships as well: to his parents,
peers, teachers, etc. Give some careful thought and attention to these, too.

"17. There are indeed a number of things to keep
in mind when working with a juvenile, but much of it boils
down to 'be yourself' and 'care sincerely about the youngster. ' We have always been confident that our volunteers
are just that kind of people. "

*   *   *   *

Report XII

CASEBOOK FOR COURT VOLUNTEERS

Assembled and Edited by
Ursula Davies and Ivan Scheier*

General Purpose and Intended Audience

About 90-95% of volunteer courts offer their volunteers some sort of orientation and training. Not many of us
do it well, however, for lack of time and resource material
in this new field. Therefore, the National Court Volunteer
Training Project is preparing court volunteer training resource material in a number of media; films, slide shows,
tapes, and as here, written. The present case material is
designed primarily for the new volunteer who will be working
directly with a probationer or parolee, either juvenile or
young adult. It is still relevant for volunteers working in
delinquency-prevention programs, but it is considerably less
relevant for volunteers working in closed settings (detention
centers, training schools, penitentiaries). Finally, it is not
of primary relevance to volunteer office workers who do not
work directly with correctional clients.

Within this audience, the purposes of this case

*Of the National Information Center on Volunteers in Courts, Boulder County
Juvenile Court, Hall of Justice, Division 3, Boulder, Colorado 80302. With
deep appreciation for the contributed experiences of the following people:
Mary Pat Boersma, Jim Carrington, Frances Furlow, Norman Gapske,
Robert Hamm, Charles F. Gardner, D. A. Haxby, Lois Johnson, James
Jorgensen, Gary Klahr, Charlotte Lefler, Kathleen Oigles, Leonard Rosen-
garten, Jack Silverstein, Kathleen Wells, Matthew Wells. Our thanks, also,
to the following groups: Boulder County Juvenile Court; Cook County
(Chicago) Juvenile Court; Denver City and County Court; Fulton County
(Atlanta) Juvenile Court; Kalamazoo County Juvenile Court; National Asso-
ciation of Probation Officers (England); National Court Volunteer Training
Project (OJD/YD); Partners of Alaska; Quincy, Massachusetts District Court;
Royal Oak, Michigan Municipal Court; Teen-Aid (Philadelphia); and VISTO
(Los Angeles County Court).

material are as follows:

 (1) To familiarize the new volunteer with typical
   kinds of probationers and typical kinds of conditions under which they live.

 (2) To familiarize the new volunteer with characteristic kinds of problems volunteers encounter in
   working with probationers, and characteristic
   kinds of solutions attempted.

 (3) To encourage in the new volunteer, a more realistic set of attitudes about his work. Thus, the
   volunteer who expects quick and easy solutions is
   usually headed for disaster.

All this is to be done in as lively and realistic manner as possible. We do know that volunteers tend to pay attention to well-prepared case material because it can indeed
convey a real-life "this is it" feeling, and allows the trainee
to identify with and relive the situation, at least vicariously.

Individualizing the Material to Your Court

While ultimately addressed to the volunteer, this casebook must first pass muster with your court's trainer of volunteers. We assume this person will not accept it just as
is, but will delete some cases, modify others, and (hopefully) add some new ones. Only then will he reprint the casebook in quantity for your court's volunteers. Please consider
that you have our full permission to do so though acknowledgment of source would be appreciated. You should always
adapt these cases to your court because no two courts in the
country have exactly the same kind of caseload, and in any
one court, the nature of the caseload will change over time.

In order to give you the broadest range to work from,
we have assembled these cases from volunteer courts all
over the country, and selected those which do seem to reflect
generally typical national patterns, many of which will be
recognizable to most courts. But we must repeat: you, the
supervisor or trainer of volunteers, must select and modify,
for the final individualizing to your court, your community
conditions, and your volunteers. And, as time goes on, you
will be able to add a heavier preponderance of illustrative
case material from your own court volunteers' experience,
as revealed in their in-service meetings, etc. The present
set is really just to "prime the pump."

Media and Other Possibilities

As presented here, the case material is written, to
be taken in through the eyes of the volunteer. Such mate-
rial-to-be-read has the advantage of being readily reproduc-
ible and easily available to the volunteer at any time. Yet,
the trainer should remember that the same kind of case
material can also be driven home in other media, which,
though perhaps more expensive, are also more dramatic--
for example, in (a) audio tapes of the probationer talking or
being interviewed, (b) slide shows and (c) films. The National Court Volunteer Training Project has produced case-
type slide shows (Report VII, parts A, B, and C); also it
has produced a directory of tapes, (Report VI), as well as
a directory of volunteer training films (Report VIII). Our
specially-produced court volunteer training film, "A Second
Chance"(Report IX), is essentially a case-study-on-film of
a volunteer working with a juvenile probationer. For the
volunteer trainer, the message is: mix your media for
maximum impact of case material.

Even within the purely verbal medium (discounting the
audio and visual possibilities described above), case material should not just be passively read by the volunteer. It
should be discussed and actively participated in. Within the
verbal realm, then, the possibilities are: (a) The volunteer
reads it, but we don't stop there; (b) The trainer as lecturer
explains, interprets, and elaborates it; (c) It is used to
stimulate give-and-take discussion questions-and-answers,
preferably in smaller groups; (d) The case material provides
the trainer with ideas for role play situations in which trainee volunteers participate directly and actively.

As indicated above, even the best case material is
only a departure point for further discussion. It cannot be
complete in itself; what it can do is stimulate discussion,
which extracts and analyzes relevant experience, develops
realistic interpretations, makes the material uniquely relevant to your current caseload, your court, your volunteers,
and directly meaningful to each individual volunteer among
them. Almost any point in these cases, however easily overlooked in mere reading, or however trivial it might seem if
left undiscussed, becomes significantly enriched by such discussion. Case material is not an end in itself, it is a
starting point for discussion, a catalyst for questions and
answers, a stimulus. Be sure you use it in this way.

Timing and Other Details of Usage

As noted before, the trainer will select, adapt, delete, and add, using the present cases only as initial resource material. Next, he will probably print in quantity
and incorporate the adapted case studies as part of the
court's "volunteer orientation manual" (alternatively, the
casebook may be printed as a separate). Note too: if you
have a lot of cases, a topic index cross-cutting actual cases,
may be helpful for ready reference use, e. g. , "family problems, " "school problems, " "runaway, " "drugs. "

Typically, the orientation manual will be given the
volunteer right after he is accepted, sometime prior to his
pre-assignment training class, or just at the beginning of it.
(See Report IV.) Urge the volunteer to read it and reflect
upon it; perhaps he can be encouraged to do so by the knowledge that he will be tested on it at some point (see Report
XV). At least he should anticipate that it will be referred
to and discussed in pre-assignment training classes. Finally, the volunteer should be allowed to keep the casebook
material during his term of service for reference and study.
Other usages, beyond just reading the cases, have been discussed in previous sections.

Increasingly, material provided from outside your
court should be replaced by more meaningful local material
from your own volunteers' ongoing experience, as brought
out in in-service case discussion meetings of volunteers or
discussion between the individual volunteer and his supervis-
or, in regard to his own case. As noted before, the present material is mainly for pre-assignment "priming the
pump. " Once the volunteer gains on-the-job experience, he
will gather the most relevant "case material" of all--from
his own case. You need only be sure you give him a chance
to air and analyze it, with others, in follow-up in-service
training.

Probationer-Minus-Volunteer, or
Probationer-Plus-Volunteer Cases

Broadly, there are two kinds of cases we might have
chosen: a description of the probationer and his life conditions, not including his interactions with a volunteer; and,
a description of the probationer and his life conditions emphasizing the relationship between the volunteer and the

probationer.

       We chose the second type, because the first type,
while certainly important, is easier to procure without our
assistance. The second type, however, describes a volunteer-probationer relationship which, in modern times, at
least, is so new that instances are hard to come by, and
we therefore felt our Project's special contacts would be
particularly useful here. Before leaving the Probationer-
Minus-Volunteer type of case, however, we would emphasize
that, though omitted here, for the reasons noted, they can
be very important, particularly in the early stages of volunteer familiarization. Indeed, it is perhaps easier for the
neophyte volunteer to cope with the "simpler" probationer-
minus-volunteer situation first, before tackling the more
complicated probationer-plus-volunteer case. Many courts
will already have a file of such probationer-minus-volunteer
cases; indeed, any court's actual case files should provide
a ready supply, with identifying information removed or dis-
guised. Secondly, any training casebook for paid professionals can usually be adapted or simplified for volunteer orientation use. Finally, a few courts have prepared probationer-
minus-volunteer cases, simplified or otherwise designed
especially for volunteer training. Perhaps the most famous
and best-tested in actual volunteer orientation are "The
Daniel Carter Case" and "The Dora Alias Case" (Report X
(A)). Professor Jorgensen or the National Information Center may have a limited number of copies of these on request. The same may be said of the case of J. A. H. (Petition # CP 6021) from Partners of Alaska. The Boulder
County Juvenile Court Orientation Manual also has a number
of shorter cases of this type, this manual being obtainable
from the National Information Center at two dollars per
copy.

Realism

       The court volunteer movement is new; therefore, pro-
bationer-plus-volunteer case material has scarcely had a
chance to be developed. Hence, our fund of cases is by no
means rich, and individual cases rarely approach the ideal
as training aids for we have all had to improvise rapidly as
we went along. Wherever possible, however, we selected
from our national files, those cases which approached the
volunteer training ideal of REALISM in these ways:

1. Sufficient detail is provided (though sometimes
   volunteers won't read too long cases, so we included a few short ones, too).
2. Artificial language, analysis, or abstraction is
   avoided. In almost every case we have left the
   case exactly as the volunteer tells it. These
   are actual cases in the words of the people who
   lived through them, full of inconsistencies, failure, and error, but full of hope, too. We have
   edited and abbreviated only where we absolutely
   had to.
3. The impression is avoided that "miraculous cures"
   are the rule. They are not. Instead, realistic
   problems and setbacks are admitted, frustration
   is prepared for, etc. The attempt is to present
   unvarnished real life in the volunteer-probationer
   relationship, as the best possible way of preparing for it.

We are deeply gratified to the many contributors of
case studies who gave us this good start towards the ideal.
We ask further help from all of you to approach it even
more closely. So please consider this a first collection to
be improved in balance and content by future contributions
from you.

SOME VOLUNTEER-PLUS-PROBATIONER CASES

Note: There is some thread of sequence and similarity as
cases are arranged in order now, but many other or-
derings are possible, to your own preference.

Alex and Mr. Hughes

The "older alcoholic"; modest expectations; persistent effort.

"Alex, a single man aged 43, whose only surviving
relative is a married sister 16 years his junior, is an alcoholic. He has several previous convictions, mainly for
petty larceny, and there is an obvious pattern to his convictions in that they all occur during periods when he is on a
drinking spree and are committed with the object of obtaining
some money to buy more drink. He has been alcoholic since
he was 16 years old and although there have been quite long
periods of sobriety, during which he has worked hard and
well, sooner or later he has started drinking again and there

has been a further relapse. When he was placed on probation for three years in February 1965, it was felt that a volunteer would be able to support him in his fight to stay sober
and he was accordingly introduced to Mr. Hughes, a 34-year-
old married man, departmental manager with a railway company, a church background but not rigidly so, and an extremely pleasant and friendly man. Mr. Hughes was able
to form a very good relationship with Alex, and for just over
15 months saw him once a week in a station cafe. During
this period there were relapses but on the whole less frequently than before. "

— — — — — — — —

Life With Father

The volunteer struggles to discover the truth with a "well-
practiced deceiver" and her equally well-practiced family, ...
the crucial relations to Daddy, who drinks and wants her
punished but whom she likes anyhow ... but Jane has lots of
achievement potential.

"When I was first working with Jane, the relationship
was very strained and she had little or nothing to say at all.
Since, she has become the 'perfect hostess' who insists on
treating me like a visiting dignitary every time I go over.
"I feel that she is a well-practiced deceiver and is
capable of effectively telling any lie she might choose. For
the most part she tells me the good side of everything and
avoids mentioning the bad.
"She was at odds with her father until about Christmas time when things started to straighten out. She had
admitted that her earlier truancies were due to a boy she
was sneaking out to see. Her father feels she has pretty
well straightened out and that he has more problems than
she does at this point.
"She has no peer associations outside of school other
than her family. She feels that most people her age are
immature. This is undoubtedly because of the responsibilities
of her role at home. Her father seems to be rarely home
evenings even when he isn't working night shift, and this
makes it impossible for me to get her away from the house
for any length of time.
"The father was drinking heavily and on one occasion
Jane called and asked me to come out at 1:00 a. m. When
I arrived I found everything from the refrigerator and kitchen
table on the floor. Jane's nightgown had been torn. Her
father left when I arrived and returned about an hour later.

At that time he promised not to drink anymore, but has continued doing so anyway.

"Jane's mother is divorced and lives separately from the father. I have asked that Jane not be allowed to stay overnight with her mother any longer and both Jane and I are in agreement with her father on this point. The mother has a habit of pairing her off with 'boyfriends' for the night, whenever Jane goes there.

"Jane has shown real interest in school and in her homework lately. She seems to be doing fairly well although I have not received the school report as yet. Recently she has mentioned college as a possibility. She is in a secretarial course and is quite interested in going on to school next year if she can get an office job half-days.

"For the most part I am still uncertain about a great many things as she and her father give me completely different stories on everything and I feel both are distorting the picture in opposite directions. The father is very definitely very punishment-minded and has on several occasions asked to have her sent to the Juvenile Home. He is willing to be involved in her probation only if it doesn't require much time or effort from him, and then primarily when it means punishing her or telling on her. He throws up everything bad she has ever done, quite frequently in front of her to me and especially to the rest of her relatives. She is very attached to him, however, and recently wrote a paper in school about how great he was to put up with her.

"I feel the thing she needs most is an opportunity to get out of the house and prove herself on her own. For this reason I have encouraged the idea of going on to school and dorm living next year. She is very capable and the administrator for whom she has been working at school recommends her highly as a good hard worker. She is highly interested in self-improvement.

"I think that solutions to the problems can be found but that it will require time and a good deal of effort on her part as well as on the parts of other persons involved. The school has been very cooperative and interested. I am hoping that the counseling services will be successful, and will be interested to hear the counselor's opinion on how badly such services are needed, and believe the father is more confused than Jane is. "

— — — — — — —

Verna

Sex and the mother as a large part of the problem.

Verna's mother was described in casework records
as "completely hopeless," and her father as completely disinterested. Psychiatric evaluation described Verna as a
love-starved girl whose intelligence is somewhat less than
average. She became involved in a series of sexual relationships and eventually became infected with a venereal
disease. Her home life is characterized by constant bicker-
ing with her mother. Her school adjustment, which has
been very poor, is characterized by extensive truancy and
repeating of grades. Verna evinced some interest in becoming a hospital worker.... Her mother has always been inclined to ridicule her efforts and discourage her. Her father
is merely there. At first the mother's ingrained posture
hampered attempts to help Verna but after numerous conferences and discussions with the family the volunteer has been
able to improve the family climate somewhat. The fact that
the mother is now able to offer a little support in place of
destructive criticism has been reflected in Verna's behavior.... The Teen-Aid volunteer, who spent much time with
this girl and her family, believes that Verna needs constant
help in order to stay out of trouble.

— — — — — — — —

Two Sisters

The girls accept a volunteer as mother-substitute for an alcoholic mother with whom they had severe conflict.

One of the first cases handled by Teen-Aid involved
two sisters who had tremendous loyalty to each other and to
an alcoholic mother.... The girls came to the Court's attention at ages 13 and 15, respectively, on their mother's
complaint of incorrigibility. Investigation revealed a seriously disturbed family situation, in which friction between the
mother and the daughters sometimes culminated in physical
brawls, followed by wild charges and counter-charges of
blame. Both girls accepted the Teen-Aid sponsor (volunteer) as a partial mother substitute and developed an obviously trusting and sincere affection for her.

Three Sisters: "Only a Witness to My Own Experience"

Working with a natural group ... some typical juvenile questions and a way of answering.

   "'Three. ' I stared at the juvenile court officer in
disbelief. 'well, it's sort of a package deal, ' she explained.
'The three are sisters--13, 14 and 15--and whether it's official or not you'll be getting involved with all of them if
you get involved with one. ' I had spent the Sunday school
hour for almost two years visiting with the girls at the Fulton
County Juvenile Detention Home located near the church I attended. When one of the matrons one Sunday asked if I'd
like to become a volunteer probation officer, I perked up ...
so I filled out the application papers, agreed to work with a
child serving probation, to be assigned to me by the court,
for at least one hour a week as a personal way of doing
something about juvenile delinquency. Now here was this
court officer springing three on me. She was right, of
course; all three girls had been picked up at one time or
another for running away from home. Their togetherness, I
was to discover, provided almost the only emotional security
they had. The Court officer went with me to their home to
introduce me and to transfer, at least symbolically, some
of her own authority.
   "The youngest I recognized from some Sunday morning
visits. The other two, it turned out, had come and gone
from the Juvenile Detention Home between Sundays or had
been there on Sundays when I was out of town. The court
officer worked out the mechanics with all of us--what night,
what time, what sort of activities, who pays for what and
how much, etc. The cooperation of their mother, divorced
and working, was essential.
   "We had some fascinating discussions: when did I
think a girl ought to start smoking? dating? drinking?
Why wasn't I married? Wasn't it better to marry and get
a divorce than not to marry at all? Wasn't it better to
marry than to finish school? Why go to college, even if
you can? That only limits your marriage possibilities.
   "With no more responsibility for them than one evening a week, I was in no position 'to lay down the law' about
their behavior except for the time we were together. Beyond that, I could only witness to my own experience and
observation and they had to evaluate my witness in the context of my own lifestyle as they had opportunity to observe
that. "

– – – – – – – –

Pot, Glue, and the Group Process

A volunteer works as counselor to a group of delinquent
girls, including Betty, who came in as "incorrigible" ...
positive peer pressure in group counseling (versus negative
peer pressure from "old friends").... The volunteer responds to the girl's attempts to manipulate and willfully dis-
tort reality....

Betty, a 16-year-old girl, had been picked up by the
police at 2 a. m. , appearing to be under the influence of
some form of drug.   Alcohol had been ruled out as there
was no smell of liquor.   She was taken to the local hospital
where she admitted to sniffing glue.   After the examination,
the police returned her to her parents.   The incident was
reported to the Juvenile Court and they carried out a home
investigation.

Betty's background revealed an upbringing in Louisiana
with the family moving to Colorado when she was 14 years.
The mother had been divorced when Betty was a small child
and remarried some years later.   The step-father did not
seem to have any attachment to Betty and appeared to be
concerned only with the inconvenience that her behavior
caused him.   There was, however, a genuine affection between Betty and her mother, although the mother exercised
very little control over her.   Betty had dropped out of
school.   The family lived in a trailer in the countryside
some 10 miles outside of a large town; the home itself was
well-furnished and in a neat and orderly condition.   Betty
hitch-hiked into the local town most days, occasionally staying overnight with boyfriends when she could not get a ride
back.

Betty was brought before the Juvenile Court as a person in need of care and protection.   During the Court hearing, Betty's mother said her daughter was beyond her control.   The Judge placed the girl on juvenile probation for
two years with strict curfew rules.

During the first three months, Betty was frequently
caught breaking curfew rules, although there was no further
evidence of glue sniffing.   In an interview with her probation
officer she was told that a "last chance" was being given to
her, the alternative would be her being sent to a detention
home.   A newly formed counseling group had been started
by the Juvenile Court where six or seven girls who had been
placed on "probation" met once a week to discuss their problems and goals.   Betty was assigned to this group which was
led by a woman volunteer from out of the community.   Betty

also met with the same woman once a week on a one-to-one basis. The supervising professional probation officer felt that she needed an association with a mature female personality--who would not be seen as an authority figure--on which, it was hoped, she would model her behavior.

Betty went to the sessions for some 10 months and over that time a distinct improvement was noticed in her behavior. During the initial weeks she attempted to manipulate the volunteer group counsellor by saying the probation officer had given her permission for extra late nights, and vice versa. These tactics were quickly discovered in the weekly phone calls the volunteer made with the probation officer. It's important that a volunteer check up on what a child says and let the child know his statements are being "reality-tested."

During discussions Betty's group had reached the conclusion that many of them had got into trouble because they did not have sufficient strength of character to go their own way rather than with the crowd when they knew their actions were illegal. This then led into trouble with the law. Betty was lucky in one escapade. She had asked permission for an extra late night out to attend the birthday party of one of her friends from the "old gang"--a group she had been told not to associate with. Permission was refused. Nevertheless Betty did go to the party and stayed for about an hour.

During this time she could see that marijuana was being smoked and she decided to leave. This move was very fortunate for her as 30 minutes later the house was raided by the police. Had she been caught she would have probably been sent to the detention home. Once Betty realized that her attempts at manipulation of the probation officer and the volunteer group leader were unsuccessful, and that the results of her being caught attending the pot party would have been disasterous for her, Betty began to show the first signs of realistic goal setting.

The verbal interaction of problems discussed by the girls in the group made Betty realize that many other teenagers also experience frustration with home and family problems, but with the guidance of the group leader, these problems could be tackled in a constructive way. In the group the girls learned socially accepted, effective ways to handle troublesome feelings such as anger, discouragement, despair, guilt.

As Betty's behavior stabilized, the one-to-one counseling stopped after some four months although she continued in group counseling for almost a year. After this time the

volunteer group leader recommended to the supervising probation officer that Betty be taken off probation and this recommendation was accepted by the department.
  The volunteer group leader kept in constant touch with
the probation officer, and the group members were aware of
this. However, the group leader was always sensitive to the
group rule of confidentiality, and they realized this contact
was as a mediator and not in any way as an informant.

- - - - - - - - - -

Life With Linda

A college volunteer doesn't really have enough time for the
job but learns some things outside of college, in a cross-
cultural match: glue sniffing, the boy friend, and the rejecting family. Doing things together, Linda found a new
world outside the slums . . . she'd slip back, but there was
new hope.

  "In my third year of college, I became a court volunteer, acting as a big sister to a 15-year-old Mexican American girl. I stayed Linda's big sister for nine months, after
which I had to drop out of the program because of a heavy
school schedule.
  "When I first met her, she didn't know what to make
of me. She had been placed on probation for incorrigibility
with a history of glue sniffing and gang involvement. To say
that she didn't trust me would be an understatement. She
viewed me as a member of the probation department and
therefore a watchguard. Indeed, after about three visits she
blurted out, 'How much are you getting paid for this?' I
told her that I wasn't getting paid anything, that I volunteered
to be her friend. Her look of disbelief changed into an extremely shy smile, and I thought I had won the first round.
  "My main problem with Linda was that I couldn't de-
vote enough time to her, due to my work and school. When
she would go places with me once a week, her hair would
be unratted and just hanging to her shoulders (i.e., more
natural and not overdone). This began happening after about
my third visit. But I discovered that if I dropped in unex-
pectedly on her, her hair would be back to the usual ratted
up 'beehive' hairdo with exaggerated makeup. Thus, I could
see it was a struggle between my influence and the influence
of her friends.
  "I wanted to show Linda things that existed outside of
her slum-neighborhood home. Due to a bad home situation
consisting of a rejecting mother and stepfather, Linda did not

have much of an opportunity to know what lay outside of her
neighborhood.   So we went together to the mountains,
beaches, to my college and dorms, entertainment centers,
etc.   Sometimes though, we'd just go out for a Coke or go
shopping, or I'd help her with her sewing.
    "We built up a trusting relationship and she confided
in me some of her problems.   One of her main problems
was an old boyfriend whom she said taught her to sniff glue.
He had been arrested and sent to camp where he couldn't
influence her.   But the time came for him to come home.
We discussed the whole situation and she decided not to see
him.   He came home and went over to her house.   She did
refuse to see him and he got himself arrested the next day
so once again he was out of the picture.   It was unfortunate
for him that he got into trouble again but it was a milestone
passed when Linda refused to see him.
    "Linda has a long way to go yet for rehabilitation.
She has the tendency to slip back into trouble.   However,
another big sister has now been assigned to her who can see
her much more frequently than I could.   I feel that with this
added support from another big sister and occasional, friendly visits from myself (I still see her), Linda can be guided
to lead a useful, law-abiding life in society.
    "I learned some things, too.   I learned that volun-
teerism not only benefits the probationer but the volunteer
as well.   The volunteer experience helped to assure me that
probation work was the right field to go into.   It made me
even more aware that probationers are human just like myself; they often have more problems and need more help than
I could ever dream of.   You establish empathy for your fellow man as a volunteer, because you develop a friendship,
and can thus see what made this girl the way she is.   But
most important, being a volunteer helped me to see that a
person who has committed a crime is not someone to be
feared and hated but is afraid himself and really needs someone just to care about him. "

- - - - - - - -

Something More Than Superficial: I Harbor No Illusions ...

A college volunteer thinks deeply about her job, trying to
clarify her role, her goals, and the best approach in the relationship with her juvenile ... high tension at the first meeting ... the probationer tests and tries to manipulate ... getting caught between the girl and her family ... unexpected
dividends from a jail crisis ... subtle changes in the relationship as the probationer takes some initiatives.

"I went to the Juvenile Court to offer my services as
a volunteer probation officer for a variety of reasons--a desire to help a child, a need to infuse meaning into my
everyday experience which was lacking in my present job.
But the motivation underlying the entire complex of reasons
was a compulsion to combat a feeling of powerlessness to
control the hostility and anonymity which pervades much of
the contemporary experience. My motivations were, then,
largely irrelevant to the goals of corrections or, more
specifically, the goal of probation.

"I was accepted as a volunteer and received a quick
briefing from the professional probation officer. She outlined the rules of probation and my role as a deputy probation officer. As a VPO I assumed the responsibilities of a
professional officer for a single child. I was to see the
child every week and report her progress to the court. I
had, then, the dual task of being both a friend and an authority figure. I awaited our first meeting with some apprehension and yet some real hope for success. In the early stage
of my volunteer experience, 'success' with my probationer
was very ill-defined for me. I thought vaguely of helping
her become a happier person.

"Our first meeting jarred this rather simple notion
of success. I arrived in the evening with the probation officer at her home. The parents, the probationer, myself,
and the juvenile officer assembled in the living room. The
atmosphere was formal and tense. The officer asked several
superficial questions concerning family relations after which
my probationer became extremely hostile, angrily denouncing
not only her parents but the probation officer and me as
well. She announced that she had no intention of seeing me
and wished we would all go to hell.

"Needless to say, this first encounter was unnerving
but it was not totally defeating. I felt I had a chance but I
lacked a definite idea of how I was going to gain her friendship. It was going to be difficult. To begin with, we had
different personalities. She was extroverted and set her
goals in terms of physical comfort, while I am restrained,
intellectual, and a graduate student. But I did not have long
to think through how I was going to establish a relationship--
the relationship was happening. Soon after our first meeting
I received a telephone call in which she sobbed the details
of an argument with her stepfather. I let her talk out her
anger, suggested several immediate solutions (i. e. , just
avoid each other for awhile).

"This pattern of telephone calls, interspersed with a
weekly meeting at which we went out for a Coke, to a

movie, or to the university campus and talked for an hour,
continued for a few weeks.   It was clear that she was testing me during this time.

"After she had initially agreed to the inevitability of
seeing me, she attempted to maneuver me into a position
where I would side with her against her parents.   During
her telephone calls she would attempt to catch me up in the
emotionalism of the moment to condemn her father's disciplinary action.   Our weekly meetings were fairly superficial.
In them she alternated between detachment and attempts to
impress me with her sexual exploits.

"During this period I attempted to maintain a reasonable neutrality.   I never interfered in the disciplinary action
of her father.   Regardless of how irrational and unfair his
actions became, I decided it would be more effective to attempt to change his attitudes in periods of calm, before
specific dictums were handed down.   At the same time, I
did not endorse his behavior.   Rather, I attempted to point
out to the girl reasons for his attitudes, ways in which she
could prevent arguments from erupting.   My goal was to
help her see, as objectively as possible, the personality and
behavior of her family.

"This pattern was interrupted when I received a telephone call that my probationer was in jail.   The authorities
felt she was no longer controllable at home.   This crisis
pulled the family down in defeat.   In their desperation, they
were willing to talk honestly about their relationships.   And
it was while my probationer was in jail, I had the first discussion with her of significant feelings about not only herself
but her family as well.   In these talks I attempted, too, to
help her realize her position in relation to the law--for
example, that when she ran away, although her parents were
hurt, she was punished.

"After a few days, she was released to the court's
group foster home where she remained for three months.
Children stay in this home for various lengths of time.   The
goal in the home is to provide children with attention in a
relatively normal family atmosphere.

"This period of our relationship was perhaps the most
frustrating.   With a deeper understanding of the psychological
nature of the family's problem, my original optimism van-
ished.   And I groped for ways to reach my probationer.   We
slogged on during these months through sheer persistence on
my part.   I tried to be pleasant but we had fallen into a
superficial routine.   I went to the Home once a week and we
either shared an activity or talked.

"This superficiality was aggravated by the fact that

living in the Home was merely a suspension of her problems: no realistic confrontation with her home problems
could be made.   Yet, in retrospect, I feel this period was
crucial in building a trusting relationship with my probationer.   Even though there was no behavior change and seemingly little insight on her part into problem solutions, we
became friends through the simple process of frequent interactions and the communication to her of my sincerity.

"When my probationer was released from the Home,
our relationship went through a subtle change.   She began
calling me and asking me to come over and talk.   I slowly
began to involve myself in family activities.   These activities
had a real effect for they assured positive family interaction, partly through the pressure of my presence.   These
activities, too, allowed for naturally occurring discussions
with the parents, giving them the opportunity to test ideas
with an outsider instead of reinforcing old patterns.   As I
became more a part of the family, the hostility between
family members subsided.

"I harbor no illusions about what I accomplished as
a volunteer.   I did not produce in my probationer a remark-
able personality change, although I finally made a friend
and established a relationship from which we both learned. "

- - - - - - - -

The Crisis is Crucial

The volunteer's response in an emergency, as a possible
turning point.

A woman probationer was assigned to a housewife
with training in psychology.   She was very distrustful at
first of her new volunteer and the first few months on probation were not successful.   Then one night the probationer's
baby took suddenly ill.   She remembered the volunteer's
suggestion to "call me anytime" and she called the volunteer
at 2:00 a. m.   Within a half hour the volunteer's own doctor
was at her residence and the baby was in the hospital shortly
thereafter.   The volunteer even paid the doctor and hospital
bill.   The probationer paid her back promptly.

The probationer's reaction to it all: "You really do
want to help me.   I won't let you down. "

- - - - - - - -

The Sixty-Sixth Visit

A college "radical" volunteers to work preventatively with a

boy, and gives us the inner workings of a relationship in
which the key was give-and-take in feelings, in communication and in attempts to understand one another.   Lots of
things are <u>done</u> together, too.   Ups and downs....

First, meet Tim.   He's ten.   His mother applied to
the project because "... it seems that his last hope for a
close relationship with men in his own family is gone."
She said he had to struggle to assert himself with three
strong-minded females.   Tim was further described as being
extremely modest, feeling unsure of himself with people and
not liking himself.   The number and intensity of his personal
problems appeared higher than the average applicant to the
project.   His teacher described him as somewhat isolated
and attention-seeking, but his classmates saw few problems
and considered him quite likeable.   He rejected professional
psychotherapy.

Now, Walt.   His peers and our staff described him
as open, warm and understanding during a selection group
session.   We hired him for these qualities.   When he joined
the project, Walt was a 20-year-old political science major
who wanted to teach in college and was active in student af-
fairs as something of a radical on "free speech" and other
issues.

Here's Walt now, "telling it like it was."

<u>First Visit</u>:   'I picked up Tim at school as we had
previously arranged and drove to the park.   We hiked in the
hills for an hour or so and then sat down to talk.   He was
eager to talk about his activities at school, particularly
sports.   I talked a little about photography but spent most
of the time listening to him...."

<u>Sixth Visit</u>:   'I met Tim after school and we drove
up to the park.   We walked around the hills, throwing rocks,
looking at things, and shouting.   Since we met, Tim seemed
to be acting as if he felt inferior to me or at least he had
to agree to my suggestions.   I told him that if we were to
be friends, we had to be able to look at each other more
as equals--this struck a responsive chord.   Later he told
me about his brother who had died last year."

<u>Eighth Visit</u>:   'He showed me an album of pictures of
his dead brother and told me how sad he was about it, which
moved me--it made me feel sad too, and I told him how I
felt; we were very close for a few moments.   We then went
out and I showed him how to ride his bike.   He did very
well and seemed happy.   I think this has been our best session so far."

<u>Twelfth Visit</u>:   'We decided to make some repairs on

Tim's bike.   He mentioned not getting along well with his
mother.   I asked him why, and he spent some time telling
me of his difficulties with her.   Then we talked more about
his family (his father left home) and he told me many of his
feelings about it.   I said that I was very interested but was
afraid to show it because he might think I was prying.   He
said 'No'--and that he felt much better after talking to me
like this.   The rest of the meeting was quiet; we worked on
his bike and then watched TV. "

<u>Fourteenth Visit</u>:   "Tim said he had some difficulty
in describing me (during an interview with a project staff
member) so I told him about my family problems and how I
felt lonesome and inferior as a boy.   He said that his description of me was indeed right and that he felt that way
too.   We talked more and more easily about feelings this
time than ever before, but I'm worried about how to handle
the situation because Tim seems to have mixed feelings about
talking.   Sometimes he really likes it--other times he is
very nervous.   Tim wanted to work on an old train set.
We worked without success for an hour or so on the train.
While we worked, Tim got talking about how he visited the
doctor the other day and how modest he is--though he knows
it's silly.   I unwittingly felt I had to tell him how I used to
be modest also.   This seemed to disappoint him as I think
he just wanted to tell me something about himself.   We then
went and played baseball for a couple or more hours.   Relaxed and enjoyed it but not talking much. "

<u>Sixteenth Visit</u>:   "He told me of his disgust at having
his head examined by a doctor, about the headaches he's
been having for several years.   We printed some photos
that we had taken.   Tim was happy about how the pictures
came out.   He told me later that he thought it was great
that he and I were friends. "

<u>Seventeenth Visit</u>:   "After the movie, he told me he
was having a tough time sleeping and said he had a lot of
problems.   I asked him 'What?', but he said he didn't want
to talk about it.   We started painting a picture together and
really enjoyed it.   He painted a picture of me with a question mark on it and said I was 'un-understandable. '   That
was, I assume, a broad hint that I should talk more about
myself--something I have rarely done. "

<u>Eighteenth Visit</u>:   "As we were carving soap he told
me he had a lot of problems but didn't want to discuss them
with me then.   I told him that I wanted to hear about them
whenever he wanted to talk about them. "

<u>Nineteenth Visit</u>:   "We went for a Coke with his
mother, brother, sister and several of her friends.   Tim

seemed very anxious to show me off as his friend. "
      Twentieth Visit: "We went to the ice skating rink.
I'd never skated before and Tim seemed anxious to teach me
something new and exciting as I taught him how to ride a
bike. I learned fairly quickly, and we enjoyed ourselves.
Tim seemed to enjoy my obvious nervousness and the opportunity it gave him to encourage and teach me.... "
      Twenty-fourth Visit: "We took pictures of Tim's dog.
Tim was rather nervous and hard to talk to. He said he
felt things too deeply and alluded to his brother's death.
But when I asked him what he meant, he quickly shifted the
subject. Tim said he was doing better in school and his
(tension) headaches were gone. "
      Twenty-seventh Visit: "We got talking about beggars--
who he said shouldn't beg. I got excited and launched into
a speech on the 'other America' and basic economics--but
ended talking about my own mother who lives rather poorly
and can't get work. Tim took the talk about my mother with
great sympathy, making me glad I had told him. We went
down and shot pool for a couple of hours afterwards. "
      Thirtieth Visit: 'One time as I was kidding him about
the mess he had made of the kite string, he said between
bursts of laughter, 'you little bastard. ' I laughed and said,
'I'm not a little bastard, I'm a big bastard. ' We laughed
some more. Funny, I never expected to find joy at someone calling me a bastard, but I felt wonderful. This was
something Tim could not have done before and it made me
feel that he liked me. I tried to tell him later that I liked
the fact that we were so open and free with each other as I
had very few people I could be open and free with and say
what I wanted. Tim said little but I felt he understood and
agreed it was good. "
      Thirty-first Visit: "While we were flying the kite,
we talked about his turtle, his father--whom he dislikes--
and sex. He wanted me to describe how it feels to have
intercourse. I tried to tell him but admitted that it was
almost impossible to give an adequate description.... We
agreed that it was important for us to be able to talk over
ideas, questions, and problems with each other....
      Thirty-seventh Visit: "Tim seemed very selfish to
me and I got angry with him. Before we left he asked what
made me mad and I told him. He said he was sorry. I
felt embarrassed and said to forget it. "
      Forty-second Visit: "During the two hours in the
darkroom we managed to print only three pictures. I get
rather perfectionistic about photography technique and though
I tried to let Tim do what he wanted, I was heavy-handed

with him and he was both bored and angry. I was angry
both at him and at myself for making the visit bad and realized both then and after that I was making the same mistake
as before: not letting things flow comfortably but trying to
structure them rigidly. We exchanged a few hot words. "

Forty-third Visit: "Tim's mother and I got into a
discussion on recent events on campus. Tim was angry because he had been ignored and told me so. I apologized. "

Forty-fourth Visit: "We rode our bikes around the
park. Tim told me about his family and his mixed feelings
towards both his mother and his father. I told him my feelings toward him and tried to explain a few things that I
thought fouled up our last couple of meetings. I also told
him how joining the project and my relationship with him
had changed my career plans. I now want to do something
where I can work directly with people. "

Forty-fifth Visit: "While we were playing chess, I
put, unthinkingly, my feet up on the coffee table. He told
me I was very rude and treated things in his house with no
respect. I was mad and told him he had hurt my feelings.
I said that he might find some way to criticize me without
making me feel that bad. He apologized and we agreed to
forget it, but it left a breach between us for the rest of the
meeting. We played chess for a while longer and, although
interested, we didn't have a very good time. "

Forty-seventh Visit: "I feel that we are not so close
now as we have been before. I don't know why and it bothers
me. I haven't brought it up yet with Tim, but I plan to
very soon. "

Fifty-third Visit: "I wanted to walk around in the
hills and talk, but he didn't. We agreed after some argument to go down and shoot some pool. We didn't have a
very good time shooting pool. Tim got depressed because
he did not do very well. As we were driving home, he
asked me how I was going to write up the visit. I told him
I would put it down as "so-so. " He felt that it was a bad
visit and said he wished we had followed my suggestion to
walk and talk. "

Fifty-fourth Visit: "Tim talked about my teaching
him how to ride a bike about five or six months ago and
said he felt I was successful where others had failed because
we were friends ... since I liked him, I was patient. This
really made me feel good and I told him. We had a bare-
knuckles sparring match for a few minutes (no hitting above
the neck or below the belt). We occasionally do this and I,
for lack of space, rarely report it to the project, but I have
noticed definite change in these sparring matches since we

started having them. At first, they bothered me a little as
Tim seemed really aggressive while at the same time scared
like he didn't trust me. Sort of hard to describe but definitely there. Now the sparring matches are a lot of fun for
both of us. I feel that he trusts me much more completely
than he used to. This is a subtle change but it's only one
example of many things which have made us more comfortable with each other. There is another change--until a few
weeks ago, Tim never asked me how I described our relationship to the project. Now we regularly talk about it. I
told him I would describe this visit as very good. Though
we had not discussed anything personal, I felt very comfortable and good with him. He said 'Yes, there is something
between us, a feeling of warmth. ' I told him that it was
great simply to be able to be with him and say whatever
came into my mind without wondering 'will he like that or
not?' which I worried about during earlier meetings. Tim
said he would call me tomorrow. This is another change.
Until about a month ago, Tim would never call me and this
hurt a little. I felt sometimes he didn't care. On the way
down to the Photo Club, Tim talked about the short time we
have left together on the project--it is very much on his
mind recently--and said he hated to lose me as I was the
only person he could talk personally to. Tim seems jealous
of time in the face of the end of the project. He really
wants to talk a lot and is unhappy when we don't. He has
always felt that our talks were the best part of our relationship, but before they just happened--now he is actively pushing them. He seems to want my understanding more than
ever before. "

     Sixtieth Visit: "As we carved our soap figures Tim
talked about his family. I just listened. He was much
more open than he had been in the past about his brother.
He said that he didn't like his brother and only realized his
affection for him when the brother died. We were quiet for
a while. Then Tim said 'how great' this session was.
Then he said 'I love you, Walt, I really like you a lot. '
I said that I thought he was right the first time in saying
'love' although it was a little embarrassing for me as well
as for him to use the term. I said that I felt that way
about him too. He nodded and said 'yes, love.... ' We
both felt completely at ease, talking as we felt like it and
working on our carvings. I felt that Tim was happy to be
able to express his feelings openly towards me, and it made
me feel good for him to be able to do so. "

     Sixty-sixth (last) Visit: After buying chemicals we
drove back to Tim's house while he talked a mile a minute

about his experiments.   He also talked about the friendship
he has with his school teacher.   He is very proud and happy
about this friendship.   When we got up to his house we talked
more about his experiments.   I told him I thought I had
changed a lot during the eight months we had been together.
I was more interested in people and had changed my career
plans.   He said that he had changed a lot too, that at the
beginning he had not liked people very much and had few
friends at school, but that just last week he formed a club
of boys and was president.   Tim wanted to mix some chemi-
cals, but I told him I didn't want to so we went outside instead.   His mother was there.   Tim told us that he thought
I was terrible the first time we met but got to like me
more as time went on until he liked me so much he couldn't
say it well.   I thought this was really important because
Tim talked so openly about himself and me in front of his
mother.   This is the first time he has done this. "

Did anything happen?   Staff said: most of Tim's problems
were still with him as the program ended even though his
mother and teacher saw the beginnings of improvement--
especially in his self-esteem and relations with other children.   One year later, the changes were more noticeable.
Tim liked himself and had more self-confidence with friends.
As for Walt, working on the project changed his career
plans and he is now a graduate student in psychology.

– – – – – – –

I Remember Ricki, and I Remember Failure

A college volunteer, overidentifying with the boy against the
Court, the police, the school, etc. ... not checking what the
boy says closely enough ... veering from overprotective to
overpunitive.

        "I began my work for the court as a volunteer proba-
tion officer, a young married university student who wanted
to help a youngster in trouble.   I was assigned a 14-year-
old boy, Ricki, who had been adjudged delinquent for a
string of burglaries and whose father was absent from the
home.
        "When I began my contacts with Ricki I emphasized
the relationship aspect of my work and underplayed the authoritarian role.   I felt that in this manner Ricki would behave himself just so he wouldn't offend me as his friend.
The meetings between Ricki and me consisted of weekly pool
sessions and fishing trips.   Things progressed well until

Ricki was picked up for stealing money from newspaper
boxes. The police put the boy in jail and I made an appointment to talk to the professional supervisor on this case.
    ''In this meeting between volunteer and professional,
I assumed the role of the irate protector and rationalizer.
I asked, 'Why was money left in the open, what rehabilitation could be gained in jail?', etc. The probation supervisor
explained to me that Ricki had responsibility in the offense
but at my insistence the boy was released to my custody.
On the way home I explained to Ricki how unjust the court
was and how I would not allow the boy to become a victim
of the system. Ricki promised he would never steal again
and everything was fine.
    ''The weekly conferences between me and my charge
proceeded for two weeks without incident until Ricki informed me that 'mean' Lieutenant Black had been hassling
him the previous day. Like any volunteer who feels that his
charge is being unjustly persecuted, I went immediately to
Lt. Black and demanded an explanation for his actions. Lt.
Black stated that he stopped Ricki during school hours headed
for a local restaurant. He further stated that the boy was
informed of the dangers of truancy and released. I now felt
that I had two adversaries, the court and the police.
    ''The third member of the trio was added on a visit
to the school. At the school, I discovered that the children
were allowed to leave the campus during study halls and
lunch. I immediately checked Ricki's attendance and found
that the boy had been absent for two weeks. Neither the
parents nor the court had been advised of the truancy so I
contacted my Ricki's probation supervisor about the situation. Much to my dismay, the probation officer immediately
had the boy arrested and placed in juvenile quarters of the
jail once again.
    ''In response, I immediately went over the probation
supervisor's head and contacted the chief probation officer
and the juvenile judge and demanded that the boy be released during the day to attend school. The request was
granted and the first day of release Ricki broke into a vend-
ing machine and ran away from home. Two weeks later he
was located and placed in jail again.
    ''By this time my whole belief in children was shat-
tered. I had been seeing Ricki now for about nine months
and felt I had at times achieved some depth of understanding
of the boy's personality and that there had been times when
Ricki had trusted me. Perhaps I did not fully realize it at
the time but my pride was receiving a blow.
    ''I contacted the supervising probation officer and

asked that the boy be institutionalized as an 'impossible
child. ' The probation officer only smiled and showed me
an application he was making out for Ricki to a private boys'
camp in the mountains.   When I settled down, I realized
that the boy wasn't unreachable, only unreachable by the
particular volunteer probation officer's approach I had used,
that I had identified too strongly with the child 'against' the
court, the school and the police, and then veered too far in
the other direction. "

— — — — — — —

Bum Rep, Bum Rap at School

The volunteer defends this boy, feels that school personnel
are responsible in being down on him too much.   The report
on Jack was received the middle of January which stated
that there were school problems.   The complaint was fighting at school.

"I first talked to the boy and his stepfather.   Then,
the following day, I talked to the school principal, to Jack's
teacher and also to the juvenile officer who investigated the
fighting incident between Jack and another boy.   The investi-
gating officer was of the opinion that this was just a 'kid's
argument' until it was aggravated by the parents--somewhat
on both sides but primarily on the side of the other boy's
parents.
"The principal and the classroom teacher both seem
to have a negative attitude towards Jack.   His teacher seems
to have less than what is needed--either puts up with whatever is happening at the moment or sends it to the principal.
The principal seems to have a tendency to exaggerate somewhat on occasions as can be shown by this incident.
"Approximately a week after the boy was assigned to
me, on a Friday afternoon, I received a call from the
principal who, in a somewhat aggravated tone, informed me
that Jack and Jeff (Jack's brother) had been writing swear
words all around the entrance of the school with some water
colors brought to school by another student.   Upon my further
questioning it was brought out that this had been reported by
some other students.   Secondly, the words had been written
by Jeff.   Thirdly, Jack, himself, had made a peace sign
and had not written any words.   I looked at the school entrance and found the words, the peace sign, and the names
of numerous other students which I am sure had been written at an earlier time.   I wondered if anything had been
done to them.

"The boy seems to me to be basically a good kid who
has just gotten into some trouble and consequently gotten a
rep for it. Now as a result, actions by him bring school
reactions faster than those by another student. His grades
are average or slightly above but he can probably do better.

"I would recommend that if at all possible the boy
finish out the school year where he is. But I think that it
would help him to be transferred to another school where he
has no rep for the next year. I would also recommend a
man teacher. One who is noted for good classroom control.
Firm but fair discipline.

"I don't think there is a necessity for the problem to
grow with the boy if handled right at the present time. "

– – – – – – – –

One Hot Dog (and Reading Problems)

A "quiet" boy, afraid of failure ... a husband and wife team
up as volunteers to work with him preventatively ... working
with the school and a mother who's given up ... all as seen
through the eyes of the volunteers' supervisor (Community
Service Officer).

Karl lives alone with his mother in the low rent housing project. The home is neat and modest. The boy is in
the ninth grade at Central Junior High. He daydreams in
his classes. His reading is extremely poor and below fourth
grade level, which is felt to be the major problem in school
and learning. There is a definite disinterest in school and
no motivation. On January 9, 1970, Karl stole one hot dog
from J. C. Penney Company. Action: Police Department
Officer released child to mother with warning.

The volunteers, Mr. and Mrs. Lowell, feel that Karl
has improved his attitude in school. Mrs. Lowell met with
the vice principal of the boy's school. He informed her that
Karl was a disciplinary problem. Two months later, when
Mrs. Lowell met with Karl's teachers, they advised that he
was not a disciplinary problem any longer. In most of his
classes Karl is very quiet and does not disrupt classes.
Also on that later date, Mrs. Lowell talked with the vice-
principal and he said that Karl's attitude had improved and
that Karl had not been in any trouble lately. The volunteers
feel that Karl's main problem in school is due to a low
reading ability. His reading level is below fourth grade
level and he does not comprehend what he reads. Karl
feels that he always fails, and the volunteers feel that, therefore, Karl is afraid to try. The Lowells are in the process

of helping Karl in his reading problem.

Both the Lowells feel that one of Karl's problems is
the relationship with his mother. She seems to be a very
negative person, who places no restrictions on him, leaving
the boy to feel that his mother does not care. Mrs. Lowell
and Karl's mother have had several joint conferences with
the school officials at which times Karl's mother presented
a passive and given-up attitude.

Mrs. Lowell and myself, as Community Service Officer, have had a joint conference with Karl's mother to
stress the role of a mother figure and what it entails. She
agreed during the conference, but so far has not demonstrated any change of behavior toward Karl that we can see.

The Lowells have met with Karl on an average of
three times a week including school and home conferences.
Activities have been camping trips, dinners in the volunteers' home, shopping trips, tutoring of school subjects, and
listening. The volunteers feel that their relationship is
steadily improving. Karl at first was shy and very quiet.
He is now becoming more spontaneous in his verbalization
with them.

The Community Service Officer strongly recommends
that the partnership continue. The volunteers should continue to present an interest in Karl's school involvement and
encourage him to practice his reading and cooperate with
the school officials. Also, the volunteers can and are willing to continue to impress upon the mother her responsibilities.

At Home With Antonio

The Baxters, Buzz and Kathy, are volunteer foster parents
for the Court, so Tony comes to live with their natural children, Larry and Susan ... there's testing, confrontation, re-
conciliation, and real communication across a cultural gap.
Here's how Kathy tells it ...

"Do a Job Well or Do it Over (Not a Threat but a Promise)

"Since Antonio's arrival in our family he has made
great positive adjustment to the new, unfamiliar demands
put upon him. My husband, Buzz, and I have stressed helping him accept his position in the family as the older boy,
but one who must still ask permission for special privileges,
who has duties to perform for his own welfare (studying) and
for the family's good (chores). For instance, we depend on

his trash disposal daily and we depend on his sharing in doing dishes daily. Our Susan, age 8, sets the breakfast table
and Larry, age 10, does breakfast dishes before going to
school. Tony's morning job is taking out trash before breakfast, and when he does dishes in the evening if they aren't
clean when I put them away he gets up at 6:00 a. m. and
does them all over.

"How could we expect this of a boy who had done for
the most part exactly as he pleased for the last seven
years? Well, he knows the rules of our house because we
have discussed them and he knows we enforce them. One
of these rules is 'Do a job well or do it over. ' And, he
had seen Larry struggle up at six a. m. to do dishes over
a few times before he, Tony, ever began sharing in this
particular job. Of course, I arranged it this way knowing
full well that Larry doesn't always get his dishes perfectly
clean, though he's learning fast that it really pays to do a
good job the first time. (It pays him an extra half hour
sleep plus a fairly made compliment to his father from me,
on the quality of his work.) Manipulation on our part?
Well ... let's call it taking advantage of a foreknown proba-
bility for a psychological purpose.

"So, the first time I woke Tony up at six a. m. , his
first objection was met with a pleasant, 'I'm sorry Tony, I
didn't do the dishes last night. You did. And what's fair
for Larry is fair for you. Maybe tonight you'll push harder
on them with the sponge instead of trying to race the clock.
Come on now, I've got to have some clean glasses and
spoons for Susan to set the table with. ' And during breakfast we talked about how people can save in the long run by
using a little more time in the first place. Innocently?
Hardly.

"We feel the benefits from this are twofold. Tony is
learning there are consequences from his own actions and
he's beginning to see he's important to the family team. He
can't get away with either total neglect of his job or with a
sloppy job. This adds to his growing security also. We
have a definite routine and he knows what's expected and
what to expect. And I found out something about him early
regarding his defiance of authority. He'll bluff you if he
can, but he responds to direct firmness, statements made in
no uncertain terms.

"You see, we took pains to make friends with him
from the very first. Buzz played chess with him many
times during which they visited, talking both about things in
general and his family problems in particular as he brought
them up himself. And I had given him free access to my

Gibson guitar even though I knew he had broken his own over
his father's head in a brawl just before he left to join his
natural mother.   Why trust him with my own instrument?
We have a theory that people are more important than things.
And my guitar was a definite tool for winning his confidence.
He had a passion for music, especially his own, and playing
guitar is the one thing he had ever succeeded in doing half
well.   (His school grades were mostly D's and F's.)   When
angry or unhappy he will sit and play for literally hours,
calming his nerves and thinking, or just escaping from reality.   But let me tell you about how the observation regarding
firmness was substantiated during our first major confrontation, in another vignette. "

"The Honeymoon is Over" (The Unmasking Begins)

'It seems to be a fact that most every foster child
is at first willing, if not eager, to please the volunteer foster parents in his new setting.   This is a 'let's get acquainted' period and is a false calm during which he or she
'cases the joint' and is cased in return.   Any event can be
chosen by the foster child as the test case for pushing the
boundaries to see who's going to call the shots or 'be boss'
from then on.   And we believe the way it's handled by the
adults is significant to the future.   Whether the honeymoon's
end is violent or mild doesn't seem to be as important as
the statement made by the child, 'This is what I'm going to
do, ' and the adult's answer: 'This is what I'm going to do,
and you're not doing that. '
'Tony and I had a major clash about six weeks after
he joined our family in which the general 'calling the shots'
issue was decided.   It was a violent incident and I know it
was the most important thing that happened determining our
specific relationship--his and mine.   He later tested my
husband in a different way, but basically Buzz had no trouble
relating to Tony in a direct way.   The Spanish culture Tony
had just come from emphasizes male dominance, and Buzz
is a strong male figure.   Being an older man and head of a
household made him Top Dog automatically in Tony's scheme
of things.
"But Tony's really big hangup was with his natural
mother.   He hadn't seen her in seven years, and his refusal
to obey her extreme authoritarian demands (which brought
him to the court's attention) was tested out on me, the sur-
rogate mother, when he finally decided not to take out the
trash anymore (or at least until Buzz should come home).
Up till then my authority with him came directly from the

fact that I was Buzz's wife. I knew this--felt it--understood
why.   But Buzz and I both figured this was a condition which
could not last if Tony was ever to learn how to accept his
mother and other women in authority or how even to be a
fair-minded man himself rather than a complete totalitarian.
So I was on guard, though not knowing exactly what to guard
against.
         "After school we were alone in the kitchen.   I chided
him gently.   'Tony, you forgot to take out the trash this
morning.' He sullenly stared at the floor, sitting at the
table.   'I'm not taking out the trash.   That's woman's work.'
I reasoned with him.   'Tony, that's your job and you should
do it without complaining.' And I waited.   Nothing.   'Well?'
And suddenly he leaped to his feet looking down at me.   He
was a tall 14 years, and I'm only 5'2".   His face got white
and he worked himself into a temper, shouting at me, 'I
won't do it!'
         'What happened next came in a split second.   Things
flashed through my mind all at the same time.   I knew I
had to win this first confrontation.   The honeymoon was
over.   I gambled on his Spanish respect for married women
plus the fact that he knew Buzz would not tolerate any vio-
lence from him toward me.   I would call his bluff.   I locked
eyes with him, drew myself up another two inches and cold-
ly, carefully said, 'You will take it out and you will take it
out now.' He pushed his face forward, starting to scream
at me and I deliberately slapped him, pretty hard.   I would
not argue with him.   He was shocked more than hurt and
stepped back in unbelief.   My own face was hard and I gazed
stonily at his eyes until he dropped them.   Then I turned
and left the room, not looking back though I wanted to.
'He'll leave and never come back,' I thought to myself.
'Boy, I really goofed maybe.   But I couldn't let him get
away with that.' And while I was thinking I found myself
really getting angry.   I had to find things to do to keep from
going in there again to tell him off.
         'In the aftermath I was furious, actually shaking in-
side, my fingers trembling.   In retrospect, while it was all
happening I was thinking clearly.   Afterwards I was confused,
doubting the rightness of my action.   And then suddenly I
was livid with so-called righteous anger!   Now, these are
some of the nasty things that went through my head, feeding
my wrath.   And mind you, no one asked me to be a volunteer.   Also, the fact is that we were better off in the house
because our girl and boy were old enough so they really had
needed rooms of their own for quite awhile.   So taking Tony
as a foster son had only been the catalyst we needed to look

for a house. O.K. Here we go. The parentheses are my
conscience reasoning back with myself. We went out of our
way for this kid. We even had to buy a house because our
apartment wasn't big enough for three kids, and rentals are
so expensive in this damn town (You really love this town,
though it's true rentals are very high in relation to other
towns). We're not even being paid to have this blankety-
blank brat disrupt our household! (It's not easy to integrate
a disturbed, hyperactive, violent natured kid with little self-
control into a family--but then, nobody said it was easy.
And be honest--nobody could pay you to do this. It's not
money you want anyway.) Imagine! Defying me in my own
home (So it's your own home? Well, you asked him into it
and you knew it wasn't going to be all roses.) Wait till I
tell Buzz. He'll really clobber him.... (Is it possible you
lost your temper just now? Relax. By the time Buzz gets
home things had better be under control. This was between
you and Tony and if you can't handle it alone you'd better
send him back to the court. Buzz had his own problems at
the office today, and it won't help him to come home to a
fight. And it won't help Tony to drag it out that far will it?
What are you doing now anyway? Feeling sorry for yourself
for the extra laundry? Aren't you letting your own nasty,
vindictive nature show? Come on, lame-brain, calm down.
You're supposed to be in control here! 'Know thyself' is
your lesson for today....)

"And when I finally was calmed down, about half an
hour later, I went back through the kitchen on a contrived
errand to the back porch, near the boy's rooms. The trash
was gone. Tony was sitting on his bed playing my guitar
softly. I ignored him and got dinner, acting as though
nothing had happened when the other children came in. Later,
in the privacy of our bedroom I told Buzz what had happened,
and laughing at myself, how I'd felt afterwards and some of
the things I'd thought which had never occurred to me to
think before. We agreed my reactions had been normal,
and quite human, and the things I'd thought must have been
lurking under my deceptive sweet-natured surface all the
time. And I'd better realize now, while it was fresh, that
even though I had had just cause to feel anger, the boy was
not obligated in any way to behave as we'd like him to.
After all, he hadn't asked to be where he was though the
circumstances of his life had brought him here. Buzz and
I had a good, long talk over this one, and overall he thought
I'd handled the situation well. At dinner we both treated
Tony normally and cheerfully. He was quiet, and got his
dishes clean that night.

'I was totally unprepared for what happened next. "

"Happy Ending to an Incident" (What Happened Then ...)

"That night all three kids said goodnight to Buzz and
me, and went to bed at 9:30 as usual.   About 10:00 Tony
called me and asked if I would come sit by him a minute.
He was shy, like a very little boy, and seemed ready to cry.
'What happened this afternoon, ' he said, 'I mean, it's hard
for me to say this--but I want to thank you for what you
did. '   I was stunned.   He was thanking me.   If I hadn't been
sitting down already I would have sat down after that one.
'That's alright, Tony, ' I smiled a little, and for the first time
since he'd been with us I voluntarily touched him, patting
his hand.   He cried then and said, 'You know Buzz would
have killed me if I'd hit you back. '   I frowned a little, 'I
knew you wouldn't hit me, Tony.   You never hit your own
mother when you were having problems with her and I think
you'll always respect ladies. '"

Tony's Natural Mother (An Explosion ...)

"Tony had mixed feelings about his natural mother,
and often got quite emotional after contacts with her.   One
time after a fight, we talked with him and thought he was
finally beginning to see things a little more in actual perspective.   He was sorry for the way he had acted.   He
wanted to call his mother on the phone and apologize.   When
he made the call I was in the kitchen and overheard his
happy, 'Mama?   This is Antonito ...   Antonito who?   Antonito, your son!'   He listened and then held the phone in his
hand, eyes big with unbelief.   I'd heard his mother's shrill
voice and the unmistakable slam on the other end.   And then
he exploded.   'She wouldn't talk to me.   She says she has
no son.   Her son is dead!   She hung up on me!   I hate her!
I hate her!   I have no mother!   My mother is dead!'"

— — — — — — — —

Man and Boy

Too much real life to summarize ...   suffice it to say the
man was the first court volunteer in the modern era, in one
large eastern state.   Though a busy businessman, he at one
time worked with a dozen juvenile probationers at once.   The
following is a report in brief form pertaining to my first
case as a volunteer and my only case at the time.   I worked
one-on-one and gave considerable time to him.   I do not

want to get involved with his emotional problems or why he
acted out. I just want to explain how I approached and
handled various situations, doing at all times what I felt
was best for the boy. The boy was first arrested at 13-1/2
for stealing a car. He was a sullen, overgrown, tough,
screwed up kid. His parents had little control over him.
The family is Catholic, low-income category, and the boy is
one of six children, next to the youngest. (Note: at no
time was I aware that subject or family resented me because
I was of a different religion and more well-to-do than they.
If anything, there seemed to be a sort of quiet respect.)

First Encounter: "Invariably, I would take the boy
for a ride in my convertible, which impressed him. When
I first met him, I tried to get him to ask me questions,
but he did not. So I talked and talked. I first explained
my position with the court and what I was trying to do as
a volunteer. I told him truthfully that what he and I talked
about was private ... just between the two of us. His response was, 'I don't care ... I don't know ... I guess so ...
Okay ...' etc. I felt I did not reach him for he did not
seem to respond to anything I said. He was not interested
in going bowling with me nor having me take him places.
"The only thing that seemed to get any sort of a reaction was when I told him stories. I started with stories
about myself and my poor youth and some of my problems.
He liked to hear about problems some other kids had in
court. I felt I came on a bit strong but explained that is
why I was there in the first place. The boy never looked
at me during this hour we were together. Consequently,
when I was about to leave, I put my hand under his chin
and turned his head to meet my eyes and I said to him
jokingly, 'How about looking at me once in a while?' That
was the first time he smiled. I saw the boy this way, in
my car, more or less for one hour a week for two years. "
Subsequent Meetings: "I did not feel the boy fully
realized my position with the court even after my explanations but he felt this was better than regular supervision at
the court so he accepted this. Many times we would stop
for a drink or ice cream. A few times I would take him
to my summer cottage at the beach where he would swim,
eat with my family, play a little, then disappear. He would
come back later with some friends as if he was looking me
over, still trying to figure me out. At all times, I tried
not to lecture him to make a point in a story. Not all my
stories to him were pleasant. I would gain his confidence
by occasionally talking about a not so nice man....

"Eventually the boy started to talk about himself but
in soft tones. He would little by little tell me about his
girl friends, his school problems, and even his ambitions
at a later date. I was pleased when he would be on time
for me and dressed neatly and combed his hair. I told him
so. I realized he did not like to play ball because he did
not play well. He did like to fight and because he was big
for his age, he fought often, but never with someone smaller
than himself.

"He began to talk about boxing for money. I knew he
couldn't at his age, but I did follow through. I explained
street fighting was not the same as ring fighting and I
planned to take him to the local police station which has a
ring that professional fighters use to train. Of course I
had to clear this with his parents first. His father was not
too happy with the idea but I explained that it was not my
intention of making a fighter out of his boy, but more interested in having him learn how to defend himself properly,
since he gets into so many fights anyhow. His father did
agree although I had the impression he felt I would do what
I wanted to anyway. The boy seemed pleased I stood up to
father and won out.

"I took my eight-year-old boy with us and the boy
took his friend. They enjoyed walking into the police station
for just a visit. Upstairs in the gym, a friend of mine was
training one of his fighters and my friend talked to both boys
at length about the art of fighting. Subject's enthusiasm
seemed to wane when he saw how hard it is to train. After
both boys put on the gloves and sparred a bit (the boy was
all business and quickly showed his friend how good he was)
the idea of boxing for money seemed to be past. We went
once again to the gym and that was that. The boy wasn't
even interested at a later date to see the boxer who was
training, fight 'for real.' I found out later on that this is
typical of such a boy. They show marked enthusiasm about
something and shortly thereafter become disinterested.

"One small thing happened early in our meetings that
is worth noting. The boy asked me if he could smoke in the
car. I told him I was not a policeman and he could do what
he likes when not with me, but when he is with me I would
rather he wouldn't. He didn't.

"Whenever the boy would postpone or try to cancel
an appointment with me, I would schedule it for later on the
same day or as soon as possible. This gave him the impression that my weekly meetings with him were important.

"The boy would be suspended from school on occasion.
His explanations always showed the teachers at fault. I

always gave him some sympathy but I never blamed the
teacher--trying to have him decide what to do if he was in
their place.   And each time I would tell him a story about
myself and how I was a wise guy when I was in the Navy
and what happened to me when I was caught.
        "The boy wanted to make money so I lined up some
cars for him to wash.   He showed up once.   He wanted the
money but did not like to wash cars to get it.   This idea
also ended quickly.
        "During all this time, I felt the boy liked me, but
more important, he would talk about me to his friends and
many times wanted me to pick him up at school in my convertible which I did.   Whenever he was with my family, and
my children asked who he was, I would only say that he was
my friend.
        "One time, I had invited him to join my family and
me on a fishing trip.   He was looking forward to it but had
to cancel out for he had a dentist appointment.   I felt he
was upset because of this and that is why he was not at
home the next time we were to meet.   However, I found out
he had gone to the local football game.   So I went there and
looked for him.   Although there was a large crowd, I did
find him.   He was impressed that I would look for him.
His excuse for not being home was a typical, 'I forgot.'   I
let it go and told him where to look for some girls.   Although I wasn't with him but a few minutes, I felt this meeting was a very important one and I proved to him my sincerity in interacting with him.
        "One time I went to see him practice football and
was told he was thrown off the team for breaking the rules.
I think it was that he wasn't as good a player as he thought
he was so he left the team in this manner.
        "I couldn't hire the boy in my store for I needed a
boy who drove.   He did eventually get a job in a shoe fac-
tory.   He didn't save much money from it.
        "The boy now talked readily to me and asked me
questions about drugs and other topics he feels I know about.
He became more affirmative on what he liked and disliked
and nowadays I seldom hear from him 'I don't know.'   I
never discouraged him in any wild idea he might have though
after proper discussion, he would lose his enthusiasm for it.
He would remember everything I ever said even though it
appeared he wasn't listening.   That is why I was glad I always told him the truth and thus never worried about what
I might have said that was false.
        "Another time with my small son present, the boy
swore.   I was angry and told him so.   He was not angry

and respected my request.

'I gave him a Christmas present: a week off from
our meetings. This was better than a material gift. However, at another time, when I took a trip, I did bring him
back a mascot. It had to be sharp and it was. I was surprised when he thanked me for I felt it wasn't easy for him.

'The boy would tell me about some of the things his
friends did wrong. I told him to get away whenever this
happened. When he told me about some minor things he
himself did wrong, I tried not to judge him. When he would
tell me he drank, I couldn't tell him not to and how wrong
it was, for I felt it would hurt our relationship. Instead, I
told him how to drink properly, like adults might do at a
cocktail party. Not chug-a-lug nor mix liquor and beer.
Since I didn't want him to drink at all, I made my point by
telling him stories about how the kids get so very sick and
picked up by the police and how I don't drink anymore for it
interferes with my wind when I jog or play handball. I know
this approach did help him when he was out with his friends
and they all drank. To the best of my knowledge, he never
got drunk after I talked to him in this manner.

'The boy entered a drum and bugle corps that had a
reputation for being one of the best. He was accepted and
was very happy about it. I explained to him he now could
gain attention without having to do something wrong. I also
explained to him that being competitive can be relative. If
two boys were competing, the one that did not win could
consider himself coming in second ... or last, depending
upon how one wants to tell the story.

'I asked the boy his advice on a few matters and
took it when it was appropriate. This pleased him. Example: what kind of car I should buy for my store deliveries
... what might be wrong with my car if it made certain
noises, etc. He liked my jokes (some were off-color) and
he liked it when I confided in him.

''As usual, when things seemed to be going well,
something happened; the boy was suspended from school for
smoking. Actually, he had a poor discipline record and this
was the last straw. He was brought back into court. I knew
in advance the punishment was going to be severe, but I did
not tell the boy. He entered court and was frightened. In
order to cover up his fear, he did not answer the judge
properly. Consequently, he was sent to the Detention Center
for five days with bail set at $300. His mother was one
step away from shock and cried bitterly, afraid to tell the
father, who drinks and does not get along with the boy, and
harps on one subject to excess. The mother's only concern

was to raise the bail money and get her son out right away.

'The judge tried to explain to the mother that what he did was best for the boy and might teach him not to be so cocky. The mother wouldn't listen. I knew how afraid the boy was about being sent away and yet felt under the circumstances, it was best for the boy. Mother wouldn't hear of it. Mother and I had a fight and it ended in a compromise. The boy was to spend one day and night in the Detention Center. I saw him before he went away. He was afraid and ashamed. I did not lecture him, but did talk to him about why he was in this jam and that it was his own doing. His mother took a second mortgage on the house and I took her the next day to the Detention Center to pick up her son.

'It was as if he was away a long time. When he came out, he was real happy to be out. I stressed to the mother not to talk of this nor should the rest of the family after he got home. However, on the way home, the boy talked of his experiences at the Center very easily. He felt the boys there with him were idiots and the judge's reasoning for sending the boy there was valid. His cockiness had been diminished. When he again appeared before the judge, he was told to 'smarten up' but no additional probation time was given. It was now my place to try to get him back into school.

'The school did not want to take him back. They listed all the bad things he had done, which were many. I did not say anything but called the boy in. He said he would stop smoking if the school would let him back. I yelled at the boy, calling him a liar. The school officials were amazed. Instead of defending the boy in order to get him reinstated, I was admonishing him. The boy was also surprised at my attitude. However, it was because of this approach that the school officials now talked directly to the boy.

'We talked openly as to how his lack of discipline had to be curtailed. The end result was that the principal, who disliked the boy, and the boy, who hated the principal, shook hands and became friends. The boy was given a three-day probation period and if in that time he was in any way smart, sarcastic, or non-cooperative, he would not be able to continue in school.

'I then had another long talk with his mother. I told her the best thing she could do for her son the next time anyone comes to her with a story about her boy is not to side with the boy, even if the story is false. She could not agree. She wanted to show the boy that his family is behind

him and that a mother cannot be mean to her son.   I felt if
she continued to bail him out of trouble, he would never
change.   I also told the boy that everyone is now out on a
limb for him and that this is the end.   No more chances.
He said he would not let us down.   And he didn't.

"Although he was disappointed in not getting into the
local trade school, and even though his drum and bugle group
lost by a fraction of a point, he did not act out again.   The
final test was when parents went away for a two-week vacation and left the boy alone at home with his married sister.
He did not get into further trouble.

"On the basis of my recommendation, the boy's case
was brought forward, his adjudication was vacated, his suspension was revoked and all cases against him were dismissed.

"I have not heard from the boy for three years.   My
Christmas cards were never acknowledged.   But he has not
been in any trouble since, to my knowledge, and that's all
I ask. "

— — — — — — —

Nearly Christmas in the Bus Station

Day-by-day and hour-by-hour--a runaway and return, and a
lie along the way. ...   The volunteer works with school
counselor and weak mother (who gives him information only
after things go bad) ... volunteer using contacts in another
town to locate the boy and give him a chance to return without official police action ... then ... sweating out the wait.

December 9, 1969:   "Received a résumé form on
Mark from Mrs. Johnson, the program supervisor.   Résumé
gave name, phone number, school grade, and birthdate of
Mark, plus parent's name and address. "

December 13, 1969:   "Talked with Mark's mother for
one and one-half hours.   She stated that Mark was rebellious,
indifferent, drank beer, tried marijuana, and had no respect
for authority.   Because of these problems, his parents had
referred Mark to the juvenile court.

"Other information related during my talk with mother:

- Mark has interest in playing the guitar and in debate
  at school.
- Mark has arguments with father.   Father doesn't think
  Mark is ambitious.   Mark's hair style bothers the
  father.
- Mark has been visiting the Halfway House and Focus

(campus).

- Mark wants very much to go on a trip with the debate team at school on the weekend of December 19.

- Mark is usually home by 11 P. M. , and spends many evenings studying.

"The talk with the boy's mother left me with the impression that she guarded her remarks. I got the impression that she tends to be overprotective and will minimize Mark's actions. "

December 18, 1969; 12:30 P. M. : "Talked with the counselor at Mark's school. Mark is not a problem at school. Attendance and grades are good. He is popular with students but only one student was named as his close friend. (Craig, who lives at the Halfway House.) Mark's tests reveal good scores in reading, math, and social studies. I. Q. is 98. The counselor indicated that the rumor at school was that Mark was going to take off for Mexico. I found out that a debate trip was not planned by the school. Mark obviously lied about this to his parents and to Mrs. Johnson, the program supervisor. "

Same Day; 1:30 P. M. : "Mark is gone. After visiting the school, I stopped to see Mrs. Johnson. She revealed that she had a tip that Mark may be at a house on Hill Street in a college town 100 miles away. Mrs. Johnson asked if I had any contacts there and I indicated that I would contact my brother in that area (hereafter referred to as town X). "

Same Day; 1:45 P. M. : "Called Mark's mother and found out nothing new except that Mark did take clothing with him when he left. "

Same Day; 9:30 P. M. : "Called my brother who happens to be a deputy sheriff in a nearby county, and asked if he had any contacts in town X. Discussion with my brother revealed that his good friend, Doug, works with the town X vice squad. The town X was a haven for runaways and a hang-out for drug addicts.

"My brother agreed to contact Doug and see if he could get a message into the house. Message would state that I wanted to have Mark call me back in his home town at any time, that I was not working with the police, and that I wanted to talk to him. "

Same Day; 10:30 P. M. : "My brother called me back and told me that his friend, Doug, drove to the house in town X and talked with the man who runs the house. He could not go in but found out that this man knew Mark. Doug told the man to deliver my message to Mark if he was there. My brother indicated that we should wait two days

for Mark to call me; if he didn't a warrant could be processed charging the man who runs the house with harboring
a 15-year-old runaway.   Concern was for Mark's safety and
exposure to drugs if he was there."
    December 19, 1969:   "Mark's mother called me at
my home.   We talked about 15 minutes.   Conversation revealed: Mark has not called home.   He had about $9 when
he left home.   Now she tells me that Mark ran away from
home before when he was 13 years old.   He was found hid-
ing in a tunnel below a church.   When the police went in,
Mark shot himself through the head.   Doctors revealed (according to Mark's mother) that it was a miracle Mark was
alive.   Mark was under psychiatric care after the incident.
I did not push for more details."
    December 20, 1969:   "Mark called home at noon.
He was in a big city near town X.   He planned to return to
town X and pick up some of his things before returning home
by bus.   Mark decided to return when he knew that his
whereabouts were known.
    "I was concerned that Mark would return to the house
in town X and be influenced to stay.   After talking with
Mrs. Johnson, program supervisor, we decided to wait until
the last bus had arrived from town X before notifying the
police to pick up Mark.   I waited seven hours in the bus
station and on the very last bus Mark arrived.   He was
taken home by his mother."
    December 22, 1969:   "I spent two hours with Mark.
See report form.   We're still working."

– – – – – – –

You Don't Win 'Em All

A volunteer shares the disappointment and heartbreak of a
long-devoted effort which suffered many reverses, the last
of which is a runaway....

    "After checking with a number of friends, we came
upon Jimmy in front of a friend's house in the neighborhood,
but before we could catch him, he started running, suit and
all.   We chased him for several hours, but then he got
away, mainly through the help of certain other friends of
his who supposedly were helping us find him, but who really
decided to help him hide out.   I still feel that if we had
been able to get Jimmy back that night, the matter still
might have been able to be worked out, although the situation at school was pretty bad and might have become impossible due to his additional ditching that day.

"As usual, his foster mother blamed me for everything, and seemed particularly upset at the idea that Jimmy
might call me and not her. She again seemed to think that
I was trying to 'seduce' Jimmy from her in some way rather
than returning him to her. In any event, he could not be
found that night or for that matter for a week. His friends
hid him out and he hid in various alleys, and although some
of them claimed to know where he was, none of them would
ever help us find him. His foster father came upon Jimmy
on a Saturday morning in a trailer where he had been living
for several days, and allegedly thought he was smoking
marijuana, but a friend distracted his attention, and Jimmy
escaped again.

"Reports started coming in of various burglaries and
car thefts in the neighborhood, which Jimmy apparently was
committing. The reports also were that Jimmy was acting
sort of like a hoodlum in 'Bonnie and Clyde' talking about
the fact that he wouldn't call us because he thought that the
lines were tapped and that the police would have to shoot
him dead before he could be captured. Obviously at this
point he was suffering extremely from guilt feelings, fear,
and a variety of other feelings, trying to tell himself that
he was getting pleasure out of what he was doing in his
final spree, but knowing that it would come to no good end.
Although I desperately tried to get his friends to have him
call me, he never did so, although there was some claim
later on that he had tried again to do so. His friends said
that he did not want to talk to me and no longer trusted me.
I think Jimmy felt like a caged lion, totally boxed in and
knowing that there was no out at that time.

"His foster mother also saw Jimmy in an alley one
day, apparently the next Monday, about the time that a
burglary was committed at a neighbor's house. Jimmy was
later charged with this and his foster mother told me that
he had admitted it, but he actually did not admit it and I'm
not at all sure that he did it, although he may have been
with another boy who did it. Due to my busy schedule, I
never did see Jimmy once during the time he was a runaway
in this period, nor did he call me. There were reports
that he had been trying to steal his foster mother's car at
night, and that he had planned to break into my apartment
or his foster parents to steal the drums that I had given
them for him, to sell them to make money for a getaway.

"It is obvious that he really didn't want to leave the
area, since he made no effort to leave the jurisdiction. In
any event, about 7:00 p.m. on Tuesday, the police captured
Jimmy. He was in a stolen car and had been riding a

stolen car at fast speeds for several days, often with other
friends. The police had found the car and staked it out
while he went out to do certain things. Jimmy at that time
was drunk, having broken into some other houses and stolen
some more liquor apparently. When he came back to the
car staked out by the police, the police captured him without
any fight, he being too drunk to do much arguing about it.
He was detained in the detention home that night along with
three other friends who were in the car with him.

"I saw Jimmy a day and a half later in the detention
home. I told him that I was quite upset with him because
he had messed up and had not even talked with me or tried
to work it out with me. He was in a very belligerent mood,
looked very bad physically, looking pale with his hair very
disheveled. Unlike the last time he was in the detention
home, he did not cry or seem remorseful, but immediately
kept saying, 'Ah, Mr. K___, come on get me out, you can
help me escape, or at least get me some cigarettes or
candy.' He kept talking about evading reality by escaping,
etc. I pointed out to him that he could not escape from his
problems any longer, that he had messed up real bad, that
letting him go would not solve anything. He said that he
could go out and leave the state if he was allowed to get out
of the detention home, or go with a friend to live with the
friend's relatives. I told him that that was very unrealistic
even if it could be arranged, and that he couldn't get away
with it, and that he had to be brought to heel.

"The probation officer came in there and we also
discussed the matter with Jimmy and suggested that he plead
guilty to the charges so that he could be committed and
possibly stay at the Youth Center if he wouldn't try to run
away. Jimmy told me privately during my visits with him
that he planned to escape, and at one point claimed that he
had weapons in the detention home to do so. At this point,
Jimmy was all belligerent veneer with none of the 'little
boy' sensitivity otherwise seen in him at other times.

"Despite our advice to Jimmy to plead guilty, he in-
sisted on pleading innocent before the referee at the arraignment on October 31. We told him he would have to
stay in the detention home that way, but Jimmy told me
that he hoped to escape in between court appearances. Apparently, no serious effort was made to escape, but later
he told me that they were watching him closely, apparently
because I told the probation officer of Jimmy's plans.

"At the November 12 adjudication hearing, Jimmy was
in a much better mood, with both his foster parents and his
mother present. The mother had not shown up for the

arraignment hearing and had earlier indicated that she didn't care what happened to him. Jimmy looked better and his attitude was much better, and he appeared much more remorseful and sobered by what he had done and what would happen to him. After the court proceedings, in which he was found innocent of both substantive charges but still committed on grounds of violation of probation for being away from home and away from school, he took it pretty well without much crying or anything like that.

"His mother and I and Kenny went to see the woman from the Department of Corrections in regard to the procedures for his commitment. The woman discussed the possibility of just where Jimmy might be sent, starting with the Youth Center and probably ending up in the training school, and explained the differences in the rules and programs of the two institutions. She emphasized that the institutions did not exist to torture or punish the boy but to help him, and that his future would be determined by how well he did at such institutions. Jimmy indicated at that time that he really appreciated what I had done for him and indicated that he no longer planned to escape or otherwise cause any more trouble. He hugged his baby sister who was with his mother and definitely said he wanted to go back with his real mother after he got out of an institution. I never saw Jimmy again until I saw him at the Youth Center three weeks later, although both his foster parents and his mother went down to see him on visiting hours the next Saturday before he was shipped out. A police officer, Mr. Farmer, went to see Jimmy about some burglary loot on another case and said that Jimmy wanted to see me, but before I could get down there, he had been sent to the Youth Center."

— — — — — — —

Help, Not Just Talk

The volunteer as an employer offering self-respect: yet another example concerns the role of any employer-volunteer. This man, the owner of a tool company, offered to employ a youngster who was on probation. This young man was not doing well on probation and was, in our opinion, "a felony looking for a place to happen." The employer spent many hours after the day's work was over talking to the young probationer. After some months, the probationer's change of attitude was evident. He got a more responsible job with the company. He enrolled in night school. He began to have faith in the fact that he was "somebody."

— — — — — — —

A Retarded Boy

How the volunteer helped him by deeds (not so much by words).

Dennis is a 14-year-old mentally retarded boy, who was abandoned by his alcoholic mother at the age of five, along with three younger children of the second marriage. The stepfather took care of the four children with the help of relatives. The stepfather was sent to the Court to gain legal guardianship, so that he would have the authority to sign for Dennis' tonsilectomy. It was found that Dennis had many problems and was not easy to take care of. His early childhood with a mother who was weak and irresponsible left him weak, insecure, and childish. When ridiculed and taunted by other children, he would defend himself by physical force and get into difficulty at school and on the street. The stepfather often thought he would have to place him in an institution. The probation officer made a study of the problem, including a diagnostic examination at our clinic, and a decision was made to provide guidance for the family in how to best deal with his outbursts and by giving Dennis individual attention. A volunteer was found through the neighborhood center--a young man with whom Dennis could identify and whom he did not have to share with his younger brothers. The volunteer helped Dennis to get into a baseball team and by attending the practice with him, he was able to forestall the clashes that Dennis would have otherwise gotten himself into. Dennis blossomed out, as he felt himself privileged by this special attention and with the increased self-confidence, he was able to hold his own with his peers, without striking at them.

— — — — — — — —

A Sample Case, Demonstrating Process and Terminology

A good training idea, we think, from a big city juvenile probation department. They use a constructed "typical case" as a natural context in which to present (1) the court terminology concepts and process flow which every volunteer must know, and (2) direct suggestions as to what the volunteer can do about the case problem presented.

Johnny Jones, 14 years old, was apprehended by police at 10:35 P. M. Tuesday night in a stolen auto that made a wrong left turn. He admitted that he had no license and the car was not his. He was advised of his legal rights and

taken to the police station where his parents were contacted
and appeared. Johnny confessed to the theft and a delinquent
petition was filed by the police alleging Johnny to be a delinquent "in that he had taken unauthorized possession of an
automobile belonging to another without the knowledge and
consent of the owner, intending to deprive said owner of its
use. "
    A court hearing was set for the Court to make a
legal determination of John's guilt or innocence. This is
called an ADJUDICATORY HEARING. Johnny and his parents
were served summons for the court hearing and Johnny was
released to his parents. At the adjudication hearing, Johnny
and his parents appeared. They were told of their legal
rights to be represented by an attorney appointed by the
Court if they could not financially afford one. They agreed
to have the case heard without a lawyer and Johnny admitted
to the charges.
    The Judge made the legal findings of delinquency and
ordered a Social Investigation to be done by the Probation
Department. He continued the case for three weeks for the
report which he uses as the basis for his decision at this
second hearing called a Disposition Hearing. The case is
then assigned to a Probation Officer who will visit in the
home with the child and parents and gather the required information about the child's total adjustment and behavior in
the home, school and community and the physical and emotional atmosphere in the home. Information about parents
and an evaluation of the situation is made to determine what
the likely chances are for this kid's not getting into trouble
again, in what areas his problems are and where he needs
help. This information is written up by the Probation Officer in a prescribed form called the Social Investigation and
is a part of the social record that is kept by the Probation
Officer in which he enters all of his contacts on the case.
    At the Disposition Hearing, the Probation Officer ap-
pears with Johnny and his parents, and gives the Judge a
condensed report of the highlights of the child's life; his total
adjustment in the home, school and community; his attitude
and motivation, and the parents' efforts and ability to help
Johnny's problems in the home and strengths within the
family.
    Hopefully, the Judge has a chance to talk briefly with
Johnny and the parents and advises Johnny he is placing him
on Probation and a Probation Officer will be visiting him.
The Judge then states a legal order of Probation of one year
or six months or whatever time he feels is indicated, or
just a straight Probation order.

Now that the kid is on Probation, the Probation Officer must immediately think about and <u>focus</u> a plan for working with and helping this child.   This <u>plan</u> is what we call the <u>Probation Plan</u> and is used as a guideline for future contacts with Johnny.   It is typed into the record.

Now here is where you, a good volunteer come in. The Probation Plan for John may be to try to motivate him towards school.   He is disgusted because he is behind and still finds the work hard.   He truants frequently.   He needs tutoring services which you may be able to get for him. Once he begins to get extra help and his grades improve, he may like school better; above all however, he needs acceptance and warm understanding of his discomforts about school. This means you.

An examination a year ago showed that he needed glasses, but he has never gone to get his eyes examined and parents have been too busy to think much about it.   You may help here in encouraging child and parents to go in, arranging for an appointment with them.   Social horizons are narrow.   He belongs to no youth groups, does not attend any community centers, has never been to the Y. M. C. A., seldom gets farther than the nearest park, has been downtown only several times in his whole life, has seen only one professional ball game, has never been to an ice show.   A good Probation Officer or Volunteer may introduce Johnny to the Neighborhood Boy's Club or Y. M. C. A., or Park Field House that offers swimming, karate, ball team tours, trips, camping experience and the like.

These are only a few of the things in the way of individual attention that are needed to demonstrate to a youngster that someone really cares about him.   Communication with adults is often difficult for the adolescent, mainly because the adult tends "to talk <u>to</u> him" and not realize that what he wants and needs, is someone to listen to what he has to say.

— — — — — — —

<u>For We Are Now Friends</u>

Pete was a dropout, alienated, a truant from the system, bright enough but unmotivated.   A young volunteer begins to get through to him....

"I got into the juvenile court volunteer program as a sociology student at the university.   The first step was a meeting with a court juvenile probation officer, Jim Morton, who was to supervise my volunteer work.   After this

preliminary interview, Mr. Morton assigned me the case of
Peter Sanford, a sixteen-year-old high school youth with a
record of truancy and running away from home. Peter became known to the court through repeated truancies and was
adjudicated a Child In Need of Supervision (CHINS) with a
probation period of two years. (A CHINS is a youth that
has not been criminally delinquent. Such a child generally
is uncontrollable by his or her parents.)

"Peter seemed to me typical of many young men and
women that have, in the last five years, become more and
more of a problem to law authorities throughout the country,
as well as to their parents. He is the kind of boy often
labeled "irresponsible," "filthy," a "hippie." I must say,
though, that to me he only seemed confused, bewildered,
searching; and behind it all, quite intelligent and sensitive.

"Mr. Morton planned to start off by setting up a
meeting between Pete and me, at the town community center.
We got off to a great start! Pete didn't even show up at
that first meeting, and the court ordered him picked up and
placed in jail (juvenile section).

"So my very first meeting with Pete was in jail,
where I went to visit him, the following day. As you might
expect, this first meeting was rather strained, especially in
the confines of the lock up. But as far as first impressions
go, it was fairly successful. Later that afternoon, Pete
was released in my custody and I took him to his home. I
was glad that things worked out in this way for when I met
his parents at home, it wasn't as cold and superficial as it
might have been with all of us sitting around Pete at a public
place like the local community center.

"During this first meeting with Mr. and Mrs. Sanford, Pete's parents, I was quickly aware of the gap between
him and his parents. Both parents were from a rural background. Mr. Sanford was a tall, rather sad but kind looking and a quiet man. He has worked for a maintenance company for 16 years. Mrs. Sanford was a frail and sickly appearing woman. But she was very vocal and clearly dominated the conversation. Pete has one brother, Frank, who
was obviously more conventional and less alienated than
Pete. The family home was a low level brick tract sub-
division model.

"After our first meeting, I generally met with Pete
once a week. He was attending school but was having
trouble scholastically. It was obvious from listening that
he was neither interested in or trying in the local school
system. It was also apparent to me that Pete's home problems were glossed over but unresolved. He told me that

after school he generally withdrew to his room and only
came down for meals.

"Several weeks passed; one day Mr. Morton called
from the court and asked me if I would be present at a
meeting with psychiatrists at the University Mental Health
Center to discuss the results of psychological tests and
future treatment. The meeting was held in a small room
with Pete, Mr. Morton, myself, the doctors, and Mr. and
Mrs. Sanford. An in-patient therapy program was recommended for Pete. The parents were somewhat hesitant and
Mrs. Sanford did most of the talking in response to questions about the family from the doctors. It was easy to
see that Pete was under pressure to commit himself; after
a long hour-and-a-half he agreed but with obvious apprehension. We adjourned. Later that evening Pete called my
home to ask for one extra late night on the weekend before
he was to be committed for treatment. I agreed. I didn't
hear anything more until the next morning when Mrs. Sanford called me to say that Pete had left a note and run in
the night. I informed Mr. Morton of the situation because
I knew I had to keep the court advised. I also called the
local high school.

"Pete returned home after a week. Upon his return
we had a long meeting (the two of us) in which we discussed
prospects for the future and alternative programs to school.
Pete decided to drop out. He was too far behind to salvage
any credits and his disenchantment with the school was so
strong that I thought, if anything, that a worthless continu-
ance would injure his success chances for a future return.
So Pete dropped his classes and began a restless few weeks
looking for a job. His age and lack of training were heavily
stacked against him and he got very discouraged. But a
couple of things did seem to get better after he dropped out
of school--family pressure eased up and he became more
open with his parents.

"Pete soon found a job in a filling station/car wash
and came to my home to tell me about his position. He
had been to my home twice before and appeared comfortable.
I believe this comfort was due to the fact that my wife and
I are young and provide a life style which not only contrasts
with that of his parents but also one to which he could relate, being closer in age and viewpoint to his own. On future
visits Pete began to bring his friends to our home, which
we accepted on an informal basis. The feelings at the time
of these meetings were congenial. However, our meetings
began to taper off and I must admit, I was delinquent in my
meeting schedule. This situation continued until Pete and I

decided to take an adult education class on social issues together. This class proved to be a significant sounding board
in which I got to know Pete and his friends better.   I believe
this experience of a shared class, in an informal atmosphere
(there were only nine of us in the class) did more to further
our relationship in the least amount of time than anything
else we ever did.   After the class ended, Pete and I continued to get together about once every two weeks.

"After a time, Pete expressed an interest in returning to school. But not school as it had been before.   He
wanted something more tangible.   So, I arranged for Pete
to meet with an instructor at the vocation school, as well as
a high school counselor, to establish how he could set up a
program.   I then met privately with Pete's parents to outline
what I had discovered.   They were receptive to any program
that would get Pete interested in education again.   At this
meeting the Sanford's and I relaxed which had never happened before, and we exchanged views on a number of significant topics in relation to their sons, the draft, education,
etc.

"Hopefully, things will begin to work out successfully
for Pete in a scholastic way soon.   For we are now friends.
His probation case comes up for review next September.
There is a good possibility that he can be released from
supervision. "

IV: RESOURCES, FEEDBACK, AND THE FUTURE

Chapter 16

MARSHALLING THE RESOURCES TO DO THE JOB

As mentioned in the preface of this book, each agency faces a distinct and unique situation as it addresses its
volunteer training needs. These individualities also must be
faced by each court as it seeks out resources in the community to help train volunteers. Hopefully, the trainer may
find that within his community he may have the locus for
training, the trainers, the technology, as well as the materials needed for training. In any event, the volunteer trainer would do well to ask himself and the court staff, "What
training resources do we have in this community?" "Do we
have a college or university?" "If so, which departments
have relevance to our program?" "What training potential
exists in private industry in this community?"

If we are to approximate the ideal training model,
where are we going to get the wherewithal to do the job?
The two basic facts of life established by the Westchester-
Boulder 1968 survey, and frequently re-established since,
are these: the typical volunteer court or institution has very
little money to spend on volunteer training, an average of
only $50-75 per year; and in the typical volunteer court,
staff supervisors lack expertise in training volunteers, or at
least they surmise that they do. This is not terribly surprising since trained volunteers are a new concept in courts.
Therefore the alternatives available to the typical volunteer
court are quite simple: go it alone and thereby acquiesce
in slipshod, incomplete training programs for volunteers, or
tap into free or nearly free training resources that are
available locally or nationally, and have a respectable training effort.

This chapter develops the latter alternative. Most
agencies will see the logic of it--that's not the problem.
However, many of us are unaware of the full range of training

resources which may be available to us in our local community, our state and nation. The possibilities will differ from court to court, from community to community, and they will certainly depend crucially on the kind of training program and model you adopt. But it is well to be exposed to the range that <u>could</u> exist. Once such resources are identified, the trainer <u>can</u> and should reach out to them for assistance in his worthy court volunteer enterprise. Indeed, effectively using available community resources is but the general case, of which court volunteerism is but one specific instance. But always, we return to realism; we assume there is little money, time, or training expertise within the court itself, yet, there is some actual precedent in some court or other for all but one or two of the "free resource" ideas presented below. Moreover, broadening our perspective to put more emphasis on informal and in-service training means we can use a wider range of outside resources. Following are our suggestions.

Within the Court or Other Volunteer-Using Agency

Whatever training expertise and time regular staff have should, of course, be used to the fullest. However widely one uses other training resources, regular staff must continue to play a central coordinating and policy role, if they want this to be their program, as it should be. Certainly, the volunteer coordinator, if there is one, must be vitally involved in training volunteers, at least in the coordinating and policy area.

The trainer, however, must be aware of the potential that the court itself offers for training. The staff of a court can and should be utilized in training, particularly in that part of training mentioned earlier regarding the court as an organization. Using court staff in training is one way of insuring continued contact between staff and volunteer. It has the added benefit of providing support in that we know that there is a human tendency to identify with and promote that which one has helped to create.

Courts range from the one-judge court where he has considerable or total administrative control of the court to the large court with many judges and where court services are relatively autonomous. Consideration of the use of judges in training will be important from an administrative and public relations standpoint.

The potential of training serving a dual purpose should
not be ignored either. Much of the training given to volunteers also has relevance to professional court staff. Economy may dictate that, where possible, staff avail themselves
of volunteer training. Beyond that, however, even where
court staff assist in a training capacity, they are forced into
learning roles. As Anna said in The King and I, "By my
students I've been taught. "

Veteran volunteers, as well as transfer volunteers
from other courts, the proven successful ones, are excellent
volunteer trainers. They needn't be professional trainers;
all they need do is describe their experiences naturally,
then freely answer questions. These may be (and usually
are) quite unstructured sessions. That is, in fact, their
strength. With caution, offenders or ex-offenders themselves may be used. People from minority or underprivi-
leged groups may also be asked to give their views.

Existing resources include tours and audits of what
you already have naturally. As mentioned in Chapter 12,
this includes observation of jails and court facilities, sitting
in on court hearings, auditing in-service volunteer meetings
or even probationer meetings, tours of high-delinquency
neighborhoods or schools or with police on patrol. Once
volunteer service begins, continuing attendance at small-
group volunteer meetings will provide inexpensive but effective training. As an extension of this, it's not too difficult to tape some volunteer in-service meetings or even
just some offenders talking, and play back the best of these
for future sessions.

Visit veteran volunteers or volunteer coordinators
from neighboring court or related agencies, or have volunteers visit in-service sessions at nearby volunteer courts or
just watch operations there or have them visit the court.

Sharing Resources in Joint Training

Obviously, combining trainee groups across agencies
means less time and energy drain on the training resources
of any participating agency and, perhaps more important, allows the trainer to use the best training people and training
aids to maximum effect. A possible disadvantage, which
should be balanced on the other side, is that combined groups
might get too large for real trainee participation.

Several neighboring courts can train their volunteers together for the basic training phase, at least: "What every court volunteer should know. " The trainees can then return home for a final session of orientation specialized to their particular court, e. g. , juvenile, adult, misdemeanant, felon, etc. Most volunteer courts today, in reasonably populated areas, do have courts so close that volunteer travel to a central place isn't a particular problem.

If there are no neighbor volunteer courts in close proximity, perhaps arrangements can be made to train together locally with agencies using volunteers in similar ways, e. g. , child welfare, mental health, school dropout programs, vocational rehab, OEO, etc.

In the plausible future, courts may combine to sponsor regional or national network ETV training shows for court volunteers. When relatively expensive speakers or training aids (e. g. films) are desirable, courts or agencies cooperating in an area can purchase or rent them jointly.

Inexpensive, Relevant Training Aids

During 1970-71 the National Court Volunteer Training Project concentrated on providing nationally adaptable core training materials and training aids for volunteer courts around the country. These are designed to be inexpensive, relevant to a core curriculum, adaptable as necessary for local use, interesting and realistic. Most of them are described in this book in Part III.

Certain other training aid materials, though not produced originally with court volunteers in mind, may nevertheless have some relevance here. The authors have therefore also attempted to identify and evaluate such materials for their court volunteer training value and have described the better ones and have informed the reader how to obtain them.

Using Your Own Community

Someone on the staff or a veteran volunteer may be recruited to keep a continual eye out for educational programs in town which may be of training value for volunteers. These may be lectures, seminars, radio or television

programs, or movies. Once they have been identified as
worthwhile for training, volunteers can be advised. Perhaps
volunteers can be induced to attend these functions as a
group with a view to discussing them later. Incidentally,
these may not always be labelled as training aids; many
commercial movies for example may carry a training message in the broadest, most creative sense.

Visits, as permitted or as volunteers are invited, to
other volunteer or even staff training sessions offer potential
for inexpensive or no-cost training. These might include
such related agencies as mental health, Office of Economic
Opportunity and related programs, vocational rehabilitation,
and public and child welfare departments. There are also
less formal, but excellent, organizations such as Synanon
which are relatively open to volunteers and which see their
mission in part being that of public education to their problem.

Speakers from other local agencies such as the above
can be induced to give training sessions for volunteers. A
"seminar series" of this type not only can give volunteers
good information for use in their court work, it can also
help familiarize them with the local social service milieu in
which they must operate. It can also help cement relations
between the court and their agency, since in helping to train
court volunteers, they develop a stake in the program. The
authors are familiar with at least one court where the whole
"contract" for training volunteers is let out to a similar service agency.

The above material refers to agencies operating in
similar service areas more or less regardless of whether
they have volunteers or not. There are also volunteer
specialists regardless of service area. Two very real possibilities to check out here, both for training volunteers and
for training staff in supervising volunteers, are local Red
Cross chapters (they are beginning to alert their local chapters to court needs), and local Volunteer Bureaus, where
they exist. Again, they can come in and help in training or
volunteers can be sent to them for the same purpose.

Local industry may be persuaded to provide their
training resources for the training of volunteer trainers as
well as rank-and-file volunteers. Many industries are doing
this kind of thing as a community service and for public relations. Indeed, some of the most creative training is

presently taking place in the corporations of America. The
potential for the use of this technology and personnel should
be explored. Ongoing training in all levels of government
might also be considered as a resource for volunteer training.

Using the College or University

Most colleges seek closeness with the community,
particularly in urban areas. Community colleges seem particularly responsive, but any college is likely to be. The
trainer of volunteers may be amazed at the things they can
and will do in the area of training if he only knows where
to ask and what to ask for. Resources here include, for
instance, college faculty people to train volunteers in any
or all of a number of corrections-related fields: counseling
and guidance, social work, sociology, psychology and social
psychology, urban planning, behavioral sciences, law, education, corrections, correctional administration, communication, etc. Quite a few colleges now actually run formal
courses to train volunteers.

College faculty or staff experts are available in training media (regardless of content) to consult or to actually
deliver training from fields such as communication, speech,
drama, radio, art, graphics, etc. For example, the graphic
arts department or a university's own graphics laboratory
can certainly provide assistance in the development of training aids such as graphs, slide shows, and even films.

Many larger colleges and universities have rather
good general film and audio-visual aid libraries of their
own. Checking their catalogs for things that might be borrowed may uncover some rich training material. Even better, some colleges subscribe to a large central audio-visual
library from which they, and the volunteer trainer through
them, can draw materials. A national audio-visual library
has been established at the University of Colorado in Boulder, for example.

The State and National Scene

A strong recent trend in the court volunteer movement is toward the development of statewide court volunteer
coordinating and resource agencies. The National

Information Center on Volunteers in Courts is currently consulting on an ongoing basis with some 40 states on their plans and operations, and whenever asked, the staff strongly suggests to the planners that a main feature of such an agency be as a resource and facilitator for local courts in the matter of training their volunteers. The state of Georgia is an example of a state where a training library is operational. It might be helpful to determine if this kind of resource is available at the state level, if not through a court volunteer coordinating agency, then through a state coordinator of (all) volunteers, or even a state volunteer coordinator for welfare or OEO programs. The National Information Center attempts to keep up-to-date lists of state coordinating contacts for volunteer courts.

A new professional breed is now on the scene: the professional trainer, the expert in design and conduct of a training package, regardless of content. Maybe they are in our future, but at present they seem too expensive for the average local court ($500-1,000 a package). Perhaps courts could jointly buy one training package and rent it around. Such packages are in fact being developed in North Carolina and in Hennepin County, Minnesota.

VISTA people assigned to communities might function as trainers of local volunteers, including court volunteers. This has in fact worked out in at least one community we know of. The National Information Center has recently developed a corps of National Court Volunteer Consultants, the outstanding experts in the field. Their consulting work, for any local court or correctional institution on request, can now be partially or fully supported by national agencies such as LEAA. Some of these national consultants are training experts, and they might be of assistance in setting up training initially or actually help to train beginning classes. Check with your regional or state LEAA planning agency for details.

National agencies such as LEAA and HEW (YD/DPA) know the whereabouts of some potentially good training materials and films. It is suggested that the reader write to the Youth Development and Delinquency Prevention Administration, Social and Rehabilitation Service, Room 2030 South, H. E. W. Building, Washington, D. C. 20201, or the Law Enforcement Assistance Administration, Department of Justice, Washington, D. C. 20530 for specific materials.

We trust that the volunteer-training specialized publications and training aids of the National Information Center
on Volunteers in Courts will increasingly be available at the
national level. Already available are Chapter 5 in Using
Volunteers in Court Settings, a book available for one dollar
from the Superintendant of Documents, U. S. Government
Printing Office, Washington, D. C. 20402, and the reports I
through XVI which have been given wide circulation and
which appear in this book. Other courts across the country
are producing training materials. The National Information
Center on Volunteers in Courts is generally aware of most
new developments.

Important Footnotes

Training of volunteers is only one of several major
management areas in court volunteerism. The best volunteer training in the world is wasted if it occurs in a context
of inept recruiting, screening, and supervising of volunteers.
Every one of the resources described in the above sections
could also help in general management areas. Note especially Volunteer Bureaus, Red Cross, local industry management training, neighboring court volunteer programs, universities (now emphasizing departments of public administration, personnel management, business administration, communications, etc.).

The National Information Center has many manuals
and guidebooks on general court volunteer program management. The basic reference is Using Volunteers in Court
Settings, but contact the Center for a complete list. Even
with all the outside help available, volunteer training takes
some money (e. g. , purchasing supplies and training aids,
mailings, etc.).   Chapter 10 of Using Volunteers in Court
Settings concentrates on financing from local and private
sources. The April, 1970, issue of the Volunteer Courts
Newsletter (Vol. 3, No. 2) has a fairly extensive piece on
potential sources of government funding.

Volunteers may be asked if they want to contribute
to bring in workshops. They may be asked who can and is
willing to do so, to pitch in to pay the necessary fee. This
may sound unusual, but it has worked in a few places, at
least.   Courts could cooperatively combine their resources
to pay fees for workshops which none of them could afford
alone.   Because a budget is a vital part of a training

program, the following budget is proposed as a realistic, if
moderate, breakdown of possible spending.

Training Aids (per year)

Film rental (or purchase per year)	$ 40.00
Acquire tape library	30.00
Books, pamphlets to take home	30.00
Slide show rental or purchase	30.00
100 orientation manuals at $1 per manual	100.00
Equipment Rental or Purchase	
Three tape cassettes	50.00
Rental slide projector	30.00
Rental 16mm film projector	40.00
Mailing notices, etc., several meetings	30.00
Refreshments at training sessions	30.00
Other Printing, placards, etc.	40.00
Honoraria for regular service of non-staff con- sultants (beyond occasional volunteer help [$25-30 per evening?])	200.00
Miscellaneous	50.00
Total	$700.00

So, at last we begin to grasp an important subtlety:
volunteers work free but volunteer training programs cost
money, even if they are bargains. It is important therefore
to figure exactly what is needed in the way of money for the
proposed training program, and consider all possibilities for
sources of support. It is probably safer not to count on
any one source for all of the training budget, but rather to
seek out a combination of resources.

Many courts successfully finance their training programs from local private sources via voluntary contributions
from churches, synagogues, foundations, service clubs, individuals, etc. Some of these organizations are looking for
worthy projects to support. In some courts volunteer training expenses have been absorbed in the regular court budget, often without special identification as such. The weak-
ness of this approach is that in some smaller volunteer
courts there is no significant staff budget. Therefore, expenses for training may endanger the expenditure of funds
for other necessary items in the court's total program.

Another approach is to have volunteer training expenses explicitly recognized as a separate additional expense
in the regular court budget, that is, in addition to, and not
taking away from, other normal court needs. We don't know

the general situation here, but we do know at least scattered
instances where some volunteer courts have gotten additional
funds from a local county budget board, earmarked especially
for volunteer programs and/or have had them approved as
extra expenses, by a state budget-controlling agency. If the
local court budget must be approved by some statewide agency
administering the courts, there is the precedent in at least
one state that they will approve extra budget especially for
court volunteer program expenses. (The statewide court
volunteer assistance agency of the future should be able to
provide seed money for new programs, but that is in the
future.) The advantage of this regular budget approach is
that volunteer budget needs can get programmed as a regular
part of the court budget, hopefully without a special frantic
scramble at the end of each and every year.

Chapter 17

EVALUATING AND ASSESSING
THE EFFECTS OF TRAINING

Introduction

The foundation assumption of this book has been that
the trained court volunteer is far more effective than the untrained one. Yet, it must be admitted, we have no convincing proof of this as yet in research which contrasts the
actual performance of the trained vs. the untrained volunteer and, beyond that, compares the relative effectiveness
of different types of training.

Fortunately, this kind of research is presently in
progress, but, it must be repeated, most of our currently
existing store of research doesn't touch this issue. Instead
it merely surveys what courts are actually doing in the way
of training volunteers, and it asks volunteers and/or professionals their opinions of current training and their suggestions about it. Some of this current research is presented
in the appendices here. Yet, at the present time each of
us goes largely blind into training volunteers, in the sense
that we have no absolute assurance that our training is producing more effective helpers, or if so, how or why. At
the same time very few of us have the time, expertise, and
money to do full-scale training research continuously on our
own programs.

Therefore, we are going to suggest some relatively
simple things any agency can do to get feedback on the effectiveness of its volunteer training from the three kinds of
people principally involved: professional supervisors of volunteers; volunteers themselves; and the clients with whom
the volunteers work.

333

Feedback: Supervising Staff

Volunteer orientation is one of the chief channels
through which staff can feel it has a stake in the volunteer
program, a means of making it reasonably accountable to
the overall objectives of the agency. Therefore, what staff
thinks of the training, where it pleases or displeases them,
is crucial. What would they like to see more emphasized,
less emphasized, etc.? We strongly suggest you ask them
regularly and systematically, and once you've asked them,
consider their suggestions very seriously. Parts of Report
XIII indicate the kinds of results that may be achieved here.

Feedback: The Volunteers Themselves

"What do you think about the training?" Obviously volunteers should be asked their opinions of the training--after
all, they're the ones it's designed to help. Again, the basic
questions would be (as specifically as possible) these: "What
do you wish had been covered in training that wasn't?"
"What did you have in training that was particularly helpful
and you would like retained? ... expanded?" "What did you
have in training that has not proven useful to you since and
hence could be de-emphasized?" "eliminated?"

"What was there too much of in kinds of presentation:
lecture? panel? tapes? films? question and answer?
written assignment? small group discussion? role play?
length in general? tours?" "What could there have been
more of in kinds of training: lecture? panel? tapes?
films? question and answer? small groups? role play?
written or reading assignments? tours? length in general?"

Note that the above questions tend to presume the
volunteer has been through training, has had a chance to reflect upon it and test it in practice.

We do think the trainer should be alert to keep a continual pulse on volunteer reactions as training progresses,
the better to adapt as possible to reactions. * We feel there
are certain limitations to this. The principal one is that the

---

*Not incidentally, such immediate feedback reactions may
differ markedly from training class to class and even from
session to session within one class. They have to be picked
up fresh each time.

volunteer trainee is by definition not yet in a position to judge decisively what's best for himself while still in early training. This lack of judgment is precisely why he is in training. But a little later, when, as noted, he's had a chance to apply his training in practice and reflect on its use to him there, he is indeed a valuable feedback resource in the improvement of training. And while a systematic small questionnaire regularly applied is very valuable for getting this all together, periodically, staff should also be alert to pick up this kind of information more informally in in-service meetings, supervisory, or other natural contacts.

A variation on feedback pickup of this type, which combines many of the best features of the formal and informal and the use of the veteran volunteer as a training-advice resource, is the training advisory council of Hennepin County Court (22 Court House, Minneapolis, Minnesota 55415, Mr. John Stoeckel, Volunteer Coordinator). This council, an amalgam of volunteers, regular staff, and expert resource people, meets regularly and not only comments on existing training, but actually takes a leading role in developing new training techniques and contents. Report XIV suggests some of the kinds of useful feedback you can get from volunteers on the reception they give to your training. This report also covers training research more broadly.

What does the volunteer know as a result of training? The volunteer's attitudes and suggestions are important, but when it comes right down to it, it's what he knows that's crucial, for training is essentially an attempt to impart specific knowledge. Presuming you have a clear idea of what knowledge you wish to impart to your volunteers, a crucial test of training is this: do your volunteers, in fact, have this knowledge after training when they didn't have it before? Basically what you must do is examine volunteers on their knowledge before training and then again after, to see what they've learned, if anything.

Clearly, this feeds back into intelligent redesign of sections of the program which are not coming across. It is also helpful in forcing trainers to think harder and more precisely as to exactly what the objectives and content of their training course should be (try constructing a test when you're vague about what you want to teach). Finally, before and after examination results are very useful for the supervisor in dealing with each individual volunteer in identifying his strengths and weaknesses.

We would note here that college and university graduate programs require theses or dissertations as part of
graduation requirements. Studies of the impact of training
have proven to be good projects for student researchers.

Appendices to this chapter describe the philosophy of
this evaluation and give the results of one such application;
this is also as close as we presently can come to a justification of court volunteer training, in the sense that it shows
how ignorant volunteers can be without it.

Feedback: The Offender

The offender is the "being done to" person, and he
is the ultimate object of training. Also, like the volunteer,
we don't have to believe everything he says about it. But
certainly one reasonable way to pitch training is toward the
problem situations and hang-ups your volunteers will commonly encounter, so that they may be prepared for them
beforehand. The offender can certainly give you some insights into these problem situations--times when he wished
the volunteer had been prepared to help him in certain ways
but couldn't, or might have done certain things but didn't.
Increasingly, too, courts are having joint meetings of groups
of volunteers and their probationers, and these are a fine
opportunity to pick up a joint appreciation of problem areas.

A Word on Research

As a general footnote to this chapter, it may seem
that developing procedures for asking staff, volunteer, and
offender feedback on training is a time-consuming process.
It might be. Yet, very recently some standard procedures
for this purpose have been suggested in the Frontier 7 publication of the National Information Center, "Everyone Should
Evaluate Their Volunteer Program--and Everyone Can."
While designed for general volunteer program feedback, these
have much specific reference to training and can easily be
adapted for even more such emphasis.

Of course, the real proof of the pudding is whether
or not the volunteer's training prepares him to do a better
job rehabilitating the offender: lower recidivism, increasing
job or school adjustment, etc., and here we come full circle
from the beginning of this chapter. But, again, we do not

as yet have clear data on the rehabilitation effectiveness of
the trained vs. the untrained correctional volunteer.   We
only believe training can probably do no harm and much good.

Yet, just as we go to press, a long step forward has
been taken in marshalling and discovering relevant research
evidence: Dr. Ernie Shelley's overview of court volunteer
research, 35 completed studies and an equal number in progress.   At least a third of these studies have some relevance
to increasing our understanding of volunteer training.   Currently it is available as Frontier 8 from the National Information Center ($3.00 per copy).   Within this publication we
particularly recommend your attention to the work of Dr.
Alex Zaphiris and his students at Denver University.

May we leave you with this thought: Evaluation of
training is only the road; it is not the destination.   It is
only a means and not an end.   The best evaluative information in the world is no help at all until implemented.   Indeed, if you lack clear go-ahead channels for converting
evaluative suggestions to actual changes in your training program, evaluation is simply a waste of time; and it may even
be a kind of cop-out.   Don't evaluate unless you intend to
do something about it.

*   *   *   *

Report XIII

PROFESSIONALS EYE VOLUNTEERS: A LOOK AT THE SYSTEM

Purpose

The National Information Center on Volunteers in
Courts (NICOVIC) conducted a study of the attitudes of professional juvenile probation officers in small communities
and a larger metropolitan area.   The goal of our study was
to unearth professionals' feelings concerning the use of volunteers in courts and volunteer training.   Implicit in this
goal is an attempt to isolate any professional resistance that
might exist to the use of volunteers and an identification of
the sources of their resistance.   It is our contention that
probation officers, who deal regularly with children in trouble, represent an untapped resource for volunteer training
program ideas.   It is further our contention that as a result
of the present national enthusiasm over volunteers, many

real problems with the use of volunteers within the judicial
system are never articulated.   It is our hope that in this
preliminary study of probation officer attitudes, these problems can be identified so that they can be dealt with by volunteer program coordinators.

Method

    We interviewed officers, who had worked with volun-
teers, from four juvenile courts.   Using an interview schedule (reprinted at the end of this report) we queried eleven
officers.   We want to emphasize that due to the very small
sample and other research limitations, to be outlined below,
this is only a pilot study.   As a result, the findings reported
here represent only the opinion of eleven professionals, as
interpreted by the author.   We need many more cases before
we can claim firm conclusions.

    A NICOVIC staff member contacted either the volun-
teer coordinator or a probation officer known to the staff in
each of the four courts.   The court contact was then asked
to find two to three probation officers who would be willing
to be interviewed by our staff for ten dollars per interview.
This selection procedure has a built-in bias, we believe,
since volunteer coordinators had an understandable tendency
to choose officers who were favorably disposed toward the
use of volunteers.   And, of course, a bias existed from the
inception of the study due to the position of staff members
who did the interviewing.   It was rather like members of the
Sierra Club interviewing Public Service officials and asking
them if they were in favor of smog.   We did assure respondents that their replies would be anonymous, thereby
protecting their confidentiality and encouraging frankness.   A
third problem area was interviewer bias.   Two interviewers
were used in an attempt to cut down the bias introduced by
the use of one researcher.   Obviously, this did not eliminate
the problem.   And lastly, the problem which is inherent in
any attitudinal survey: do attitudes necessarily match behavior?   We, of course, have no way of assessing this last
and, perhaps, most significant question.

    Given all these limitations, the reader may ponder
why the study was carried out.   In defense of our effort we
feel that systematically asking probation officers how they
felt about volunteers and their training has never been done
before to our knowledge, and, therefore, was in itself a

useful task.   After the conclusion of the study, our suspicion
was confirmed.   We found probation officers glad to have
the chance to express themselves concerning volunteers, and
secondly, the probation officers seemed open about their
feelings.

Program Descriptions

Now that we have established a background for the
study, it is useful to describe the volunteer programs we
investigated: the source of volunteers, the function of volunteers, the structure of the volunteer program, and the
degree of staff commitment to the use of volunteers.

In three of the four courts investigated, volunteers
were drawn from the community.   Two of the four courts
used a large proportion of college students.   And one court
drew volunteers from VISTA and an autonomous, religiously-
oriented volunteer program, as well.   In general, community
members were most consistently favored.   We found, in two
programs, college students and VISTA's worked least well.
According to the probation officers interviewed, students did
not maintain a consistent contact with the juveniles on probation and the VISTA's over-identified with the probationers:
they were too alienated from the Establishment to work within
the court system.

In all four courts, the major volunteer job was working with a juvenile in a one-to-one relationship.   One program had, in addition, tutor, foster parent, and group discussion programs.   Two courts were initiating volunteer
tutor programs.   The consistent trend in all courts was for
the volunteer to act as a friend.   Volunteers could not, then,
make alterations in terms of probation and the ultimate responsibility for the child rested with the probation officer.
(Foster parents are an important exception; they have responsibility for the child.)   Although in all four courts, if,
in the judgment of the probation officer, the volunteer can
deal appropriately with the probationer, the probation officer
does not see the probationer on a regular basis.

All four courts studied had a volunteer coordinator on
the staff who was responsible for the recruitment, selection,
and training of volunteers.   However, in all courts the probation officer functioned independently of the volunteer coordinator: the probation officer chose, from the volunteer

pool, the number and kind of volunteers he wished; he matched the volunteer with the appropriate probationer, and, in general, determined the kind and amount of communication the volunteer would have with him. Indeed, several professionals chose to use personal friends as volunteers, not only by-passing the volunteers selected by the court but also many of the problems associated with volunteer usage.

The degree of commitment to the use of volunteers varied with each professional interviewed. As a result, we shall report general attitudinal trends. In two courts there was limited staff commitment to volunteers. The most consistent source of professional alienation appeared to be an envisioned threat by volunteers to their professional status. Bad experiences with volunteers centering around their lack of consistent contact with probationers and immature volunteer behavior played a role in their rejection by professionals. Parenthetically, we found that younger probation officers tend to be more accepting of volunteer usage. And there seems to be evidence to indicate that those probation officers who resist volunteers have had the least contact with them.

In the other two courts, volunteers were well accepted by the staff. Indeed, the volunteer concept was so well established in one court that volunteers verged on the point of not being taken seriously. In the author's opinion, respondents answered more often with the "right" answers concerning volunteers than with meaningful answers.

In the remainder of our report we shall outline probation officer attitudes regardless of court in three areas: the volunteer-probationer relationship; the volunteer-court relationship; and the volunteer training issue.

The Volunteer Probationer Relationship

Within the area of volunteer-probationer relationships, we queried the professionals on the following dimensions:

1. The needs of the probationer the volunteer can satisfy.
2. The motivation of volunteers; why do volunteers volunteer?
3. The sophistication of volunteers about the "type" of child with which they will be dealing.

We found that professionals tended to agree that volunteers can fulfill the need of a probationer for a model as well as taking the role of an empathic friend. Professionals identify the desire to make a contribution on the part of the volunteer as his primary motivation, although there was some evidence that probation officers find that some volunteers are of the "do-gooder" genre and that they resent this kind of volunteer. We found eight out of 11 probation officers felt that volunteers were unsophisticated about the kind of child and problems with which they would be dealing. This "volunteer naivete" seems to imply the need for reality-oriented volunteer training.

The Volunteer-Court Relationship

Our second area of concern, volunteer-court relations, was investigated by examining the following dimensions:

1. The kind of supervision probation officers extend over volunteers.
2. The manner in which officers kept in touch with volunteers.
3. The advantages and disadvantages of using volunteers in a court system.
4. The overlap between the volunteer and probation officer roles.

We found that half the officers questioned relied on a scheduled reporting system for supervising their volunteers while the other half relied upon the Director of the volunteer program. Nearly all the probation officers kept in touch with their volunteers through an (approximately) monthly volunteer meeting. From the point of view of the professionals, communication problems did not exist between the volunteer and officer. (In other studies, though, we have found that the volunteer does often feel there are communication problems here.)

Professionals identified a variety of advantages and disadvantages of the volunteer working within a court system. The advantages fall in two categories: advantages to the probation officer and advantages to the probationer. Advantages to the probation officer were indicated as follows. The probation officer is freed, through the use of volunteers, to work with the probationers who need them most, although

several professionals stated that volunteers do not save the
officer time.   The professional must spend time working
with the volunteers, as he would the child.   The advantage
of volunteers is that for every hour the officer spends with
the volunteer, the volunteer multiplies in time spent with the
probationer.   A second advantage of volunteers to probationers, is that because they are not officials, volunteers can
relate to the probationers in a one-to-one relationship on a
more meaningful level.

The advantages given for using volunteers are, after
several years of national enthusiasm over volunteers, ones
we had expected and have heard before, officially and unofficially.   We found the disadvantages of volunteers more
pertinent to the actual functioning of the volunteer within
juvenile court.   The following were indicated by our interviewees as disadvantages:

    --the volunteer doesn't stay with his job;
    --volunteers over-identify with probationers;
    --they have problems working with the probationer and
      his family;
    --inability to handle serious problems;
    --the volunteer attempts to reap too much personal gain
      from his relationship with the probationer;
    --he becomes too dependent upon the probation officer or,
      conversely, tries to take his place.

Further, the professionalism of probation officers is threatened by volunteers; the officer feels he tends to lose contact
with the probationer, and lastly, the probation officer notes
that he must continue to deal with a probationer, even though
the volunteer may have failed.   It is imperative to ask: why
do these malfunctions occur?   Are they due to the nature of
some volunteers, all volunteers, some probationer officers,
all probation officers, the volunteer program, the court
system?   Indeed, we hope future research will address these
important problems.

We queried professionals as to the amount of overlap
between volunteer and probation officer roles.   Somewhat to
our surprise, we found most officers agreed there was little
overlap (officers were officials with authority), although we
found many officers threatened by the use of volunteers.
Volunteers, by their very presence, imply that traditional
probation has not worked.   We suggest that fear of job replacement is not the source of threat: it is the recognition

that volunteers have come in because professionals and the system have not been entirely effective.

The Volunteer Training Issue

Our third area of investigation, probation officers' views on volunteer training, was investigated by asking professionals the following questions:

1. How much money do you have for training?
2. How much time per month do you spend in training and orientation of your volunteers?
3. What techniques do you use in training?
4. Ideally, what should be the focus and structure of training? What are the best techniques to promote the most effective training?

Collectively, probation officers have little or no idea how much money or time is spent on volunteer training in their court. They have a general impression of volunteer training--the majority of training techniques being lecture with discussion periods, with on-going training being volunteer monthly meetings. One court did use role-playing and video-tapes as regular training techniques. It was highly significant to note the lack of professional sophistication regarding training. When asked to suggest or construct an ideal volunteer training program, nearly all were satisfied with what they had. (Some mention was made that more emphasis was needed upon the legal system, and the availability of films and audio-visual aids.) Many officers stated, instead, general training goals, for example honesty, achieving communication between volunteer and probationer; but none articulated actual training techniques that would help achieve these goals, with partial and minor exceptions noted (legal system, training aids, etc.). It is possible that the dearth of training sophistication of courts has a direct relationship to the multitude of volunteer problems outlined earlier.

We would like to add that other research has been done in the area of professional reaction to volunteers. We refer the reader to: (1) Dr. Leonard E. Flynn, Director of Community Services, Florida Probation and Parole Commission, Room 235, Doyle E. Carlton Building, Tallahassee, Florida 32304. And (2) Dr. Leonard Pinto, Sociology Department, University of Colorado, Boulder, Colorado 80302.

Interview Schedule

1. What is the total number of regular, active volunteers in your court at the present time?

2. How do you use volunteers; what are their jobs?

3. What kind of responsibility do your volunteers have concerning their probationers?

4. What needs of the probationer can the volunteer satisfy?

5. Why do you feel volunteers volunteer?

6. From your experience, what level of knowledge do volunteers have when they first come to court about the "type" of child with which they will be dealing?

7. What kind of supervision do you extend over your volunteers; if you have no authority over them, who does?

8. How do you keep in touch with your volunteers?

9. Could you list the two main advantages and disadvantages of using volunteers in a court system?

10. Do you see the volunteer and yourself overlapping in your respective efforts?

11. How much money do you have for training volunteers, per year?

12. How much time per month do you spend in training and orientation of your volunteers?

13. What techniques do you use in training?

14. Ideally, what should be the focus and structure of training; what are the best techniques to promote the most effective training?

*   *   *   *

Report XIV

VOLUNTEER TRAINING IN COURTS: AN OVERVIEW

Purpose

The purpose of this report is to summarize the available evidence and observations relating to court volunteer training. Reactions, as opposed to content descriptions, to training will be the focal point of the analysis. Professional as well as volunteer reactions will be probed. An underlying assumption of our discussion of court volunteer training programs is that training is an essential tool with which to maximize volunteer effectiveness. In the pioneer days of court volunteers, the early 1960's, a few sensitive judges began using hand-picked volunteers in small programs. The "mystique" of volunteer involvement sustained the effort. As volunteerism mushrooms and less experienced personnel assume the task of volunteer management, training becomes a necessary imperative to success. Before delineating the training data, it is illuminating to analyze the implications of volunteer involvement for society and the court system.

Volunteerism today is being hailed as the reservoir of pure citizen participation that will spout forth and cure the nation of deep-seated social maladies. Court volunteerism is a segment of a larger movement; juvenile delinquency is but a fragment of wider societal breakdown. Volunteer involvement is pitted against insidious and monumental social ills. In spite of the pervasive quality of social disorganization and juvenile delinquency, in particular, volunteer participation has made significant gains in rehabilitating youngsters to a more productive life style. But the glimmer of success cannot blind corrections to the realities of volunteer misuse. Society cannot afford the luxury of waiting ten years for research to formulate solutions; corrections does not have the time passively to contemplate the nature of volunteer programs. The National Information Center on Volunteers in Courts estimates one court per day is initiating a court volunteer program. Analysis of court volunteers reveals that they are motivated by the desire to help. Responsible citizens are responding to the social crises. Corrections must be not only responsive to their involvement but also ready with sophisticated training programs.

In order for corrections to meet the challenge, fundamental philosophical questions concerning the use of volunteers must be confronted by corrections: what is the role
of the volunteer; what is his relationship to the professional;
what is his relationship to the probationer?   Given the role
of the volunteer, what kind of training best prepares him
for his job.   These are not easy questions to answer.   Honest consideration of these issues involves a redefinition of
professionalism.   Indeed, the volunteer effort can be interpreted as saying, in effect, to the professional: we are
here because you have not done your job well enough and
there are not enough of you to do the job well.

Historical Perspective

Before describing reactions to volunteer training it
is necessary to put the court volunteer movement in the
proper perspective.   It is important to know the extent of
the movement, the level of acceptance of the movement, and
the integration of training into the court philosophy.   It is
significant, too, to contrast the current trends in the court
volunteer movement with volunteerism in other fields throughout the country.   Although the National Information Center
on Volunteers in Courts has a complex of impressionistic
data concerning the movement, the Joint Commission on Correctional Manpower and Training polls, Corrections 1968, A
Climate for Change, and Volunteers Look at Corrections,
will be used as the source for a descriptive accounting of
the present situation.   Research findings will be drawn from
social work to evaluate the state of volunteerism outside of
corrections.

In spite of the population explosion of court volunteers
in the last two years, the movement is still confined to a
minority of correctional agencies.   Furthermore, among
those agencies who do not employ volunteers, there is resistance to their introduction.   Resistance to volunteers is
attributed primarily to their lack of qualifications and the
most oft cited reason that they are not helpful is that they
lack training.   Even among those agencies who have adopted
volunteers, volunteers are not perceived as central to the
rehabilitative process.   They are most often used, according
to the survey, in clerical positions.   "Giving personal attention to the offender" ranks second.   Of those agencies
who use volunteers, they are accepted: 71% of the adminis-
trators would like to use more volunteers compared with

42% of the line workers. It is interesting to note that acceptance of volunteers increases with the educational level
and job status of the correctional worker. Evaluating the
professional reaction to volunteers, the survey concludes:

> If this community resource is to be tapped more
> effectively, it is clear that not only must the vol-
> unteer come to expect a rewarding experience in
> a correctional agency, but also corrections must
> learn to appreciate the real value volunteers can
> offer.

Volunteers Look at Corrections reflects the lack of
agency commitment to not only volunteers but also volunteer
training. Two-thirds of the volunteers interviewed contacted
the agency. Screening is casual at best: 41% were interviewed by someone in the agency, 25% provided written information, 18% provided references, 15% satisfied no type of
requirement. Training is minimal. Only 50 per cent received any kind of initial orientation and training; only 20%
received training for their present job. The lack of training
is made even more significant when the correctional expertise
of the volunteer is considered: less than 20% of the volunteers had any correctional experience and only 30% experienced any concern about working in corrections. Given this
situation it is particularly relevant to investigate the motivational determinants of volunteer participation. The vast
majority of individuals volunteer for reasons that are irrelevant to the goals of the agency. For example, they want to
help others, recognize a need to participate, and anticipate
personal benefit. And it was found that 67% felt that training was unnecessary. It is clear that the volunteer is not
only inexperienced and overconfident but he is also more interested in broad societal goals than specific correctional
aims. Training, in view of the dimensions of the volunteer
preparation for correctional work, becomes even more imperative. But at the present time corrections has not met
the challenge. The survey results suggest that: "The low
levels of orientation, job training, and evaluation make the
following conclusion obvious; most correctional agencies have
not made a real commitment to their volunteer programs. "

Before beginning an analysis of the program research,
it is relevant to establish an appropriate frame of reference
for the discussion. It is fruitful to conceptualize training in
three dimensions: volunteer reactions to training, professional staff reactions to training, and probationers' reactions

to volunteers and the resulting implications for training.

Volunteer Training Outside Corrections

        The initiation of the Peace Corps in the early 1960's
publicized the growing volunteer movement in America. Today, volunteers are significantly involved in not only countries abroad but also in domestic community actions through
VISTA, mental health organizations, and hospitals. The
Social Work Associate Program, (January 1964 to August
1965) a demonstration project using volunteers sponsored by
the Big Sister Association, the Youth Development Project
of Minneapolis, and the Training Center for Community Programs at the University of Minnesota, is fashioned on the
social work model. This program has been chosen to represent volunteer action outside corrections for several reasons: (1) The work done by social work associates parallels
court volunteer efforts. SWA's are trained to establish supportive relationships with deprived adolescent girls and their
families. Although this relationship lacks the sometimes
more punitively oriented responsibilities of the court volunteer, both approaches share the fundamental goal of rehabilitating a troubled youngster through a meaningful one-to-one
relationship with a volunteer. (Court volunteers, of course,
can adopt a variety of roles, a close relationship with a
probationer is but one of them.) (2) The SWA project has
a well developed volunteer training program which is a
striking contrast to the primitive court volunteer training
that has just been described. It is important to note here
that the brief description of not only the SWA program
(which will follow) and the remaining program descriptions
in this discussion in no way does justice to the work. For
a complete report, it is best to refer to the original documents listed at the end of the paper in the bibliography.

        Before delineating reactions to training, it is useful
to describe, briefly, the form and content of the training
program. Volunteers received forty hours of training: one
day per week over an eight week period. The sessions
were conducted as small seminars, each member discussing
lectures and reading assignments, accompanied by films,
guest lecturers, and field trips to relevant agencies. The
primary goal of the training was two-fold: to enable the
volunteer to build a trusting relationship with her client and
to provide the volunteer with opportunities for personal
growth and development. To achieve those ends training

focused upon: explicating the cause and nature of poverty, contrasting the culture of poverty with middle class values, spotlighting the differences and similarities between the two value systems. An attempt was made, in particular, to increase volunteer's insight into his own value system. The nature of behavior dynamics, in general, was discussed. Group meetings were held to not only share experiences but also provide mutual volunteer support. Post-test survey results reveal that both volunteers and professionals gave a complete endorsement to not only the training program but also the effects of the volunteer upon the child and the agency. It is useful to begin with the volunteer reactions to training. Background material on the culture of poverty was rated the most helpful aspect of the course. And the majority of respondents found nothing to criticize in the program. The suggestions for program change were made, then, within the context of genuine overall satisfaction with the program. Volunteers suggested the following topics should receive more coverage:

1. More case material including films on cases and training in writing up case histories.
2. Opportunity to meet girls in advance.
3. More practical discussion of the nature of community resources.
4. More practice in interviewing.
5. More on employment opportunities.
6. More on family structure of minority groups.

Suggestions for organizational changes focused upon the need for more inter-personal techniques to promote good relationships with their children: more practice in role playing and interviewing, an earlier introduction of material about clients, and a more definite understanding concerning the volunteer role. It was suggested that a reference guide, containing lists of community resources, case histories, and methodological suggestions for a total approach to family problems, be developed as a tool with which volunteers could work for a better relationship with their children.

The professional reaction to SWA training that was cited in the program research centered around an articulation of their role in the training process. The program supervisors agreed that: "The quality of supervision is the heart of a program using nonprofessional persons." According to the staff, effective supervisors must assume the following responsibilities. Supervisors must be most active in the

diagnostic effort.   The supervisor must teach the volunteer
critical diagnostic skills.   The professional must insure
maintenance, by the volunteer, of professional confidentiality.
Although the volunteer is trusted, the staff member must be
alert to the necessity of taking over certain volunteer responsibilities.   The professional must keep in continual contact with the volunteer.   The fundamental problem was perceived not as the complexity of the client's problem but as
a choice of an appropriate associate for each child.   In order
to achieve staff expectations concerning their responsibilities
in the training process, it was necessary to have an on-going
training process.   An integral part of this process was continuing volunteer evaluation.   "It is after all, a recognition
that the service she performs merits the time and effort to
examine it carefully to pull together what has been learned,
to assess, and to set goals for the future. "

        A key to staff success was their recognition of the
special problems involved in using nonprofessionals: the
diversity of ability among volunteers, appropriate volunteer
use of supervision, volunteer frustration and their "crisis
in confidence. "   The staff not only recognized these problems but also dealt with them, through extensive volunteer-
staff contact, in their training structure.

        The SWA program is suggestive of training techniques
that could be incorporated into court volunteer training programs: lengthy and continuous training, seminar format involving discussion of sociological and psychological processes
involved in delinquency, use of films and field trips, close
integration of staff into the training process with well-defined
responsibilities of both the professional and the volunteer.

Volunteer Training in Corrections

        We can now turn to an evaluation of court volunteer
training programs.   There is limited data from which to
construct our analysis.   Indeed, the research deficit is an
indication of the lack of hard evidence concerning the form
and structure of programs.   The Westchester Citizen's Committee Survey (Gary Auslander), Volunteer Probation Counselors in the Denver County Court (MA group thesis, Denver
University), and the Report on Tutorial Project (sponsored
by Delinquency Control Training Center, Wayne State University and the Trade Union Leadership Council of Detriot, by
Muriel Rosenbaum), and an unpublished analysis of

volunteer-staff relations (Dr. Leonard Pinto and Mrs. Barbara Farhar), form the core of research on court volunteer training. It is our understanding that the Texas Adult Probation Department received a grant to investigate court volunteer training. Their research is not available for inclusion in the discussion at this time. There are two significant studies of volunteers involved in correctional settings, although not in one-to-one relationships with probationers, The Jewish Board of Guardians Evaluation and a study of Junior League involvement in a detention home.

It is fruitful to begin with the Westchester Citizen's Committee Survey. This survey was sent out in September, 1968, under the auspices of the Committee and the Boulder County Juvenile Court to 500 different courts. The survey was intended to tap court training needs. Before citing the survey response it is important to put the answers in the proper perspective: only thirty-six out of the 500 questionnaires mailed were returned. It is not irrelevant that the response was poor. It can be hypothesized that either the courts polled lacked volunteer programs or if they had them, did not train volunteers, or that they were uninterested in sharing their information. Of those who did reply the majority felt that preparation of nationally relevant training materials would be helpful. Only two courts indicated there were no "gaps" in their existing training program. The remaining respondents cited the training deficiencies given in Table A.

These knowledge-gaps point to not only the need for volunteer training but also the need for techniques, "counseling and treatment techniques," for example, that foster close volunteer-probationer relationships. This pressing need for training is again reflected in the responses citing "additional training materials that would be useful." "Training and films" and "supervision and training" are number one and two on the list. They are followed by case histories, almost anything, orientation, counseling and interviewing techniques, information about successful programs, materials, and material about social and emotional problems. Mr. Auslander points to the interesting phenomenon that many courts indicate training material needs, while they fail to relate gaps in their own program. In league with the limited amount of training is the limited financing of volunteer programs. Only half of the responding courts had financing and those who did had a minimal amount.

Table A.   Gaps Cited in Present Training Program

Gaps	Number of Courts
Not that far along	8
Counseling and treatment techniques	5
Training	5
Supervision	5
"Key" Volunteer	3
Time	3
No answer	3
Sociological and Psychological	3
Orientation	2
Professional-Volunteer relations	2
None, so far	2
Tape recordings	1
Definition of goals	1
Delineation of roles	1
Use of resources	1
Not applicable	1
Inappropriate answer	1
Total	47

     The survey attempted to assess, too, the training material currently in use.   There are a variety of materials used by courts.   Printed material is most often used.   The remaining responses, lectures, conferences, individual orientation, slides, and tapes, received a few votes apiece. Although there were eight courts who lacked material, these same courts indicated they would like training material. The weighted use of literature in training is related to the number of hours courts spent in volunteer training.   It takes much less court involvement to hand the volunteer pamphlets, than it does to coordinate seminars, films, field trips, lectures, and group experiences.   And the survey did find that most courts spend less than four hours in the initial training phase.   In terms of on-going training, survey results found that there was no real provision for continuing volunteer training.

     It is evident from the survey that training materials would have to be tailored to small programs: 19 out of 34 courts had 25 volunteers or less and only four out of 34 had more than 100 volunteers.   It is evident, too, that training should be devoted to providing the volunteer with the knowledge and techniques necessary to establish a meaningful relationship with a probationer, for the majority of courts

replied that they use volunteers on a one-to-one basis, although they did not limit their program to one type of volunteer job.   Half of the courts had more than one program to
offer the volunteer.   If the majority of courts use volunteers
on a one-to-one basis with probationers, it is clear that
training must focus upon: How does a volunteer develop a
meaningful relationship with a probationer.   In reality courts
do not make a significant attempt to achieve this goal!   It
is pertinent to quote Mr. Auslander's survey conclusion:

> The overall general response to the survey seems
> to indicate that the volunteer court movement, if
> it can be called such, may not be as widespread
> and sophisticated as previously thought.   Many of
> the courts seem to be quite underdeveloped as to
> number of volunteers, amount of available funds,
> sufficiency of training materials, and the overall
> effort and time that is put into training volunteers.
> The implications are that most of the volunteer
> courts are beginning volunteer programs without
> well thought out plans and are therefore in desper-
> ate need of information and training materials that
> could be made available from more sophisticated
> court programs.

In spite of the pressing national situation, there are
courts that are running successful training programs.   Denver County Court, a large urban court in Colorado, is not
only a leader in the court volunteer movement but also a
leader in program analysis.   They commissioned the University of Denver to research and evaluate their court training
program.   In May, 1966, the Denver County Court applied
to the Law Enforcement Assistance Administration project; a
grant was awarded for a two-year study.   And the Denver
Court set out to test the hypothesis that individualized contact with adult misdemeanants by volunteer lay counselors
would reduce recidivism.   At the end of the two-year period
Denver concluded:

> From the amount of data presented in the report,
> we must conclude that the primary goal of the
> project, the reduction of criminal activity meas-
> ured by arrests, was achieved to a statistically
> significant degree.   The amount of success is the
> amazing fact.

This positive result was attributed to the use of lay counselors

whose success, in turn, was a function of the volunteer training program. Before analyzing the training program it is
helpful to give a brief description of the format. The training sessions, which were conducted by the Denver University
School of Social Work, were run in three consecutive evenings on a monthly basis.

Night I, Session I (7:30-10:00 p. m.):
A general orientation to the philosophy and programs of
the court is provided by a county judge. This presentation is followed by a twenty-five minute film, "Price of a
Life," which sets the tone for perceiving probation as a
viable alternative to imprisonment. The documentary is
followed by a detailed lecture from a D. U. professor concerning the personality structure of many probationers:
the character disorder.

Night II, Session II (7:30-10:00 p. m.):
The appropriate context has been provided in Session 1
for an understanding of the court and its relationship to
social deviants. The second session describes for the
lay volunteer techniques of counseling that enable him to
effect positive personality change in the misdemeanant.

Night III, Session III (7:30-10:00 p. m.):
The third session underscores the first session's emphasis: a realistic understanding of the life style of the
misdemeanant. The session opens with the film, 'The
Revolving Door," a documentary dealing with the dimensions of misdemeanant behavior. A case study of a
"typical" misdemeanant is then presented for class analysis. After the initial presentation the class is broken
into smaller units to extensively probe the case. The
class then reconvenes to share ideas. The use of the
case study as a teaching device is completed after a
class member, playing the role of the protagonist in the
case study, is interviewed by the instructor to not only
illustrate helpful interviewing techniques but also to involve the class more actively in the conceptualization of
misdemeanant behavior. The final training session concludes, after a list of valuable community resources that
are available for the probationer are given to the volunteer.

Attention can now be turned to the research, Volunteer Probation Counselors in the Denver County Court (A
Study of the Opinions of Ninety-Five Probation Counselors

About the Training Program, the Project and Probation),
which focuses upon volunteers' reaction to training.   This
report is weighted from one point of view but the remaining
perspectives will be later probed.   Pre- and post-training
attitudes were calculated from interviews with volunteers.
Pre-test attitudes will be discussed first.   The majority of
trainees approached training with interest and expected useful information.   Their anticipations were rewarded for the
overwhelming response to training was positive.   Evaluation
of differential approval of the training program was rated in
the following manner: five sections of the training were
ranked as "positive, " "negative, " or "no response" by the
volunteers.   The ranks are schematized in Table B.

Table B

		Ratings		
Ranking	Program Section	Positive	Negative	No Response
1	Principles of counseling	84	8	1
2	Orientation to court and project	82	9	4
3	Psychology and Sociology of the character disorder	81	12	2
4	Getting started with the probationer	75	14	6
5	Description of community resources	55	35	6

Moving from an evaluation of the training material to
training attitudinal impact, it was found that 9 out of 10
counselors had an accepting attitude toward probationers.
More than half the trainees reported tolerance prior to
training.   One-half of the non-tolerant trainees become more
tolerant as a result of training.   More significantly, 80%
indicated they found the training program "very helpful" in
actual work with probationers and further, more than three-
fourths indicated the training succeeded in giving them an
accurate portrayal of probationers.

Although the trainees found the program valuable,
they did recommend change.   Trainees regularly suggested
the following restructuration: more time to explore material

presented, feedback from experienced lay counselors; a consistent split appeared between those who sought a more
practical orientation and those who desired a more theoretical orientation. Several suggestions pertaining to program
additions were made: continuing group discussions for counselors in which they could share ideas, the necessity of ongoing training, more contact with the staff to provide adequate structure and more complete diagnostic evaluation.
These suggestions are a call for more training. Volunteers
want more knowledge, support, and structure. Indeed, they
want continual training throughout their volunteer experience.

    A significant proportion of court volunteers are tutors.
Tutors, in contrast with volunteer counselors, work within
a structured framework. Their job is to evaluate and repair
the child's educational skills. The Delinquency Control
Training Center at Wayne State University in May, 1964,
conducted a volunteer tutor training program. Although these
tutors were not dealing with juvenile delinquents, they were
working with the same type of children: adolescent youngsters who were not doing well in school. Before revealing
training reactions, the training program will be summarized.
The training sessions consisted of eight bi-weekly sessions
and two supervised sessions with the tutorees. The group
did not exceed twenty-five people and operated within a classroom structure. The lectures focused upon specific techniques necessary to teach basic educational skills. These
techniques were accompanied by an orientation to the psychological environment of the children.

    Both volunteer and professional reactions to training
were diagrammed in the tutorial report. The majority of
volunteers were found to be pleased with the program. They
did make some suggestions for improvement: more time to
absorb the material, a more extensive training period, early
introduction to the students so that the training would be
more meaningful, (the possibility of an internship). The
professional staff was more cautious. They stated it was
too soon to make a definitive assessment of the success of
the program, as measured by the childrens' improvement in
school. But they wholeheartedly endorsed the willingness of
the tutors to learn. They did suggest alterations, if the
program were to be repeated: two additional sessions for
demonstrations and review, increased opportunity for class
interaction, use of video tapes and real children. They proposed, too, the institution of a minimal screen process; they
found that individuals with lower educational levels were less

satisfactory as tutors.

The Westchester Citizen's Committee Survey reflected
the need for training; the Denver study provided an example
of a successful training program; the Detroit analysis revealed the usefulness of specialized tutor training.   In contrast, Dr. Pinto's data on volunteer staff relations   articu-
lates volunteer reactions to a lack of training.   These reactions obtained through intensive interviews (February 1966
- July 1968) with ten volunteers, alert staff to valuable clues
concerning what volunteers need in a training program.   This
descriptive analysis was made along the satisfied-dissatisfied
dimension.   Interview data from satisfied volunteers was
contrasted with interview data from dissatisfied volunteers.

It is useful to look first at those volunteers who were
satisfied with their court involvement.   Their most salient
trait is that they had a clear conception of their role within
the court structure.   This "clearness" was a function of
their program involvement and staff support.   Specifically,
staff supported those volunteer programs and the individuals
in them that were of concrete value to the court: tutoring,
psychological testing, vision test, for example.   Further,
professional acceptance of these programs resulted in increased willingness to deal with volunteer problems and volunteer attempts at role proliferation.

There are several significant variables in discriminating the satisfied and dissatisfied volunteer experience.   The
fundamental distinction, however, was that the professional
staff did not offer support for those individuals committed to
the development of long-lasting relationships with juveniles.
Professional resistance to these efforts spawned a variety of
interrelated problems: volunteers lacked clear definitions of
how their work fit into the court program as a whole and an
understanding of their specific volunteer role.   Furthermore,
professional resistance to these volunteer programs produced
confused or minimal communication between the staff and the
volunteers.   These blocked communication channels, and
prohibited satisfactory problem-solving by the volunteers.
Further, volunteer efforts to initiate new programs, due to
a lack of precise understanding of what was to be done, were
blocked by the staff.   As the report succinctly states: "The
staff had not taken, in many cases, positive action in directing volunteers; thus they were forced into negative, blocking
action. "

An additional factor contributing to misunderstanding
was conflicting staff and volunteer goals. Professionals supported volunteer programs out of a conviction that the community should be sensitized, through volunteers and the volunteer process, to the problems of juvenile delinquency.
This goal was in direct conflict with the prime motivational
goal of the majority of volunteers, that is, to develop a
meaningful relationship with children in trouble.

In many ways, this data is a description of a volunteer program failure. We must extract from this experience
what can be done to avoid further difficulties. Needless to
say, before volunteer training is initiated staff must face the
volunteer issue squarely: what are the program goals, what
is the role of the volunteer in this scheme and, further,
what is the role of the professional. It is only after the
entire professional staff has arrived at a consensus on the
objectives that training can begin. Training the volunteer becomes, then a process of imparting program objectives to
the volunteer. But it is not only that. From the experience
cited above it is clear that training must be conceptualized
as an on-going process. Volunteers need channels through
which they can have a continuous dialogue with the staff and
a forum where their suggestions can be considered and acted
upon.

The third but more elusive sphere of volunteer training is the probationer reaction to volunteers and what it
means for training. We again turn to Dr. Pinto's data for
research. His recently published data, A Case Study of
Volunteerism in the Juvenile Court: Problems and the Probationer, review how probationers perceive volunteers. The
findings are not complex: probationers like volunteers who
know exactly what they are and still want to help. It has
been found that the majority of volunteers volunteer not because they are dedicated to the goals of the court but because they want to help others. Given these two variables:
probationer reaction to volunteers and volunteer knowledge
of corrections, training must be a process of familiarizing
the volunteer to what probationers are like and court procedure and philosophy concerning the children.

Volunteer Training in Non-Probation Correctional Settings:

The program to Train Volunteers to Serve Children
and Families in Social Crisis in the Court (January, 1968)

prepared by the Research and Development Center of the
Jewish Board of Guardians is the source for the following
discussion.   The Board received a three year grant from
the State Department of Mental Health to develop a volunteer
training program.   Their goal in the program was threefold:

1. To demonstrate the value of volunteers.
2. To develop a prototype training program that could
    be adapted by other agencies.
3. To sensitize the community to the positive work that
    could be achieved by volunteers.   They recruited
    eleven volunteers from a cross-section of NYC social
    agencies to take part in the training program.   Each
    volunteer was recommended from her original agency.
    Their training goal was to make them "paraprofes-
    sional volunteer mental health aides. "

The training program began in January, 1968.   Sessions were run for nine weeks with classes meeting two full
days a week.   One day was spent in class; the second day
was spent in a field placement in one of the JBG court
liaison and referral service offices located in the Juvenile
Term Court.   In these placements the volunteers served in
the following capacities:

1. Offering services to families and children appearing
    in the Juvenile Term Court by "standing by" before,
    during, and after, a court appearance until a dis-
    position is made.
2. In situations where a referral for professional ser-
    vices is necessary, the volunteer gives a preliminary
    intake interview with the family as part of the refer-
    ral process.
3. In situations where a referral has been made, the
    volunteer serves as a liaison between the agency, the
    client, and the court.   He obtains the necessary back-
    ground information essential to the disposition of the
    case and formulation of the treatment plan.
4. In situations where a family problem comes to the
    court that doesn't lie within the jurisdiction of the
    court, the volunteer assists them in getting to the
    appropriate community agency.

The functions of the Jewish Board of Guardians volunteers differ from the long-term relationships cultivated by
the court volunteer counselor or tutor.   But their training
program parallels court probation volunteer programs.

Specifically, their program stressed instruction in personality theory, "crisis-intervention" and problem-solving techniques, and familiarization with community resources.

After this review of program structure and goals, it is significant to turn to an evaluation of volunteer and staff reactions to training. It was found that volunteer response was not a total endorsement of the training program. Volunteers responded that their court experience had not been sufficient to prepare them to function as court workers. The program was too short and the field experience did not provide enough experience. In evaluating their training, volunteers suggested a variety of program changes. Increased class structure was needed via definite reading assignments and participation by all class members. Furthermore, lecture material should have been more selectively screened for relevance. They felt the need for techniques to enable them to work more effectively with their clients: how to recognize major problems and what direction to take once these problems have been identified. They cited the need for guidelines, in the form of a reference work to which they could turn for more specific information and suggestions.

On the other hand, staff reactions to training offered a striking parallel to volunteer reactions. Both groups suggested similar changes and both groups split on the relative value of field work as opposed to class lectures. However, both groups did agree that a better integration of the field experience and seminars was needed. Additionally, staff suggestions for improvement centered around the need for more information about the structure and function of the agency, a better operational understanding by the volunteer of the referral sources available to the client. In hindsight, the staff realized a better thinking through of the consequences of each program would have produced a more effective training program. The Jewish Board of Guardians work points to the need for structured, well thought out training programs in which the didactic and practical are brought together in a meaningful relationship.

Although there was some goal confusion in this program, the significant implication of the research is that when the staff and volunteers share a consistent conception of the role of the volunteer, the staff share in the expectations of the volunteers concerning the training program. It is possible that role definition is easier to achieve in the

prediagnostic sphere of volunteerism than it is in probation
court volunteers.   But that cannot obscure the issue.   Staff
must confront and answer the question: "What do we want
from the volunteer?" before training can begin.

The involvement of Junior League Volunteers in the
Hennepin County Home School, a juvenile detention center in
Minnesota, represents a special case of volunteer involvement in a correctional setting.   The setting as well as the
existence of an organized volunteer structure, the Junior
League, are the unique features of this program.   The overall goals of these volunteers were:

1.   To help the individual child increase his self-respect.
2.   To make the school and living environment a richly
       endowed community.
3.   To extend help to the young person as he leaves the
       County Home School.

These goals were to be realized through appropriate volun-
teer-child interaction accompanied by volunteer training.
Staff training was conceived as an integral counterpart of
volunteer training.   Specifically, staff were oriented to the
use of volunteers; staff needs and expectations regarding
volunteers were assessed and, furthermore, what staff were
willing to contribute to the volunteers.   An advisory committee was organized as a forum where opinions on the volunteer program were voiced.   Volunteers and staff rotated
positions on the committee.

The report, which covered a period from 1968 through
1969, gives a scant review of the training process.   Training was conducted in four four-hour sessions by Dr. Konopka
from the Training Center for Community Programs at the
University of Minnesota and selected faculty from the Home
School.   Training centered upon providing instruction in the
problems of delinquency and skills to enable the volunteers
to deal with these problems.   An evaluation of the training
is not presented.   The remainder of the report focuses upon
volunteer-staff relations during the first year.   This review
of the interactions is valuable for it points to ways professionals can insure smooth and effective program functioning.
The following recommendations were made by the report for
improved volunteer-staff functioning.

1.   A greater emphasis upon closer collaboration between
       permanent staff and the volunteers.

2. The first year volunteers and staff should play a significant part in the orientation of new staff and volunteers for the second year.

3. A more flexible arrangement for the "shifting" of a volunteer from one setting to another so that the stigma of failure can be avoided and a volunteer may, where helpful, follow a child from one institutional sphere to another.

4. A specific description of Junior League goals and their commitment should be presented to the Home School staff.

5. Records of volunteer involvement should be kept for the research staff.

6. The training program should be continued for the volunteers with increasing participation of the veteran volunteer in such programs.

7. A new effort should be made by staff and volunteers to pinpoint objectives for volunteer involvement in the Home School Program.

Volunteer Training: A Look to the Future

The program research used in this review is the ground from which future research can grow. In spite of the real contributions made by these efforts, the field of court volunteer training remains virtually unexplored. Given the growth rate of volunteer courts and the dismal lack of sophistication concerning training, research must act quickly to avert inevitable program failures. "Program failure" is but an academic euphemism for continued waste of human resources--those of both the volunteer and the person in trouble.

Research must, then, dissect volunteer usage: specifically, professional and volunteer involvement in the training process. The following research designs incorporate the missing links in systematic data. The real test of volunteer training is behavior. We must contrast the performance of a trained group of volunteers with a matched control group who do not receive training. In this way the overall effectiveness of training can meaningfully be evaluated. But a simple rejection of endorsement of a training program is not enough. Research must probe the impact of diverse training media and training structure. Assuming staff consensus exists upon the content of training, the effects of training media must be analyzed. What techniques are more effective in imparting training goals: are films more powerful than lectures, are sensitivity groups useful in volunteer training or a waste of time. Further, what are the effects of these specific media upon content retention over time; for example, does training that is essentially experiential in nature have a more long lasting effect than printed literature? What kind of training correlates with specific attitude change in volunteers? The nature of training media in the court volunteer movement is riddled with unknowns. But a positive aspect of being in the dark is that there is unlimited room for improvisation! Training structure is, too, available for experimentation. For when considering structure, a second large complex of question arises. For example, should training be concentrated in one initial exposure to the volunteer or is it more effectively presented throughout volunteer experience. What is the role of initial screening as a training device and what is the role of matching as a technique to sensitize the volunteer to probationer-type.

Bibliography*

Auslander, Gary, "The Volunteer in the Court, A Review of the Literature and a Survey of Training Needs with an Analysis for Future Exploration, " M. A. thesis, University of Illinois, 1969.

Cohn, Miriam R., "The Social Work Associate Program, Report of a Demonstration Project, " August, 1966.

Denver County Court, "The Use of Volunteer Probation Counselors: A Special Demonstration Project, " Report on LEAA Grant #037, 1968.

Denver University, "Volunteer Probation Counselors in the Denver County Court: A Study of the Opinions of Ninety-Five Probation Counselors about the Training Program, the Project and Probation, " Group thesis presented to the Graduate School of Social Work, Denver University, June, 1968.

Jewish Board of Guardians, Research and Development Center, "Program to Train Volunteers to Serve Children and Families in Social Crisis in the Court, Evaluation Report, " April, 1969.

*References are abstracted in the Centers' overview of research and evaluation (Frontier 8).

Joint Commission on Correctional Manpower and Training,
    Report of a Survey made by Louis Harris and Associates,
    "Corrections 1968, A Climate for Change, " August, 1968.

Joint Commission on Correctional Manpower and Training,
    Report of a Survey made by Louis Harris and Associates,
    "Volunteers Look at Corrections, " February, 1969.

Pinto, L. J. , "Volunteerism in the Juvenile Court: A Case
    Study. "

Pinto, L. J. , and Barbara Farhar, "Volunteer-Staff Rela-
    tions, " unpublished report.

Rosenbaum, Muriel, "Report on Tutorial Project, Program
    for Training Volunteer Tutors, " May, 1964.

Wiebler, James, "An Overview: The Involvement of Junior
    League Volunteers in a Program of Cultural Enrichment
    at the Hennepin County Home School, Glen Lake, Minne-
    sota, 1968-1969 (First Year). "

*   *   *   *

Report XV

VOLUNTEER EXAMINATION

There are many problems involved in any volunteer
training program for the person responsible for directing the
program.   Unlike trainers in other areas, a volunteer trainer
is faced with people from very diverse backgrounds and educational levels whom he must train on a wide spectrum of
topics ranging from very general attitudinal concerns to very
specific case techniques.   If a subject area already familiar
to the volunteer is presented a valuable hour may well be
lost.   On the other hand, if material unfamiliar to a volunteer is omitted, maximum development of a valuable resource
may well result.   The most important problem to any volunteer trainer then is how to make maximum effective use of
his "training hour. "

Maximization of training time is a very difficult problem.   We feel that the solution to the problem lies in:
planning for training sessions; preparation of volunteers for
training; assessment of training program; and assessment of
individual volunteer training needs.

One approach currently being explored in the area of volunteer training is the Volunteer Exam. It is felt that an exam, if properly applied, will allow volunteer coordinators to solve many of the training problems or at least pinpoint areas where problems exist.

Advantages of the Volunteer Exam

(1) It is an aid to staff planning: before an examination is devised to measure volunteer knowledge, the examiner must have in his own mind a concrete idea of what information is being transmitted to the volunteer. This first step may seem to be common sense, but how many volunteer trainers can list exactly what information they desire the volunteer to absorb? The preparation of a volunteer examination then first requires that the volunteer trainer prepare a specific program for presentation. He himself must know the volunteer function, the volunteer requirements and the volunteer needs of his own program.

(2) It prepares volunteers for training; training preparation is an important concept not often dealt with in volunteers programs. Many programs begin with an interview, a "how to do it" manual and an invitation to a training session. Volunteers may enter and leave their duties wondering "what should I have learned?" A volunteer exam, used in both a pre- and post-fashion allows a volunteer at the pre-phase to see exactly what he should learn from training. The volunteer then can prepare to seek out the information at training sessions and take an active part in abolishing his own informational deficit.

(3) It allows assessment of the overall training program; perhaps the most important function of the volunteer exam is assessment of the overall training program. A volunteer trainer who has planned his sessions, prepared his volunteers and proceeded with the training sessions must have some way to tell whether volunteers actually absorbed the desired information. Perhaps more important he must assess which parts of the training sessions were more productive. When comparing pre vs. post where a pre test is used, it can indicate what increases have been made in particular areas of volunteer knowledge. Armed with this information, the volunteer trainer then can adapt his training program to correct for test-revealed weaknesses and make plans to refine the program.

(4)   It allows assessment of individual volunteer
needs: a point of concern for any volunteer trainer is the
concern for individual volunteers.   In any training program
some volunteers will be at a more advanced training level
than other volunteers.   It would be helpful then to know by
use of a pre-post exam what the volunteer already knows,
in what areas he needs more knowledge and if knowledge has
been obtained.   If, for example, it is determined at the end
of a training program that volunteer X needs more information on community resources and volunteer Y needs more
information on the Children's Code it would be easy for the
volunteer trainer to have them repeat a session, talk to him
individually or seek out the information by themselves.

Weak Points of the Volunteer Exam

(1)   It is a tax on the training hour: a volunteer
exam may take from one to two hours of valuable training
time.   If the exam is a productive one it may well be worth
the time spent.   A non-productive exam, however, will be
doubly expensive.

(2)   It could be objectionable to the volunteer: some
volunteers may not like the idea of an examination.   They
may feel it is too academic, too vague and generally a
waste of time.   On the other hand, many volunteers may
take the exam to mean that the Court takes the volunteer
seriously and demands good work.

(3)   Exams may be misleading;   an exam question regarding volunteer attitude may produce in the volunteer the
idea that only one attitude or only one point of view is correct.   In most volunteer jobs there is room for many differing attitudes and approaches to the same subject and examin-
ers should be careful to make this point clear.

Conclusion

The concept of volunteer examination is an exciting
consideration for anyone currently training volunteers.   The
concept itself is important and anyone considering use of an
exam should deal with the overall idea before accepting or
rejecting it.   If you accept the concept, then begin to organize and set up your program around the idea of examination
both before and after volunteer training.   The sample exam

which follows is only a very unrefined exam (in a compacted form here for reasons of space) currently being used by the Boulder Juvenile Court. It was prepared by Robert D. Hamm, Volunteer Program Coordinator, Boulder Juvenile Court, Kathleen Wells, Research Assistant, NICOVIC, and Dr. Scheier. If you decide to examine your volunteers, design your own exam around your own program. Try the exam on your volunteers and if the information proves useful to you, use it. If, on the other hand, the exam proves to be just another way of gaining useless information delete it from your program.

BOULDER JUVENILE COURT VOLUNTEER EXAMINATION

Name_____

Date _____

Pre Service_____

Post Service_____

Length of Service_____

Volunteer Assignment_____

EXAM

A.   PHILOSOPHY

1.   What would you say are the main points of the philosophy of Boulder County Juvenile Court?

2.   Elaborate some of these points by contrasting it with the philosophy of an <u>adult</u> Court.

3.   What factors contribute to delinquency?
     (a)   Generally speaking
     (b)   For your charge.

4.   What is the child trying to accomplish through delinquent behavior?

5.   How can delinquent behavior be most effectively changed?
     (a)   Generally speaking.
     (b)   For your charge.

6.   What are some of the things we hope to accomplish by putting youngsters on probation?

7.   What kind of relationship do you hope for or have

with the probationer?

8. What do you think is the particular "probationer type?"

9. What are some of the things Boulder's diagnostic program can tell you about your probationer?

10. What are some of the things it <u>can't</u> tell you?

B. SUPERVISORS

1. For each of the following positions within the Juvenile Court Probation Department give the person's full name, correctly spelled and where their office is.

    Top Supervision, policy maker _____ _____
    Chief Juvenile Officer _____ _____
    Volunteer Program Coordinator _____ _____
    Chief VPO _____ _____
    Chief Tutor Volunteer (Longmont) _____ _____
                          (Boulder) _____ _____
    Staff person directly supervising _____ _____
    my work (if known)
    Intake Officer _____ _____

2. Below is a list of typical problems volunteers may run into in their work.
    (1) Your probationer runs away.
    (2) Your probationer tells you he is selling illegal drugs.
    (3) Your probationer tells you his father beat him up.
    (4) Your probationer doesn't attend school for 3 days.
    (5) Your probationer doesn't report for his meeting.
    (6) Your probationer gets straight F's in school.
    (7) Your probationer won't talk to you.

    For each problem, say:
        (a) Would you try to handle it yourself?
        (b) Would you consult with someone in the Department?
        (c) If the latter, who first?
        (d) If the latter, who ultimately?

3. What are usual office hours at the Juvenile Probation Department?

4. What's the best procedure when you can't contact your staff supervisor during working hours?

5. What's a good procedure for this <u>after</u> working hours?

C. LAWS REGARDING JUVENILES

1. What's the title of the main body of law applicable to your work in the Juvenile Court?

2. What are the age limits, lower and upper, for being a delinquent in this state?

3. In what sense is a juvenile delinquent a criminal or not?

4. What's the intention of the distinction between the CHINS and the delinquent?

5. Under what kinds of circumstances might a child be declared "Dependent" and "Neglected" rather than CHINS or delinquent?

6. Can the Court deal with a youngster who is not formally in any of these three categories, and if so, under what circumstances and conditions?

7. When may a child be:
   (a) Placed in custody?
   (b) Placed in detention?

8. Briefly distinguish between "custody" and "detention?"

9. Would you describe residence at Attention Home as "custody" or "detention?" Give reasons.

10. Where are the various facilities in which Boulder Juvenile Court youngsters may be detained?

11. What are the rules and procedures involved in:
    (a) Placing a child in detention?
    (b) Removing him from detention?

12.   Who may participate in decisions regarding changes in probation rules and how?

13.   Who ultimately is responsible for the decision in these changes?

14.   What is revocation, why may it be used, and what alternative things can happen when it is used?

D.   INVESTIGATIVE PROGRAM

15.   Below is a list of terms.   Rank them in order of time of occurrence from 1 to 5:
Revocation
Adjudicatory hearing
Referral
Parole
Development of probation plan
(Some don't belong at all)

16.   How do you see yourself and your relationship to your probationer?

17.   List the five most important responsibilities of your volunteer job.
1.
2.
3.
4.
5.

18.   List three things that are not primarily the responsibility of your volunteer job in relation to the juvenile.

Whose responsibility are they?

19.   At your regular meetings with your staff supervisor what sorts of things and information should you have ready if he or she wants them?

20.   What kinds of things may be asked of you in your job in addition to your direct contact with your juvenile?

21.   What kinds of support in your work may you expect:
(a)   From Court staff?
(b)   From your immediate staff supervisor?

E.   COMMENTS (for post-service volunteers)

    1.   What aspects of your work with the Court should
have been emphasized more in training?

    2.   What aspects should have been emphasized less?

    3.   Comments:
[A significant variation on volunteer examination is given at
Oakland County Juvenile Court, Pontiac, Mich. It is a self-
quiz for the volunteer following each section of the orientation
manual. According to his scores, the volunteer is then directed
to re-study the section, or go on to the next section.]
*   *   *   *

Report XVI

VOLUNTEERS' KNOWLEDGE OF COURTS
PRIOR TO TRAINING: A SURVEY

       In the development of a training program for volun-
teers in courts, it is essential that the trainer have cognizance of the familiarity of the court volunteer with the court
and the correctional process in order that training objectives
can be developed and individualized for each volunteer.

       A class of volunteers is not unlike a class in any oth-
er setting, in that there are among the individual trainees
diverse levels of knowledge and preparation.   Some volunteers present themselves for training very much misinformed;
some have good intentions but little information, while others
possess a great deal of information.   The only real justification for training is to provide minimum knowledge about certain subject matter and to provide the opportunity for attitude
change.   A training program then, if it is to have relevance
for a class of diverse individuals, must have within it something for each trainee.

       One means of assessing the knowledge of volunteers
is through the administration of a simple paper-and-pencil
test given before volunteer training has begun.   The previous
report of the National Court Volunteer Training Project provides one model of such a test.   It is recognized that in
utilizing such a test there are obvious limitations, particularly when dealing with questions where the answer is not necessarily right or wrong but rather reveals an attitude on the
part of the volunteer.   Research points to the conclusion

that attitudes toward a subject, as expressed verbally, are not necessarily correlated with similar <u>behavior</u> toward that subject.   As a result, it is necessary to suggest here that paper-and-pencil tests be used as only one means of assessment, and that observation of behavior in experiential training also be used in order to supplement our knowledge of the volunteer's training needs.

Hoping to learn more about volunteer training needs by establishing a baseline of volunteer knowledge prior to training, and keeping in mind the above-recognized limitations, Dr. Ivan Scheier devised a preliminary paper-and-pencil test.   This test was administered to two novice volunteer training groups which had been recruited and screened, but had not yet begun formal pre-assignment training.   The groups were screened, but had not yet begun formal pre-assignment training.   The groups were comprised of 31 "Partners," a group of mostly college-age young people undergoing training to serve as volunteers to delinquent children coming before the Denver Juvenile Court, and 31 community volunteers with a wider age spread preparing to serve the Denver County Court as Probation Counselors for adult misdemeanants.   The responses of the 62 people were categorized by a rater.   Thus the responses to follow are not necessarily verbatim statements from the volunteers. The procedure followed in administration of the test was as follows.   When the class was assembled and settled in their seats, the trainer began.

"We would like you to answer a few questions before the training class begins.   Please just do the best you can on them.   We fully realize that you can't possibly know all or even most of the answers until training is completed. We also realize some of your answers might be different after training.   Write the number of the question down on your paper as I read it, and then the answer.   We do not need your name on the paper.   We're just interested in group averages.   Answer each question fully.   No more than a sentence or two perhaps.   If you don't know the answer, simply write 'don't know'. "

The Test Questions

1.   Have you ever been a volunteer in a court before?   Yes - No
2.   Have you ever been through a training session

for court volunteers? Yes - No

3. Have you read any volunteer orientation materials yet?
   (a) Just scanned it.
   (b) Really studied it.
   (c) Not looked at it.

4. Briefly what do you think "probation" means?

5. How does probation differ from parole?

6. In your opinion what is the purpose of probation?

7. What would you guess are the four most frequent crimes or offenses of people brought before this court?

8. What is the average age of people brought before this court?

9. What is the youngest age at which a person can be brought before this court?

10. What is the difference between a misdemeanor and a felony?

11. How many hours <u>a month</u> do you think the court expects you to put in on your volunteer job? Choose one of the following options:
   (a) No fixed minimum.
   (b) Two hours minimum.
   (c) Five hours minimum.
   (d) Ten hours minimum.
   (e) Fifteen hours maximum allowed.

12. Can you give the full names of the following people?
   (a) Judge closely associated with this volunteer program.
   (b) The person who heads this probation department.
   (c) The person most directly responsible for this program.

13. As for the volunteer program in this court:
   (a) How long has it been in existence?
   (b) How many volunteers have worked in it?

The Responses

Responses to question 1 clearly show that the vast majority of the volunteers tested had never before been volunteers in courts prior to the training sessions. Out of 62 examinees, only four of the Partners and one of the Denver County Court volunteers had in fact been volunteers in other court programs. Consistent with this finding was the response to question 2. Here only two volunteers answered

"yes" to the question, "Have you ever been through a training session for court volunteers?" The fact that volunteer
programs in courts are relatively new would probably be the
main reason for the small number of volunteers with previous court volunteer experience. It is quite clear that a
group with nominal exposure to volunteer experience and/or
training does require a program of orientation and training.
A key point also established here is that these are in fact
naive pre-training volunteers, so the test is getting at what
court volunteers know or don't know prior to any training.

The authors do not feel that a justification for court
volunteer training is any longer a point of contention. If
we are indeed intent on using lay citizens as change agents
for offenders, they must be equipped with knowledge of the
goals of the court, how the court is organized to achieve its
goals, the role of the court in the larger community, as
well as knowledge of the people who are under the court's
jurisdiction. Specific training about purposeful use of self
in relation to the offender is now a common part of volunteer training for courts.

With the exception of one person, the volunteers either
had only scanned the written orientation materials given them
or had not looked at it at all prior to being surveyed. This
was not terribly surprising, due to the time factor involved,
but it does lend credence to the fact that the trainees' information about the court and corrections was not particularly
enhanced by exposure to written study materials presented to
the class prior to training.

Thirty-eight of the trainees responded to the query,
"Briefly what do you think 'probation' means?" by making
reference to the "trial period" connotation of probation.
Twelve other respondents were inclined to see probation as
surveillance, while eight individuals emphasized the counseling motif of probation. Only three trainees admitted that
they didn't know what probation was. The general understanding of probation, while reflecting a differential in emphasis, was considered to be positive and generally accurate.
Training would thus need to be directed toward more specific
understanding for this group but it does not appear that the
naive trainees were victims of basic misinformation about
the concept of probation.

In order to get at a clearer picture of volunteers'
ability to distinguish probation from parole, the question

asked was, "How does probation differ from parole?" These
two terms which are commonly confused and misunderstood
by many laymen were also confusing to our sample of court
volunteers prior to training. Fully 26 of the 62 trainees
frankly admitted they did not know the answer to this question or their responses were so vague as to convince the
raters that they could not differentiate the two. Twenty-nine
of the sample group responded in such language as to reveal
a clear differentiation of the two processes, while the remaining seven of the trainees reflected partial understanding
in that they saw the difference largely in terms of the goals
set for the offender or a difference in the severity of the
penalty.

The 6th question, "In your opinion what is the purpose of probation?" demonstrated that the trainees generally
had rehabilitation-oriented opinions about the purpose of probation to the extent that only four respondents answered
"don't know." Nineteen felt probation was a chance for the
offender to prove himself; 20 saw probation as counseling of
some sort; and 19 indicated it was a process of adjustment.
It is interesting to note that none of the volunteers saw probation as a sentence, a penalty, or punishment.

Question 7 was designed to indicate the pre-training
sensitivity of the volunteer to the types of offenses being
committed by offenders coming before the courts to which
they were offering their services. It was recognized that the
news media may have the effect of distorting the accuracy
with which a volunteer may perceive the incidence of certain
types of crimes. Further, it was felt that neophyte volunteers may be apprehensive about and preparing for a more
aggravated type of offender than is actually placed on probation. According to 1968 statistics, the four most common
offenses in the Denver Juvenile Court were burglary, joy-
riding, shoplifting, and assault and battery. The Partners
Volunteers, according to their responses, underestimated the
occurrence of joyriding, shoplifting, and assault and battery.
They correctly surmised that burglary was prevalent among
juveniles, and they overestimated the extent of narcotics as
a reason for coming before the court. Denver County Court
Volunteers were inclined to overestimate the degree to which
narcotics is a County Court problem, and they were also
overly prepared to deal with offenders convicted of various
kinds of theft. They correctly defined drunkenness as a major problem of the court.

For the most part, the trainees were correct in their assumptions regarding the average age of the offender coming before the court. The average age of children appearing in Denver Juvenile Court is 14.7 years. Only five of the Partners responded to this question with an expectation of dealing with a younger age group. The Denver County Court Volunteers also in large measure correctly anticipated working with a youthful age group of 18-21. There was, however, an evident lack of clarity regarding the youngest age at which an offender can be brought to the court. This probably reflects the differing policies in various states with which the volunteers are familiar and the obvious confusion about which courts have jurisdiction over various age groups. The youngest age at which a child can be brought to Juvenile Court in Denver is ten, yet only ten of 31 Partners knew this. Similarly, 17 of 31 of the Denver County Court Volunteers were incorrectly operating under the assumption that an adult misdemeanant court had jurisdiction over juveniles. Only 12 of 31 correctly understood age 18 to be the minimum age for this court.

A slight majority of the 31 Denver County Court Volunteers saw the distinction between a felony and a misdemeanor as being the seriousness of the offense. Eighteen trainees responded in this vein, while 24 of the 31 Partners elicited a similar distinction. It is recognized that the complexity of this distinction from jurisdiction to jurisdiction negates more precise responses. However, the fact that the majority of the volunteers understood the basic concept in this distinction is indicative of a level of sophistication not anticipated by many, from the average layman.

Question 11 was designed to determine to what extent the trainees and the court were in agreement as to what was expected of the volunteer in terms of time commitment. Partners expects considerably more time from their volunteers than the Denver County Court, asking for a minimum of 12 hours per month. The Denver County Court asks for a minimum of one hour per week or four hours per month.

Fifteen of the 31 Denver County Court Volunteers were expecting to give the exact number of hours expected, while the remainder were expecting to give more in varying amounts. Partners volunteers were extremely close to their agency's time expectations. Two expected no fixed minimum time; 22 out of 31 expected to give a ten-hour monthly minimum time commitment, while three expected to give at least

15 hours.   One respondent admitted he didn't know. The conclusion that might be drawn from this finding is indeed encouraging in that the volunteers clearly expected to give as
much or more time to the offender than is in fact being
asked of them.

The 12th question was geared to inquire into the pre-
trained volunteer's knowledge of key court personnel involved
with the volunteer program.   Correct answers here would
perhaps reflect internal knowledge of the court.   Thus trainees were asked if they could list the names of the judge associated with the program, the person heading the probation
program, and the person responsible for the volunteer program.   Half of the Partners could identify Judge Philip
Gilliam as one of two judges in the Juvenile Court, but not
a single one of them could name the Director of Probation,
while only 18 of 31 correctly identified the Director of the
Partners by name.

Denver County Court, having 13 judges, provided the
volunteer with a more formidable task.   Only seven of 31
correctly identified the judge most closely associated with
their volunteer program, while 21 said they did not know.
Since a new Director of Probation had just assumed office
at the time of this survey, the fact that only eight people
could identify him by name is understandable.

The last question regarding the length of time the
volunteer programs have operated and the number of volunteers having participated, revealed that the volunteers
seemed to be generally aware of the size of the organizations
they were joining as well as the length of their operation.
Thus, a clear majority of the volunteers knew that the Denver volunteer program had operated for four years and had
utilized over 1500 volunteers.   Partners trainees also had
a clear understanding of the fact that this organization was
two years old and included nearly 200 volunteers.

Implications

Rather than attempt to form firm conclusions, the
authors would suggest some inferences that may be drawn
from the above material.   They are:

(1)   The volunteers had not, at the time of training,
performed volunteer services in another court nor had they

received training to do so. Thus, courts are not yet at the point where they can expect to recruit many experienced volunteers who are graduates of other related programs elsewhere. If courts want trained volunteers, each court must do it for themselves.

(2) Untrained court volunteers have a <u>generalized</u> idea of probation that is accurate and in keeping with the goals of probation. On the other hand, they lack <u>specific</u> understanding in more technical areas.

(3) Court volunteers, prior to training, like the rest of the population, are probably more sensitive to the more publicized offenses and expect to be working with offenders who commit these offenses.

(4) Neophyte court volunteers, in substantial numbers, seem confused about the jurisdiction of the various courts, as reflected in their uncertainty regarding such items as minimum age and types of offenses handled in the two courts in the present study.

(5) Untrained court volunteers are prepared to spend time working with offenders consistent with or in excess of the expectations of the court. Again, within the limitations of the present verbal testing procedure, the inference is that they are prepared to be serious about their volunteer work, if you are.

(6) The volunteer prior to training does not seem to be familiar with the names of key court personnel, although he has accurate general knowledge about the volunteer program he is joining.

This test as it stands can be utilized to provide the trainer with a general picture of each class, and in that sense can make him more sensitive to the training needs of that class. However, the present test does not seek to identify volunteer attitudes toward the judicial system, although the reader is urged to refer to Report XV as a beginning step in this direction. Obviously there is a need for more sophisticated test instruments in relation to both knowledge and attitudes, which in turn could provide court volunteer trainers with a better-guided and researched training design.

Chapter 18

LOOKING BACKWARD AND LOOKING FORWARD

Having conveyed through the written word our ideas
about training court volunteers, we would like to re-empha-
size the tentative nature of what has been stated here. Writing a "how-to-do-it" book in a time of an explosion in knowledge, ideas, and technology is dangerous business. To do
so is to invite the prospect of presenting something that
may be obsolete in the very near future.

Then, too, to suggest "how-to-do-it" is also to invite
someone else to suggest an easier and better way. This invitation is heartily extended by your authors. Our purpose
in writing this book stems from thousands of individual requests we have received from all over the United States and
in some cases outside the U. S. for specific information on
"how to" perform specific volunteer training tasks. If this
book proves to be of help, then it will possibly serve to get
us out of the letter writing business for a while.

We have attempted to provide in this book a rationale
for volunteer training if indeed that is necessary, a view of
the needs of a total training program, the opportunities for
training in points of time, and the ways and means of delivering training and evaluating its effectiveness. Finally,
we have discussed the kinds of resources necessary for a
successful training program.

It is our hope that this book will have the effect of
giving the would-be trainer, lacking in self-confidence, the
support to initiate training programs for court volunteers.
For to ignore this dimension is to miss an opportunity to
help citizens understand the problems of crime, delinquency,
and the criminal justice system. To ignore training is to
ignore the link between knowledge and action. Our society
in the 1970's is in need of people who better understand the
crime-producing society in which they live, the offenders in
that society, and the criminal justice and correctional

apparatus that is charged with socialization of the offender. It further needs citizens who are willing to take the initiative by entering into a helping relationship with these offenders with a view to helping them reap the benefits of society. That is the reason for training court volunteers and the only reason for this book.

We will be expecting some of our readers to write more advanced books on this subject in the not too distant future.

INDEX